fbForth 2.0

A File-Based Cartridge Implementation of TI Forth

Lee Stewart

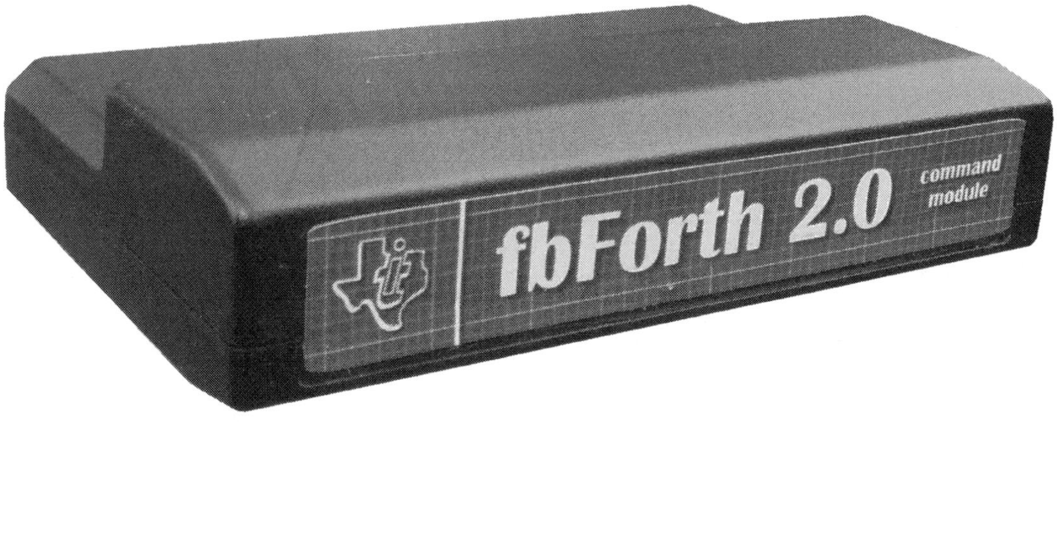

Based on the *TI Forth Instruction Manual* (1983) by Leslie O'Hagan, Leon Tietz and John T. Yantis

and the **fbForth 1.0** *Manual* (2014) by Lee Stewart

Published by Lee Stewart

Author's website: *fbforth.stewkitt.com*

Cover design by Lee Stewart

Printed by CreateSpace, Charleston SC, an Amazon.com company

ISBN-13: 978-1973932673
ISBN-10: 1973932679

Original Dedication of TI Forth

This diskette-based Forth Language system for the Texas Instruments TI-99/4A Home Computer was adapted by Leon Tietz and Leslie O'Hagan of the TI Corporate Engineering Center from Ed Ferguson's TMS9900 implementation of the Forth Interest Group (FIG) standard kernel. This system was placed in the public domain "as is" by Texas Instruments on December 21, 1983, by sending one copy of this *TI Forth Instruction Manual* and the TI Forth System diskette to each of the TI-recognized TI-99/4A Home Computer User Groups as of that date. There were no more copies made, and none are available from Texas Instruments. TI Forth had not undergone the testing and evaluation normally given a product which is intended for distribution at the time TI withdrew from the Home Computer market. Although both the diskette and this manual may contain errors and omissions, TI Forth for the TI-99/4A Home Computer ***will not be supported by*** TI in any way, shape, form or fashion. What is contained in this manual and on the accompanying TI Forth System diskette is all that exists of this system, and is its sole reference.

Texas Instruments Incorporated (hereinafter "TI") hereby relinquishes any and all proprietary claims to the software language known as "TI Forth" to the public for free use thereof, without reservations on the part of TI. It should be understood that the TI Forth software language is not subject to any warranties of fitness, either express or implied, by TI, and TI makes no representations as to the fitness of the TI Forth software language for any intended application by the user. Any use of the TI Forth software language is specifically at the discretion of the user who assumes the entire responsibility for such use.

—from the original TI Forth Manual

To Anna Roth Stewart, the love of my life,
whose tolerance and encouragement
have made this book possible

Table of Contents

1 Introduction

1.1 Original Introduction to TI Forth

The Forth language was invented in 1969 by Charles Moore and has continually gained acceptance. The last several years have shown a dramatic increase in this language's following due to the excellent compatibility between Forth and mini- and microcomputers. Forth is a threaded interpretive language that occupies little memory, yet, maintains an execution speed within a factor of two of assembly language for most applications. It has been used for such diverse applications as radio telescope control to the creation of word processing systems. The Forth Interest Group (FIG) is dedicated to the standardization and proliferation of the Forth language. TI Forth is an extension of the fig-Forth dialect of the language. The fig-Forth language is in the public domain. Nearly every currently available mini- and microcomputer has a Forth system available on it, although some of these are not similar to the FIG version of the language.

The address for the Forth Interest Group is:

Forth Interest Group
P. O. BOX 1105
San Carlos, CA 94070

This document will cover some of the fundamentals of Forth and then show how the language has been extended to provide easy access to the diverse features of the TI-99/4A Computer. The novice Forth programmer is advised to seek additional information from such publications as:

Starting FORTH (1st Ed.)
by Leo Brodie
published by Prentice Hall

Using FORTH
by Forth Inc.

Invitation to FORTH
by Katzan
published by Petrocelli Books

In order to utilize all the capabilities of the TI-99/4A, it is necessary to understand its architecture. It is recommended that the user who wants to use Forth for graphics, music, access to Disk Manager functions or files have a working knowledge of this architecture. This information is available in the *Editor/Assembler Manual* accompanying the Editor/Assembler Command Module. All the capabilities addressed in that document are possible in Forth and most have been provided by easy-to-use Forth words that are documented in this manual.

Forth is designed around a virtual machine with a stack architecture. There are two stacks: The first is referred to variously as the data stack, parameter stack or stack. The second is the return stack. The act of programming in Forth is the act of defining procedures called "words", which are defined in terms of other more basic words. The Forth programmer continues to do this until a single word becomes the application desired. Since a Forth word must exist before it can be referenced, a bottom up programming discipline is enforced. The language is structured and contains no GOTO statements. Successful Forth programming is best achieved by designing top down and programming bottom up.

Bottom-up programming is inconvenient in most languages due to the difficulty in generating drivers to adequately test each of the routines as they are created. This difficulty is so severe that bottom-up programming is usually abandoned. In Forth, however, each routine can be tested interactively from the console and it will execute identically to the environment of being called by another routine. Words take their parameters from the stack and place the results on the stack. To test a word, the programmer can type numbers at the console. These are put on the stack by the Forth system. Typing the word to be tested causes it to be executed and when complete, the stack contents can be examined. By writing only relatively small routines (words) all the boundary conditions of the routine can easily be tested. Once the word is tested (debugged) it can be used confidently in subsequent word definitions.

The Forth stack is 16 bits wide. [***Author's Note:*** **In Forth, a 16-bit value is known as a *cell*. Hence the stack is one cell wide.**] When multi-precision values are stored on the stack they are always stored with the most significant part most accessible. The width of the return stack is implementation dependent as it must contain addresses so that words can be nested to many levels. The return stack in TI Forth is 16 bits wide.

[***Author's Note:*** **This paragraph's use of DR0, DR1, *etc.* does not obtain for fbForth because those words have been eliminated from fbForth**] Disk drives in TI Forth are numbered starting with 0 and are abbreviated with “DR” preceding the drive number: DR0, DR1, etc. Other TI languages (TI Basic, TI Extended Basic, TI Assembler, etc.) and software refer to disk drives starting with 1 and the abbreviation “DSK” preceding the disk (drive) number: DSK1, DSK2, *etc*. From this you can see that DR0 and DSK1 refer to the same disk drive. When referring to the disk drives by device names, they will always be DSK1, …, such as part of a complete file reference, *e.g.*, DSK1.MYFILE.

Keyboard key names in this document will be offset with “<>” and set in the italicized font of the following examples: ***<ENTER>***, ***<CTRL+V>***, ***<FCTN+4>***, ***<BREAK>*** and ***<CLEAR>***. Incidentally, the last three key names listed refer to the same key.

—from original TI Forth Manual

1.2 Author's Introduction

My source for the text of the original *TI Forth Instruction Manual*, much of which is included in this document, was a series of sixteen files named A, B, C, …, P in TI-Writer format, which I had purchased from the MANNERS (Mid-Atlantic Ninety-NinERS) TI Users Group shortly after TI put TI Forth into the public domain. I do not know who deserves the credit for originating these files, but it was always my understanding they came from TI and that the printed document we all received with the TI Forth system was prepared in and printed from TI Writer. However, the A – P files have differences from the original printed document. I have taken the liberty of incorporating most of the original into this **fbForth 2.0**: *A File-Based Cartridge Implementation of TI Forth.*

Chapters 1 – 11 have the same topics and much of the same structure as the original *TI Forth Manual*. The same goes for the seven original appendices, except for the insertion of the current Appendix E "Differences: fbForth 2.0, fbForth 1.0 and TI Forth", which shifts the original Appendices E – I to F – J.

Forth screens are now referred to as blocks, in line with the current Forth convention.

Though not new since **fbForth 1.0**, Chapter 12 "fbForth 2.0 Dictionary Entry Structure" bears mentioning here to remind you of its existence and to note the addition of § 12.5 "Notes on Resident Dictionary Words", which describes how the resident dictionary's structure in ROM differs from the user's dictionary in RAM.

Also noteworthy additions since the original TI Forth are

- Appendix K "Diskette Format Details".
- Appendix L "Notes on Radix-100 Notation", which describes in detail the radix-100 (base-100) notation implemented for floating point numbers on the TI-99/4A.

New to **fbForth 2.0** are

- The facility for loading your own font in place of the default font in the cartridge (see Chapter 13 "Screen Fonts and the Font Editor"). Chapter 13 also provides instruction for using the author's Font Editor. New words are **SCRFNT** , **FNT** , **USEFFL** and **FONTED** .
- A stack-based string library has been added to FBLOCKS and is fully described in Chapter 14 "The Stack-based String Library".
- Chapter 15 "TI Forth Block Utilities" describes a set of utilities added to FBLOCKS for browsing/reading/writing TI Forth blocks.
- Chapter 18 "Signed Integer Division" discusses signed integer division and the different methods available in **fbForth 2.0** for its implementation. The ANS Forth words, **SM/REM** and **FM/MOD** , now part of **fbForth 2.0**, are discussed in detail, as is the User Variable **S|F** that allows the user to specify which method of signed integer division **fbForth 2.0** should use.
- Several software packages, previously requiring loading from FBLOCKS, are now part of the resident dictionary:
  - 40/80 Column Editor, rewritten in TMS9900 Assembly Language (ALC) for efficiency, now including an on-screen menu.
  - Floating Point Math Library, which no longer uses the console GPL/XML-based library, and contains several new words, including **FFMT.** (includes a formatted print

option for 3-digit E-notation), **>DEG** , **>RAD** , **CEIL** , **DEG/RAD** , **EXP10** , **EULER_E** , **F>R** , **FABS** , **FCONSTANT** , **FMT.** , **FLOOR** , **FMINUS** , **FP1** , **FP10** , **FRAC** , **FROT** , **FVARIABLE** , **LN10INV** , **LOG10** , **R>F** , **RAD/DEG** and **TRUNC** .

  - File I/O Library.
  - **BSAVE**—Binary Save Routine.
  - All Graphics modes, including **VMODE** , an all-purpose mode-changing word.
  - Graphics Primitives Library, much of it rewritten in ALC.

- **.BASE**—a new word for displaying the current radix (number base) in decimal: This is useful because, regardless of the current radix, executing **BASE @ .** will always display **10**—not particularly useful! For example, **HEX .BASE** yields **16** , which is much more informative.
- **DIR**—new disk cataloging word in FBLOCKS that uses the DSR's catalog "file" to get disk and file information. The actual byte size of PROGRAM files is unavailable with this word.
- **CAT**—new disk cataloging word in FBLOCKS that uses the disk's VIB, FDIR and FDRs to get disk and file information. The actual byte size of PROGRAM files is displayed.
- Many new words have been added and many words have been removed. Many of them are noted in this "Author's Introduction". See Appendix E "Differences: fbForth 2.0, fbForth 1.0 and TI Forth" for a detailed list.
- SAMS memory expansion (1024 KiB) is supported with **SAMS?** , **SAMS!** , **S0&TIB!** and **>MAP** .
- Sound for the four separate sound generators is supported with **SOUND** .
- **fbForth 2.0** ISR has been extensively modified to support interrupt driven speech and sound lists.
  - The sound lists include sound list #1, which can be interrupted by sound list #2. Sound list #1 will not be paused, but rather will be muted. These sound lists are implemented with **PLAYING?** and **PLAY** .
  - The TI Speech Synthesizer is supported with **TALKING?** , **SAY** and **STREAM** .
- Scrollable panels (windows) are supported with **PANEL** , **WRAP** and **SCROLL** .
- **ASM: … ;ASM** and **CODE: … ;CODE** provide clearer ways of defining words with Assembly Language and machine code, respectively.
- **DOES>ASM: … ;ASM** and **DOES>CODE: … ;CODE** provide clearer ways of coding the runtime behavior of defining words with Assembly Language and machine code, respectively.
- **N>S** pushes to the stack the next number in the input stream. This word is required to get a number to the stack within **CODE: … ;CODE** and **DOES>CODE: … ;CODE** constructs.
- The **DATA[…]DATA** construct allows for quickly compiling a block of cells to HERE or into a word definition. This is particularly useful for character (**DCHAR**) and sprite (**SPDCHAR**) patterns as well as sound lists, *etc.*
- Users of the nanoPEB or CF7+ devices manufactured by Jaime Malilong, occasionally available on *eBay.com*, (see website: *webpages.charter.net/nanopeb* for description) can use the Compact Flash utilities (**CF?** , **CFVOLS** and **CFMOUNT**), added to FBLOCKS to

discover what volume numbers are mounted as DSK1, DSK2 and DSK3, as well as to mount a specific volume in DSK1, DSK2 or DSK3.

You will notice at startup that a revision number appears following a ':' after the version number. The current version:revision is displayed as **fbForth 2.0:9**. Using a revision number allows for minor builds that correct errors and fix bugs. Until a version-number change, this document will continue to use **fbForth 2.0** without the revision number in most instances.

Please note that the SI unit "KiB" is used in this document to denote a byte-multiple of $2^{10} = 1024$, where "KB" had been so used. This is because the old unit is now an SI unit that denotes a byte-multiple of $10^3 = 1000$.

Though, in coding **fbForth 2.0**, I have been careful with my modifications of TI Forth in converting it to use file I/O for reading and writing **fbForth** blocks, as with anything else in this document, you assume responsibility for any use you make of it. Please, feel free to contact me with comments and corrections at *lee@stewkitt.com*.

—Lee Stewart
August, 2017
Silver Run, MD
fbforth.stewkitt.com

1.3 Acquiring fbForth 2.0

A cartridge with the current version of **fbForth 2.0** is available at *fbforth.stewkitt.com*, the author's website. There, you will also find current versions of FBLOCKS and FBFONT; source code and binaries for **fbForth 2.0**; and much more **fbForth**-related information.

1.4 Starting fbForth 2.0

To operate the **fbForth 2.0** System, you must have the following equipment or equivalent:

TI-99/4A Console
Monitor
Memory Expansion
Disk Controller
1 (or more) Disk Drives
fbForth 2.0 Module (cartridge available from the author via *fbforth.stewkitt.com*)
RS232 Interface (optional)
Printer (optional)

See the manuals accompanying each item for proper assembly of the TI-99/4A system.

The **fbForth 2.0** system consists of the **fbForth 2.0** cartridge along with the system blocks file (FBLOCKS) and the default font file (FBFONT) on the system disk. **fbForth 2.0** will complain if it does not find FBLOCKS, but will start perfectly well without it. The useful utilities in FBLOCKS make it advantageous to the user to keep an up-to-date version on the system disk.

To begin, power up the system. The TI Color-Bar screen should appear on your monitor. If it does not, power down and recheck all connections. Press any key to continue. A new screen will appear, displaying choices for TI Basic and two **fbForth 2.0** variants. To use **fbForth 2.0**, select one of its menu options. Pressing and holding a number key immediately following the menu selection will cause the startup code to look for the system files on that disk number. Pressing and holding ***<ENTER>*** instead will prevent loading of FBLOCKS, but not DSK1.FBFONT.

fbForth 2.0 boots and displays the following welcome screen if DSK1.FBLOCKS and DSK1.FBFONT are found. Note that the revision number now appears after the ':':

```
fbForth 2.0:9        (c) 2016 Lee Stewart
 ...a file-based TI Forth implementation

FBLOCKS mod: 19APR2017

Type MENU for load options.


fbForth 2.0:9
█
```

Note that the current modification date of FBLOCKS is displayed. Typing "MENU" per the startup instructions will display the following menu:

```
Load Options (19APR2017)  fbForth 2.0:9

Description                   Load Block
----------------------------------------
CPYBLK -- Block Copying Utility.......4
CRU Words.............................5
64-Column Editor......................6
Memory Dump Utility..................16
TRACE -- Colon Definition Tracing....18
Printing Routines....................19
TMS9900 Assembler....................21
More Useful Stack Words etc..........41
Stack-based String Library...........42
DIR -- Disk Catalog Utility..........36
CAT -- Disk Catalog Utility..........58
TI Forth Block Utilities.............61
ASM>CODE -- Code Output Utility......39
Compact Flash Utilities..............69
TMS9900 Assembler (v2.0:9 binary)....27
64-Column Editor (v2.0:9 binary).....32
String Library (v2.0:9 binary).......52

Type <block> LOAD to load.    ok:0
█
```

Loading a block in the "Load Block" column in the above menu loads all routines necessary to perform the task(s) described.

To load a particular package, simply type its load-block number, exactly as it appears in the menu, followed by **LOAD** . For example, to load the **fbForth 2.0** TMS9900 Assembler, type **21 LOAD** and press *<ENTER>*. You may load more than one package at a time.

The list of load options may be displayed at any time by typing the word **MENU** and pressing *<ENTER>*. See Appendix G for a detailed list of what each option loads.

1.5 fbForth 2.0 *Terminal Response*

With few exceptions after typing *<ENTER>*, **fbForth** responds with:

```
ok:n
```

where the number ***n*** following **ok:** is the depth of the parameter stack, *i.e.*, the count of numbers or cells on the stack. For example, if the stack were empty and you typed three numbers followed by *<ENTER>*, the following would obtain:

```
2 4 6  ok:3
```

Note that above and elsewhere in this manual the computer's responses are underlined.

1.6 Changing How fbForth 2.0 *Starts*

When **fbForth 2.0** boots up, it always looks for DSK1.FBLOCKS and complains if it does not find it. Upon finding it, **fbForth 2.0** always loads block 1, the first block in the file. This provides you a way to change what happens at that point in the **fbForth** boot process. You can design your own blocks file that loads your favorite words, including those you create. All you need to do is to eventually rename the file "FBLOCKS" and place it in DSK1 when you want **fbForth 2.0** to load it after it boots up.

The boot process also looks for DSK1.FBFONT, which contains the default startup font. This font has true lowercase letters with descenders. If this font file is not found, the console font is loaded, with its small-caps letters instead of true lowercase letters.

1.7 Startup Changes

This section will detail the startup changes made to **fbForth 2.0** since **fbForth 2.0:2**, many of which are significant.

1.7.1 The Opening Menu

The opening menu has two choices for **fbForth 2.0** as shown in the screen shot as shown on the next page:

- Option 2 will open in 40-column Text mode, **TEXT** .
- Option 3 will open in 80-column Text mode, **TEXT80** , which must not be selected unless the user has installed an F18A, V9938 or similar video display processor capable of 80-column Text mode. Otherwise, the display will be corrupted and VRAM will not be set up properly.

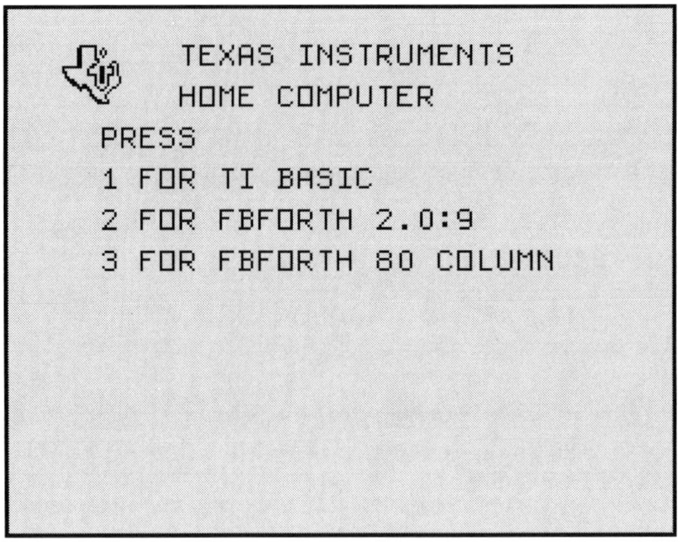

1.7.2 Enabling 1024 KiB SAMS Mapping

After selection of one of the **fbForth 2.0** options, the first thing that the initialization code does is to set up 1024 KiB SAMS, whether or not a SAMS card is present! It then tests for proper SAMS operation by writing a 16-bit value to an arbitrary address, mapping another SAMS bank to the 4 KiB segment containing the written value and, finally, testing for the written value. If the written value is found, the SAMS mapping did not work. If it is not found, SAMS mapping obviously worked. The SAMS flag is set to 0 or 1, accordingly. It is this flag that is tested by **SAMS?** , see Appendix D "The fbForth 2.0 Glossary".

1.7.3 Changes to the fbForth 2.0 ISR

The **fbForth 2.0** ISR is now enabled at startup so that the new speech (**SAY** and **STREAM**) and sound (**PLAY**) words will work. The speech and sound word ISRs are driven by the **fbForth 2.0** ISR. It is easy enough to disable it if the user does not use speech, sound or a user ISR and wants to recover the little bit of time it takes for the **fbForth 2.0** ISR to check for non-existent ISRs to service. See Chapter 10 "Interrupt Service Routines (ISRs)" for details.

1.7.4 Changes to COLD

COLD is the last routine executed by the **fbForth 2.0** startup code. Formerly, it was a high-level Forth word that called another high-level Forth word (**BOOT**) at its conclusion. They have both been combined into a single ALC routine that (re)sets the Forth environment to the default startup conditions.

Holding down a key immediately upon execution of **COLD** will force **COLD** to look for FBLOCKS from that disk. If the user executed **COLD** , the last loaded font is reloaded regardless of the new disk selection indicated by the held key. Whereas, at startup, the held key depressed immediately after the menu selection, will, in fact, also cause the search for FBFONT on the held key's disk. Both invocations of **COLD** will not attempt to load FBLOCKS if ***<ENTER>*** is the held key.

If *<ENTER>* was held down at powerup or after execution of **BOOT** (see next section), the default disk drive for both FBLOCKS and FBFONT is DSK1. Though DSK1.FBLOCKS is not loaded, DSK1.FBFONT *is* loaded (or, at least, attempted). For the next go-round with **COLD** executed by the user, if no key is held down then, both DSK1.FBLOCKS and DSK1.FBFONT will be loaded if found.

User changes to the following settings will survive a user-executed **COLD** :

- Display font (see **USEFFL** , **SCRFNT** , **FNT** for how to change font)
- Default colors for all VDP modes (see definition of **DCT** for how to change)
- Default VDP mode, which should be limited to **TEXT80** (0) or **TEXT** (1) (see definition of **DCT** for how to change)
- Default **S0** and **TIB** changed by **S0&TIB!** .

1.7.5 Redefinition of BOOT

BOOT has been redefined to restart **fbForth 2.0** at the cartridge startup code. The desired default VDP text mode of **TEXT80** or **TEXT** may be set by pushing to the stack 0 or 1, respectively, prior to executing **BOOT** :

```
0 BOOT
```

will set the default VDP text mode to **TEXT80** and reboot **fbForth 2.0** just as though the user had made the selection on the opening screen.

BOOT may also be executed with nothing on the stack:

```
BOOT
```

which will set the default VDP text mode to **TEXT** as though the user had executed

```
1 BOOT
```

Holding a disk-selection key or *<ENTER>* will have the same effect as at powerup selection.

1.8 Acknowledgments

The author would like to thank the following for their help with the development of **fbForth 2.0**:

- Tim Tesch for the source code of the MDOS L10 Floating Point Library (FPL) and encouragement and permission in this effort to adapt it to do the heavy lifting for the **fbForth 2.0** Floating Point Library.
- Beery Miller for permission to use the MDOS L10 FPL.
- 9640News and all of the MDOS contributors who developed the TMS9900 code for the MDOS L10 FPL, which the author adapted for use with **fbForth 2.0** on the TI-99/4A.
- Mark Wills for his assistance, encouragement, permission to use code from **TurboForth**[1] and porting his **TurboForth** String Stack Library to **fbForth 2.0**.
- Matthew Splett for his assistance in debugging the **fbForth 2.0** kernel code as well as proofreading and assistance with editing this manual.

1 See Mark Wills' website: *turboforth.net*.

2 Getting Started

This chapter will familiarize you with the most common words (instructions, routines) in the Forth Interest Group version of Forth (fig-Forth). The purpose is to permit those users that have at least an elementary knowledge of some Forth dialect to easily begin to use **fbForth 2.0**. Those with no Forth experience should begin by reading a book such as *Starting FORTH, (1st Ed.)* by Leo Brodie. Appendix C "How fbForth 2.0 differs from Starting FORTH (1st Ed.)" is designed to be used side by side with *Starting FORTH, (1st Ed.)* and lists the differences between the Forth language described in the book (polyForth) and **fbForth 2.0**.

A word in Forth is any sequence of characters delimited (set off) by blanks or a carriage return (***<ENTER>***). In this document, all Forth words will be set in a bold mono-spaced font that distinguishes the digit '**0**' from the capital letter '**O**' and will always be followed by a blank, even when punctuation such as a period or a comma follows. For example, **DUP** is such a Forth word and is shown also at the end of this sentence to demonstrate this practice: **DUP** . This obviously looks odd, but this notation is necessary to avoid ambiguity when discussing Forth words because many of them either end in or, in fact, are such punctuation marks themselves. For example, the following, space-delimited character strings are all Forth words:

`. : , ' ! ; C, C! ;CODE ? ." ASM:`

The following convention will be used when referring to the stack in Forth:

(n_1 n_2 --- n_3)

This diagram shows the stack contents before and after the execution of a word. In this case the stack contains two values, n_1 and n_2, before execution of a word. The execution is denoted by "---" and the stack contents after execution is n_3. The most accessible stack element is always on the right. In this example, n_2 is more accessible than n_1. There may be values on the stack that are less accessible than n_1 but these are unaffected by the execution of the word in question.

When the return stack is manipulated by a word, it will be shown beside the parameter stack (the stack) with a preceding "R:":

(*n* ---) (R: --- *n*)

When the input stream is used by a word, it will be indicated next to the stack signatures with a preceding "IS:":

(*n* ---) (IS:*string*")

In addition, the following symbols are used as operands for clarity:

SOME SYMBOLS USED IN THIS DOCUMENT

n, n_1, ...	16-bit signed numbers
d, d_1, ...	32-bit signed double numbers
u	16-bit unsigned number
ud	32-bit unsigned double number
f	8-byte, 4-cell, radix-100 floating-point number
addr, $addr_1$, ...	memory addresses

b	8-bit byte (in right half of cell)
c	7-bit character (in right end of cell)
flag	Boolean flag (0 = false, non-0 = true)
|	separates alternate results

2.1 Stack Manipulation

The following are the most common stack-manipulation words:

-DUP	(*n* --- *n n* | *n*)	Duplicate only if non-zero
.S	(---)	Non-destructively display stack contents
>R[2]	(*n* ---) (R: --- *n*)	Move top item on stack to return stack
DEPTH	(--- *stack-depth*)	Number of cells on parameter stack
DROP	(*n* ---)	Discard top of stack
DUP	(*n* --- *n n*)	Duplicate top of stack
OVER	(n_1 n_2 --- n_1 n_2 n_1)	Make copy of second item on top
R	(--- *n*) (R: *n* --- *n*)	Copy top item of return stack to stack
RP!	(---)	Clear return stack, resetting it to its base **R0**. *Be extremely careful using this word!*
R0	(--- *addr*)	User Variable with return stack base address
R>[2]	(--- *n*) (R: *n* ---)	Move top item on return stack to stack
RP@	(--- *addr*)	Leave address of top of return stack
ROT	(n_1 n_2 n_3 --- n_2 n_3 n_1)	Rotate third item to top
SP!	(---)	Clear stack, resetting it to its base **S0**
S0	(--- *addr*)	User Variable containing stack base address
SP@	(--- *addr*)	Leave address of top of stack
SWAP	(n_1 n_2--- n_2 n_1)	Exchange top two stack items

2.2 Arithmetic and Logical Operations

The following are the most common arithmetic and logical operations:

*****	(n_1 n_2 --- n_3)	Multiply
***/**[3]	(n_1 n_2 n_3 --- *quot*)	Like ***/MOD** but giving *quot* only
***/MOD**[3]	(n_1 n_2 n_3 --- *rem quot*)	n_1 * n_2 / n_3 with 32-bit intermediate

2 **>R** and **R>** must be used with caution as they may interfere with the normal address stacking mechanism of Forth. Make sure that each **>R** in your program has an **R>** to match it in the same word definition.

`+`	(n_1 n_2 --- n_3)	Add
`-`	(n_1 n_2 --- n_3)	Subtract ($n_1 - n_2$)
`/`[3]	(n_1 n_2 --- n_3)	Divide n_1 by n_2 and leave quotient n_3
`/MOD`[3]	(n_1 n_2 --- *rem quot*)	Divide n_1 by n_2 giving remainder & quotient
`1+`	(n_1 --- n_2)	Increment by 1
`2+`	(n_1 --- n_2)	Increment by 2
`1-`	(n_1 --- n_2)	Decrement by 1
`2-`	(n_1 --- n_2)	Decrement by 2
`ABS`	(n --- $\|n\|$)	Absolute value
`AND`	(n_1 n_2 --- n_3)	Bitwise logical AND giving n_3
`D+`	(d_1 d_2 --- d_3)	Add double precision numbers
`D+-`	(d_1 n --- d_2)	Negate double number d_1 if sign of n is negative
`DABS`	(d --- $\|d\|$)	Absolute value of 32-bit number
`DMINUS`	(d_1 --- d_2)	Leave two's complement of 32-bits
`FM/MOD`	(*d n* --- *rem quot*)	Mixed-magnitude, floored divide
`MAX`	(n_1 n_2 --- n_1 | n_2)	Maximum
`MIN`	(n_1 n_2 --- n_1 | n_2)	Minimum
`M*`	(n_1 n_2 --- d)	Multiply 2 single numbers giving double result
`M/`[3]	(*d n* --- *rem quot*)	Mixed-magnitude divide
`M/MOD`	(*ud u* --- *urem udquot*)	Unsigned mixed-magnitude divide
`MINUS`	(n_1 --- n_2)	Leave two's complement
`MOD`[3]	(n_1 n_2 --- n_3)	Modulo (remainder from n_1 / n_2)
`OR`	(n_1 n_2 --- n_3)	Bitwise logical OR n_3
`SGN`	(n --- -1 | 0 | +1)	Sign of n as -1 | 0 | +1
`SLA`	(n_1 n_2 --- n_3)	Shift n_1 left arithmetic n_2 bits giving n_3
`SM/REM`	(*d n* --- *rem quot*)	Mixed-magnitude, symmetric divide
`SRA`	(n_1 n_2 --- n_3)	Shift n_1 right arithmetic n_2 bits giving n_3
`SRC`	(n_1 n_2 --- n_3)	Shift n_1 right circular n_2 bits giving n_3
`SRL`	(n_1 n_2 --- n_3)	Shift n_1 right logical n_2 bits giving n_3
`SWPB`	(n_1 --- n_2)	Swap the bytes of n_1 producing n_2

3 The division performed by this word will be symmetric if user variable `S|F` = 0 (the default) or floored if `S|F` $\neq$ 0. See entry for `M/` in Appendix D "The fbForth 2.0 Glossary" and Chapter 18 "Signed Integer Division" for details.

XOR	(n_1 n_2 --- n_3)	Bitwise logical exclusive OR n_3
U*	(u_1 u_1 --- ud_2)	Unsigned * with double product
U/	(u_1 u_2 --- *urem uquot*)	Unsigned / with remainder

2.3 Comparison Operations

The following are the most common comparisons (*flag* = 1 for true; *flag* = 0 for false):

<	(n_1 n_2 --- *flag*)	True if $n_1 < n_2$ (signed)
=	(n_1 n_2 --- *flag*)	True if $n_1 = n_2$
>	(n_1 n_2 --- *flag*)	True if $n_1 > n_2$
0<	(*n* --- *flag*)	True if top number is negative
0=	(*n* --- *flag*)	True if top number is 0
0>	(*n* --- *flag*)	True if top number is positive
U<	(u_1 u_2 --- *flag*)	True if $u_1 < u_2$ (unsigned)

2.4 Memory Access Operations

The following operations are used to inspect and modify memory locations anywhere in the computer:

!	(*n addr* ---)	Store *n* at address (store a cell)
+!	(*n addr* ---)	Add *n* to contents of address
>MAP	(*bank addr* ---)	Maps SAMS memory *bank* to *addr*.
?	(*addr* ---)	Print the contents of address (same as **@ .**)
@	(*addr* --- *n*)	Replace word address by its contents
C!	(*b addr* ---)	Store *b* at address (store a byte)
C@	(*addr* --- *b*)	Fetch the byte at *addr*
CMOVE	(*from_addr to_addr u* ---)	Block move *u* bytes.
BLANKS	(*addr u* ---)	Fill *u* bytes with blanks beginning at *addr*
ERASE	(*addr u* ---)	Fill *u* bytes beginning at *addr* with 0s
FILL	(*addr u b* ---)	Fill *u* bytes with *b* beginning at *addr*
MOVE	(*from_addr to_addr u* ---)	Block move *u* cells.

2.5 Control Structures

The sets of words detailed in the following sections are used to implement control structures in **fbForth**. They are used to create all looping and conditional structures within the definitions of **fbForth** words. These structures may be nested to any depth that the return and parameter stacks can tolerate. If they are nested improperly an error message will be generated at compile time and the word definition will be aborted.

It can be very difficult for programmers new to Forth to understand how control structures work in Forth because of the stack-oriented nature of the language. Using these control structures will be a piece of cake once you understand that the value tested or otherwise consumed by **IF**, **UNTIL**, **WHILE**, **CASE**, **OF**, **ENDCASE** or **DO** must be on the stack *before* the word is executed rather than following the word inline as with most other programming languages. The sections that follow show details and examples of each control structure to give you a better idea of how they work. Some of the examples are taken from the resident dictionary of **fbForth 2.0** while others are from nonresident words that are part of the default system blocks file, FBLOCKS.

2.5.1 IF ... THEN

IF ... THEN **IF** (*flag* ---)	**IF** tests the top of stack and if non-zero (*true*), the words between **IF** and **THEN** are executed. Otherwise, they are skipped and execution resumes after **THEN**.
ENDIF	Synonym for **THEN**.

The words **IF** and **THEN** enclose code that will be executed when **IF** finds a nonzero value for *flag* on the stack. Consider the following example that simply takes the number on top of the stack and makes sure it is even, adding 1 if it is not:

: EVEN	« Define word **EVEN** to insure top of stack contains an even number. Add 1 if not.
(n_1 --- n_1 | n_1+1)	« In: n_1. Out: n_1 or n_1+1.
DUP 1 AND	« Duplicate n_1. Check if odd, *i.e.*, LSb (least-significant bit) set.
IF	« Is n_1 odd? (**IF** tests the number left on the stack in the above line).
1+	« Yes. Add 1 to n_1 to make it even.
THEN	
;	

2.5.2 IF ... ELSE ... THEN

IF ... ELSE ... THEN **IF** (*flag* ---)	**IF** tests the top of stack and if non-zero (*true*), the words between **IF** and **ELSE** are executed. If the top of the stack is zero (*false*), the words between **ELSE** and **THEN** are executed. Execution then continues after **THEN**.

The **IF … ELSE … THEN** structure causes execution of one of two alternatives. The following example is part of the **fbForth 2.0** resident dictionary. **CLOAD** loads a block from the current blocks file only if the word that follows **CLOAD** in the input stream cannot be found in the dictionary. It is a state-smart word that can be used in a word definition as well as on the command line. It is used in the following way:

20 CLOAD MYWORD,

where **20** is the block that will be loaded from the current blocks file if **MYWORD** is not found in the dictionary.

```
: CLOAD                   « Define CLOAD to conditionally load a block from blocks file.
   ( blk# --- )           « Load blk# if word after CLOAD not found.
   [COMPILE] WLITERAL     « Force immediate word WLITERAL to compile into definition
                            of CLOAD so it executes when CLOAD executes.
   STATE @                « Get compilation state for IF to test.
   IF                     « Are we compiling?
      COMPILE <CLOAD>     « Yes. Defer execution of runtime procedure <CLOAD> by
                            compiling it into word invoking CLOAD in its definition.
   ELSE
      <CLOAD>             « No. Execute it.
   THEN
;   IMMEDIATE             « Make CLOAD immediate, i.e., execute even if compiling.
```

2.5.3 BEGIN … AGAIN

BEGIN … AGAIN	Creates an infinite loop, continually re-executing the words between **BEGIN** and **AGAIN**[4].

The **BEGIN … AGAIN** infinite loop is the simplest looping structure in **fbForth** because there are no tests—it just repeats forever the words between **BEGIN** and **AGAIN** . The only way the loop can be exited is if **QUIT** or **ABORT** gets executed within the loop or another word drops the top of the return stack.[4] Generally, however, if you wish to provide a normal exit from the loop, you should use one of the conditionally looping structures described in sections following this one.

The following example is the primary loop in **fbForth**. The last thing the **fbForth** boot process does is to execute **QUIT** . **QUIT** is an endless loop whose primary function is to repeatedly call the interpreter, which is itself an endless loop:

```
: QUIT   ( --- )          « Define QUIT with no inputs or outputs.
   0 BLK !                « Store 0 in BLK to set up input from the terminal.
   [COMPILE] [            « Compile immediate word [ into QUIT 's definition; [ will
                            set system to interpret state when QUIT executes.
   BEGIN                  « Start infinite, top-level loop.
      RP! CR              « Clear return stack. Put screen cursor at start of next line.
      QUERY               « Get a line of text.
      INTERPRET           « Interpret input text.
      STATE @             « Get compilation state.
```

4 This loop may be exited by executing **R> DROP** one level below.

```
      0= IF                  « Are we interpreting, i.e., STATE = 0?
         ."  ok:" DEPTH .    « Yes. Echo " ok:" to the terminal followed by stack depth.
      THEN
   AGAIN                     « Repeat loop.
;
```

2.5.4 BEGIN ... UNTIL

BEGIN ... UNTIL — Loop that executes the words between **BEGIN** and **UNTIL**, which must leave *flag* to be tested by **UNTIL**, until *flag* is non-zero (true).

UNTIL (*flag* ---)

END — Synonym for **UNTIL** .

The following example is from the resident dictionary. **VLIST** lists words in the **CONTEXT** vocabulary starting with the last defined word pointed to by **CONTEXT** and following the linked list of words and vocabularies until it finds the first word at the top of the chain that has a pointer (link field address or *lfa*) of 0. This topmost word will always be **EXECUTE** in **fbForth**. See Chapter 12 "fbForth 2.0 Dictionary Entry Structure" for an explanation of **fbForth** word fields and their abbreviations (*lfa*, *nfa*, *cfa* and *pfa*). If you know the *pfa*, you can get the other three field addresses for a given word. You can get the *pfa* if you know the *nfa*. These facts are used in the following example:

```
: VLIST                      « Define VLIST to list the CONTEXT vocabulary.
   ( --- )                   « Takes no parameters and leaves none.
   80 OUT !                  « Store maximum expected  character count in OUT .
   CONTEXT @ @               « Get nfa of last defined word in CONTEXT vocabulary.
   0 SWAP                    « Start word counter at 0 and swap nfa to top of stack.
   BEGIN                     « Start indefinite loop.
      DUP C@ 3F AND          « Dup nfa. Get length byte's least-significant 5 bits.
      OUT @ +                « Add name length to OUT .
      SCRN_WIDTH @ 3 -       « Get screen width – 3 for spaces and end of line.
      > IF                   « Will line be too long?
         CR 0 OUT !          « Yes. Go to next line and zero character count.
      THEN
      DUP ID.                « Dup nfa. Display name.
      SWAP 1+ SWAP           « Get word count to top. Increment it. Swap nfa back.
      PFA LFA @              « Get lfa from pfa. Get next word's nfa from lfa.
      SPACE                  « Emit a space (updates OUT in the process).
      DUP 0=                 « Dup new nfa. Leave true if 0, else false.
      PAUSE                  « Pause if keystroke. Return true if <BREAK>, else false.
   OR UNTIL                  « OR above flags. Exit loop if true, else repeat.
   DROP CR . ." words listed" « Drop leftover nfa. Display word count on next line.
;
```

2.5.5 BEGIN … WHILE … REPEAT

BEGIN … WHILE … REPEAT

WHILE (*flag* ---)

Executes words between **BEGIN** and **WHILE** , which must leave *flag* to be tested by **WHILE**. If *flag* is non-zero (*true*), executes words between **WHILE** and **REPEAT** , then jumps back to **BEGIN** . If *flag* is zero (*false*), continues execution after the **REPEAT** .

The following example starts with a **BEGIN … UNTIL** loop that waits for the left joystick's fire button to be depressed, after which it starts a counter and enters the **BEGIN … WHILE … REPEAT** loop. That loop waits for the fire button to be released, counting the number of times through the loop while that is not happening. After the fire button is released, the **WHILE** clause is not executed and the loop exits. **FIREDOWN** finishes with the display of the number of iterations through the **BEGIN … WHILE … REPEAT** loop:

```
: FIREDOWN                      « Define FIREDOWN to display loop iterations between press
                                  and release of left joystick's fire button.
   ( --- )                      « No parameters in or out.
   BEGIN                        « Start indefinite loop awaiting fire button press.
      1 JOYST DROP DROP         « Get state of joystick/keyboard #1. Save only char value.
   18 = UNTIL                   « Repeat loop until char is fire-button value (18).
   0                            « Initialize counter on stack.
   BEGIN                        « Start indefinite loop awaiting release of fire button.
      1 JOYST DROP DROP         « Get state of joystick/keyboard #1. Save only char value.
   18 = WHILE                   « Continue with loop while char value = 18, else exit.
      1+                        « Increment loop counter on stack.
   REPEAT                       « Repeat loop.
   CR . ."  iterations."        « Display # of iterations on next screen line.
;
```

2.5.6 DO … LOOP

DO … LOOP

DO (*lim strt* ---)

DO sets up a loop with a loop counter. The stack contains the first and final values of the loop counter. The loop is executed at least once. **LOOP** causes a return to the word following **DO** unless termination is reached.

I (--- *n*)

Used between **DO** and **LOOP**. Places value of loop counter on stack.

J (--- *n*)

Used when **DO LOOP**s are nested. Places value of next outer loop counter on the stack.

LEAVE (---)

Causes loop to terminate at next **LOOP** or **+LOOP**.

The following example could have been written more efficiently, but this version makes use of all of the above words. The word **8X8SRCH** defined below looks on the stack for the address of an 8x8 array *addr* of numbers to search and a number *n* to match. The result will be only a *false* flag if there is no match, but a *true* flag, row *r* and column *c* of the array if there is a match.

You will notice that the stack depth is stored on the return stack before entering the outer **DO** loop and moved to the parameter stack when that loop is exited to then calculate the difference. The reason for this maneuver is that there is no way for **8X8SRCH** to anticipate how many cells there may be on the stack below *n* before **8X8SRCH** executes:

```
: 8X8SRCH                     « Define 8X8SRCH to search an 8x8, row-major array for a
                                number.
   ( n addr --- F | c r T )   « In: n = number to match; addr = array address. Out:
                                false (0), if not found—or c = column; r = row; true
                                (non-zero), if found.
   DEPTH >R                   « Store stack depth to return stack to check at end.
   8 0 DO                     « Array row loop.
      8 0 DO                  « Array column loop.
         OVER OVER            « Copy n and addr to top of stack.
         J 8 * I +            « Convert row r and column c to address offset into array.
         + @                  « Add offset to addr and get value at that location.
         = IF                 « Do we have a match to n?
            DROP DROP         « Yes. DROP top 2 numbers from the stack.
            I J 1 LEAVE       « Leave column c, row r and 1 for outer loop test. Leave
                                inner loop when we next get to LOOP .
         ELSE                 «
            0                 « No. Leave 0 for outer loop test.
         THEN
      LOOP                    « Inner loop end.
      IF                      « Did we have a match?
         1                    « Yes. Leave true (1) [stack now: c r 1].
         LEAVE                « Leave outer loop at LOOP .
      THEN
   LOOP                       « Outer loop end.
   DEPTH R> -                 « Get current stack depth, previous depth and difference.
   2 = IF                     « # cells on stack out of loops = 2?
      DROP DROP 0             « Yes. Loop exhausted with no match. DROP everything
                                and leave only false (0).
   THEN
;
```

The following example from the graphics primitives of the resident dictionary uses decimal numbers instead of hexadecimal. It initializes the screen in multicolor graphics mode.

Note that **I** (containing loop's index) on the fourth line is the same index as **J** (next outer loop's index) on the eighth line and *not* the same as **I** on the eighth line. The definitions of **I** and **J** are not equivalent, but in this situation they reach the same cell on the return stack to get the index of the outer loop:

```
: MINIT   ( --- )          « Define MINIT to initialize multicolor mode. It takes no
                             parameters and leaves none.
   24 0 DO                 « Row loop: 24 = loop limit; 0 = index start.
      0                    « Initialize column counter on stack for use in inner loop.
      I 4 / 32 *           « Calculate inner loop index start from current value of outer
                             loop's index I .
```

```
      DUP 32 +              « DUP it and add 32 to get inner loop limit.
      SWAP                  « Now, inner loop index start is on top of stack.
      DO                    « Char# loop.
         DUP J 1 I HCHAR    « Get 4 values to stack for use by HCHAR : DUP column
                              counter, get row from index J of outer loop; 1 char; char# I .
         1+                 « Increment column counter left on stack.
      LOOP                  « Inner loop end.
      DROP                  « DROP column counter still on stack.
   LOOP                     « Outer loop end.
;
```

2.5.7 DO ... +LOOP

DO ... +LOOP

DO (*lim strt* ---)

+LOOP (*n* ---)

DO as above. **+LOOP** adds top stack value to loop counter (index).

There may be times you will want your loop index to step by more than 1 or to step down instead of up. For that, you need **+LOOP** .

The following example from the resident dictionary is the definition of the **fbForth** word **.S** , which nondestructively displays the stack contents. **.S** starts by displaying "| " to indicate the bottom of the stack. It then displays the numbers starting at the bottom of the stack, which is marked by the value in user variable **S0** .

The reason we need **+LOOP** is that, though we say that **S0** marks the bottom of the stack, in actuality it is a roof because the stack grows downward from high memory. The first cell on the stack is the first step below this roof. If there is at least one number on the stack and you want to read it, you would need to *subtract* 2 from the value in **S0** to get its address. The upshot of all this is that we need a loop that decrements the stack address by 2:

```
: .S   ( --- )     « Define .S to nondestructively display the stack contents. It takes no
                     parameters and leaves none.
   CR              « Start display on new line.
   SP@ 2-          « Get address of top of stack and go 1 cell beyond, which will be the
                     loop limit.
   S0 @ 2-         « Get address of stack base and adjust to address of first cell, which will
                     be the loop index start.
   ." | "          « Display "| ".
   OVER OVER       « Duplicate loop limit and start.
   = 0= IF         « Are they =? If they are, the stack is empty and we don't want to go
                     through the loop, so we test that result for falsity with 0= . Now the
                     question for IF is, "Are they ≠?"
      DO           « Yes—they are ≠.
         I @ U.    « The index I is the address of the current stack cell. Get its contents
                     and display it as an unsigned number in the current radix.
      -2 +LOOP     « Loop end. Add -2 to the loop index to get the next stack cell's address
   ELSE            « No—we have an empty stack.
```

```
      DROP DROP      « DROP the 2 numbers DO didn't get to use so we don't pollute the stack.
   THEN
;
```

2.5.8 CASE ... ENDCASE

The **CASE** structure allows you to select one of many courses of action based on a single value. It is much neater and easier to read than what would result if you attempted the same thing with a series of **IF** and **ELSE** clauses. It is also much less prone to error.

The catchall **ELSEOF … ENDOF** clause (see § 2.5.8.2 below) was added as of **fbForth 2.0:8** to make it easier for the programmer to deal with the default case.

2.5.8.1 Without ELSEOF ... ENDOF

CASE
   n_1 **OF … ENDOF**
   n_2 **OF … ENDOF**
   …
   n_m **OF … ENDOF**
   …
ENDCASE

CASE (*n* ---)

Looks for a number (n_1, n_2, …, n_m) matching *n*. If there is a match, executes the code between the **OF … ENDOF** set that immediately follows the matching number, proceeding then to the code following **ENDCASE** . If there is no match, the code after the last **ENDOF** is executed, with **ENDCASE** dropping *n* from the stack. Execution then continues after **ENDCASE** . Code after the last **ENDOF** may use *n*, which is still available, but it must not consume *n*. Otherwise, **ENDCASE** will drop whatever was under *n*, adversely affecting program logic and possibly causing a stack underflow.

2.5.8.2 With ELSEOF ... ENDOF

CASE
   n_1 **OF … ENDOF**
   n_2 **OF … ENDOF**
   …
   n_m **OF … ENDOF**
   ELSEOF … ENDOF
ENDCASE

CASE (*n* ---)

Looks for a number (n_1, n_2, …, n_m) matching *n*. If there is a match, executes the code between the **OF … ENDOF** set that immediately follows the matching number, proceeding then to the code following **ENDCASE** . If there is no match before reaching **ELSEOF** , **ELSEOF** forces a match by duplicating *n* and calling **OF** . This has the effect of preventing **ENDCASE** or any code immediately preceding it from ever executing and is obviously a lot easier on the programmer.

The following example is from the graphics primitives that are now part of the resident dictionary. It uses the console's keyboard scanning routine KSCAN to check for joystick and fire-button status of left and right joysticks or corresponding keys on left and right sides of the keyboard:

```
HEX                                « Use radix 16.
: JKBD                             « Define JKBD to scan for joystick input.
   ( kbd --- chr xst yst )         « In: Keyboard kbd = 1 or 2. Out: Value chr of key
                                     struck, joystick x-status xst and y-status yst.
```

```
   8374 C!                                  « Store kbd for keyboard # to scan.
   ?KEY DROP 8375 C@                        « Check for keystroke. DROP char returned and get
                                              KSCAN's returned value.
   DUP 12 =                                 « Duplicate chr and check for fire button.
   OVER 0FF =                               « Duplicate chr again and check for "no keystroke".
   OR IF                                    « Was fire-button or no key depressed?
      8377 C@ 8376 C@                       « Yes. Leave xst and yst on stack on top of chr.
   ELSE                                     « No.
      DUP                                   « Duplicate chr for input to CASE .
      CASE
         04 OF 0FC   4 ENDOF                « chr = 4 (NW)?   xst = FCh,   yst = 4
         05 OF   0   4 ENDOF                « chr = 5 (N)?    xst = 0,     yst = 4
         06 OF   4   4 ENDOF                « chr = 6 (NE)?   xst = 4,     yst = 4
         02 OF 0FC   0 ENDOF                « chr = 2 (W)?    xst = FCh,   yst = 0
         03 OF   4   0 ENDOF                « chr = 3 (E)?    xst = 4,     yst = 0
         0F OF 0FC 0FC ENDOF                « chr = Fh (SW)?  xst = FCh,   yst = FCh
         00 OF   0 0FC ENDOF                « chr = 0 (S)?    xst = 0,     yst = FCh
         0E OF   4 0FC ENDOF                « chr = Eh (SE)?  xst = 4,     yst = FCh
         ELSEOF DROP 0 0 0 ENDOF            « Illegal chr: Drop chr and leave three 0s.
      ENDCASE                               « Never executed due to use of ELSEOF
   THEN
   0 8374 C!                                « Restore previous keyboard #.
;
```

A more extensive example of the **CASE** structure appears in FBLOCKS in the 64-column editor (**EDT** in block 12). **EDT** is set up with an infinite **BEGIN … AGAIN** loop that continuously monitors the keyboard until the exit key, ***<FCTN+9>***, is struck. ***<FCTN+9>***'s ASCII value is **0Fh**, so the **OF** clause that follows **0Fh** executes its contents, ultimately executing **QUIT** to get back to the terminal command line interpreter.

2.6 Input and Output to/from the Terminal

The most common type of terminal input is simply to enter a number at the terminal. This number will be placed on the stack. The number which is input will be converted according to the number base stored at **BASE** . **BASE** is also used during numeric output. **.BASE** is the best way for the user to determine the current radix because **BASE @** will always display **10** .

.	(*n* ---)	Print a signed number
."	(---)	Print a string terminated by **"**
.BASE	(--- *n*)	Print the decimal value of the current radix (number base)
.R	(n_1 n_2 ---)	Print n_1 right-justified in field of width n_2
?KEY	(--- *n*)	Read keyboard. No key? *n* = 0. Key? *n* = ASCII keycode.
?TERMINAL	(--- *flag*)	Test if ***<BREAK>*** (***<CLEAR>*** on TI-99/4A) pressed
BASE	(--- *addr*)	System variable containing number base. To set some base (*e.g.*, Octal) use the following sequence from any base above Octal: **8 BASE !**

CLS	(---)	Clears screen.
COUNT	(*addr* --- *addr*+1 *n*)	Move length byte from a packed character string[5] at *addr* to stack and increment *addr*—suitable for **TYPE**
CR	(---)	Perform a Carriage Return + Line Feed
D.	(*d* ---)	Print double-precision (DP) number
D.R	(*d n* ---)	Print DP number right-justified in field of width *n*
DECIMAL	(---)	Sets the base to Decimal (Base 10)
EMIT	(*c* ---)	Type character from stack to terminal
EXPECT	(*addr n* ---)	Read *n* characters (or until **CR**) from terminal to *addr*
GOTOXY	(*col row* ---)	Places cursor at designated column and row of screen.
HEX	(---)	Sets the base to Hexadecimal (Base 16)
KEY	(--- *c*)	Wait for a keystroke and put its ASCII value on the stack.
PAGE	(---)	Clears screen and places cursor at top left of screen.
PANEL	(*x y w h* ---)	Sets up panel (window) on screen for **SCROLL** .
SCROLL	(*dir* ---)	Scrolls screen panel set up with **PANEL** in direction *dir*.
SPACE	(---)	Type 1 space
SPACES	(*n* ---)	Type *n* spaces
TYPE	(*addr n* ---)	Type *n* characters from *addr* to terminal
U.	(*u* ---)	Print an unsigned number
WORD	(*c* ---)	Read one word from input stream delimited by *c*
WRAP	(--- *wrap*)	A user variable containing the wrapping flag for **SCROLL** .

2.7 Numeric Formatting

Advanced numeric formatting control is possible with the following words:

NUMBER	(*addr* --- *d*)	Convert string at *addr* to a double number *d*
<#	(---)	Start output string conversion
#	(d_1 --- d_2)	Convert next, least-significant digit of d_1 leaving d_2
#S	(*d* --- 0 0)	Convert all significant digits from right to left
SIGN	(*n d* --- *d*)	Insert sign of *n* into number
HOLD	(*c* ---)	Insert ASCII character *c* into string
#>	(*d* --- *addr u*)	Terminate conversion, ready for **TYPE**

5 A packed character string is a string of characters with a leading length byte. Several **fbForth** words expect or produce such strings.

Formatting is always right to left. Consider that you wish to display a formatted Social Security Number that is on the stack as the double number, 123456789. The following would do the trick:

```
<# # # # # 45 HOLD # # 45 HOLD # # # #> CR TYPE
123-45-6789 ok:0
```

Note that the format as you read the Forth code is the reverse of what is displayed and that 45 is the decimal value for the ASCII character '-'. See the individual definitions, especially **<#**, in Appendix D "The fbForth 2.0 Glossary" for more information.

2.8 Block-Related Words

The following words assist in maintaining source code in the current blocks file on disk as well as implementing the Forth virtual memory capability:

B/BUF	(--- *n*)	Constant: Block size in bytes (always 1024 in **fbForth**)
BLK	(--- *addr*)	User variable containing current block number (contains 0 for terminal input)
BLOAD	(*blk* --- *flag*)	Loads binary image at *blk* created by **BSAVE** and returns flag = 0 for successful load. Otherwise, flag = 1.
BLOCK	(*n* --- *addr*)	Leave address of block *n*, reading it from the current blocks file if necessary
BSAVE	(*addr* blk_1 --- blk_2)	Copies to block blk_1 *ff.* of current blocks file the binary image from *addr* to **HERE**, leaving the next available block blk_2.
CLEAR	(*n* ---)	Fill block *n* with blanks
CLR_BLKS	(n_1 n_2 ---)	**CLEAR** a range of blocks from block n_1 to block n_2
CLOAD	(*blk* ---) (IS:*word*)	Load block *blk* if *word* not in **CONTEXT** vocabulary.
CPYBLK	(---) (IS:n_1 n_2 $file_1$ n_3 $file_2$)	Copy range of blocks from a blocks file to the same or different blocks file based on input stream (IS)
EMPTY-BUFFERS	(---)	Erase all buffers
FLUSH	(---)	Write all updated (dirty) buffers to disk
LIST	(*n* ---)	List block *n* to terminal
LOAD	(*n* ---)	Interpret block *n*
MKBFL	(---) (IS: *file n*)	Create blocks file from string and number in IS
SCR[6]	(--- *addr*)	User variable containing block number most recently referenced by **LIST** or **EDIT**
UPDATE	(---)	Mark last buffer accessed as updated (dirty)
USEBFL	(---) (IS: *file*)	Select a different blocks file from IS

2.9 Defining Words

The following are defining words. They are used not only to create new Forth words, but in the case of words using **<BUILDS** , to create new defining words.

: xxx	(---)	Begin colon definition of **xxx**[7]
;	(---)	End colon definition
VARIABLE xxx	(*n* ---)	Create variable with initial value *n*
xxx	(--- *addr*)	Returns address when executed
FVARIABLE xxx	(*f* ---)	Create floating-point (FP) variable with initial value *f*
xxx	(--- *addr*)	Returns address when executed
CONSTANT xxx	(*n* ---)	Create constant with value *n*
xxx	(--- *n*)	Returns *n* when executed
FCONSTANT xxx	(*f* ---)	Create FP constant with value *f*
xxx	(--- *n*)	Returns *f* when executed
FILE xxx	(va_1 *ad* va_2 ---)	Define a file reference word and associate PAB address va_1, RAM buffer address *ad* and VRAM buffer address va_2 with it
xxx		Makes current the file referenced by **xxx** by setting **PAB-ADDR** , **PAB-BUF** , **PAB-VBUF** to va_1, *ad*, va_2, respectively
USER xxx	(*n* ---)	Create user variable with offset *n* bytes from base address of user variable table
xxx	(--- *addr*)	Returns address *addr* of user variable **xxx**
ASM: xxx … ;ASM	(---)	Define assembly-language primitive named **xxx**
CODE: xxx … ;CODE	(---)	Define machine-code primitive named **xxx**
: xxx <BUILDS … DOES>ASM: … ;ASM		Create new defining word **xxx** with execution-time, assembly-language routine

6 The name of the word **SCR** is a throwback to Forth systems like TI Forth that used low-level disk block I/O for Forth blocks/screens. It is so named to refer to an editable Forth screen because a screen was not required to be equivalent to a block in fig-Forth. A block was defined as the chunk (block) of disk space read/written in the process of accessing Forth screens and was not required to be as large as a screen. A screen was composed of one or more disk blocks. For **fbForth**, 'block' is synonymous with 'screen' and contains exactly 1024 bytes regardless of the chunk (now a 128-byte file record instead of a disk block) read/written from/to a blocks file. Each **fbForth** block access processes 8 records/block. **SCR** was retained simply because it made coding **fbForth** easier.

7 If you wish to **FORGET** an unfinished definition, the word likely will not be found. If it is the last definition attempted, you can make it findable by executing **SMUDGE** and then **FORGET**ting it.

: xxx <BUILDS … DOES>CODE: … ;CODE	Create new defining word **xxx** with execution-time, machine-code routine
: xxx <BUILDS … DOES> … ;	Create new defining word **xxx** with execution-time, high-level-Forth routine

2.10 Miscellaneous Words

The following words are relatively common, but don't fit well into any of the above categories:

' xxx	(--- *addr*)	Leave parameter field address (*pfa*) of **xxx**. If compiling, compile address. (tick)
(	(---)	Begin comment. Terminated by **)**
****	(---)	Begin line comment.
,	(*n* ---)	Compile *n* into the dictionary (comma)
ABORT	(---)	Error termination
ALLOT	(*n* ---)	Leave *n*-byte gap in dictionary
CONTEXT	(--- *addr*)	Leave address of pointer to context vocabulary (searched first)
CURRENT	(--- *addr*)	Leave address of pointer to current vocabulary (new definitions placed there)
DATA[	(--- *addr n*) (IS:n_1 … n_n)	Compile numbers until **]DATA**. Leave address and number of cells *n* on stack or in word definition.
DEFINITIONS	(---)	Set **CURRENT** to **CONTEXT**
FORGET xxx	(---)	Forget all definitions back to and including **xxx**[7]
FORTH	(---)	Set **CONTEXT** to main Forth vocabulary.
HERE	(--- *addr*)	Leaves address of next unused byte in the dictionary
IN	(--- *addr*)	User variable containing offset into input buffer.
PAD	(--- *addr*)	Leaves address of scratch area (68 bytes above **HERE**)
PLAY	(*addr flag* ---)	Starts sound list at *addr*, depending on *flag*.
S"	(--- *addr* | [ ]) (IS:*string*")	Store string as packed string at **PAD** or within a word definition. Leaves address of length byte.
SAY	(*addr n* ---)	Speaks *n* Speech-Synthesizer words from *addr*.
SOUND	(*pitch vol ch#* ---)	Starts sound generator *ch#* at *pitch* and volume *vol*.
STREAM	(*addr n* ---)	Speaks *n* cells of raw speech data from *addr*.
VOCABULARY xxx	(---)	Define new vocabulary.
]DATA	(---)	Ends number compilation started with **DATA[** and updates cell count on stack or in word definition.

Many additional words are available in **fbForth 2.0**. The user should consult the remaining chapters in this manual as well as the glossary (Appendix D) for a complete description. Many of these words are defined in FBLOCKS and must be loaded by the user via the load options, which are viewable by typing **MENU** , before they become available. The word's description in the glossary will indicate whether the word is in the resident dictionary or needs to have its definition loaded from FBLOCKS. If it needs to be loaded, the block where it resides is identified.

3 How to Use the fbForth 2.0 Editors

Words introduced in this chapter:

CLEAR	**EDIT**	**TEXT**
CLR_BLKS	**EMPTY-BUFFERS**	**TEXT80**
CPYBLK	**FLUSH**	**USEBFL**
ED@	**MKBFL**	**WHERE**

In the Forth language, programs are divided into blocks. Each Forth block is 16 lines of 64 characters and has a number associated with it. A single-sided single-density (SSSD) TI-99/4A disk that contains a single DF128[8] blocks file that fills the disk can hold 89 Forth blocks (numbered 1[9] – 89). There will actually be one sector (256 bytes) left because disk and file overhead occupy 3 sectors and the blocks file occupies 356 sectors (89 · 4), which leaves one sector of a possible 360 unoccupied. A program may occupy as many Forth blocks as necessary.

If you plan to edit the system blocks file, FBLOCKS, you should back it up with a suitable disk manager program or a combination of **MKBFL** (see below) and **CPYBLK** (see § 3.5 "Block-Copying Utility") before modifying it.

The editor uses the current blocks file, which is DSK1.FBLOCKS at system startup. You can change the current blocks file to one of your choosing, *e.g.*, DSK2.MYBLOCKS, with **USEBFL** by typing on the terminal:

```
USEBFL DSK2.MYBLOCKS  ok:0
```

If DSK2.MYBLOCKS does not exist, you must first create it with an appropriate number of blocks by executing **MKBFL** , being careful not to exceed the capacity of the disk, followed by **USEBFL** :

```
MKBFL DSK2.MYBLOCKS 80  ok:0
USEBFL DSK2.MYBLOCKS  ok:0
```

Now you are ready to begin editing the selected blocks file.

3.1 Forth Block Layout Caveat

As indicated above, Forth blocks are laid out in 16 lines of 64 characters each. However, you should be aware that the lines have no actual delimiters, *i.e.*, there are no carriage-return or line-feed characters at the end of a Forth-block line. This means that one line wraps around to the next line with no intervening white-space such that a word ending on one line will be concatenated with a word that starts on the next line if there is no intervening space. This will usually be nonsense to the system and generate an error message when the block is loaded, indicating that the unintended word has not been defined. Worse, it can result in an unintended existing word such as **-DUP** instead of **- DUP** or **+LOOP** instead of **+ LOOP** .

8 DF128 refers to the file format: **D**isplay data type, **F**ixed record length, **128**-byte logical record length

9 For **fbForth**, the first block of a blocks file is always numbered 1. This is different from most fig-Forth systems, including TI Forth, which start at block number 0.

3.2 The Two fbForth *Editors*

There are two Forth editors available in **fbForth 2.0**. The first, which is in the resident dictionary, operates in **TEXT** or **TEXT80**[10] mode. It will be referred to as the 40/80-column editor[11]. Each block is displayed in roughly two halves (left and right) in normal sized characters in **TEXT** mode.

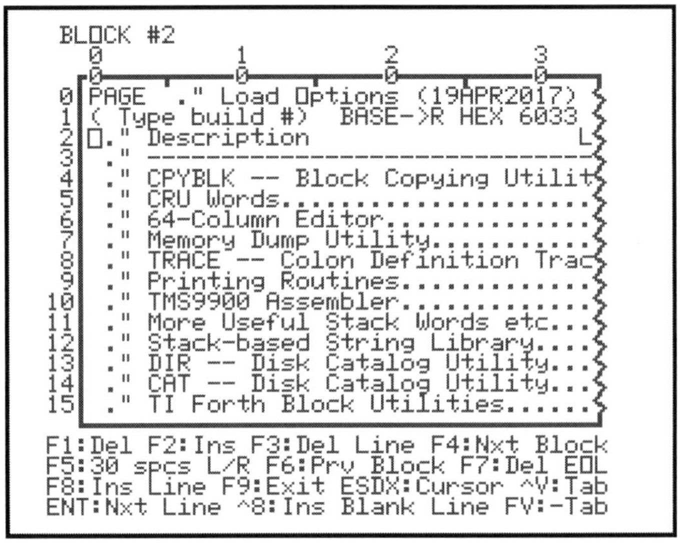

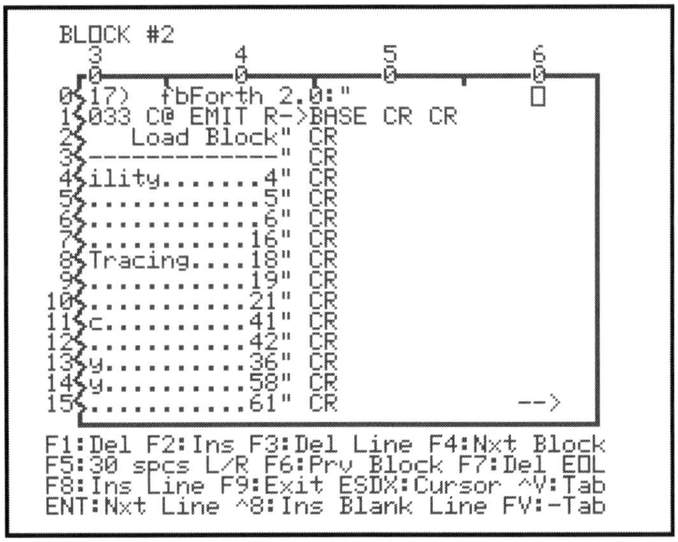

The full block is displayed in **TEXT80** mode.

10 **TEXT80** mode should only be invoked if your computer is equipped with a VDP that can display 80 columns of text. No harm is done to VRAM except that what shows on the screen will be unpredictable. You can easily restore 40-column mode by executing **TEXT** , even though you may not be able to see what you are typing.

11 The 40/80-column Forth editor may only be used when the computer is in **TEXT** or **TEXT80** mode (see Chapter 6). For example, if the 40/80-column editor is loaded, don't type **EDIT** while you are in **SPLIT** or **SPLIT2** mode because the screen will be corrupted and the computer will likely need to be restarted.

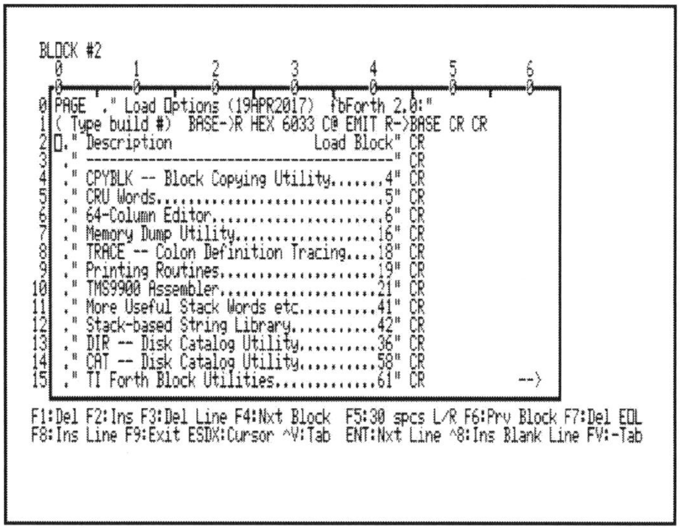

The second, which is loaded by **6 LOAD**, operates in **SPLIT** mode, a modified bitmap mode. It allows you to view an entire block at once on a 40-column screen. However, the characters are very small. It will be referred to as the 64-column editor.

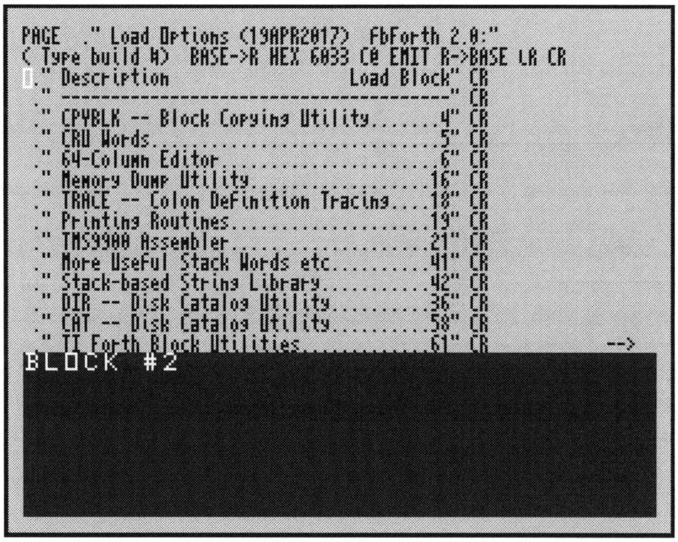

If you load the 64-column editor, that is the only one you will be able to use. If, after you load it, you wish to use the 40/80-column editor, you will need to remove the 64-column editor with

```
FORGET TCHAR  ok:0
```

or by restarting with **COLD** or **MON**. Use whichever editor you prefer. Editing instructions are identical for each.

3.3 Editing Instructions

You should insure that the blocks you are editing are filled with only displayable characters (blanks, if starting from scratch). If you just created the file you are editing with **MKBFL** , all blocks have already been filled with blanks. A single block may be filled with blanks before it is edited by typing a block number and **CLEAR** :

1 CLEAR ok:0

will prepare block 1 for use by the editor.

A range of blocks may be cleared to blanks by executing **CLR_BLKS** with the first and last blocks of the range on the stack:

1 5 CLR_BLKS ok:0

You may begin writing on block 1 or on any block you wish. To bring a block from the file into the editor, type the block number followed by the word **EDIT** :

1 EDIT

The above instruction will bring the contents of block 1 into view. If you did not **CLEAR** the block before entering the editor and the block contains non-displayable characters or other undesirable information, it may be easier to simply exit the editor temporarily and clear the block before writing to it. To exit the editor, press the ***<BACK>*** (***<FCTN+9>***) function key on your keyboard. To clear the block, type the block number and the word **CLEAR** as above.

To re-enter the editor, you do *not* have to type **1 EDIT** again. A special Forth word,

ED@

will return you to the last block you were editing.

Upon entering the editor, the cursor is located in column 0 of line 0. It is customary to use line 0 for a comment describing the contents of that block. Type a comment that says "**PRACTICE BLOCK**" or something to that effect. Do not forget that all comments must begin **(** [12] and end with a **)** . You may also use \ to start a rest-of-line comment.

If you are using the 40/80-column editor in **TEXT** mode, you have probably noticed that only 35 columns (0–34) of the 64 available columns are visible on your terminal. To see the rest of the block, type any characters on line 1 until you reach the right margin. Now type a few more characters. Notice that the block is now displaying columns 29 – 63. Press ***<ENTER>*** to move to the beginning of the next line.

In the 40/80-column editor, you will notice that a keystroke menu is displayed at the bottom of the screen just below the editing window. Though it is cryptic, it should aid in remembering the keystrokes for the editing commands. This feature was inspired by Mark Wills' **TurboForth**[1] and the idea and some code was used with his permission.

12 The left parenthesis *must* be followed by at least 1 space. Press ***<ENTER>*** to move to the next line.

The function keys on your keyboard each perform a special editing function:

key	**function**
<FCTN+S>, (←)	moves the cursor one position to the left.
<FCTN+D>, (→)	moves the cursor one position to the right.
<FCTN+E>, (↑)	moves the cursor up one position.
<FCTN+X>, (↓)	moves the cursor down one position.
<DELETE> (*<FCTN+1>*)	deletes the character on which the cursor is placed.
<INSERT> (*<FCTN+2>*)	inserts a space to the left of the cursor moving the rest of the line right one space. Characters may be lost off the end of the line.
<AID> (*<FCTN+7>*)	erases from the cursor to the end of a line and saves the erased characters in **PAD**. They may be placed at the beginning of a new line by pressing *<REDO>*. *<REDO>* inserts a line just above where the cursor is and places the contents of **PAD** there.
<BEGIN> (*<FCTN+5>*)	**40/80-column editor:** in **TEXT** mode, moves the cursor 29 positions to the right if the cursor is on the left half of a block. Otherwise, it moves the cursor 29 positions to the left. This key can be used to toggle between the left and right half of a block. In **TEXT80** mode, places the cursor in the upper left corner. **64-column editor:** places the cursor in the upper left corner
<ERASE> (*<FCTN+3>*) *<REDO>* (*<FCTN+8>*)	are used in combination to pick up lines and move them elsewhere on the screen. *<ERASE>* picks up one line while erasing it from view. *<REDO>* inserts this line just above the line on which the cursor is placed. Both *<ERASE>* and *<REDO>* may be used repeatedly to erase several lines from view or to insert multiple copies of a line.
<CTRL+8>	will insert a blank line just above the line the cursor is on.
<CTRL+V>	will tab forward by words.
<FCTN+V>	will tab backwards by words.

Experiment with these features until you feel you understand each of their functions. Erase the line you typed from the screen and type a sample program for practice.

The Forth editor allows you to move forward or backward a block without leaving the editor. Pressing *<CLEAR>* (*<FCTN+4>*) will read in the succeeding block. Pressing *<PROCEED>* *(<FCTN+6>)* will read in the preceding block.

If an error occurs during a **LOAD** command, typing the word **WHERE** will bring you back into the editor and place the cursor immediately after the word causing the error, *i.e.*, just in front of the word that was next to be read if there had been no error.

The word **FLUSH** is used to force the disk buffers that contain data no longer consistent with the copy in the blocks file to be written to the file. Use this word at the end of an editing session to be certain your changes are written to the disk. The word **EMPTY-BUFFERS** can be used to clear all Forth buffers and thereby undo any unsaved changes. This is not guaranteed to work except on the current block due to how the editors function when acquiring buffer space.

One last note about blocks: Though your word definitions can span more than one block, you should try to insure that any given word is defined in a single block. This aids in clarity and the good Forth-programming practice of keeping word definitions short.

3.4 Changing Foreground/Background Colors of 64-Col Editor

The black-on-gray color scheme of the 64-column editor and the white-on-dark-blue colors of the 8-line text area at the bottom of the screen can be changed to whatever foreground/background combinations you would like by making minimal changes to Forth code on block 12 of FBLOCKS. There are three chunks of commented-out code on lines 1 and 2 (see following) that offer templates for changing the editor's colors, the screen background color and the 8-line text area, in that order:

```
1: : EDT   VDPMDE @ >R  SPLIT  ( 0 1000 040 VFILL)  ( 0F 7 VWTR)
2: ( 1000 800 01B VFILL)  CINIT !CUR R/C CGOTOXY
```

If you want to change the editor's colors to dark blue on transparent, un-comment the first chunk of code,

```
( 0 1000 040 VFILL)
```

by removing the parentheses:

```
0 1000 040 VFILL
```

For some other combination, change **040** to **0XY**, where **X** is the desired hexadecimal digit for the foreground color and **Y** is the desired background color digit.

To change the screen color (including the border color), un-comment the second chunk of code,

```
( 0F 7 VWTR)
```

which will change the screen color to white:

```
0F 7 VWTR
```

If you do not want white, change the **0F** to the screen color of your choice.

The final chunk of commented code,

```
( 1000 800 01B VFILL)
```

only requires un-commenting to get black on yellow for the bottom 8-line section:

```
1000 800 01B VFILL
```

Change the **01B** to any desired combination of colors as described above for the editor's colors.

You may also want to change the color of the 64-column editor's cursor from white to some other color that makes sense with your new color scheme. If so, you will need to change the color of the cursor sprite in the word **CINIT** (block 7) from **0 1 F 5 0 SPRITE** to **0 1 *new_color* 5 0 SPRITE**, where ***new_color*** is your new color (see § 6.3 "Color Changes").

3.5 Block-Copying Utility

You can copy a range of blocks to the same or another blocks file with **CPYBLK** . This utility is not part of the resident dictionary, so you will need to load block 19 (**19 LOAD**) from FBLOCKS. Typing **MENU** will show you this option as well as ensure that FBLOCKS is the current blocks file. Usage instructions are displayed after **CPYBLK** is loaded:

```
19 LOAD

CPYBLK copies a range of blocks to the
same or another file, e.g.,
      CPYBLK 5 8 DSK1.F1 9 DSK2.F2
will copy blocks 5-8 from DSK1.F1 to
DSK2.F2 starting at block 9.
 ok:0
```

It should be noted that **CPYBLK** will safely copy overlapping source and destination block ranges when the source and destination files are the same. First, **CPYBLK** checks to see whether the source and destination files are the same. If they are, it next checks to see whether the ranges overlap. If they do, it checks to see whether the number of blocks to be copied exceeds the distance between start blocks of source and destination. If it does, then, and only then, it will change the direction of copying to be end to start blocks. It will also reverse the start and end block numbers if you enter a larger number for the start block than for the end block.

If something goes wrong, you may need to restore to current status the blocks file you were using before you invoked **CPYBLK** . See **USEBFL** in Appendix D .

4 Memory Maps

The following diagrams illustrate the memory allocation in the TI-99/4A system. For more detailed information, see the *Editor/Assembler Manual*.[13]

The VDP memory can be configured in many ways by the user. The **fbForth 2.0** system provides the ability to set up this memory for each of the VDP's 5 modes of operation (Text80, Text, Graphics, Multicolor and Graphics2). The allocation of memory for these modes is shown on the VDP Memory Map. The first four modes are shown on the left side of the figure, the Graphics2 mode on the right side. The area at **03C0h** is used by the GPL transcendental functions in all modes for a rollout area, which was a problem for TI Forth and **fbForth 1.0**. Fortunately, you do not need to worry about this now because **fbForth 2.0**'s floating point math package does not use them (see Chapter 7 The Floating Point Support Package). Note that the VDP RAM is accessed from the 9900 only through a memory mapped port and is not directly in the processor's address space.

The only CPU RAM on a true 16-bit data bus is in the console at **8300h**. Because this is the fastest RAM in the system, the Forth Workspace and the most frequently executed code of the interpreter are placed in this area to maximize the speed of the **fbForth 2.0** system. The use of the remainder of the RAM in this area is dictated by the TI-99/4A's resident operating system.

The 32 KiB memory expansion is divided into an 8 KiB piece at **2000h** and a 24 KiB piece at **A000h**. The small piece contains BIOS and utility support for **fbForth 2.0** as well as 4 KiB of disk buffers, the Return Stack and the User Variable area. The large piece of this RAM contains the user dictionary, the Parameter Stack and the Terminal Input Buffer.

4.1 VDP Memory Map

Address	Graphics & Multicolor		Text Mode (40 Columns)	Text Mode (80 Columns)	Graphics2		Address
0000h	Graphics & Multicolor Screen Image Table *bytes:*	**300h**	Text Screen Table	Mode Image Table	Bitmap Color Table	**1800h**	**0000h**
0300h	Sprite Attribute List	**80h**	40 Columns	80 Columns			
0380h	Color Table	**20h**	**TEXT**	**TEXT80**			
03A0h	Unused	**20h**	**3C0h**	**780h**			
03C0h	VDP Rollout Area	**20h**					
03E0h	Value Stack	**80h**					
0460h	PABS etc.	**320h**					
0780h	Sprite Motion Table	**80h**	*[Value Stack for* **TEXT80***]*				

13 Hexadecimal (base 16) notation for integers in this manual is indicated when a string of 1 – 4 hexadecimal digits (`0` – `9`, `A` – `F`) is followed by '`h`'. For example, `2F0Eh` is a hexadecimal integer equivalent in value to decimal integer 12046 and `Ah` is decimal 10. The '`h`' is never typed into the Forth terminal or on Forth blocks. It is used in this manual only to avoid confusion. The notation used in the *Editor/Assembler Manual* (use of a preceding '>' instead of a trailing '`h`') is only used in Chapter 9 for the conventional assembler examples, where it is required as input to the Editor/Assembler module.

Address	Contents	Size
0800h	Pattern & Sprite Descriptor Tables 0 – 127	**400h**
0C00h	128 – 255	**400h**
1000h	**fbForth**'s Disk Buffer	**80h**
1080h	PAB: User Screen Font File	**46h**
10C6h	PAB: Current Blocks File	**46h**
110Ch	PAB: Second Blocks File	**46h**
1152h	Unused *[PABS points here for* **TEXT80***]*	**2686h**
37D8h	Disk Buffer Region for 3 Simultaneous Disk Files	**828h**
3FFFh		

Contents	Size	Address
Bitmap Screen Image Tab.	**300h**	**1800h**
Sprite Attribute List	**80h**	**1B00h**
fbForth's Disk Buffer	**80h**	**1B80h**
PAB: User Screen Font File	**46h**	**1C00h**
PAB: Current Blocks File	**46h**	**1C46h**
PAB: Second Blocks File	**46h**	**1C8Ch**
User PABs, *etc.*	**2EEh**	**1CD2h**
Stack for VSPTR	**40h**	**1FC0h**
Bitmap Pattern Descriptor Table	**1800h**	**2000h**
Sprite Descriptor Table	**1DEh**	**3800h**
Disk Buffer Region: 2 Files	**622h**	**39DEh**
		3FFFh

4.2 CPU Memory

Address	
0000h	Console ROM
2000h	Low Memory Expansion **fbForth 2.0** Block Buffers, User Variable Table, System Support, Return Stack
4000h	Peripheral ROMs for DSRs
6000h	**fbForth 2.0** ROMs (including Resident Dictionary) in Command Module
8000h	Memory-mapped Devices for VDP, GROM, SOUND, SPEECH, CPU Scratchpad RAM at **8300h** – **83FFh**
A000h **FFFFh**	High Memory Expansion User Dictionary (up to Parameter Stack & TIB at high end) Parameter Stack, Terminal Input Buffer (TIB)

4.3 CPU RAM Pad

Address[14]			
8300h **831Fh**	**fbForth**'s Workspace (see § 9.2)		
8320h **832Dh**	–FREE–[15]	**Eh**	
832Eh **8347h**	**fbForth**'s Inner Interpreter, etc.		
8348h **8349h**	–FREE– (unless using Floating Point Library)	**2**	
834Ah **8351h**	FAC (Floating Point Accumulator)		
8354h	Floating Point Error		
8355h	Floating Point String↔Number	Conversion	Options make use of these 3 bytes
8356h **8357h**	Subroutine Pointer for DSRs		
835Ch **8363h**	ARG (Floating Point Argument Register)		
836Eh **836Fh**	VSPTR (Value Stack Pointer)		
8370h **8371h**	Highest Available Address of VDP RAM		
8372h	Least Significant Byte of Data Stack Pointer		
8373h	Least Significant Byte of Subroutine Stack Pointer		
8374h	Keyboard Number to be Scanned		
8375h	ASCII Keycode Detected by Scan Routine		
8376h	Joystick Y-status		
8377h	Joystick X-status		
8379h	VDP Interrupt Timer		
837Ah	Number of Sprites that can be in Automotion		
837Bh	VDP Status Byte	Bit 0[16] Bit 1 Bit 2 Bits 3-7	On during VDP Interrupt On when 5 Sprites on a Line On when Sprite Coincidence Number of 5th Sprite on a Line
837Ch	GPL Status Byte	Bit 0 Bit 1 Bit 2 Bit 3 Bit 4	High Bit Greater than Bit On when Keystroke Detected (COND) Carry Bit Overflow Bit
837Dh	VDP Character Buffer		
837Eh	Current Screen Row Pointer		
837Fh	Current Screen Column Pointer		
8380h	Default Subroutine Stack		
83A0h	Default Data Stack		

14 Locations omitted are not used by **fbForth**, but may be used by system routines.

15 This "free" block is not always available to the user. It is used for temporary storage by the text/font editors, the Floating Point Library and the following resident words: **EXPECT WORD USEFFL DATA[**

16 Bit 0 = high order bit.

Address			
83C0h	Random Number Seed (Begin Interrupt Workspace)	C	R0
83C2h	Flag Bit 0 Disable All of the Following	o	R1
	Bit 1 Disable Sprite Motion	n	
	Bit 2 Disable Auto Sound	s	
	Bit 3 Disable System Reset Key (Quit)	o	
83C4h	Link to ISR Hook	l	R2
83C6h	Default keyboard argument – 3 (*i.e.*, 0 – 2)	I e	R3
83C7h	Keyboard column 0 (special keys)	S	
83C8h	Scan code of current key, whatever keyboard type	R	R4
83C9h	Ditto for keyboard type 4 (Pascal)	W	
83CAh	Ditto for keyboard type 5(Standard) [Keyboard Debounce?]	o	R5
83CCh	Sound List Pointer (VDP RAM)	r	R6
83CEh	Sound List Initiation (set to **01h**) & Countdown Byte	k	R7
83D0h	Search Pointers for GROM & ROM	s	R8 – R9
83D4h	Contents of VDP Register 1	p	R10
83D6h	Screen Timeout Counter	a	R11
83D8h	Return Address Saved by Scan Routine	c	R12
83DAh	Player Number Used by Scan Routine	e	R13 – R15
83E0h	G	R0	«Data (Src)
83E2h	P	R1	«Address (Src)
83E4h	L	R2	«Data (Dst)
83E6h	W	R3	«Address (Dst)
83E8h	o	R4	«MSB: (Src Flag) LSB: (Dst Flag)
83EAh	r	R5	«MSB: Word Command Flag
83ECh	k	R6 – R8	
83F2h	s	R9	«MSB: GPL Code
83F4h	p	R10 – R12	
83FAh	a	R13	«Current GROM Port (**9800h**)
83FCh	c	R14	«Timer Tick & Flags
83FEh	e	R15	«VDPWA (**8C02h**)

4.4 Low Memory Expansion

2000h	XML Vectors	**0010h** bytes
2010h	**fbForth** Block Buffers (4)	**1010h**
3020h	System Support for **fbForth**	**0698h**
36B8h	User Variable Table	**0080h**
3738h	Assembler Support , Trampoline Code, ...	**03AEh**
3AE6h 3FFFh	↑ Return Stack	**051Ah**

4.5 High Memory Expansion

A000h	End of Resident **fbForth** Vocabulary	**0030h**
A030h	User Dictionary Space ↓ ↑ Parameter Stack	**5F70h**
FFA0h FFF1h	Terminal Input Buffer	**0052h**

5 System Synonyms and Miscellaneous Utilities

Words introduced in this chapter:

`'`	`RANDOMIZE`	`VFILL`
`,`	`RND`	`VLIST`
`.S`	`RNDW`	`VMBR`
`:` (traceable)	`SEED`	`VMBW`
`C,`	`TRACE`	`VMOVE`
`CLS`	`TRIAD`	`VOR`
`DSRLNK`	`TRIADS`	`VSBR`
`DUMP`	`TROFF`	`VSBW`
`GPLLNK`	`TRON`	`VWTR`
`INDEX`	`UNTRACE`	`VXOR`
`MYSELF`	`VAND`	`XMLLNK`

Several utilities are available to give you simple access to many resources of the TI-99/4A Home Computer. These are defined as system synonyms[17].

Also included in this chapter are block-listing utilities, special trace routines, random number generators and a special routine that allows recursion.

The descriptions that follow in tabular form include the abbreviation "instr" for "instruction".

5.1 System Synonyms

The system synonyms are part of the resident dictionary in **fbForth 2.0**. These utilities allow you to

- change the display;
- access the Device Service Routines for peripheral devices such as RS232 interfaces and disk drives;
- link your program to GPL and Assembler routines; and
- perform operations on VDP memory locations.

17 The term "system synonym" was coined by the developers of TI Forth and likely means "system utilities identical to Editor/Assembler utilities in name and function". A handful of the system synonyms here are actually enhanced utilities, but are still based on Editor/Assembler utilities.

5.1.1 VDP RAM Read/Write

The first group of instructions enables you to read from and write to VDP RAM. Each of the following **fbForth 2.0** words implements the Editor/Assembler (E/A) utility with the same name. Two words have no equivalent E/A utility: **VFILL** was introduced in TI Forth and **VMOVE** was new in **fbForth 1.0**.

VSBW (*b vaddr* ---)

Writes a single byte to VDP RAM. It requires 2 parameters on the stack: a byte *b* to be written and a VDP address *vaddr*.

base	*byte*	*vaddr*	instr
HEX	**A3**	**380**	**VSBW**

The above line, when interpreted will change the base to hexadecimal, push **A3h** and **380h** onto the stack and, when **VSBW** executes, places the value **A3h** into VDP address **380h**.

VMBW (*addr vaddr count* ---)

Writes multiple bytes to VDP RAM. You must first place on the stack a source address at which the bytes to be written are located. This must be followed by a VDP address (or destination) and the number of bytes to be written.

base	*addr*	*vaddr*	*count*	instr
HEX	**PAD**	**808**	**4**	**VMBW**

reads 4 bytes from PAD and writes them into VDP RAM beginning at **808h**.

VSBR (*vaddr* --- *byte*)

Reads a single byte from VDP RAM and places it on the stack. A VDP address is the only parameter required.

base	*vaddr*	instr
HEX	**781**	**VSBR**

places the contents of VDP address **781h** on the stack.

VMBR (*vaddr addr count* ---)

Reads multiple bytes from VDP and places them at a specified address. You must specify the VDP source address, a destination address and a byte count.

base	*vaddr*	*addr*	*count*	instr
HEX	**300**	**PAD**	**20**	**VMBR**

reads 32 bytes beginning at **300h** and stores them into PAD.

VFILL (*vaddr count byte* ---)

If you wish to fill a group of consecutive VDP memory locations with a particular byte, a **VFILL** instruction is available. You must specify a beginning VDP address, a count and the byte you wish to write into each location.

base	*vaddr*	*count*	*byte*	instr
HEX	**300**	**20**	**0**	**VFILL**

fills 32 (**20h**) locations, starting at **300h**, with zeroes.

VMOVE (*vaddr*$_1$ *vaddr*$_2$ *count* ---)

Copies *count* bytes from one location (*vaddr*$_1$) in VDP RAM to another (*vaddr*$_2$).

base	*vaddr*$_1$	*vaddr*$_2$	*count*	instr
HEX	**1500**	**1640**	**100**	**VMOVE**

copies 256 (**100h**) bytes from *vaddr*$_1$ to *vaddr*$_2$. If the ranges overlap, it is only safe to copy from a higher address to a lower address because the copy proceeds from the lowest address of the source block to the highest. If the copy were in the other direction, all the bytes in the overlapping region would be trashed before they could be copied.

5.1.2 Extended Utilities: GPLLNK, XMLLNK and DSRLNK

The next group of instructions allows you to implement the Editor/Assembler instructions GPLLNK, XMLLNK and DSRLNK. To assist the user, the Forth instructions have the same names as the Editor/Assembler utilities. Consult the *Editor/Assembler Manual*, § 16.2.2 – § 16.2.4 for more details.

GPLLNK (*addr* ---)

Allows you to link your program to Graphics Programming Language (GPL) routines. You must place on the stack the address vector of the GPL routine to which you wish to link as well as provide what additional information that routine may require.

base	set up FAC for call	*addr*	instr
HEX	**900 834A !**	**16**	**GPLLNK**

branches to the address of the GPL routine indicated by address vector **16h**, which loads the TI-99/4A standard character set into VDP RAM. It then returns to your program.

XMLLNK (*addr* ---)

Allows you to link a Forth program to any executable machine-code routine with vectors in ROM or low-RAM (2000h) or to branch to a routine located in high RAM (8000h – FFFFh). The instruction expects to find on the stack an address vector encoding either the address of and offset into a ROM/low-RAM table or a high-RAM address.

base	*addr*	instr
HEX	**800**	**XMLLNK**

accesses the floating-point (FP) multiplication routine, located in console ROM. The *addr* value (**800h**) in this case is a reference to offset **10h** into the console-ROM table for FP routines that starts at **0D1Ah**. **0D1Ah** is the first table pointed to in the XML jump table (**0CFAh**) in console ROM. Offset **10h** (**0D2Ah**) of the FP table contains the address in console ROM of said FP multiplication routine, which executes and returns to your program.

Note: The above FP multiplication routine requires the FP multiplier in FAC and the FP multiplicand in ARG. The product is returned in FAC. The **fbForth 2.0** FP library (Chapter 7 "The Floating Point Support Package") *no longer* uses the code in the above example for FP multiplication.

DSRLNK (---)

Links a Forth program to any Device Service Routine (DSR) in ROM. Before this instruction is used, a Peripheral Access Block (PAB) must be set up in VDP RAM. A PAB contains information about the file to be accessed. See the *Editor/Assembler Manual* and Chapter 8 "Access to File I/O Using TI-99/4A Device Service Routines" of this manual for additional setup information. **DSRLNK** needs no parameters on the stack.

The Editor/Assembler version of DSRLNK also allows linkage with a subroutine in the DSR, but the **fbForth 2.0** version does not. If you need this functionality, you might define the following word (**DSRLNK-SP**) in decimal mode:

```
DECIMAL  : DSRLNK-SP 10 14 SYSTEM ;
```

See the *Editor/Assembler Manual* for details on this form of the call to the DSRLNK utility. You will also need to consult the DSR's specifications because this form of access is at a lower level, with each subroutine usually requiring information that differs from the PAB set up for **DSRLNK** .

5.1.3 VDP Write-Only Registers

The VDP contains 8 special write-only registers. In the Editor/Assembler, a VWTR instruction is used to write values into these registers. The Forth word **VWTR** implements this instruction.

VWTR (*b n* ---)

VWTR requires 2 parameters; a byte *b* to be written and a VDP register number *n*.

base	*b*	*n*	instr
HEX	**F5**	**7**	**VWTR**

The above instruction writes **F5h** into VDP write only register number 7. This particular register controls the foreground and background colors in text and text80 modes. The foreground color is ignored in other modes. Executing the above instruction will change the foreground color to white and the background color to light blue.

5.1.4 VDP RAM Single-Byte Logical Operations

VAND , **VOR** and **VXOR** (*b vaddr* ---)

The Forth instructions **VAND** , **VOR** and **VXOR** greatly simplify the task of performing a logical operation on a single byte in VDP RAM. Normally, 3 programming steps would be required: a read from VDP RAM, an operation, and a write back into VDP RAM. The above instructions each get the job done in a single step. Each of these words requires 2 parameters, a byte *b* to be used as the second operand and the VDP address *vaddr* at which to perform the operation. The result of the operation is placed back into *vaddr*.

base	*b*	*vaddr*	instr
HEX	**F0**	**804**	**VAND**
HEX	**F0**	**804**	**VOR**
HEX	**F0**	**804**	**VXOR**

Each of the above instructions reads the byte stored at **804h** in VDP RAM, performs an AND, OR or XOR on that byte and **F0h**, and places the result back into VDP RAM at **804h**.

5.2 Disk Utilities

FORTH-COPY , **DTEST** , **DISK-HEAD** and **FORMAT-DISK** are not supported in **fbForth 2.0**. If you need the functionality of these words, use one of the various disk manager cartridges or programs available such as TI's Disk Manager 2 cartridge, CorComp's Disk Manager, Quality 99 Software's Disk Manager III or Fred Kaal's Disk Manager 2000 (available on his website, *www.ti99-geek.nl*). You can, of course, use the above words in TI Forth.

SCOPY and **SMOVE** have been replaced by **CPYBLK** , which is described in § 3.5 "Block-Copying Utility".

5.3 Listing Utilities

There are three words defined in **fbForth 2.0** starting in block 19 of FBLOCKS, which make listing information from a Forth blocks file very simple. The following descriptions refer to FBLOCKS dated 01SEP2014 or later to insure that you can print the first 3 blocks. If the file contains a number of blocks not evenly divisible by 3, printing the last 1 or 2 blocks will cause a file error message to be printed when **TRIAD** tries to read past the end of the blocks file.

TRIAD (*blk* ---)

The first, called **TRIAD**, requires a block number on the stack. When executed, it will end with a block number evenly divisible by three. Blocks that contain non-printable information will be skipped. If your RS232 printer is not on Port 1 and set at 9600 Baud, you must modify the word **SWCH** on your System disk.

TRIADS (blk_1 blk_2 ---)

The second instruction, called **TRIADS**, may be thought of as a multiple **TRIAD**. It expects start and end block numbers on the stack. **TRIADS** executes **TRIAD** as many times as necessary to cover the specified range of blocks.

INDEX (*blk*$_1$ *blk*$_2$ ---)

The **INDEX** instruction allows you to list to your terminal line 0 (the comment line) of each of a specified range of blocks. **INDEX** expects start and end block numbers on the stack. If you wish to temporarily stop the flow of output in order to read it before it scrolls off the screen, simply press any key. Press any key to start up again. Press *<BREAK>* (*<CLEAR>* or *<FCTN+4>*) to exit execution prematurely.

5.4 Debugging

5.4.1 Dump Information to Terminal

Loading block 16 loads the useful **fbForth** word **DUMP** for getting information for debugging purposes. **DUMP** is 80-column aware if you have successfully executed **TEXT80** (see Chapter 3 "How to Use the fbForth 2.0 Editors" for some discussion of 80-column text mode).

DUMP (*addr count* ---)

The **DUMP** instruction allows you to list portions of memory to your terminal. **DUMP** requires two parameters, an address *addr* and a byte count *count*. For example,

base	*addr*	*count*	instr
HEX	**2010**	**20**	**DUMP**

will list 32 (**20h**) bytes of memory beginning at address **2010h** to your terminal:

```
2010:  0001  2820  6662  466F  ..( fbFo
2018:  7274  6820  5745  4C43  rth WELC
2020:  4F4D  4520  5343  5245  OME SCRE
2028:  454E  2D2D  2D4C  4553  EN---LES
 ok:0
```

Press any key to temporarily stop execution in order to read the information before it scrolls off the screen. Press any key to continue. To exit this routine, press *<BREAK>*.

Two other useful words, **VLIST** and **.S** , are now part of **fbForth 2.0**'s resident dictionary and are available at any time.

VLIST (---)

VLIST is 80-column aware and lists to your terminal the names of all words currently defined in the **CONTEXT** vocabulary. This instruction requires no parameters and may be halted and started again by pressing any key as with **INDEX** in the previous section. When finished or aborted with *<BREAK>*, **VLIST** displays the number of words listed.

.S (---)

The Forth word **.S** allows you to nondestructively view the parameter stack contents. It may be placed inside a colon definition or executed directly from the keyboard. The word **SP!** should be typed on the command line before executing a routine that contains **.S** . This will clear any garbage from the stack. The '**|**' symbol is printed to represent the bottom of the stack. The number appearing farthest from the **|** is the most accessible stack element, *i.e.*, top of the stack:

```
.S
| 1 8 189  ok:3
```

5.4.2 Tracing Word Execution

This section is based on the following article available at *www.forth.org* :

Paul van der Eijk. 1981. Tracing Colon-Definitions. *Forth Dimensions* **3**:2, p. 58.

A special set of instructions in block 18 of FBLOCKS allows you to trace the execution of any colon definition. Executing the **TRACE** instruction will cause all following colon definitions to be compiled in such a way that they can be traced. In other words, the Forth word **:** takes on a new meaning. To stop compiling under the **TRACE** option, type **UNTRACE**. When you have finished debugging, recompile the routine under the **UNTRACE** option.

After instructions have been compiled under the **TRACE** option, you can trace their execution by typing the word **TRON** before using the instruction. **TRON** activates the trace. If you wish to execute the same instruction without the trace, type **TROFF** before using the instruction.

The actual trace will print the word being traced, along with the stack contents, each time the word is encountered. This shows you what numbers are on the stack just before the traced word is executed. The **|** symbol is used to represent the bottom of the stack. The number printed closest to the **|** is the least accessible while the number farthest from the **|** is the most accessible number on the stack. Here is a sample **TRACE** session:

```
DECIMAL  ok:0
TRACE  ok:0                        (compile next definition with TRACE option)
: CUBE DUP DUP * * ;  ok:0         (routine to be traced)
UNTRACE  ok:0                      (don't compile next definition with TRACE option)
: TEST CUBE ROT CUBE ROT CUBE ;  ok:0
TRON  ok:0                         (want to execute with a TRACE)
5 6 7 TEST                         (put parameters on stack and execute TEST)
CUBE                               (TRACE begins)
| 5 6 7                            (stack contents upon entering CUBE)
CUBE
| 6 343 5                          (stack contents upon entering CUBE)
CUBE
| 343 125 6  ok:3
.S                                 (check final stack contents)
| 343 125 216  ok:3                (stack contents after final CUBE )
```

5.4.3 Recursion

Normally, a Forth word cannot call itself before the definition has been compiled through to a **;** because the smudge bit is set, which prevents the word from being found during compilation. To allow recursion, **fbForth 2.0** includes the special word **MYSELF** .

MYSELF (---)

The **MYSELF** instruction places the *cfa* of the word currently being compiled into its own definition thus allowing a word to call itself.

The following, more complex, **TRACE** example uses a recursive factorial routine for illustration:

```
DECIMAL  ok:0
TRACE  ok:0                  (compile following definition under TRACE option)
: FACT DUP 1 > IF DUP 1 - MYSELF * THEN ;  ok:0
UNTRACE  ok:0
TRON  ok:0
5 FACT                       (put parameter on stack and execute FACT)
FACT                         (TRACE begins)
| 5
FACT
| 5 4
FACT
| 5 4 3
FACT
| 5 4 3 2
FACT
| 5 4 3 2 1  ok:1
.S                           (check final stack contents)
| 120  ok:1
```

Each time the traced **FACT** routine calls itself, a **TRACE** is executed.

5.5 Random Numbers

Two different random number functions are available in **fbForth**. They are part of **fbForth**'s resident dictionary.

RNDW (--- *u*)

The first random number function, **RNDW**, generates an unsigned random integer *u*. No range is specified for **RNDW**. A 5-bit circular right shift of (**6FE5h** * *seed* + **7AB9h**) is stored at **83C0h** as the new value for *seed* and returned as *u* on the stack such that $0 \leq u \leq$ **FFFFh**. Only the rightmost 16-bit value of the unsigned result of **6FE5h** * *seed* is used in the above calculation. Overflow is ignored for all operations.

```
RNDW  ok:1
```

will place on the stack an unsigned integer from **0** to **FFFFh**.

RND (n_1 --- n_2)

The second, **RND**, generates a positive random integer between 0 and a specified range n_1 by taking the absolute value of the result for **RNDW** above, dividing it by n_1 and leaving the remainder on the stack as n_2, such that $0 \leq n_2 < n_1$.

```
DECIMAL 13 RND  ok:1
```

will place on the stack an integer n_2, such that $0 \leq n_2 < 13$. Beware negative n_1! If n_1 is negative, regardless of its value, n_2 will be equivalent to executing

```
RNDW ABS  ok:1       0 ≤ n ≤ 32767
```

RANDOMIZE (---)

To guarantee a different sequence of random numbers each time a program is run, the **RANDOMIZE** instruction must be used. **RANDOMIZE** places an unknown seed into the random number generator. The seed is calculated by clearing the VDP status register by reading it at **8802h** and entering a counter loop that increments the counter and checks the VDP status register for the next VDP interrupt, (essentially racing the console ISR for it) at which point it exits the loop and stores the counter in the seed location **83C0h**.

SEED (*n* ---)

To place a known seed into the random number generator, the **SEED** instruction is used. You must specify the seed value.

```
4 SEED  ok:0
```

will place the value 4 into the random number generator seed location **83C0h**. This is particularly useful during testing because **RND** and **RNDW** will generate the same series of pseudo-random numbers every time they are started with the same seed.

5.6 Miscellaneous Instructions

' (--- *pfa*)

' (tick) searches the **CONTEXT** vocabulary and then the **CURRENT** vocabulary in the dictionary for the next word in the input stream. If it is found, **'** pushes the word's parameter field address *pfa* onto the stack. Otherwise, an error message is displayed and, if the result of loading a block, the contents of **IN** and **BLK** are left on the stack.

, (*n* ---)

, (comma) stores *n* at **HERE** on an even address boundary in the dictionary, which includes the current value of **HERE** , and advances **HERE** one cell to the next even address. Comma is the primary compiling word in Forth.

C, (*b* ---)

C, stores *b* at **HERE** . **C,** is the byte equivalent of **,** . Care must be taken when using **C,** to compile bytes into the dictionary because most storage to the dictionary is cell-oriented. If **HERE** is left on an odd address, a word like **,** will overwrite the previously stored byte!

CLS (---)

CLS is part of **fbForth**'s resident dictionary. Use this word to clear the display screen. **CLS** clears the display screen by filling the screen image table with blanks. The screen image table runs from **SCRN_START** to **SCRN_END** . **CLS** may be used inside a colon definition or directly from the keyboard. **CLS** will not clear bitmap displays or sprites.

PAGE (---)

PAGE clears the screen and places the cursor at the top left of the screen. It is a shortcut for the following code:

```
CLS
0 0 GOTOXY
```

6 An Introduction to Graphics

Words introduced in this chapter:

#MOTION	**DELALL**	**JCRU**	**SCREEN**	**SPRPAT**
BEEP	**DELSPR**	**JKBD**	**SPCHAR**	**SPRPUT**
CHAR	**DOT**	**JMODE**	**SPDCHAR**	**SSDT**
CHARPAT	**DRAW**	**JOYST**	**SPLIT**	**TEXT**
COINC	**DTOG**	**LINE**	**SPLIT2**	**TEXT80**
COINCALL	**GCHAR**	**MAGNIFY**	**SPRCOL**	**UNDRAW**
COINCXY	**GRAPHICS**	**MCHAR**	**SPRDIST**	**VCHAR**
COLOR	**GRAPHICS2**	**MINIT**	**SPRDISTXY**	**VDPMDE**
DATA[	**HCHAR**	**MOTION**	**SPRGET**	**VMODE**
DCHAR	**HONK**	**MULTI**	**SPRITE**	**]DATA**

Graphics words in **fbForth 2.0** are now much faster than in TI Forth and **fbForth 1.0** because most of the graphics primitives have been rewritten in Assembly Language. **LINE** probably enjoys the greatest speed increase. Its high-level Forth code in TI Forth and **fbForth 1.0** rendered it nearly useless.

6.1 Graphics Modes

The TI Home Computer possesses a broad range of graphics capabilities. Seven screen modes are available to the user:

0) **Text80 Mode**—This is the same as text mode described below except that, in text80 mode, the screen is 80 columns by 24 lines. The user should insure that the system in use is capable of displaying 80-columns before invoking it, *i.e.*, it should be equipped with an F18A VDP (available at *codehackcreate.com*) or similar device.

1) **Text Mode**—Standard ASCII characters are available, and new characters may be defined. All characters have the same foreground and background color. The screen is 40 columns by 24 lines. Text mode is used by the Forth 40/80-column screen editor.

2) **Graphics Mode**—Standard ASCII characters are available, and new characters may be defined. Each character set may have its own foreground and background color.

3) **Multicolor Mode**—The screen is 64 columns by 48 rows. Each standard character position is now 4 smaller boxes which can each have a different color. ASCII characters are not available and new characters cannot be defined.

4) **Bitmap Mode (Graphics2)**—This mode is available only on the TI-99/4A. Bitmap mode allows you to set any pixel on the screen and to change its color within the limits permitted by the TMS9918a. The screen is 256 columns by 192 rows.

5) **Split Mode**—This mode is one of two unique graphics modes created by using graphics2 mode in a non-standard way. Split2 [see (6)] is the other non-standard variation of

graphics2 mode. Split and split2 modes allow you to display text while creating bitmap graphics. Split mode sets the top two thirds of the screen in graphics2 mode and places text on the last third. Split mode is used by the 64-column editor.

6) **Split2 Mode**—This mode is the other of the two unique graphics modes created by using graphics2 mode in a non-standard way [see (5)]. Split2 sets the top one sixth of the screen as a text window and the rest in graphics2 mode.

Split and split2 modes provide an interactive bitmap graphics setting. That is, you can type bitmap instructions and watch them execute without changing modes.

Sprites (moving graphics) are available in all modes except text and text80. The sprite automotion feature is not available in graphics2, split, or split2 modes.

You may place the computer in the above modes by executing one of the following instructions:

TEXT80 (---)

TEXT (---)

GRAPHICS (---)

MULTI (---)

GRAPHICS2 (---)

SPLIT (---)

SPLIT2 (---)

VMODE (*n* ---) where *n* is one of the above VDP mode numbers (0 – 6).

The following resident user variable holds a number corresponding to one of the above modes as enumerated above. It can be useful for programmatically determining the graphics mode:

VDPMDE (--- *addr*)

Executing one of the mode-setting words puts the corresponding number into **VDPMDE** as can be seen in the following:

```
GRAPHICS VDPMDE @ .
2  ok:0
```

6.2 fbForth 2.0 *Graphics Words*

Many **fbForth** words have been defined to make graphics handling much easier for the user. As many words are mentioned, an annotation will appear underneath them denoting which of the modes they may be used in (T G M B). These denote text, graphics, multicolor and bitmapped (graphics2, split, split2) modes, respectively—'T' includes text80.

In several instruction examples, a base (**HEX** or **DECIMAL**) is specified. This does not mean that you must be in a particular base in order to use the instruction. It merely illustrates that some instructions are more easily written in hexadecimal than in decimal. It also avoids ambiguity.

6.3 Color Changes

The simplest graphics operations involve altering the color of the screen and of character sets. There are 32 character sets (0 – 31), each containing 8 characters. For example, character set 0 consists of characters 0 – 7, character set 1 consists of characters 8 – 15, *etc*. Sixteen colors are available on the TI Home Computer.

Color	Hex Value	Color	Hex Value
transparent	0	medium red	8
black	1	light red	9
medium green	2	dark yellow	A
light green	3	light yellow	B
dark blue	4	dark green	C
light blue	5	magenta	D
dark red	6	gray	E
cyan	7	white	F

SCREEN (*color* ---)

The Forth word **SCREEN** following one of the above table values will change the screen color to that value. The following example changes the screen to light yellow:

base	*color*	instr	
HEX	**B**	**SCREEN**	or
DECIMAL	**11**	**SCREEN**	
		(T G M B)	

For text modes, the color of the foreground also needs to be set and should be different from the background color so that text is visible. The foreground color must be in the leftmost 4 bits of the byte passed to **SCREEN**. It is easier to compose the byte in hexadecimal than decimal because each half of the byte is one hexadecimal digit. To set the foreground to black (**1**) and the background to light yellow (**Bh**), the following sequence will do the trick:

```
HEX 1B SCREEN  ok:0
```

COLOR (*fg bg charset* ---)

The foreground and background colors of a character set may also be easily changed:

base	*fg*	*bg*	*charset*	instr	
HEX	**4**	**D**	**1A**	**COLOR**	or
DECIMAL	**4**	**13**	**26**	**COLOR**	
				(G)	

The above instruction will change character set 26 (characters 208 – 215) to have a foreground color of dark blue and a background color of magenta.

6.4 Placing Characters on the Screen

HCHAR (*col row count char* ---)

To print a character anywhere on the screen and optionally repeat it horizontally, the **HCHAR** instruction is used. You must specify a starting column and row position as well as the number of repetitions and the ASCII code of the character you wish to print.

Keep in mind that both columns and rows are numbered from zero!!!

For example,

base	*col*	*row*	*count*	*char*	instr	
HEX	**A**	**11**	**5B**	**2A**	**HCHAR**	or
DECIMAL	**10**	**17**	**91**	**42**	**HCHAR**	
					(T G)	

will print a stream of 91 *s, starting at column 10, row 17, that will wrap from right to left on the screen.

HCHAR does *not* check to see whether (*col,row*) is within the screen buffer or whether count will overrun VRAM after the screen buffer. This is the same behavior as in TI Forth. This behavior will be changed in the next build of **fbForth 2.0** to conform to how TI Basic and TI Extended Basic implement this function, *i.e.*, in the next build, **HCHAR** will throw an error if it would start outside the screen buffer and it will wrap to the start of the screen buffer upon reaching the end of the screen buffer.

VCHAR (*col row count char* ---)

To print a vertical stream of characters, the word **VCHAR** is used in the same format as **HCHAR** . These characters will wrap from the bottom of the screen to the top of the same column.

VCHAR does *not* check to see whether (*col,row*) is within the screen buffer. Upon reaching the end of the screen buffer, it wraps to the top of the same column. This is different from TI Forth, which wraps to the next column and then to (0,0), filling the screen buffer if *count* is high enough. This behavior will be changed in the next build of **fbForth 2.0** to conform to how TI Basic and TI Extended Basic implement this function, *i.e.*, in the next build, **VCHAR** will throw an error if it would start outside the screen buffer and it will wrap to (0,0) upon reaching the end of the screen buffer, as it does now.

GCHAR (*col row* --- *char*)

The **fbForth** word **GCHAR** will return on the stack the ASCII code of the character currently at the specified position on the screen. If the above **HCHAR** instruction were executed and followed by

base	*col*	*row*	instr	
HEX	**F**	**11**	**GCHAR**	or
DECIMAL	**15**	**17**	**GCHAR**	
			(T G)	

2Ah or 42 would be left on the stack.

6.5 Defining New Characters

Each character in graphics mode is 8 x 8 pixels in size. Each row makes up one byte of the 8-byte character definition. Each set bit (1) takes on the foreground color while the others remain the background color.

In text mode, characters are defined in the same way, but only the left 6 bits of each row are displayed on the screen.

For example, these 8 bytes:

	3C66h	DBE7h	E7DBh	663Ch
Rows	0 – 1	2 – 3	4 – 5	6 – 7

define this character:

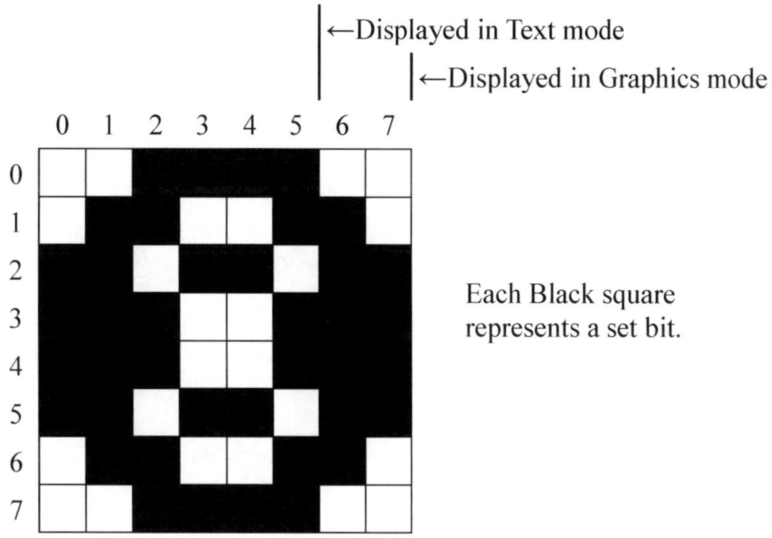

Each Black square represents a set bit.

CHAR (n_1 n_2 n_3 n_4 *char* ---)

The **fbForth** word **CHAR** is used to create new characters. To assign the above pattern to character number 123, you would type

base	n_1	n_2	n_3	n_4	*char*	instr	
HEX	**3C66**	**DBE7**	**E7DB**	**663C**	**7B**	**CHAR**	or
DECIMAL	**15426**	**56295**	**59355**	**26172**	**123**	**CHAR** (T G)	

As you can see, it is more natural to use this instruction in **HEX** than in **DECIMAL** .

DCHAR (*addr cnt char* ---)

DCHAR can be used to create several contiguous characters at once. For example, to create five such characters starting with character number 123, you would first set up an array of 20 16-bit numbers for the required 40 bytes (8 bytes or 4 cells for each character's pattern), place the array's start address *addr* and cell count *cnt* on the stack followed by the character code *char* (123 in this case). You would then type

base	*addr*	*cnt*	*char*	instr	
HEX	**AC34**	**14**	**7B**	**DCHAR**	or
DECIMAL	**44084**	**20**	**123**	**DCHAR**	
				(T G)	

An easy way to set up the array for the above is to use the **DATA[…]DATA** construct, which will leave the address and cell count of the array on the stack. Add *char* to the stack and launch **DCHAR**. The following example defines characters 123 – 127 to each have the same pattern as the **CHAR** example above:

```
HEX DATA[ 3C66 DBE7 E7DB 663C
          3C66 DBE7 E7DB 663C
          3C66 DBE7 E7DB 663C
          3C66 DBE7 E7DB 663C
          3C66 DBE7 E7DB 663C ]DATA  ok:2
7B DCHAR  ok:0
```

See Appendix D "The fbForth 2.0 Glossary" for the details of **DATA[** and **]DATA**.

CHARPAT (*char* --- n_1 n_2 n_3 n_4)

To define another character to look like character 65 ('A'), for example, you must first find out what the pattern code for 'A' is. To accomplish this, use the **CHARPAT** instruction. This instruction leaves the character definition on the stack in the proper order for a **CHAR** instruction. Study this line of code:

HEX	**41**	**CHARPAT**	**7E**	**CHAR**	or
DECIMAL	**65**	**CHARPAT**	**126**	**CHAR**	
				(T G)	

The above instructions place on the stack the character pattern for 'A' and assigns the pattern to character 126. Now both character 65 and 126 have the same shape.

6.6 Sprites

Sprites are moving graphics that can be displayed on the screen independently and/or on top of other characters. Thirty-two sprites are available.

6.6.1 Magnification

Sprites may be defined in 4 different sizes or magnifications:

Magnification Factor	Description
0	Causes all sprites to be single size and unmagnified. Each sprite is defined only by the character specified and occupies one character position on the screen.

Magnification Factor	Description
1	Causes all sprites to be single size and magnified. Each sprite is defined only by the character specified, but this character expands to fill 4 screen positions.
2	Causes all sprites to be double size and unmagnified. Each sprite is defined by the character specified along with the next 3 characters. The first character number must be divisible by 4. This character becomes the upper left quarter of the sprite, the next characters are the lower left, upper right, lower right respectively. The sprite fills 4 screen positions.
3	Causes all sprites to be double size and magnified. Each sprite is defined by 4 characters as above, but each character is expanded to occupy 4 screen positions. The sprite fills 16 positions.

The default magnification is 0.

MAGNIFY (*n* ---)

To alter sprite magnification, use the **fbForth** word **MAGNIFY** .

n	instr
2	**MAGNIFY** (G M B)

will change all sprites to double size and unmagnified.

6.6.2 Sprite Initialization

DELALL (---)

DELALL
(G M B)

should be used to initialize all sprites. It removes all sprites from the screen and from memory. It also zeroes the Sprite Motion Table, except in bitmap modes. **DELALL** takes no parameters. Only the Sprite Descriptor Table will remain intact after this instruction is executed. The VDP mode must be set before using this word.

If you wish to change the Sprite Descriptor Table to a location different from the default for a given VDP mode, use **SSDT** , which follows.

SSDT (*vaddr* ---) ***This word is optional in **fbForth 2.0*****

SSDT changes the location of the Sprite Descriptor Table from its default location, set by the VDP mode changing words. As of **fbForth 2.0**, **SSDT** is no longer required to initialize sprites. **SSDT** does call **DELALL** before moving the location of the Sprite Descriptor Table, so sprites do not need to be initialized with **DELALL** after executing **SSDT** . If you *do* use this word, the computer must be set into the VDP mode you wish to use with sprites before executing it. Recall that *sprites are not available in text mode*.

With this word, you have a choice of overlapping your sprite character definitions with the standard characters in the Pattern Descriptor Table (see VDP Memory Map in Chapter 4) or moving the Sprite Descriptor Table elsewhere in memory. This move is highly recommended (except in bitmap modes) to avoid confusion. **2000h** is usually a good location, but any available 2 KiB (**800h**) boundary will do.

base	*vaddr*	instr	
HEX	**2000**	**SSDT**	or
DECIMAL	**8192**	**SSDT**	
		(G M B)	

will move the Sprite Descriptor Table to **2000h**.

6.6.3 Using Sprites in Bitmap Mode

SATR (--- *vaddr*)

When using sprites in any of the bitmap modes (graphics2, split, split2) and after entering the desired VDP mode, the location of the Sprite Attribute List will have already been changed to **1B00h**. This can be verified in split or split2 mode as follows:

HEX SATR U. **1B00** **ok:0**

The base address of the Sprite Descriptor Table will also have been changed to the required **3800h**, which can be verified in split or split2 mode with

HEX SPDTAB U. **3800** **ok:0**

Only 59 character numbers will be available for sprite patterns in the bitmap modes because otherwise you will interfere with the disk buffering region at the top of VRAM. **SPCHAR** may only be used to define patterns 0 – 58. (See the following section for information on **SPCHAR**.) If you really need more than 59 sprite patterns available and you don't need to open any files other than blocks files like FBLOCKS, you can change from 2 simultaneous files to 1 with **1 FILES** after changing the VDP mode because **fbForth 2.0** only opens one blocks file at a time, and then, only to read or write a single block. This will allow 65 more patterns (0 – 123).

Note: If you have mass storage in addition to diskettes (hard disk, nanoPEB, CF7+, *etc.*), it is possible that more than you expect of upper VRAM is used for buffering. In this case, check location **8370h** for the highest VRAM address available, subtract **3800h** from it, divide by 8 and truncate the quotient to get the number of sprite patterns available.

3800h	Sprite Patterns 0-58
39DDh	**01DEh**
39DEh	Start of Disk Buffer Region for 2 files

6.6.4 Creating Sprites

The first task involved in creating sprites is to define the characters you will use to make them. These definitions will be stored in the Sprite Descriptor Table mentioned in the above section.

SPCHAR (n_1 n_2 n_3 n_4 *char* ---)

A word identical in format to **CHAR** is used to store sprite character patterns. If you are using a magnification factor of 2 or 3, do not forget that you must define 4 consecutive characters for *each* sprite. In this case, the character # of the first character must be a multiple of 4.

base	n_1	n_2	n_3	n_4	*char*	instr	
HEX	**0F0F**	**2424**	**F0F0**	**4242**	**0**	**SPCHAR**	or
DECIMAL	**3855**	**9252**	**61680**	**8770**	**0**	**SPCHAR**	
						(G M B)	

defines character 0 in the Sprite Descriptor Table. If your Pattern and Sprite Descriptor Tables overlap, use character numbers below 127 with caution.

SPDCHAR (*addr cnt char* ---)

SPDCHAR can be used to create several contiguous sprite characters at once. **SPDCHAR** is identical to **DCHAR** , (see § 6.5 "Defining New Characters" above) but for sprite pattern definitions because SPDTAB does not always start at the same VRAM address as PDT. Here is the same example as for **DCHAR** in § 6.5 to create five identical sprite characters numbering 123 – 127, with pattern array of *cnt* cells starting at *addr*:

base	*addr*	*cnt*	*char*	instr	
HEX	**AC34**	**14**	**7B**	**SPDCHAR**	or
DECIMAL	**44084**	**20**	**123**	**SPDCHAR**	
				(G M B)	

As with **DCHAR** , you can facilitate setting up the pattern array with **DATA[…]DATA** . See the **DCHAR** example in § 6.5 above.

SPRITE (*dotcol dotrow color char spr* ---)

To define a sprite, you must specify the dot column and dot row at which its upper left corner will be located, its color, a character number and a sprite number (0 – 31).

base	*dotcol*	*dotrow*	*color*	*char*	*spr*	instr	
HEX	**6B**	**4C**	**5**	**10**	**1**	**SPRITE**	or
DECIMAL	**107**	**76**	**5**	**16**	**1**	**SPRITE**	
						(G M B)	

defines sprite #1 to be located at column 107 and row 76, to be light blue and to begin with character 16. Its size will depend on the magnification factor.

Once a sprite has been created, changing its pattern, color or location is trivial.

SPRPAT (*char spr* ---)

base	*char*	*spr*	instr	
HEX	**14**	**1**	**SPRPAT**	or
DECIMAL	**20**	**1**	**SPRPAT**	
			(G M B)	

will change the pattern of sprite #1 to character number 20.

SPRCOL (*color spr* ---)

base	*color*	*spr*	instr	
HEX	**C**	**2**	**SPRCOL**	or
DECIMAL	**12**	**2**	**SPRCOL**	
			(G M B)	

will change the color of sprite #2 to dark green.

SPRPUT (*dotcol dotrow spr* ---)

base	*dotcol*	*dotrow*	*spr*	instr	
HEX	**28**	**4F**	**1**	**SPRPUT**	or
DECIMAL	**40**	**79**	**1**	**SPRPUT**	
				(G M B)	

will place sprite #1 at column 40 and row 79.

6.6.5 Sprite Automotion

In graphics or multicolor mode, sprites may be set in automotion. That is, having assigned them horizontal and vertical velocities and set them in motion, they will continue moving with no further instruction. Sprite automotion is only available in graphics and multicolor modes.

Velocities from 0 to **7Fh** are positive velocities (down for vertical and right for horizontal) and from **FFh** to **80h** are taken as two's complement negative velocities.

MOTION (*xvel yvel spr* ---)

base	*xvel*	*yvel*	*spr*	instr	
HEX	**FC**	**6**	**1**	**MOTION**	or
DECIMAL	**-4**	**6**	**1**	**MOTION**	
				(G M)	

will assign sprite #1 a horizontal velocity of -4 and a vertical velocity of 6, but will not actually set them into motion.

#MOTION (*n* ---)

After you assign each sprite you want to use a velocity, you must execute the word **#MOTION** to set the sprites in motion. **#MOTION** expects to find on the stack the highest sprite number you are using + 1.

n	instr
6	**#MOTION**
	(G M)

will set sprites #0 – #5 in motion.

n	instr
0	**#MOTION**

will stop all sprite automotion, but motion will resume when another **#MOTION** instruction is executed.

SPRGET (*spr --- dotcol dotrow*)

Once a sprite is in motion, you may wish to find out its horizontal and vertical position on the screen at a given time.

spr	instr
2	**SPRGET**
	(G M B)

will return on the stack the horizontal (*dotcol*) and vertical (*dotrow*) positions of sprite #2. The sprite does *not* have to be in automotion to use this instruction.

6.6.6 Distance and Coincidences between Sprites

It is possible to determine the distance d between two sprites or between a sprite and a point on the screen. This capability comes in handy when writing game programs. The actual value returned by each of the **fbForth** words, **SPRDIST** and **SPRDISTXY** , is d^2. Distance d is the hypotenuse of the right triangle formed by joining the line segments, d, $x_2 - x_1$ (the horizontal x-distance difference in dot columns) and $y_2 - y_1$ (the vertical y-distance difference in dot rows). The squared distance between the two sprites or the sprite and screen point is calculated by squaring the x-distance difference and adding that to the square of the the y-distance difference, *i.e.*, $d^2 = (x_2 - x_1)^2 + (y_2 - y_1)^2$.

SPRDIST (spr_1 spr_2 --- n)

spr_1	spr_2	instr
2	**4**	**SPRDIST**
		(G M B)

returns on the stack the square of the distance between sprite #2 and sprite #4.

SPRDISTXY (*dotcol dotrow spr --- n*)

base	*dotcol*	*dotrow*	*spr*	instr
DECIMAL	**65**	**21**	**5**	**SPRDISTXY**
				(G M B)

returns the square of the distance between sprite #5 and the point (65,21).

A coincidence occurs when two sprites become positioned directly on top of one another. That is, their upper left corners reside at the same point. Because this condition rarely occurs when sprites are in automotion you can set a tolerance limit for coincidence detection. For example, a tolerance of 3 would report a coincidence whenever the upper left corners of the two sprites came within 3 dot positions of each other.

COINC (spr_1 spr_2 *tol --- flag*)

To find a coincidence between two sprites, the **fbForth** word **COINC** is used.

spr_1	*spr_2*	*tol*	instr
7	**9**	**2**	**COINC**
			(G M B)

will detect a coincidence between sprites #7 and #9 if their upper left corners passed within 2 dot positions of each other. If a coincidence is found, a true flag is left on the stack. If not, a false flag is left.

COINCXY (*dotcol dotrow spr tol --- flag*)

Detecting a coincidence between a sprite and a point is similar.

base	*dotcol*	*dotrow*	*spr*	*tol*	instr
DECIMAL	**63**	**29**	**8**	**3**	**COINCXY**
					(G M B)

will detect a coincidence between sprite #8 and the point (63,29) with a tolerance of 3. A true or false flag will again be left on the stack.

Both of the above instructions will detect a coincidence between non-visible parts of the sprites. That is, you may not be able to *see* the coincidence.

COINCALL (*--- flag*)

Another instruction is used to detect only *visible* coincidences. It, however, will not detect coincidences between a select two sprites, but will return a true flag when any two sprites collide. This instruction is **COINCALL** , and takes no arguments.

6.6.7 Deleting Sprites

As you might have noticed, sprites do not go away when you clear the rest of the screen with **CLS** . Special instructions must be used to remove sprites from the display,

DELSPR (*spr ---*)

spr	instr
2	**DELSPR**
	(G M B)

will remove sprite #2 from the screen by altering its description in the Sprite Attribute List (see VDP Memory Map in Chapter 4). It sets sprite #2 to sprite pattern #0 and sets the sprite off screen at $\boldsymbol{x} = 1$, $\boldsymbol{y} = 192$. It zeroes the velocity of sprite #2 in the Sprite Motion Table, but does not alter the number of sprites the computer thinks are defined by virtue of not setting y = **D0h**, the y-value that undefines all sprites with numbers greater than or equal to the lowest-numbered sprite with that value.

DELALL (---)

DELALL
(G M B)

on the other hand, will remove all sprites from the screen and from memory. See § 6.6.2 Sprite Initialization above for more details.

6.7 Multicolor Graphics

Multicolor mode allows you to display kaleidoscopic graphics. Each character position on the screen consists of 4 smaller squares which can each be a different color. A cluster of these characters produces a kaleidoscope when the colors are changed rapidly.

MINIT (---)

After entering multicolor mode, it is necessary to initialize the screen. The **MINIT** instruction will accomplish this. It takes no parameters.

When in multicolor mode, the columns are numbered 0 – 63 and rows are numbered 0 – 47. A multicolor character is ¼ the size of a standard character. Therefore, more of them fit across and down the screen.

MCHAR (*color col row* ---)

To define a multicolor character, you must specify a color and a position (column, row) and then execute the word **MCHAR** :

base	*color*	*col*	*row*	instr	
HEX	**B**	**1A**	**2C**	**MCHAR**	or
DECIMAL	**11**	**26**	**44**	**MCHAR**	

The above instruction will place a light yellow square at (26,44).

To change a character's color, simply define a different color with **MCHAR** with the same position. In other words, cover the existing character.

6.8 Using Joysticks

JOYST (n_1 --- [*char* n_2 n_3] | n_2)

The **JOYST** instruction allows you to use joysticks in your **fbForth** program. **JOYST** accepts input from joystick #1 and the left side of the keyboard ($n_1 = 1$) or from joystick #2 and the right side of the keyboard ($n_1 = 2$). Return values depend on the value in **JMODE** (see below). If **JMODE** = 0 (default), **JOYST** executes **JKBD** (see below for more detail), which returns the character code *char* of the key pressed, the ***x*** status n_2 and the ***y*** status n_3. If **JMODE** ≠ 0, **JOYST** executes **JCRU** , which checks only the joysticks and returns a single value with 0 or more of the 5 least significant bits set. See **JCRU** below for their meaning.

JMODE (--- *addr*)

JMODE is a user variable that uses offset **26h** of the user variable table. It is used by **JOYST** to determine whether to execute **JKBD** (= 0) or **JCRU** (≠ 0). The default value is 0. See **JOYST** , **JKBD** and **JCRU** in this section.

JKBD (n_1 --- *char* n_2 n_3)

Executed by **JOYST** when **JMODE** = 0, **JKBD** allows input from joystick #1 and the left side of the keyboard (n_1 = 1) or from joystick #2 and the right side of the keyboard (n_1 = 2). Values returned are the character code *char* of the key pressed, the x status n_2 and the y status n_3. A "Key Pad" exists on each side of the keyboard and may be used in place of joysticks. Map directions (N, S, E, W, NE, *etc.*) are used on the diagrams below to indicate the corresponding display-screen directions (up, down, right, left, diagonally-up-and-right, *etc.*) The following diagrams show which keys have which function.

When Joystick #1 is specified, these keys on the left side of the keyboard are valid

The function of each key is indicated below the key and is followed by the character code returned as *char* on the stack.

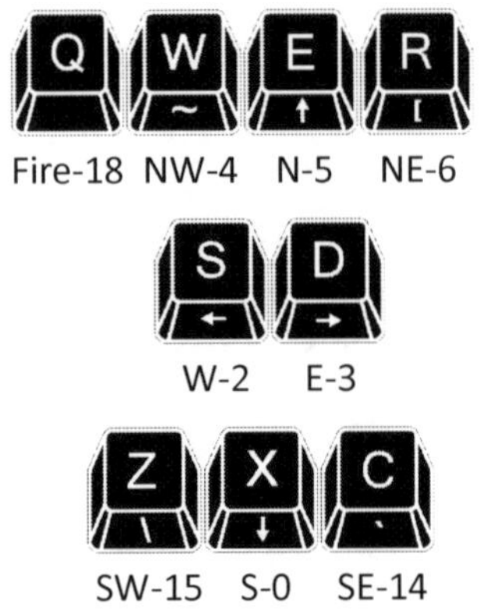

When Joystick #2 is specified, these keys on the right side of the keyboard are valid

The function of each key is indicated below the key and is followed by the character code returned as *char* on the stack.

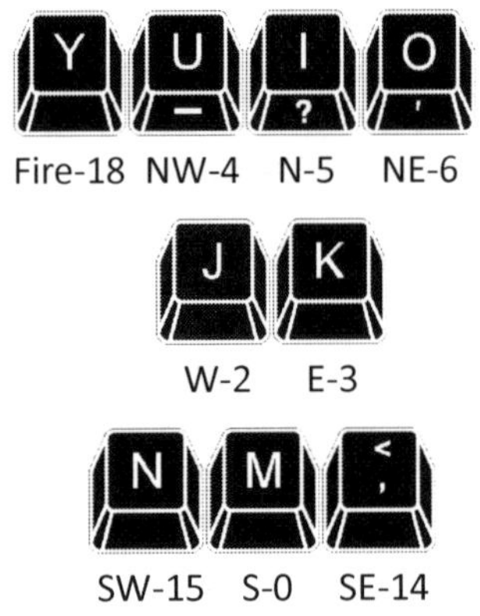

The **JKBD** instruction (or **JOYST** with **JMODE** = 0) returns 3 numbers on the stack: a character code *char* on the bottom of the stack, an x-joystick status n_2 and a y-joystick status n_3 on top of the stack. The joystick positions are illustrated in the diagram on page 62.

FCh equals decimal 252. The capital letters and ',' separated by '|' indicate which keys on the left and right side of the keyboard return these values. *Note:* The character value of all fire buttons is 18 (**12h**).

If no key is pressed, the returned values will be a character code of 255 (**FFh**), and the current x- and y-joystick positions. If a valid key is pressed, the character code of that key will be returned along with its translated directional meaning (see diagram). If an illegal key is pressed, three zeroes will be returned.

If the fire button is pressed while using the keyboard, a character code of 18 (**12h**) along with two zeroes will be returned. If the fire button is pressed while using a joystick, a character code of 18 (**12h**) along with the current *x*- and *y*-joystick positions will be returned.

If you are using **JKBD** (or **JOYST** with **JMODE** = 0) in a loop, do not forget to **DROP** or otherwise use the three numbers left on the stack before calling **JKBD** or **JOYST** again. A stack overflow will likely result if you do not.

You will notice that the *x* and *y* values left by **JKBD** (or **JOYST** with **JMODE** = 0) for joystick status use **FCh** for left and down as described on page 250 of the *Editor/Assembler Manual*. If you are used to the value -4, which is the value returned for the same directions in TI Basic and TI Extended Basic, you can change **JKBD** 's return of **FCh** to -4 in block 39, where it is defined. You will need to change every instance of '**0FC**' to '-4' in the definition of **JKBD**—there are six of them.

The reason, of course, that **FCh** is used in **fbForth** (and TI Forth before it) is that **FCh** is how -4 is represented in a single byte in the byte-oriented GROM joystick table where it is stored.

JCRU (n_1 --- n_2)

Executed by **JOYST** when **JMODE** ≠ 0, **JCRU** allows input from joystick #1 (n_1 = 1) or #2 (n_1 = 2). The value n_2 returned will have 0 or more of the 5 least significant bits set for direction and fire-button status. Bit values are 1 = Fire, 2 = W, 4 = E, 8 = S and 16 = N. Two-bit directional combinations are 18 = NW (N + W or 16 + 2), 20 = NE, 10 = SW and 12 = SE.

If you are using **JCRU** (or **JOYST** with **JMODE** ≠ 0) in a loop, do not forget to **DROP** or otherwise use the number left on the stack before calling **JCRU** or **JOYST** again. A stack overflow will likely result if you do not.

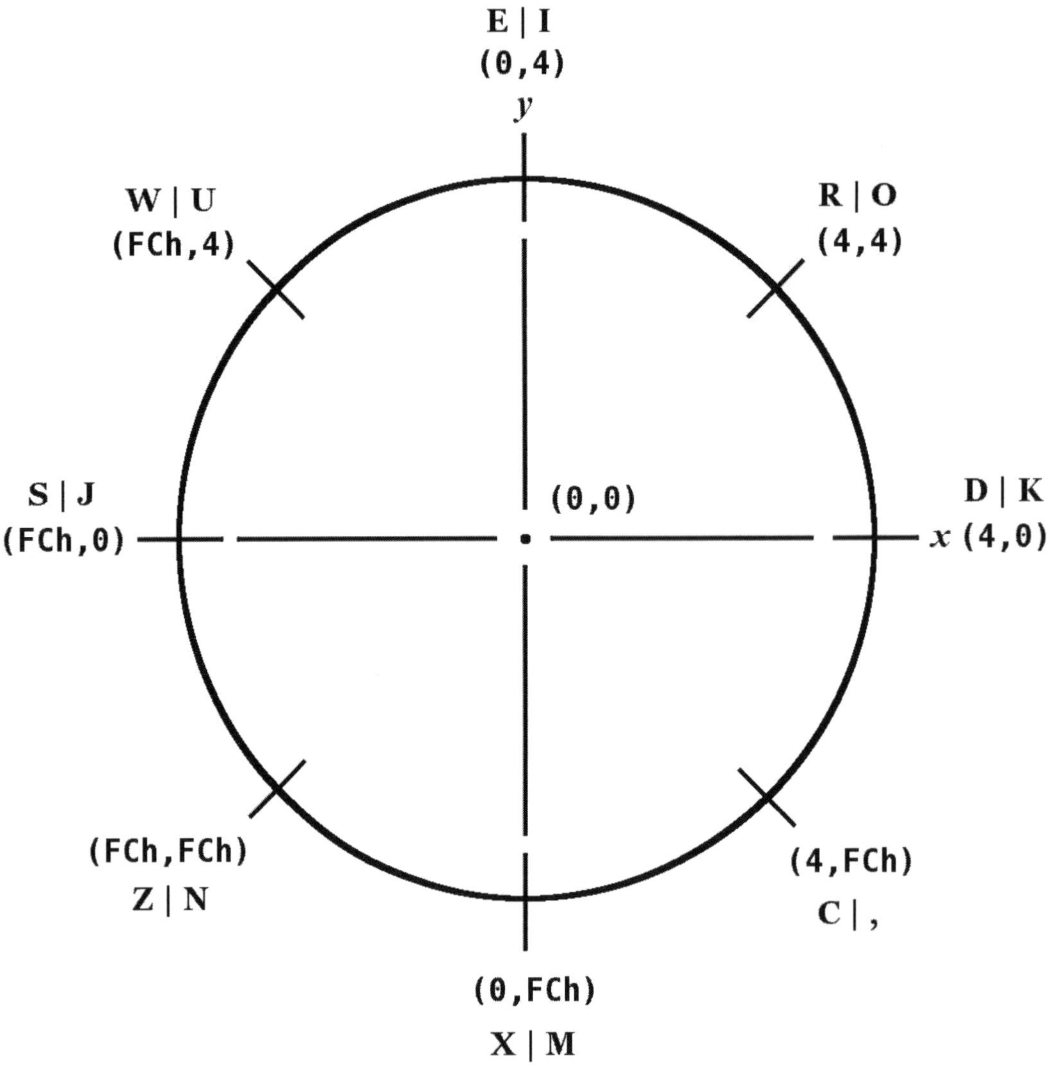

Joystick positions and values left by **JKBD** *(or* **JOYST** *with* **JMODE** *= 0)*

6.9 Dot Graphics

High resolution (dot) graphics are available in graphics2, split and split2 modes. In graphics2 mode, it is possible to independently define each of the 49152 pixels on the screen. Split and split2 modes allow you to define the upper two thirds or the lower five sixths of the pixels.

Three dot drawing modes are available:

DRAW (---)

stores 0 in **DMODE** , which causes **DOT** to plot dots in the 'on' state.

UNDRAW (---)

stores 1 in **DMODE** , which causes **DOT** to plot dots in the 'off' state.

DTOG (---)

stores 2 in **DMODE** , which causes **DOT** to toggle dots between the 'on' and 'off' state. If the dot is 'on', **DOT** will turn it 'off' and vice versa.

DMODE (--- *addr*)

The value of a variable called **DMODE** controls which drawing mode **DOT** is in. If **DMODE** contains 0, **DOT** is in **DRAW** mode. If **DMODE** contains 1, **DOT** is in **UNDRAW** mode, and if **DMODE** contains 2, **DOT** is in **DTOG** mode.

DOT (*dotcol dotrow*---)

To actually plot a dot on the screen, the **DOT** instruction is used. You must specify the dot column and dot row of the pixel you wish to plot:

base	*dotcol*	*dotrow*	instr
DECIMAL	**34**	**12**	**DOT**

will plot or unplot a dot at position (34,12), depending on the value of **DMODE** .

DCOLOR (--- *addr*)

DCOLOR is short for "dot color" and should contain either one byte of foreground-background (FG-BG) color information or -1. The default is -1, which means that **DOT** will use the FG and BG colors of the byte in the Bitmap Color Table where the dot will be plotted/unplotted. These colors are black on transparent when the bitmap graphics modes are initialized. The screen color default is gray. To alter the FG and BG colors of the dots you plot, you must modify the value of the variable **DCOLOR** . The value of **DCOLOR** should be two hexadecimal digits, where the first digit specifies the FG color and the second specifies a BG color. Why do you need a BG color for a dot? There is a simple explanation: Each dot represents one bit of a byte in memory. Any 'on' bit in that byte displays the FG color while the others take on the BG color. Usually, you would specify the background color to be transparent so that all 'off' dots will have the screen's color.

LINE ($dotcol_1$ $dotrow_1$ $dotcol_2$ $dotrow_2$ ---)

The **fbForth** instruction **LINE** allows you to easily plot a line between *any* two points on the bitmap portion of the screen. You must specify a dot column and a dot row for each of the two points.

base	$dotcol_1$	$dotrow_1$	$dotcol_2$	$dotrow_2$	instr
DECIMAL	**23**	**12**	**56**	**78**	**LINE**

The above instruction will plot a line from left to right between (23,12) and (56,78). The line instruction calls **DOT** to plot each point. Therefore, you must set **DMODE** and **DCOLOR** before using **LINE** if you do not want different plotting mode and FG-BG dot colors.

6.10 Special Sounds

Two special sounds can be used to enhance your graphics application. To use these noises in your program, simply type the name of the sound you want to hear. No parameters are needed.

BEEP (---)

The first is called **BEEP** and produces a pleasant high pitched sound.

HONK (---)

The other, called **HONK**, produces a less pleasant low tone.

6.11 Constants and Variables Used in Graphics Programming

The following constants and variables are defined in the graphics routines. In **fbForth 2.0**, the values of **COLTAB**, **PDT**, **SATR** and **SPDTAB** are now changed by the mode changing words and do not require intervention by the user.

				bitmap modes		
name	**type**	**description**	**default**	**4**	**5**	**6**
DMODE	variable	Dot graphics drawing mode	0	0|1|2		
SMTN	constant	VDP address of Sprite Motion Table	780h	N/A	N/A	N/A
COLTAB	constant	VDP address of Color Table	380h	0	0	0
PDT	constant	VDP address of Pattern Descriptor Table	800h	2000h	3000h	2000h
SATR	constant	VDP address of Sprite Attribute Table	300h	1B00h	1B00h	1B00h
SPDTAB	constant	VDP address of Sprite Descriptor Table	800h	3800h	3800h	3800h

7 The Floating Point Support Package

Words introduced in this chapter:

>DEG	F!	F>	FOVER	LOG10
>F	F*	F>R	FP1	PI
>RAD	F+	F@	FP10	R>F
?FLERR	F-	FABS	FRAC	RAD/DEG
ATN	F->S	FCONSTANT	FROT	S->F
CEIL	F.	FDROP	FSWAP	SIN
COS	F/	FDUP	FVARIABLE	SQR
DEG/RAD	FO<	FFMT.	INT	TAN
EXP	FO=	FLERR	LN10INV	TRUNC
EXP10	F<	FLOOR	LOG	^
EULER_E	F=	FMINUS		

The floating point package is designed to make it easy to use the Radix 100 floating point package available in ROM in the **fbForth 2.0** cartridge. Normal use of these routines does not require the user to understand the implementation. You should consult Appendix L "Notes on Radix-100 Notation" to get a better understanding of how floating point numbers are managed on the TI-994A computer by the routines discussed in this chapter.

All floating point operations that have results that exceed the maximum or minimum representable floating point numbers convert the result to the maximum representable floating point number ($\pm$ 9.9999999999999 $\cdot$ 10^{127}) for numbers that are too large and to 0 for numbers that are too small.

7.1 Floating Point Stack Manipulation

The floating point numbers in the TI-99/4A occupy 4 16-bit cells (8 bytes) each. In order to simplify stack manipulations with these numbers, the following stack manipulation words are presented. They have the same functions as their 16-bit, 1-cell counterparts that appear in this manual without the '**F**' in their names:

FDUP (f --- f f)

FDROP (f ---)

FOVER (f_1 f_2 --- f_1 f_2 f_1)

FSWAP (f_1 f_2 --- f_2 f_1)

FROT (f_1 f_2 f_3 --- f_2 f_3 f_1)

F>R (f ---) (R: --- f)

R>F (--- f) (R: f ---)

7.2 Floating Point Defining Words

The following words create new floating point variables and constants. They both require an 8-byte floating-point number on the stack to place in the parameter field of the newly defined variable or constant:

FVARIABLE xxx	(*f* ---) (IS: *varName*)	Create variable with initial value *f*
xxx	(--- *addr*)	Returns *pfa* of **xxx** when executed
FCONSTANT xxx	(*f* ---) (IS: *constName*)	Create constant with value *f*
xxx	(--- *f*)	Returns *f* (contents of **xxx**'s *pfa*) when executed

7.3 Floating Point Fetch and Store

Floating point numbers can be stored and fetched by using

F! (*f addr* ---)

F@ (*addr* --- *f*)

The user must ensure that adequate storage is allocated for these numbers (*e.g.*, define a floating point variable: **>F 0 FVARIABLE nnnn** could be used. **FVARIABLE** allots 8 bytes in the variable **nnnn** 's parameter field.)

7.4 Floating Point Conversion Words

The following words convert numbers on the stack to and from floating point numbers:

S->F (*n* --- *f*)

A 16-bit number can be converted to floating point by using **S->F** . It functions by replacing the 16-bit number on the stack by a floating point number of equal value.

F->S (*f* --- *n*)

This is the inverse of **S->F** . It starts with a floating point number on the stack and leaves a 16-bit integer.

7.5 Floating Point Number Manipulation

FABS (*f* --- |*f*|)

converts *f* to its absolute value.

FMINUS (*f* --- −*f*)

negates *f* by negating the most significant word (topmost cell on the stack).

FLOOR (f_1 --- f_2)

finds the closest integer f_2 less than or equal to f_1.

CEIL (f_1 --- f_2)

finds the closest integer f_2 greater than or equal to f_1.

TRUNC (f_1 --- f_2)

truncates f_1, leaving the integer portion f_2 of f_1 on the stack.

FRAC (f_1 --- f_2)

truncates f_1, leaving the fractional portion f_2 of f_1 on the stack.

This word has a bug that causes a system crash. It will be fixed in the next revision of **fbForth 2.0**. In the meantime, you can redefine **FRAC** as follows:

```
: FRAC FDUP TRUNC F- ; FRAC isn't unique.  ok:0
```

You will get the indicated response because the word is already defined.

7.6 Floating Point Number Entry

In addition, the word

>F (--- f)

can be used from the console or in a colon definition to convert a string of characters to a floating point number. Note that **>F** is independent of the current value of **BASE** .

The string is always terminated by a blank or carriage return. The following are examples:

```
>F 123          or   123 S->F
>F 123.46
>F -123.46
>F 1.23E-006
>F 9.88E+091
>F 0            or     0 S->F
```

7.7 Built-in Floating Point Constants

DEG/RAD (--- f)

pushes the constant 57.295779513082 (degrees/radian) to the stack.

EULER_E (--- f)

pushes the constant $e = 2.718281828459$ to the stack.

FP1 (--- f)

pushes the constant 1 to the stack as a floating point number. It is equivalent to **>F 1** .

FP10 (--- f)

pushes the constant 10 to the stack as a floating point number. It is equivalent to **>F 10** .

LN10INV (--- f)

pushes the constant 1/ln(10) = 1/2.302… = 0.43429448190325 to the stack.

PI (--- f)

pushes the constant π = 3.141592653590 to the stack.

RAD/DEG (--- f)

pushes the constant 0.01745329251994 (radians/degree) to the stack.

7.8 Floating Point Arithmetic

Floating point arithmetic can now be performed on the stack just as it is with integers. The four arithmetic operators are:

F+ (f_1 f_2 --- f_3)

puts on the stack the result (f_3) of $f_1 + f_2$.

F- (f_1 f_2 --- f_3)

puts on the stack the result (f_3) of $f_1 - f_2$.

F* (f_1 f_2 --- f_3)

puts on the stack the result (f_3) of $f_1 \times f_2$.

F/ (f_1 f_2 --- f_3)

puts on the stack the result (f_3) of f_1 / f_2.

7.9 Floating Point Comparison Words

Comparisons between floating point numbers and testing against zero are provided by the following words. They are used just like their 16-bit counterparts except that the numbers tested are floating point.

F0<	(f --- *flag*)	*flag* is true if f on stack is negative
F0=	(f --- *flag*)	*flag* is true if f on stack is zero
F>	(f_1 f_2 --- *flag*)	*flag* is true if $f_1 > f_2$
F=	(f_1 f_2 --- *flag*)	*flag* is true if $f_1 = f_2$
F<	(f_1 f_2 --- *flag*)	*flag* is true if $f_1 < f_2$

7.10 Formatting and Printing Floating Point Numbers

F. (f ---)

The word **F.** is used to print the floating point number on top of the stack to the terminal in TI Basic free format. **F.** is the simplest printing word for floating point numbers. It is exactly the same as **0 FFMT.** (see next definition) and is the only floating point print word retained from TI Forth and **fbForth 1.0** because of its likely common use and to maintain some backward compatibility:

1) Integers representable exactly are printed without a trailing decimal,
2) Fixed point format is used for numbers in range and
3) Exponential format (scientific notation) is used for very large or very small numbers.[18]

The following screen shows examples of all the above situations:

```
>F 8  ok:4
F.  8 ok:0
>F 123.45690123456  ok:4
F.  123.4569012 ok:0
>F -123.456789  ok:4
F. -123.456789 ok:0
>F 12.34567E89  ok:4
F.  1.23457E+90 ok:0
>F 12.3456789E-56  ok:4
F.  1.23457E-55 ok:0
>F 12.3456789E120  ok:4
F.  1.23457E+** ok:0
>F 12.3456789E127  ok:4
F.  9.99999E+** ok:0
```

The words **F.R** , **FF.** and **FF.R** are no longer defined in **fbForth 2.0**, but can be defined in terms of **FFMT.** below.

FFMT. (*f* [*intLen fracLen*] *optMask* ---)

FFMT. handles all of the formatting and printing of floating point numbers. The integer length *intLen* and the fraction length *fracLen* are required if and only if the options mask *optMask* $\neq 0$. To avoid confusion, you should always use **F.** (*optMask* = 0) for free format output and limit use of **FFMT.** to fixed-format output (*optMask* $\neq 0$). Then you may think of this word as *requiring* all four stack entries in the above stack signature.

The output field width consists of *intLen* + *fracLen* (the significand field width) plus the exponent field width (always 4 characters for E-notation or 5 characters for extended E-notation). The significand field width cannot exceed 16 characters or an error message that the field is too big will be printed. If the number cannot be formatted for the requested output field width and *intLen* + *fracLen* ≤ 16, the field will be filled with asterisks.

The following table details the various formats, free and fixed, that are possible and the input stack entry parameters required for **FFMT.** :

18 The exponential format of the output string provided by TI in its GPL routine allows for just two digits for the power of ten. It is puzzling that TI did this because the exponent can be as high as 127 and as low as -128. This means that perfectly legitimate three-digit exponents appear as "**" in the output! This was one of the reasons for the Author's adaptation of the Geneve MDOS L10 Floating Point Math Library (with permission from Beery Miller of 9640 News) to run on the TI-99/4A in cartridge ROM space.

Parameter			Description
f :			Floating point number to be formatted
intLen :			Number of places before decimal point, including sign
fracLen :			Number of places after decimal point, including decimal point
optMask :			Output options mask—
	bit 0:	0 =	Free form TI Basic style. No other bits should be set. There should be ***no*** other numbers on the stack except *f* and *optMask* = 0.
		1 =	Fixed format, requiring four parameters on the stack, *f*, *intLen*, *fracLen* and *optMask*
	bit 1:	2 =	Explicit sign
	bit 2:	4 =	Show '+' for positive number instead of space. Bit 1 must also be set.
	bit 3:	8 =	E-notation. There will be 4 additional places in the output not accounted for by *intLen* and *fracLen*.
	bit 4:	16 =	Extended E-notation. Bit 3 must also be set. There will be 5 additional places in the output not accounted for by *intLen* and *fracLen*.

Several examples of the output possible with **FFMT.** are shown in the following screen:

```
>F 123  ok:4
2 15 1 FFMT. field too big! ok:0
>F 123  ok:4
2 14 1 FFMT. **************** ok:0
>F 123  ok:4
4 12 1 FFMT.  123.00000000000 ok:0
>F 123.45678901234  ok:4
2 14 9 FFMT.  1.2345678901230E+02 ok:0
>F -1.2345678901234E120 FDUP  ok:8
2 14 9 FFMT. -1.2345678901230E+** ok:4
2 14 25 FFMT. -1.2345678901230E+120 ok:0

█
```

7.11 Transcendental Functions

The following transcendental functions are also available:

>DEG	(f_1 --- f_2)	is the conversion of f_1 radians to f_2 degrees
>RAD	(f_1 --- f_2)	is the conversion of f_1 degrees to f_2 radians

INT	(f_1 --- f_2)	Returns greatest integer not greater than input
^	(f_1 f_2 --- f_3)	f_3 is f_1 raised to the f_2 power
SQR	(f_1 --- f_2)	f_2 is the square root of f_1
EXP	(f_1 --- f_2)	f_2 is e (2.71828...) raised to the f_1 power
EXP10	(f_1 --- f_2)	f_2 is 10 raised to the f_1 power
LOG	(f_1 --- f_2)	f_2 is the natural log of f_1
LOG10	(f_1 --- f_2)	f_2 is the common log ($\log_{10}$) of f_1
COS	(f_1 --- f_2)	f_2 is the cosine of f_1 (in radians)
SIN	(f_1 --- f_2)	f_2 is the sin of f_1 (in radians)
TAN	(f_1 --- f_2)	f_2 is the tangent of f_1 (in radians)
ATN	(f_1 --- f_2)	f_2 is the arctangent (in radians) of f_1

7.12 Interface to the Floating Point Routines

The floating point routines use two memory locations in the console CPU RAM as floating point registers. They are called FAC (for floating point accumulator) and ARG (for argument register). Though **fbForth 2.0** uses them for floating point calculations, the following words are no longer defined in **fbForth 2.0**:

>ARG	**FAC**	**FAC>ARG**	**FMUL**	**SETFL**
>FAC	**FAC->S**	**FADD**	**FSUB**	**VAL**
ARG	**FAC>**	**FDIV**	**S->FAC**	

7.13 Handling Floating Point Errors

FLERR (--- n)

FLERR is used to fetch the contents of the floating point error register (**8354h**) to the stack. It can be used to get more specific information about the error than you get with **?FLERR** below. See the next section for error codes. The *Editor/Assembler Manual* may also be helpful because, even though the console routines it describes are no longer used in **fbForth 2.0**, they were the basis of the current routines and still use location **8354h** for storing the error.

?FLERR (---)

?FLERR issues the following error message if the last floating point operation resulted in an error:

?FLERR ? floating point error

Note: All of the floating point operations in **fbForth 2.0** reset the floating point error location, **8354h**, before they run. You no longer need to insure it is reset yourself as with the GPL routines.

You do, however, need to check for an error before another floating point operation clears it. Also, the message is meaningless if no floating point operation has yet occurred.

7.14 Floating Point Error Codes

The following table lists the possible error codes reported in the byte at location **8354h** after floating-point operations:

Code	Error Description
01	Overflow
02	Syntax
03	Integer overflow on conversion
04	Square root of a negative number
05	Negative number to non-integer power
06	Logarithm of a negative number
07	Invalid argument in a trigonometric function

8 Access to File I/O Using TI-99/4A Device Service Routines

Words introduced in this chapter:

APPND	**INPT**	**PABS**	**SQNTL**
CLSE	**INTRNL**	**RD**	**STAT**
DIR	**LD**	**REC-LEN**	**SV**
DLT	**OPN**	**REC-NO**	**SWCH**
DSPLY	**OUTPT**	**RLTV**	**UNSWCH**
F-D"	**PAB-ADDR**	**RSTR**	**UPDT**
FILE	**PAB-BUF**	**SCRTCH**[19]	**VRBL**
FXD	**PAB-VBUF**	**SET-PAB**	**WRT**

This chapter will explain the means by which different types of data files native to the TI-99/4A are accessed with **fbForth 2.0**. To further illustrate the material, two commented examples have been included in this chapter. The first (§ 8.7) demonstrates the use of a relative disk file and the second (§ 8.8) a sequential RS232 file.

A group of Forth words has been included in the resident dictionary of **fbForth 2.0** to permit a Forth program to reference common data with Basic or Assembly Language programs. These words implement the file system described in the *User's Reference Guide* and the *Editor/Assembler Manual*. Note that the **fbForth 2.0** system (as opposed to TI Forth) uses only normally formatted disks for the system blocks file (FBLOCKS) and that you may perform file I/O to/from any disks, including the system disks, as long as they are properly initialized by a Disk Manager and there is enough room. You should avoid writing to TI Forth disks that contain TI Forth blocks (screens) because you will likely destroy them.

8.1 Switching VDP Modes After File Setup

You must be careful switching VDP modes after you set up access to a file (discussed in following sections) because switching to/from bitmap and 80-column text modes moves the PAB and file-setup areas (PABS) in VRAM. *This will destroy access to the file!* You can, however, switch safely among graphics, text and multicolor modes without losing access to your file information.

8.2 The Peripheral Access Block (PAB)

Before any file access can be achieved, a Peripheral Access Block (PAB) must be set up that describes the device and file to be accessed. Most of the words in this chapter are designed to make manipulation of the PAB as easy as possible.

19 **SCRTCH** , is *not* part of **fbForth**. It is mentioned because it was defined in TI Forth. TI, however, never implemented **SCRTCH** in any DSR for the TI-99/4A. Its use always resulted in a file I/O error.

A PAB consists of 10 bytes of VDP RAM plus as many bytes as the device name to be accessed. An area of VDP RAM has been reserved for this purpose (consult the VDP Memory Map in Chapter 4). The user variable **PABS** points to the beginning of this region. Adequate space is provided for many PABs in this area. More information on the details of a PAB are available in the *Editor/Assembler Manual*, page 293*ff*. The following diagram illustrates the structure of a PAB:

<table>
<tr><td>Byte 0
I/O Opcode</td><td>Byte 1
Flag/Status</td></tr>
<tr><td colspan="2">Bytes 2 & 3
Data Buffer Address in VDP</td></tr>
<tr><td>Byte 4
Logical Record Length</td><td>Byte 5
Character Count</td></tr>
<tr><td colspan="2">Bytes 6 & 7
Record Number</td></tr>
<tr><td>Byte 8
Screen Offset (Status)</td><td>Byte 9
Name Length</td></tr>
<tr><td colspan="2">Byte 10+
File Descriptor
•
•
•</td></tr>
</table>

8.3 File Setup and I/O Variables

All Device Service Routines (DSRs) on the TI-99/4A expect to perform data transfers to/from VDP RAM. Since **fbForth 2.0** is using CPU RAM, it means that the data will be moved twice in the process of reading or writing a file. Three variables are defined in the file I/O words to keep track of these memory areas.

PAB-ADDR (--- *addr*)

Holds address in VDP RAM of first byte of the PAB.

PAB-BUF (--- *addr*)

Holds address in CPU RAM of first byte in **fbForth**'s memory where allocation has been made for this buffer.

PAB-VBUF (--- *addr*)

Holds address in VDP RAM of the first byte of a region of adequate length to store data temporally while it is transferred between the file and **fbForth**. The area of VDP RAM which is used for this purpose is labeled "Unused" on the VDP Memory Map in Chapter 4. If working in bitmap mode, be cautious where **PAB-VBUF** is placed.

There is practically no available space in bitmap mode. There are a couple of things you can do. You can set simultaneous files to 1 with **1 FILES** to free up 518 bytes between the old value in **8370h** and the new value put there after executing **1 FILES** . This should be safe as long as you do not read/write blocks because **fbForth** only opens a file to read/write one block. The blocks file is closed the rest of the time.

The other thing you can do is to temporarily use the bitmap color and/or screen image tables by saving and restoring the area you want to use. It might even be rather entertaining to watch your file I/O happen on the screen!

FILE (*vaddr*$_1$ *addr vaddr*$_2$ ---)

The word **FILE** is a defining word and permits you to create a word which is the name by which the file will be known. A decision must be made as to the location of each of the buffers before the word **FILE** may be used. The values to be used for those locations are contained in the above variables and are placed on the stack in the above order followed by **FILE** and the file name (not necessarily the device name). For example:

Using The Defining Word, FILE

0 VARIABLE MY-BUF 78 ALLOT	(Create 80-character RAM buffer)
PABS @ 10 +	(PAB starts 10 bytes into VRAM region for PABS and this address will be stored in **PAB-ADDR**)
MY-BUF	(RAM address to be stored in **PAB-BUF**)
6000	(A free area at **1770h** in VRAM to be stored in **PAB-VBUF**)
FILE JOE	(Whenever the word **JOE** is executed, the file I/O variables, **PAB-ADDR** , **PAB-BUF** and **PAB-VBUF** , will be set as defined here.)
JOE	(Use the file's identifying word (FID) before using any other file I/O words)

SET-PAB (---)

The word that creates the PAB skeleton is **SET-PAB** . It creates a PAB at the address shown in **PAB-ADDR** and zeroes the first ten bytes. It then places the contents of the variable **PAB-VBUF** into its PAB location at bytes 2 and 3. Obviously, **PAB-ADDR** and **PAB-VBUF** must be set up before **SET-PAB** is invoked, which is done by executing the file identifying word (**JOE** , in the above example) before **SET-PAB** . **SET-PAB** should be executed only once for each file and should immediately follow the first invocation of the file ID word.

8.4 File Attribute Words

Files on the TI-99/4A have various characteristics that are indicated by keywords. The following table describes the available options. The example in the back of the chapter will be helpful in that it shows at what time in the procedure these words are used. Use only the attributes which apply to your file and ignore the others. Remember, if you are using multiple files, then the file referenced is the file whose name word was most recently executed.

	Options From		
Attribute Type	**TI Basic**	**fbForth**	**Description**
File Type	SEQUENTIAL	**SQNTL***	Records may only be accessed in sequential order
	RELATIVE	**RLTV**	Accessed in sequential or random order. Records must be of fixed length
Record Type	FIXED	**FXD***	All records in the file are the same length
	VARIABLE	**VRBL**	Records in the same file may have different lengths
Data Type	DISPLAY	**DSPLY***	File contains printable or displayable characters
	INTERNAL	**INTRNL**	File contains data in machine or binary format
Mode of Operation	INPUT	**INPT**	File contents can be read from, but not written to
	OUTPUT	**OUTPT**	File contents can be written to, but not read from
	UPDATE	**UPDT***	File contents can be written to *and* read from
	APPEND	**APPND**	Data may be added to the end of the file, but cannot be read

* Default if attribute is not specified

REC-LEN (*b* ---)

To specify the record length for a file, the desired length byte *b* should be on the stack when the word **REC-LEN** is executed. The length will be placed in the current PAB.

F-D" (---)

Every file must have a name to specify the device and file to be accessed. This is performed with the **F-D"** word, which enters the File Description in the PAB. **F-D"** must be followed by a string describing the file and terminated by a **"** mark. Here are a few examples of the use of **F-D"** :

```
F-D" RS232.BA=9600"  ok:0
F-D" DSK2.FILE-ABC"  ok:0
```

8.5 Words that Perform File I/O

The actual I/O operations are performed by the following words. The table gives the usual TI Basic keyword associated with the corresponding **fbForth** word. Here, as in the previous table, the **fbForth** words are spelled differently than the TI Basic words to avoid conflict with one or more existing **fbForth** words.

From TI Basic	From fbForth	DSR Opcode
OPEN	**OPN**	0
CLOSE	**CLSE**	1
READ	**RD**	2
WRITE	**WRT**	3
RESTORE	**RSTR**	4
LOAD	**LD**	5
SAVE	**SV**	6
DELETE	**DLT**	7
STATUS	**STAT**	9

OPN (---)

opens the file specified by the currently selected PAB, which is pointed to by **PAB-ADDR** .

CLSE (---)

closes the file whose PAB is pointed to by **PAB-ADDR** .

REC-NO (*n* ---)

Before using the **RD** and **WRT** instructions with a relative file, you must place the desired, zero-based record number *n* into the PAB. To do this, place the record number *n* on the stack and execute the word **REC-NO** . If your file is sequential, you need not do this.

RD (--- *n*)

The **RD** instruction will transfer the contents of the next record from the current file into your **PAB-BUF** via your **PAB-VBUF** and leave a character count *n* on the stack.

WRT (*n* ---)

takes a character count *n* from the stack and moves that number of characters from your **PAB-BUF** via your **PAB-VBUF** to the current file.

RSTR (*n* ---)

takes a record number *n* from the stack and repositions (restores) a relative file to that record for the next access.

LD (*n* ---)

used to load a program file of maximum *n* bytes into VDP RAM at the address specified in **PAB-VBUF** . **OPN** and **CLSE** need not be used.

SV (*n* ---)

used to save *n* bytes of a program file from VDP RAM at the address specified in **PAB-VBUF** . **OPN** and **CLSE** need not be used.

DLT (---)

is used to delete the file whose PAB is pointed to by **PAB-ADDR** .

STAT (--- *b*)

returns the status byte *b* (PAB+8, labeled "Screen Offset" in the PAB diagram above) of the current device/file from the PAB pointed to by **PAB-ADDR** after calling the DSR's STATUS opcode (9), which actually gets the status and writes it to PAB+8. Incidentally, the term "Screen Offset" for PAB+8 is from its use by the cassette interface, which must put prompts on the screen, to get the offset of screen characters with respect to their normal ASCII values. The table below, excerpted from the *Editor/Assembler Manual*, p. 298, shows the meaning of each bit of the status byte:

	Status Byte Information When Value is	
Bit	**1**	**0**
0	File does not exist.	File exists. If device is a printer or similar, always 0.
1	Protected file.	Unprotected file.
2		Reserved for future use. Always 0.
3	INTERNAL data type.	DISPLAY data type or program file.
4	Program file.	Data file.
5	VARIABLE record length.	FIXED record length.
6	At physical end of peripheral. No more data can be written.	Not at physical end of peripheral. Always 0 when file not open.
7	End of file (EOF). Can be written if open in APPEND, OUTPUT or UPDATE modes. Reading will cause an error.	Not EOF. Always 0 when file not open.

Almost all of the file I/O support words of TI Forth and **fbForth 1.0** are no longer available in **fbForth 2.0** as high-level Forth definitions. They have been defined in TMS9900 Assembly Language as part of the resident dictionary and are no longer directly executable. If the user desires more information from a file I/O error condition than the fact that a file I/O error occurred, the following definition can be used to retrieve the flag/status byte from the file's PAB:

```
: GET-FLAG   PAB-ADDR @ 1+ VSBR ;
```

The following describes in detail the information that can be obtained with **GET-FLAG** :

GET-FLAG (--- *b*)

retrieves to the stack the flag/status byte *b* from byte 1 the current PAB. The high-order 3 bits are used for DSR error return, except for "bad device name". With the "bad device name" error, this error return will be 0, but the GPL status byte (**837Ch**) will have the COND bit set (**20h**). The low-order 5 bits are set by routines that set the file type prior to calling **OPN** , which reads these bits. See table below for the meaning of each bit of the flag/status byte:

Flag/Status Byte of PAB (Byte 1)

Bits	Contents	Meaning
0–2	Error Code	0 = no error. Error codes are decoded in table below.
3	Record Type	0 = fixed-length records; 1 = variable-length records.
4	Data Type	0 = DISPLAY; 1 = INTERNAL.
5–6	Mode of Operation	0 = UPDATE; 1 = OUTPUT; 2 = INPUT; 3 = APPEND.
7	File Type	0 = sequential file; 1 = relative file.

Error Codes in Bits 0–2 of Flag/Status Byte of PAB

Error Code	Meaning
0	No error unless bit 2 of status byte at address **837Ch** is set (then, bad device name).
1	Device is write protected.
2	Bad OPEN attribute such as incorrect file type, incorrect record length, incorrect I/O mode or no records in a relative record file.
3	Illegal operation; *i.e.*, an operation not supported on the peripheral or a conflict with the OPEN attributes.
4	Out of table or buffer space on the device.
5	Attempt to read past the end of file. When this error occurs, the file is closed. Also given for non-extant records in a relative record file.
6	Device error. Covers all hard device errors such as parity and bad medium errors.
7	File error such as program/data file mismatch, non-existing file opened in INPUT mode, *etc.*

Examples of file I/O in use are shown in § 8.7 , § 8.8 and block 19*ff* in FBLOCKS (dated 01SEP2014 or later, which has definitions of the alternate I/O capabilities for printing to the RS232 interface).

8.6 Alternate Input and Output

When using alternate input or output devices, the 1-byte buffer in VDP memory must be the byte immediately preceding the PAB for **ALTIN** or **ALTOUT** .

The words

SWCH (---) and

UNSWCH (---)

make it possible to send output that would normally go to the monitor to an RS232 serial printer. For example, the **LIST** instruction normally outputs to the monitor. By typing

SWCH 45 LIST UNSWCH

you can list block 45 of the current blocks file to the printer. If your RS232 printer is not on port 1 and set at 9600 baud or you would rather print via the parallel port, you must modify the word **SWCH** in block 19 of FBLOCKS.

The user variables

ALTIN (--- *vaddr*) and

ALTOUT (--- *vaddr*)

contain values which point to the current input and output devices. The value of **ALTIN** is 0 if input is coming from the keyboard. Otherwise, its value is a pointer to the VDP address where the PAB for the alternate input device is located. The value of **ALTOUT** is 0 if the output is going to the monitor. Otherwise, it contains a pointer to the PAB of the alternate output device.

8.7 File I/O Example 1: Relative Disk File

Instruction	Comment
HEX	Change number base to hexadecimal
0 VARIABLE BUFR 3E ALLOT	Create space for a 64 byte buffer which will be the **PAB-BUF**
PABS @ A +	PAB starts 10 bytes into **PABS** . This will be the **PAB-ADDR**
BUFR 1700	Place the **PAB-BUF** and **PAB-VBUF** on stack in preparation for **FILE**
FILE TESTFIL	Associates the name **TESTFIL** with these three parameters
TESTFIL	File name must be executed before using any other File I/O words
SET-PAB	Create PAB skeleton
RLTV	Make **TESTFIL** a relative file
DSPLY	Records will contain printable information
40 REC-LEN	Record length is 64 (**40h**) bytes
F-D" DSK2.TEST"	Will create the file descriptor "DSK2.TEST" in the PAB for **TESTFIL** .
OPN	Open the file in the default (UPDATE) mode. This will create the file on disk unless it already exists.

To write more than one record to the file, it is necessary to write a procedure. This routine may be composed in a Forth block beforehand and loaded at this time.

: FIL-WRT TESTDATA	**TESTDATA** is assumed to be the beginning memory address of the information to be written to the file
10 0 DO	Want to write 16 (**10h**) records

`DUP`	Duplicate address
`BUFR 40 CMOVE`	Move 64 bytes of information into the **PAB-BUF**
`I REC-NO`	Place record number into PAB
`40 WRT`	Write one 64-byte record to the disk
`40 +`	Increment address for next record
`LOOP DROP`	Clear stack
`;`	End definition

`FIL-WRT`	Execute writing procedure
`4 REC-NO RD`	Choose a record number to read (4 is chosen here) to verify correct output. A byte count will be left on the stack and the read information will be in **BUFR**
`BUFR 40 DUMP`	Print out the read information to the monitor. (**DUMP** routines must be loaded from block 16 of FBLOCKS)
`CLSE`	Close the file

8.8 File I/O Example 2: Sequential RS232 File

Instruction	Comment
`HEX`	Change number base to hexadecimal
`0 VARIABLE MY-BUF 4E ALLOT`	Create an 80-character **PAB-BUF**
`PABS @ 30 +`	Skip all previous PABs. This will be the **PAB-ADDR**
`MY-BUF 1900`	Place the **PAB-BUF** and **PAB-VBUF** on stack in preparation for **FILE**
`FILE PRNTR`	Associates the name **PRNTR** with these three parameters
`PRNTR`	File name must be executed before using any other File I/O words
`SET-PAB`	Create a PAB skeleton
`DSPLY`	**PRNTR** will contain printable information
`SQNTL`	**PRNTR** may be accessed only in sequential order
`VRBL`	Records may have variable lengths
`50 REC-LEN`	Maximum record length is 80 char.
`F-D" RS232.BA=9600"` or `F-D" PIO"`	**PRNTR** will be an RS232 serial "file" with baud rate = 9600 or a parallel printer "file".
`OPN`	Open the file

A procedure is necessary to write more than one record to a file. A file-write routine may be composed in a Forth block beforehand and loaded at this time. The following is a simple example:

`: PRNT FILE-INFO`	**FILE-INFO** is assumed to be the beginning memory address of the information to be sent to the printer
`20 0 DO`	Will write 32 records

`      DUP`	Duplicate address
`      MYBUF 50 CMOVE`	Move 80 characters from **FILE-INFO** to **MY-BUF**
`      50 WRT`	Write one record to printer
`      50 +`	Increment address on stack
`    LOOP DROP`	Clear stack
`;`	End definition

`PRNT`	Execute write program
`CLSE`	Close the file called **PRNTR**

8.9 Disk Catalog Utilities

Two different disk cataloging utilities are available in FBLOCKS dated 19JUN2015 and later.

8.9.1 DIR

DIR is adapted, with permission, from Mark Wills' **TurboForth**[1] and, though available in FBLOCKS dated as early as 17OCT2014, only the version that first appears in the 19JUN2015 edition should be used:

DIR (---)

> **DIR** catalogs to the output device the disk device name that follows it in the input stream. The disk device name must be terminated with a period. **DIR** gets its information from the DSR's catalog "file" (see Chapter 8 "Catalog File Access" in TI's *Software Specifications for the 99/4 Disk Peripheral*). **DIR** will not load if **CAT** (below) is loaded. Use **MENU** to show what block to load for **DIR** .
>
> Usage: **DIR DSK1.**

Example:

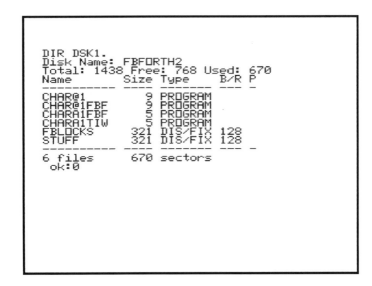

```
DIR DSK1.
Disk Name: FBFORTH2
Total: 1438 Free: 768 Used: 670
Name         Size Type     B/R P
------------ ---- -------- --- -
CHAR@1          9 PROGRAM
CHAR@1FBF       9 PROGRAM
CHARA1FBF       5 PROGRAM
CHARA1TIW       5 PROGRAM
FBLOCKS       321 DIS/FIX  128
STUFF         321 DIS/FIX  128
------------ ---- -------- --- -
6 files       670 sectors
 ok:0
```

8.9.2 CAT

CAT (*n* ---)

CAT catalogs to the output device the disk number *n* on the stack for the current DSR.

CAT reads the Volume Information Block (VIB) to get the disk name, total sectors and free sectors. The free sectors are calculated by adding all the zero bits in the allocation bitmap found in the VIB.

Next, **CAT** reads the File Descriptor Index Record (FDIR) and finds each file's File Descriptor Record (FDR) from the sector pointers in the FDIR.

Each FDR has the file's name, file type, sectors occupied by the file, protection and EOF byte offset in the last sector. The EOF offset and the sector count are used to calculate the actual size in bytes of a PROGRAM file. The sector size that **CAT** displays for a file is one more than the size of the file body to account for the file's FDR. See Appendix K , "Diskette Format Details" for more specific information about the VIB, FDIR and FDR.

CAT will not load if **DIR** is loaded.

Usage: **2 CAT** to catalog DSK2.

Example:

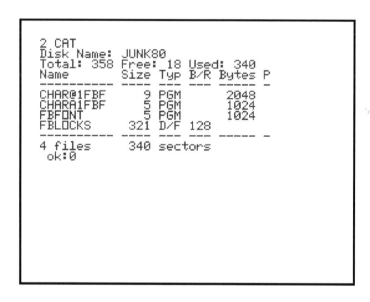

```
2 CAT
Disk Name: JUNK80
Total: 358 Free: 18 Used: 340
Name       Size Typ B/R Bytes P
---------- ---- --- --- ----- -
CHAR@1FBF     9 PGM      2048
CHARA1FBF     5 PGM      1024
FBFONT        5 PGM      1024
FBLOCKS     321 D/F 128
---------- ---- --- --- ----- -
4 files     340 sectors
 ok:0
```

9 The fbForth 2.0 TMS9900 Assembler

The assembler supplied with your **fbForth 2.0** system is typical of assemblers supplied with fig-Forth systems and is almost identical with the TI Forth assembler—there are some enhancements. It provides the capability of using all of the opcodes of the TMS9900 as well as the ability to use structured assembly instructions. It uses no labels. The complete **fbForth 2.0** language is available to the user to assist in macro type assembly, if desired. The assembler uses the standard Forth convention of Reverse Polish or Postfix Notation for each instruction. For example, the instruction to add register 1 to register 2 is:

```
R1 R2 A,
```

As can be seen in the above example, the 'add' instruction mnemonic is followed by a comma. Every opcode in this Forth assembler is followed by a comma. The significance is that when the opcode is reached during the assembly process, the instruction is compiled into the dictionary. The comma is a reminder of this compile operation. It also serves to assist in differentiating assembler words from the rest of the words in the **fbForth 2.0** language. A complete list of Forth-style instruction mnemonics is given in the next section.

Before going on, it would be a good idea to familiarize yourself with Chapter 12 "fbForth 2.0 Dictionary Entry Structure" to ensure you understand the structure of **fbForth 2.0** words.

9.1 TMS9900 Assembly Mnemonics

A,	JGT,	RTWP,
AB,	JH,	S,
ABS,	JHE,	SB,
AI,	JL,	SBO,
ANDI,	JLE,	SBZ,
B,	JLT,	SETO,
BL,	JMP,	SLA,
BLWP,	JNC,	SOC,
C,	JNE,	SOCB,
CB,	JNO,	SRA,
CI,	JOC,	SRC,
CKOF,	JOP,	SRL,
CKON,	LDCR,	STCR,
CLR,	LI,	STST,
COC,	LIMI,	STWP,
CZC,	LREX,	SWPB,
DEC,	LWPI,	SZC,
DECT,	MOV,	SZCB,
DIV,	MOVB,	TB,
IDLE,	MPY,	THEN,
INC,	NEG,	X,
INCT,	ORI,	XOP,
INV,	RSET,	XOR,
JEQ,	RT,	

These words are available when the assembler is loaded. Only the words `C,` and `R0` (see later) conflict with the existing **fbForth 2.0** vocabulary.

Most assembly code in **fbForth 2.0** will probably use **fbForth 2.0**'s workspace registers. The following table describes the register allocation. The user may use registers R0 through R7 for any purpose. They are used as temporary registers only within **fbForth** words which are themselves written in TMS9900 assembly/machine code (ALC).

9.2 fbForth 2.0's Workspace Registers

Register Name		
Original	**Alternate**	**Usage**
0	R0	These registers are available. They are used only within **fbForth** words written in ALC.
1	R1	
2	R2	
3	R3	
4	R4	
5	R5	
6	R6	
7	R7	
UP	R8	Points to base of User Variable area
SP	R9	Parameter Stack Pointer
W	R10	Inner Interpreter current Word pointer
11	R11	Linkage for subroutines in ALC routines
12	R12	Used for CRU instructions
IP	R13	Interpretive Pointer
RP	R14	Return Stack Pointer
NEXT	R15	Points to the next instruction fetch routine

9.3 Loading and Using the Assembler

The **fbForth 2.0** TMS9900 Assembler is located in blocks 21 – 26 of FBLOCKS and is loaded by typing **21 LOAD**. The words **ASM:** , **DOES>ASM:** , **CODE:** , **DOES>CODE:** and **;CODE** are in the resident dictionary and part of the Forth vocabulary. When the assembler is loaded, it is loaded into the Assembler vocabulary. To use the assembler, it must be the context vocabulary, which may be effected by typing **ASSEMBLER** or by using the words **ASM:** or **DOES>ASM:** , each of which makes Assembler the context vocabulary.

There are only two words in the Assembler vocabulary that are part of the resident dictionary, namely, **;ASM** and its synonym, **NEXT,** . After defining words that use **ASM:** or **DOES>ASM:** , it is advisable to execute **FORTH** to restore the context vocabulary to Forth, unless such use is immediately followed by **:** (beginning a colon definition), which restores the context vocabulary to the current vocabulary (usually Forth). The important point is that Forth must be the context vocabulary before the Forth words **C,** and **R0** can be executed because **C,** and **R0** are the only

Assembler vocabulary words that conflict with Forth vocabulary words of the same name.

The use of **CODE** , **;CODE** and **NEXT,** , though still supported, is deprecated in favor of the identical but clearer **ASM:** , **DOES>ASM:** and **;ASM** , respectively. Please keep this in mind when attempting to compare **fbForth 2.0** code using them with TI Forth code, which, obviously can only use the former.

An Assembly definition begins with **ASM:** . It is followed by assembly mnemonics and terminated with **;ASM** . **ASM:** is used in the following way:

```
ASM: EXAMPLE <assembly mnemonics> ;ASM
```

Equivalently, machine code, which does not require the Assembler, may be used in place of assembly mnemonics with

```
CODE: EXAMPLE <machine code> ;CODE
```

Each defines a Forth word named **EXAMPLE** with an execution procedure defined by the assembly mnemonics or machine code that follow **EXAMPLE** , which must terminate with **;ASM** . The assembly code ends with ;**ASM** , so the **fbForth 2.0** inner interpreter can get to the next word to be executed. There are several examples using **ASM:** in the sections that follow.

DOES>ASM: is used with **<BUILDS** to create the execution procedure of a new defining word very much like the word **DOES>** except that **DOES>ASM:** does not cause the *pfa* of newly defined words to be left on the stack for the consumption of the code following **DOES>ASM:** as is the case with **DOES>** . **DOES>ASM:** is used as follows:

```
: DEF-WRD <BUILDS … DOES>ASM: <assembly mnemonics> ;ASM
```

Just as with **ASM:** , assembly code following **DOES>ASM:** must end with **;ASM** . Later, when the newly created defining word **DEF-WRD** is executed in the following form, a new word is defined:

```
DEF-WRD TEST
```

This will create the word **TEST** which has as its execution procedure the code following **DOES>ASM:** . An example using **DOES>ASM:** is shown in § 9.10 .

Just as with **CODE:** , **DOES>CODE:** can be used to create the same defining word without needing to load the Assembler (see example in § 9.11):

```
: DEF-WRD <BUILDS … DOES>CODE: <machine code> ;CODE
```

9.4 fbForth 2.0 *Assembler Addressing Modes*

We will now introduce those words that permit this assembler to perform the various addressing modes of which the TMS9900 is capable. Each of the remaining examples will show the **fbForth 2.0** assembler code (column 1) for various instructions, the TI Forth code (column 2) and the conventional Assembler (column 3) method of coding the same instructions. The Wycove Forth equivalents of the **fbForth 2.0** addressing mode words may also be used. The TI Forth code can be used in **fbForth 2.0** with no changes.

;ASM is defined as

```
: ;ASM *NEXT B, ;
```

and is equivalent to the following assembly code:

```
B       *R15
```

9.4.1 Workspace Register Addressing

The registers in the **fbForth 2.0** code below can be referenced directly by number. However, we are using the alternate, easier-to-read R designation:

fbForth 2.0	TI Forth	Conventional Assembler		
`HEX`	`HEX`			
`ASM: EX1`	`CODE EX1`		DEF	EX1
`  R1 R2 A,`	`  1 2 A,`	EX1	A	R1,R2
`  R3 INC,`	`  3 INC,`		INC	R3
`  R3 FFFC ANDI,`	`  3 FFFC ANDI,`		ANDI	R3,>FFFC
`;ASM`	`NEXT,`		B	*R15

9.4.2 Symbolic Memory Addressing

Symbolic addressing is done with the `@()` word (Wycove Forth equivalent: `@@`). It is used after the address.

fbForth 2.0	TI Forth	Conventional Assembler		
`0 VARIABLE VAR1`	`0 VARIABLE VAR1`	VAR1	BSS	2
`5 VARIABLE VAR2`	`5 VARIABLE VAR2`	VAR2	DATA	5
`ASM: EX2`	`CODE EX2`		DEF	EX2
`  VAR2 @() R1 MOV,`	`  VAR2 @() 1 MOV,`	EX2	MOV	@VAR2,R1
`  R1 2 SRC,`	`  1 2 SRC,`		SRC	R1,2
`  R1 VAR1 @() S,`	`  1 VAR1 @() S,`		S	R1,@VAR1
`  VAR2 @() VAR1 @() SOC,`	`  VAR2 @() VAR1 @() SOC,`		SOC	@VAR2,@VAR1
`;ASM`	`NEXT,`		B	*R15

9.4.3 Workspace Register Indirect Addressing

Workspace Register Indirect addressing is done with the `*?` word (Wycove Forth equivalent: `**`). It is used after the register number to which it pertains. In line 4 below we use the clearer definition of § 9.4.6 for **fbForth 2.0**. TI Forth must use `*?` .

fbForth 2.0	TI Forth	Conventional Assembler		
`HEX 2000 CONSTANT XRAM`	`HEX 2000 CONSTANT XRAM`	XRAM	EQU	>2000
`ASM: EX3`	`CODE EX3`		DEF	EX3
`  R1 XRAM LI,`	`  1 XRAM LI,`	EX3	LI	R1,XRAM
`  *R1 R2 MOV,`	`  1 *? 2 MOV,`		MOV	*R1,R2
`;ASM`	`NEXT,`		B	*R15

9.4.4 Workspace Register Indirect Auto-increment Addressing

Workspace Register Indirect Auto-increment addressing is done with the `*?+` word (Wycove Forth equivalent: `*+`). It is also used after the register to which it pertains. In line 4 below we use the clearer definition of § 9.4.6 for **fbForth 2.0**. TI Forth must use `*?+` .

fbForth 2.0	TI Forth	Conventional Assembler		
`HEX 2000 CONSTANT XRAM`	`HEX 2000 CONSTANT XRAM`	XRAM	EQU	>2000
`ASM: EX4`	`CODE EX4`		DEF	EX4
`  R1 XRAM LI,`	`  1 XRAM LI,`	EX4	LI	R1,XRAM
`  *R1+ R2 MOV,`	`  1 *?+ 2 MOV,`		MOV	*R1+,R2
`;ASM`	`NEXT,`		B	*R15

9.4.5 Indexed Memory Addressing

The final addressing type is Indexed Memory addressing. This is performed with the `@(?)` word (Wycove Forth equivalent: `()`) used after the Index and register as shown below. Here we use the clearer definition of § 9.4.6 for **fbForth 2.0**. TI Forth must use `@(?)` .

fbForth 2.0	TI Forth	Conventional Assembler		
`HEX 2000 CONSTANT XRAM`	`HEX 2000 CONSTANT XRAM`	XRAM	EQU	>2000
`ASM: EX5`	`CODE EX5`		DEF	EX5
`  XRAM @(R1) R2 MOV,`	`  XRAM 1 @(?) 2 MOV,`	EX5	MOV	@XRAM(R1),R2
`  DECIMAL`	`  DECIMAL`			
`  XRAM 22 + @(R2)`	`  XRAM 22 + 2 @(?)`		MOV	@XRAM+22(R2),@XRAM+26(R2)
`   XRAM 26 + @(R2) MOV,`	`   XRAM 26 + 2 @(?) MOV,`			
`;ASM`	`NEXT,`		B	*R15

9.4.6 Addressing Mode Words for Special Registers

In order to make addressing modes easier for the **W** , **RP** , **IP** , **SP** , **UP** and **NEXT** as well as all the numbered registers (**R0** – **R15**), the following words are available and eliminate the need to enter the register name separately. The register number (0 – 15) in the last entry is represented by ***n*** :

Register Address	Indirect	Indexed	Indirect Auto-increment
W	*W	@(W)	*W+
RP	*RP	@(RP)	*RP+
IP	*IP	@(IP)	*IP+
SP	*SP	@(SP)	*SP+
UP	*UP	@(UP)	*UP+
NEXT	*NEXT	@(NEXT)	*NEXT+
R*n*	*R*n*	@(R*n*)	*R*n*+

9.5 Handling the fbForth 2.0 Stacks

Both the parameter stack and the return stack grow downward in memory. This means that removing a cell from the top of either stack requires *incrementing* the stack pointer after consuming the cell's value. Conversely, adding a cell requires *decrementing* the stack pointer. The **fbForth 2.0** Assembler word ***SP+** references the contents of the top cell of the parameter stack and then increments the stack pointer **SP** to reduce the size of the stack by one cell. The following code copies the contents of the stack's top cell to register 0 and reduces the stack by one cell:

```
*SP+ R0 MOV,
```

The following code adds a cell to the top of the stack and copies the contents of register 1 to the new cell:

```
SP DECT,
R1 *SP MOV,
```

The same procedures obtain for the return stack using ***RP+** , **RP** and ***RP** . If you must manipulate the return stack, be very careful that you restore it properly when you are finished and before the system needs it.

9.6 Structured Assembler Constructs

Though you may certainly use the jump instructions in your programming (see § 9.9 "Jump Instructions (If You Must!)"), the Forth Assembler permits you to write structured code, *i.e.*, code that does not use labels. This is done in a manner very similar to the way that **fbForth 2.0** implements conditional constructs. The major difference is that rather than taking a value from the stack and using it as a true/false flag, the processor's condition register is used to determine whether or not to jump. The following structured constructs are implemented:

IF, … THEN, [also **IF, … ENDIF,**]

IF, … ELSE, … THEN, [also **IF, … ELSE, … ENDIF,**]

BEGIN, … UNTIL,

BEGIN, … AGAIN,

BEGIN, … WHILE, … REPEAT,

Note that **THEN,** is a synonym for TI Forth's **ENDIF,** . **THEN,** is used in the **fbForth 2.0** Assembler example below, but the **ENDIF,** of the TI Forth example works, as well. Be sure you have FBLOCKS dated 01SEP2014 or later before you attempt to use **THEN,** .

The three conditional words in the previous list (**IF, UNTIL, WHILE,**) must each be preceded by one of the jump tokens in the next section.

9.7 Assembler Jump Tokens

Token	Comment	Conventional Assembler Used	Machine Code Generated
EQ	True if =	JNE $+2	1600h
GT	True if signed >	JGT $+4 JMP $+2	1501h 1000h
GTE	True if signed > or =	JLT $+2	1100h
H	True if unsigned >	JLE $+2	1200h
HE	True if unsigned > or =	JL $+2	1A00h
L	True if unsigned <	JHE $+2	1400h
LE	True if unsigned < or =	JH $+2	1B00h
LT	True if signed <	JLT $+4 JMP $+2	1101h 1000h
LTE	True if signed < or =	JGT $+2	1500h
NC	True if No Carry	JOC $+2	1800h
NE	True if equal bit not set	JEQ $+2	1300h
NO	True if No overflow	JNO $+4 JMP $+2	1901h 1000h
NP	True if Not odd Parity	JOP $+2	1C00h
OC	True if Carry bit is set	JNC $+2	1700h
OO	True if Overflow	JNO $+2	1900h
OP	True if Odd Parity	JOP $+4 JMP $+2	1C01h 1000h

9.8 Assembly Example for Structured Constructs

The following example is designed to show how these jump tokens and structured constructs are used:

fbForth 2.0	TI Forth	Conventional Assembler
`( GENERALIZED SHIFTER )`	`( GENERALIZED SHIFTER )`	`* GENERALIZED SHIFTER`
`ASM: SHIFT`	`CODE SHIFT`	`DEF SHIFT`
`*SP+ R0 MOV,`	`*SP+ 0 MOV,`	`SHIFT MOV *SP+,R0`
`NE IF,`	`NE IF,`	`JEQ L3`
`*SP R1 MOV,`	`*SP 1 MOV,`	`MOV *SP,R1`
`R0 ABS,`	`0 ABS,`	`ABS R0`
`GTE IF,`	`GTE IF,`	`JLT L1`
`R1 R0 SLA,`	`1 0 SLA,`	`SLA R1,0`
`ELSE,`	`ELSE,`	`JMP L2`
`R1 R0 SRL,`	`1 0 SRL,`	`L1 SRL R1,0`
`THEN,`	`ENDIF,`	
`R1 *SP MOV,`	`1 *SP MOV,`	`L2 MOV R1,*SP`
`THEN,`	`ENDIF,`	
`;ASM`	`NEXT,`	`L3 B *R15`

One word of caution is in order. The structured constructs shown above do not check to ensure that the jump target is within range (+127, -128 words). They do, however, force the jump target to that range by masking off any high-order bits exceeding one byte, which will certainly not be what you intend. This will be a problem only with very large assembly language definitions and will violate the Forth philosophy of small, easily understood words.

9.9 Jump Instructions (If You Must!)

This section is provided only for the sake of completeness. It is easier and better to use the structured programming described in § 9.6 "Structured Assembler Constructs". Using the jump instructions (**JEQ,** , **JGT,** , **JH,** , **JHE,** , **JL,** , **JLE,** , **JLT,** , **JMP,** , **JNC,** , **JNE,** , **JNO,** , **JOC,** and **JOP,**) is not recommended for a couple of reasons:

1. As already mentioned, a better programming style is available.
2. Their use in the Forth Assembler is not comparable to the Editor/Assembler version and is, thereby, error prone.

For the Editor/Assembler version, you give the jump instruction the value of a label as the jump target, *e.g.*:

```
        JEQ  LABEL2
         :
LABEL2 ...
```

and the Assembler calculates the jump distance and direction for you and stores the value in the LSB of the jump instruction's machine code..

For the Forth Assembler, you must first calculate the jump distance and direction by taking the difference between the jump target's address and the address of the instruction following the jump instruction. Then, you must divide by 2 to convert to a word distance and direction. Finally, you should insure the value fits in a single byte. In other words, you must manually assemble part of the instruction's machine code. You will likely need to define your Forth Assembler word first, using a placeholder for the jump distance and direction, to make it easier to find the jump distance and direction. Then, **FORGET** the word just defined so you can replace the placeholder with the actual value. Here is an example, using **FFh** as a placeholder:

```
HEX
0FF JEQ,
```

9.10 Assembly Example with DOES>ASM:

Before giving an example of defining an **fbForth 2.0** defining word that uses **DOES>ASM:** , an explanation of why you might want to use it in the first place is in order.

The defining words that are part of the **fbForth 2.0** kernel are **:** (paired with **;**), **VARIABLE** , **CONSTANT** , **USER** , **VOCABULARY** , **<BUILDS** (with **DOES>** , **DOES>ASM:** or **DOES>CODE:**), **ASM:** , **CODE:** and **CREATE** . Of course, most words you would ever need to define can be created with the first three (**:** , **VARIABLE** and **CONSTANT**). However, you too can use **<BUILDS** and **CREATE** , the same words used for defining most of the above, for the eventuality that these do not suffice.

In **fbForth 2.0**, it is not useful to use **CREATE** on the command line unless you really know what you are doing because it creates a dictionary header in which the smudge bit is set and the code field points at the parameter field with no storage allotted for it. This means that the parameter field must be allotted with executable code (or the code field changed to point to some) and the smudge bit must be reset so a dictionary search can find the word. The same discussion obtains for **<BUILDS** except for the smudge bit because **<BUILDS** is defined in **fbForth 2.0** as

```
: <BUILDS CREATE SMUDGE ;
```
(**SMUDGE** toggles the smudge bit.)

This situation is made easier by using **<BUILDS** , **DOES>** and **DOES>ASM:** within colon definitions as

```
: NEW_DEFINING_WORD <BUILDS … DOES> … ;
```

or

```
: NEW_DEFINING_WORD <BUILDS … DOES>ASM: … ;ASM
```

You simply replace the first "…" with words you want to execute when **NEW_DEFINING_WORD** is compiling a new word, *e.g.*, to reserve space for and store a value in the first cell of the parameter field using **,** . You then replace the second "…" with code to be executed when the new word actually executes. It will be this code to which the code field of the new word will point.

Here, now, is an example of the use of **DOES>ASM:** in the definition of a defining word, *i.e.*, a word that creates new words:

CONSTANT is an **fbForth 2.0** word that defines a word, the value of which is pushed to the stack when the word is executed.

```
9 CONSTANT XXX
```

defines the word **XXX** with 9 in its parameter field and the address of the execution code of **CONSTANT** in its code field. **fbForth 2.0** defines **CONSTANT** in high-level Forth essentially as

```
: CONSTANT <BUILDS , DOES> @ ;
```

Using **DOES>ASM:** , it could also be defined with Assembler code as

: CONSTANT	Start colon definition of **CONSTANT** .
<BUILDS	**CONSTANT** will create a dictionary header for the word appearing after it in the input stream when **CONSTANT** is executed. The new word's *cfa* will point to the address immediately following the *cfa*. This will be the new word's *pfa*, but no space will be allocated for the *pfa*.
,	Comma expects a number on the stack, which it will store at the *pfa* of the new word, allocating space for it.
DOES>ASM:	The new word's *cfa* will be changed to point to machine code that follows **DOES>ASM:** here in **CONSTANT** . The following machine code is what will run when the new word is executed:
SP DECT,	Make space on the stack.
***W *SP MOV,**	Copy current (newly defined) word's parameter field contents to the stack. [**W** (R10) contains the current word's *pfa*.]
;ASM	Return to the interpreter.

which, once you know the machine code, can be coded without the Assembler loaded as

```
HEX
: CONSTANT <BUILDS , DOES>CODE: 0649 C65A ;CODE
```

For **CONSTANT** , the first, high-level definition is easier to understand. They are both the same length. In this case, they both create words of the same length. However, there may come a time when only Assembler will do your bidding and **DOES>ASM:** offers that facility.

9.11 ASM: and DOES>ASM: without the Assembler

fbForth 2.0 words using **ASM:** or **DOES>ASM:** can be written without the 3208-byte overhead of the **fbForth 2.0** Assembler by using the machine code equivalent to assembly code.

Important Note: **ASM>CODE** (see entry in Appendix D) can be used to convert words written using **ASM:** to their **CODE:** counterparts. Unfortunately, this convenience does not extend to words that use **DOES>ASM:** .

This section details how you can convert by hand words that use **ASM:** or **DOES>ASM:** to **CODE:** or **DOES>CODE:** , respectively. It is much more painful than with **ASM>CODE** for **ASM:** to **CODE:** , but explains the gory details. And, of course, you have no choice with the conversion of **DOES>ASM:** to **DOES>CODE:** .

Until you have tested and debugged your work, it is probably best to work with one Forth word at a time in an **fbForth 2.0** block.

1. Write, test and debug your Forth word using the **fbForth 2.0** Assembler. Here, we'll use **EX5** from § 9.4.5 for the **ASM:** example and **CONSTANT** (renamed **CONST2** to avoid confusion) from § 9.10 for the **DOES>ASM:** example.
2. Ensure that the **fbForth 2.0** Assembler is loaded by executing **21 LOAD** .
3. Ensure that the dump routines are loaded by executing **16 LOAD** .
4. Load the screen that contains the definition of your Forth word and continue with (5) in the appropriate section below.

9.11.1 ASM: without the Assembler

Refer to the example in § 9.4.5 for the following:

5. Use **'** to find the *pfa* of **EX5** and dump from the *pfa* to the end of the word:

   ```
   HERE ' EX5 SWAP OVER - DUMP
   ```

   will dump this to the screen:

   ```
   AE52:  C0A1  2000 C8A2  2016   .. .... .
   AE5A:  201A  045F               .._
   ok:0
   ```

   The column at the left indicates the addresses in RAM where the hexadecimal cells to the right are located. The 8-character, right-hand column is their ASCII representation.
6. The last cell should be **045Fh**, corresponding to the **;ASM** instruction.
7. Write the high-level part of the word with **CODE:** instead of **ASM:** (**CODE: EX5**) followed by the machine code after **EX5** using the dump above to transcribe the

hexadecimal value for each cell starting with the first cell (parameter field) and ending with **;CODE** (instead of **045Fh**) as follows:

```
HEX
CODE: EX5 C0A1 2000 C8A2 2016 201A ;CODE
```

You may have noticed that the machine code between **CODE:** and **;CODE** is not compiled with **,** as it is in TI Forth. This is because **CODE:** employs its own interpreter to attempt to first convert tokens in the input stream to numbers, whereas the Forth outer interpreter first tries to find the tokens in the dictionary. The upshot of this is that you must now use **N>S** between **CODE:** and **;CODE** if you need a number pushed to the stack.

8. If all the code was assembly code, you're done. Otherwise, you need to replace values that can vary from one load to the next, such as variables, named constants and dictionary entries not part of the resident dictionary, with the high-level code used in the word's assembly language definition and compile them into the definition yourself. In the above example, the constant **XRAM** was used, so we need to replace the value **2000h** with the reference that put it there. In this case **XRAM** is used three times to get the cells with **2000h**, **2016h** and **201Ah**. We need to replace the **2000h** with **XRAM**, the **2016h** with **XRAM 16 +** and the **201Ah** with **XRAM 1A +** to get

```
HEX
CODE: EX5
        C0A1 XRAM , C8A2 XRAM N>S 16 + , XRAM N>S 1A + ,
;CODE
```

which can now be entered in an **fbForth 2.0** block to be loaded without the Assembler overhead.

Notice the use of **,** and **N>S** in the code above. **XRAM** is not recognized as a number by **CODE:**, so you must compile it with **,** . **16** is a number we want on the stack to add to **XRAM** before compiling the result, so we must prevent **CODE:** from compiling it by using **N>S** to push it to the stack. The same situation obtains for **XRAM N>S 1A + ,** .

You should test your new version of the word to verify that it is identical to the original assembly version.

9.11.2 DOES>ASM: without the Assembler

We need to do more work with **DOES>ASM:** than we did with **ASM:** above. We must find the *cfa* of **(;CODE)** that **DOES>ASM:** compiled into our word and retrieve the machine code that follows it. Refer to the example in § 9.10 (which we've renamed here as **CONST2** to avoid confusion) for the following:

5. Use **'** and **CFA** to find the *cfa* of **(;CODE)** so you can find the cell within the definition of **CONST2** that contains it:

```
HEX ' (;CODE) CFA U.
```

will display this on the screen:

```
7254  ok:0
```

6. Use **'** to find the *pfa* of **CONST2** and dump from the *pfa* to the end of the word:

```
HERE ' CONST2 SWAP OVER - DUMP
```

will dump this to the screen:

```
AE4A:  71CC  6616  7254 0649  q.f.rT.I
```

```
AE52:  C65A  045F              .Z._
ok:0
```

The column at the left indicates the addresses in RAM where the hexadecimal cells to the right are located. The 8-character, right-hand column is their ASCII representation.

7. The last cell should be **045Fh**, corresponding to the **;ASM** instruction.
8. Write the high-level part of the word through **DOES>ASM:** , replacing **DOES>ASM:** with **DOES>CODE:** , followed by the machine code after **7254h** [the *cfa* of **(;CODE)** we found above in (5)]. Use the dump above for guidance to place the hexadecimal value for each cell as follows, replacing **045Fh** with **;CODE** :

```
HEX
: CONSTANT <BUILDS , DOES>CODE: 0649 C65A ;CODE
```

which can now be entered on an **fbForth 2.0** screen to be loaded with only **DOES>CODE:** and **;CODE** and without the Assembler overhead.

9. If all the code was assembly code, as it is here, you're done. Otherwise, you need to replace values that can vary from one load to the next, such as variables, named constants and dictionary entries not part of the resident dictionary, with the high-level code used in the word's assembly language definition. See (8) in § 9.11.1 for an example with a named constant.
10. You should test your new version of the word to verify it is identical to the original assembly version.

10 Interrupt Service Routines (ISRs)

As of **fbForth 2.0:8**, the **fbForth 2.0** ISR is enabled by default so that it may process the new **fbForth 2.0** speech and sound routines. Though the **fbForth 2.0** ISR may be disabled by the user as it used to be by default, doing so will disable the new speech and sound routines.

The method of servicing a user's ISR written in Forth is basically the same as in past builds of **fbForth 2.0**.

10.1 Overview of fbForth 2.0*'s ISR*

Though the user may disable it[20], **fbForth 2.0**'s ISR is now hooked at startup and is executed for every interrupt. There are three entry points into **fbForth 2.0**'s ISR. Their ALC (Assembly Language Code) labels are **INT1**, **INT2** and **INT3**.

INT1 is where the console ISR branches at the end of its interrupt processing. It processes any pending speech (started with **SAY** or **STREAM**) and sound (started with **PLAY**). It then looks to see whether a user ISR is installed in user variable **ISR** . If so, it modifies the **fbForth 2.0** inner interpreter's **NEXT** (R15) to re-enter at **INT2**.

Re-entry at **INT2** will restore **NEXT** and set up re-entry yet again at **INT3** for cleanup just before branching to the user ISR.

When the user ISR finishes, **fbForth 2.0**'s ISR is re-entered at **INT3** for cleanup via the inner interpreter. Upon exit, the inner interpreter will resume processing Forth words where it was interrupted.

A user ISR will be executed only if the user has installed an ISR using the steps detailed in § 10.3 "Installing a User ISR".

10.2 A Detailed Look at fbForth 2.0*'s ISR*

The console ISR branches to the contents of **83C4h** (R2 of the console ISR workspace [**83C0h**]) if it is non-zero. As of **fbForth 2.0:8**, **83C4h** contains the address of ISR entry point **INT1** (currently, **3020h**) mentioned in the last section. This same entry point is in user variable **INTLNK** , as well. This means that the console ISR will branch to the **fbForth 2.0** ISR with **BL *R12** through the GPL workspace (**83E0h**), R12 containing the ISR's entry point.

Upon entry at **INT1** from the console ISR, the **fbForth 2.0** ISR does the following:

- Checks for pending speech and sound. If found, the following ISR branch stack is set up and executed:
  - Relevant speech ISR address, if speech pending;
  - Sound list #1 ISR address, if pending;
  - Sound list #2 ISR address, if pending;
  - **fbForth 2.0** ISR return address.
- Restores interrupted bank.

20 **fbForth 2.0**'s ISR may be disabled by zeroing **83C4h** with **HEX 0 83C4 !** .

- Checks user variable **ISR** for a non-zero value, implying a user ISR is installed. If a user ISR is defined, modifies **NEXT** to re-enter **fbForth 2.0**'s ISR at **INT2** at the next branch through **NEXT** via **B *NEXT** or **B *R15**, which will set up to execute the user ISR.
- Exits the **fbForth 2.0** ISR by changing to the ISR workspace (**83C0h**) and returning to the caller of the console ISR.

Upon entry at **INT2** (because we have a user ISR defined), the **fbForth 2.0** ISR does the following:

- Disables interrupts via **LIMI 0**.
- Disables VDP interrupt.
- Restores **NEXT** to its value before it was changed at **INT1**.
- Sets the **fbForth** "pending interrupt" flag.
- Pushes current IP (next word pointer) to the return stack.
- Changes IP to **INT3** for cleanup re-entry to **fbForth 2.0** ISR.
- Copies the value in **ISR** to W (current word pointer) so inner interpreter will execute the user ISR.
- Branches to inner interpreter to execute user ISR via **DOEXEC**.

Upon entry at **INT3** (because we are returning from executing the user ISR), the **fbForth 2.0** ISR does the following:

- The inner interpreter actually branches to the address 4 bytes after **INT3**, which pops the saved IP from the return stack.
- Clears the **fbForth** "pending interrupt" flag.
- Clears the pending VDP interrupt by reading VDP status.
- Re-enables VDP interrupt.
- Re-enables interrupts via **LIMI 2**.
- Branches to inner interpreter via **NEXT** to continue executing the interrupted list of word addresses.

If the user's ISR (see below) is properly installed, **fbForth 2.0**'s ISR, at interrupt, modifies **NEXT** so that the very next time **B *NEXT** or **B *R15** is executed from **fbForth 2.0**'s workspace, **fbForth 2.0**'s ISR is re-entered to disable interrupts and to insert execution of the user ISR and its cleanup into the **fbForth 2.0** inner interpreter's list of execution addresses (*cfa*s).

The TI-99/4A has the built-in ability to execute an interrupt routine every 1/60 second. This facility has been extended by the **fbForth 2.0** system so that the routine to be executed at each interrupt period may be written in Forth rather than in assembly language. This is an advanced programming concept and its use depends on the user's knowledge of the TI-99/4A.

10.3 Installing a User ISR

The user variables **ISR** and **INTLNK** are provided to assist the user in using ISRs. Initially, **INTLNK** contains the address of the **fbForth 2.0** ISR handler and **ISR** is set to 0 to indicate no user ISR. To correctly use user variable **ISR** , the following steps should be followed:

	Step	Forth Code
1)	Create and test an **fbForth 2.0** routine to perform the function. Let's call it **MYISR** :	**: MYISR … ;**
2)	Clear the **fbForth 2.0** ISR hook to temporarily disable it:	**HEX 0 83C4 !**
3)	Determine the Code Field Address (*cfa*) of the routine in (1):	**' MYISR CFA**
4)	Write the *cfa* from (3) (still on the stack) into user variable **ISR** :	**ISR !**
5)	Write the contents of **INTLNK** into **83C4h** (33732) to re-enable the **fbForth 2.0** ISR:	**HEX INTLNK @ 83C4 !**

The ISR linkage mechanism is designed so that your interrupt service routine will be allowed to execute immediately after each time the **fbForth 2.0** system executes the instruction whose address is in **NEXT** (as it does at the end of each code word). In addition, the **KEY** routine has been coded so that it also executes through **NEXT** after every keyscan whether or not a key has been pressed. The execution of the "NEXT" instruction in the inner interpreter is actually coded in TI Assembler as **B *NEXT** or **B *R15** because **fbForth 2.0** workspace register 15 (**R15** or **NEXT**) always contains the address of "NEXT" (**MOV *IP+,W**) except, of course, when we temporarily force its change by installing a user ISR. This executes the same procedure as the **fbForth 2.0** Assembler words **;ASM** and **NEXT,** (see Chapter 9"The fbForth 2.0 TMS9900 Assembler").

Before installing an ISR, you should have some idea of how long it takes to execute, keeping in mind that for normal behavior it should execute in less than 16 milliseconds. ISRs that take longer than that may cause erratic sprite motion, speech and sound because of missed interrupts. In addition it is possible to bring the **fbForth 2.0** system to a slow crawl by using about 99% of the processor's time for the ISR.

The ISR capability has obvious applications in game software as well as for playing background music or for spooling blocks from file to printer while other activities are taking place. This final application will require that file buffers and user variables for the spool task be separate from the main Forth task or a very undesirable cross-fertilization of buffers may result. In addition it should be mentioned that disk activity causes all interrupt service activity to halt.

ISRs in **fbForth 2.0** can be written as either colon definitions or as **ASM:** definitions. The former permits very easy routine creation, and the latter permits the same speed capabilities as routines created by the Editor/Assembler. Both types can be used in a single routine to gain the advantages of both.

10.4 Example of a User ISR: DEMO

An example of a simple ISR is given below. This example also illustrates some of the problems associated with ISRs and how they can be circumvented. The problems are:

1) A contention for PAD between a normal Forth command and the ISR routine.
2) Long execution time for the ISR routine. (Even simple routines, especially if they include output conversion routines or other words that nest Forth routines very deeply, will not complete execution in 1/60 second.)

The problem listed in (1) is overcome by moving PAD in the interrupt routine to eliminate the interference between the foreground and the background task. An example of problem (2) would be attempting to use the built-in number formatting routines, which are quite general and hence pay a performance penalty. **DEMO** performs this conversion rather crudely, but fast enough that there is adequate time remaining in each 1/60 second to do meaningful computing.

```
0 VARIABLE TIMER                    (TIMER will hold the current count)
: UP 100 ALLOT ;                    (move HERE and thus PAD up 100 bytes)
: DOWN -100 ALLOT DROP ;            (restore PAD to its original location)
: DEMO UP                           (move PAD to avoid conflict)
    1 TIMER +! TIMER @              (increment TIMER , leave on stack)
    PAD DUP 5 +                     (ready to loop from PAD + 5 down to PAD + 1)
    DO
      0 10 U/                       (make positive double, get 1st digit)
      SWAP 48 +                     (generate ASCII digit)
      I C!                          (store to PAD )
    -1 +LOOP                        (decrement loop counter)
    PAD 1+ SCRN_START @ 5 VMBW      (write to screen)
    DOWN ;                          (restore PAD location)
```

10.4.1 Installing the DEMO ISR

To install this ISR, the following code should be executed:

```
HEX 0 83C4 !      (clear console ISR hook)
' DEMO CFA        (get cfa of the word to be installed as user ISR)
ISR !             (place it in user variable ISR )
INTLNK @          (get the fbForth 2.0 ISR address to the stack)
HEX 83C4 !        (re-install fbForth 2.0 ISR into console ISR hook)
                  (Note: the cfa of DEMO must be in user variable ISR
                   before writing to 83C4h)
```

10.4.2 Uninstalling the DEMO ISR

To reverse the installation of the ISR, the following code should be executed:

```
HEX 0 83C4 !      (clear console ISR hook)
0 ISR !           (disable user ISR by zeroing user variable ISR )
INTLNK @          (get the fbForth 2.0 ISR address to the stack)
HEX 83C4 !        (re-install fbForth 2.0 ISR into console ISR hook)
```

10.5 Some Additional Thoughts Concerning the Use of ISRs

ISRs are uninterruptible. Interrupts are disabled by the code that branches to your ISR routine and they are not enabled until just before branching back to the foreground routine. *Do not enable interrupts in your interrupt routine.*

1) Caution must be exercised when using PABs, changing user variables or using disk buffers in an ISR, as these activities will likely interfere with the foreground task unless duplicate copies are used in the two processes.
2) An ISR must never expect nor leave anything on the stacks. It may however use them in the normal manner during execution.
3) Disk activity disables interrupts as do most of the other DSRs in the TI-99/4A. An ISR that is installed will not execute during the time interval in which disk data transfer is active. It will resume after the disk is finished. Note that it is possible to **LOAD** from disk while the ISR is active. It will wait for about a second each time the disk is accessed. The dictionary will grow with the resultant movement of **PAD** without difficulty.

11 Potpourri

Your **fbForth 2.0** system has a number of additional features that will be discussed in this chapter. These include a facility to save and load binary images of the dictionary so that applications need not be recompiled each time they are used, a group of CRU (Communications Register Unit) instructions and some additional words that make the stack easier to manipulate.

11.1 BSAVE and BLOAD

BSAVE (*addr* blk_1 --- blk_2)

The word **BSAVE** is used to save binary images of the dictionary. It has been made part of the resident dictionary in **fbForth 2.0**, so you no longer need to load it from FBLOCKS. **BSAVE** requires two entries on the stack:

1) The lowest memory address *addr* in the dictionary image to be saved to disk.
2) The Forth block number blk_1 to which the saved image will be written.

BSAVE will use as many **fbForth 2.0** blocks as necessary to save the dictionary contents from the address given on the stack to **HERE**. These are saved with 1000 bytes per **fbForth 2.0** block until the entire image is saved. **BSAVE** returns on the stack the number blk_2 of the first available Forth block after the image.

Each Forth block of the saved image has the following format:

Byte #	Contents
0–1	Address at which the first image byte of this Forth block will be placed
2–3	DP for this memory image
4–5	Contents of **CURRENT**
6–7	Contents of **CURRENT @**
8–9	Contents of **CONTEXT**
10–11	Contents of **CONTEXT @**
12–13	Contents of **VOC-LINK**
14–15	Pointer to last word defined in Forth vocabulary
16–17	Pointer to last word defined in Assembler vocabulary
18	The letter ‘t’
19	The letter ‘i’
20–23	Not used
24–1023	Up to 1000 bytes of the memory image

BLOAD (*blk --- flag*)

BLOAD is part of your **fbForth 2.0** kernel and does not have to be loaded before you can use it. It reverses the **BSAVE** process and makes it possible to bring in an entire application in seconds. **BLOAD** expects an **fbForth 2.0** block number *blk* on the stack. Before performing the **BLOAD** function the 18th and 19th bytes are checked to see that they contain the letters "ti". If they do, the load proceeds and **BLOAD** returns a flag of 0 on the stack signifying a successful load. If the letters "ti" are not found, then the **BLOAD** is not performed and a flag of 1 is returned. This facility permits a conditional binary load to be performed and if it fails (wrong disk, *etc.*), other actions can be performed.

Because the **BLOAD** / **BSAVE** facility is designed to start the save (and hence the load) at a user-supplied address, a complete overlay structure can be implemented. ***Very important:*** The user must ensure that, when part of the dictionary is brought in, the remainder of the dictionary (older part) is identical to that which existed when the image was saved.

11.1.1 Using BSAVE to Customize How fbForth 2.0 Boots Up

You may find that you use the same **MENU** choices frequently and would like to load them automatically and quickly each time you boot **fbForth 2.0**. You can do this by using the Forth word **TASK** as a reference point for **BSAVE** . A no-operation word or null definition, **TASK** is the last word defined in the resident Forth vocabulary of **fbForth 2.0** and the last word that *cannot* be forgotten using **FORGET** . Its definition is simply

```
: TASK ;
```

Its address can be used to **BSAVE** a personalized **fbForth 2.0** system disk by using **' TASK** as the address on the stack for **BSAVE** . If part of your personalized system includes the 64-column editor, you can use the 37 empty blocks of FBLOCKS, starting with block 27, to save your system image:

```
' TASK 27 BSAVE .
```

(*Be sure to back up the original FBLOCKS file before trying this!*). It is important that you ensure that this procedure does not compromise **fbForth 2.0** system blocks you may need for your new personalized system. The **.** after **BSAVE** will report the next available block from the value left on the stack. Subtracting the starting block number (27, in this case) from that number will tell you how many blocks it took to save the binary image in the above **BSAVE** line.

You now need to add the code to block 1 to load what you have just saved the next time you boot your system. You currently have lines 5 – 15 to add your code as long as it eventually ends with **27 BLOAD** for the above case. You also must remove (or put at the end of your added code) the **;S** at the end of line 4 because **;S** exits loading and interpreting the block. This will load your **BSAVE**d system and it will happen a lot faster than loading the text blocks because they now don't need to be interpreted.

11.1.2 An Overlay System with BSAVE and BLOAD

As mentioned above, you can implement a complete overlay structure using **BSAVE** and **BLOAD** . It can be a bit tedious to set up, however, because you must ensure that the dictionary structure older than what you load with **BLOAD** is identical to what it was when the binary image was saved with **BSAVE** . If your application always uses **TASK** as the reference point, as in the previous section, for saving and loading all overlays you set up for your application, the situation is actually pretty simple. If, on the other hand, you wish to have the most efficiently running application possible with minimum load/reload times, you will want to load as overlays only those parts of your application that can be considered mutually exclusive or, at least, not redundant functions.

Such an application might be set up as follows:

1. Anticipate blocks where overlays will be saved with **BSAVE** .
2. Set up storage (variables, arrays, ...) that is common to two or more overlays.
3. Set up the overlay-loading mechanism in your application to use **BLOAD** to load them. The following example illustrates such a mechanism using the **CASE … ENDCASE** construct:

```
0 VARIABLE OVLY    \ track current ovly#
: OVLY_LD ( ovly# --- )
      DUP
      CASE
         1 OF 120 BLOAD ENDOF
         2 OF 130 BLOAD ENDOF
         3 OF 140 BLOAD ENDOF
         ELSEOF -1 ENDOF   \ wrong overlay choice!
      ENDCASE
      \ 2 cells to here. Top cell: -1|0|1
      CASE
         -1 OF ." No choice for overlay " . CR ENDOF
          0 OF OVLY ! ENDOF   \ Success! Save new #
          1 OF ." Failed to load overlay " . CR ENDOF
      ENDCASE ;
```

4. Program a method for determining which overlay is needed for a particular function or set of functions and use **OVLY** to determine whether that overlay needs to be loaded.
5. As the last word of your application before any overlays, define **OVERLAYS** as a null definition to be a reference point for **BSAVE** and make it unforgettable:

```
: OVERLAYS ;
' OVERLAYS NFA FENCE !
```

6. Begin each overlay with the following null definition as a **FORGET** reference point for loading the next overlay source block prior to saving its binary image with **BSAVE** :

```
: OVLY_STRT ;
```

7. After the successful load (with **BLOAD**) of an overlay, set **OVLY** to its number as in the example in (3) above.

After programming and debugging the application, save the application and its overlays as follows:

1. Remove all system components from the dictionary that are not required by your application and that are newer than **TASK** . To start with a dictionary with only resident words:

a) Execute **VLIST** to get the name of the word immediately following **TASK**. Remember that **VLIST** lists the dictionary from **HERE** back to older words.

b) **FORGET** that word to leave only the resident dictionary. If the word following **TASK**, *i.e.*, listed just before **TASK** by **VLIST** , is **XXX** , then execute **FORGET XXX** .

2. Load all system components required to run your application.
3. Load application.
4. Load first overlay.
5. **BSAVE** application using the address of **TASK** to a free Forth block:

    ' TASK 30 BSAVE .

6. **BSAVE** first overlay using the address of **OVERLAYS** to a free Forth block:

    ' OVERLAYS 40 BSAVE .

7. For each overlay following the first do the following:

    a) **FORGET OVLY_STRT**

    b) **100 LOAD** (100 should be where the Forth block for next overlay resides.)

    c) **' OVERLAYS 50 BSAVE .** (Obviously, 50 should be a different block for each additional overlay.)

11.1.3 An Easier Overlay System in Source Code

The above **BSAVE / BLOAD** method for setting up an overlay system can be very difficult to maintain because of the unforgiving nature of **BLOAD** . Any changes in the application other than the overlay section will almost certainly necessitate re-saving *all* of the overlays. An easier method to maintain is one such as described in *Starting FORTH (1st Ed.)*, p. 80*ff.* It will be necessarily slower to load overlays because it involves interpreting source blocks. You can still save a binary image of the application as above with the first, presumably most used, overlay to minimize load time, but it still may be better for software changes to **BSAVE** the application without an overlay.

Because you are not using **BSAVE** to save the overlays, you can dispense with one of the null definitions. Let us say you are using **OVERLAYS** , as the word to **FORGET** each time another overlay is loaded. **OVERLAYS** will now separate the main application from the current overlay and should, of course, be the last word of the main application. **OVERLAYS** should obviously not be made unforgettable! The first **fbForth 2.0** block of each overlay should begin with

```
FORGET OVERLAYS          : OVERLAYS ;
```

You can use the same mechanism (**OVLY_LD**) as in the previous section for loading the overlays, but you will need to change all instances of **BLOAD** to **LOAD** and, of course, the blocks will be text blocks, not binary images. You will also need to change the code that expects a flag on the stack from **BLOAD** because **LOAD** does not leave a flag.

11.2 Conditional Loads

CLOAD (*blk* ---)

The word **CLOAD** has been included in your system to assist in easily managing the process of loading the proper support routines for an application without compiling duplicates of support routines into the dictionary.

CLOAD calls the words **<CLOAD>** , **WLITERAL** , and **SLIT** . Their functions are described briefly as follows:

<CLOAD> (---)

performs the primary **CLOAD** function and is executed or compiled by **CLOAD** depending on **STATE** .

SLIT (--- *addr*)

is a word designed to handle string literals during execution. Its purpose is to put the address of the string on the stack and step the **fbForth 2.0** Instruction Pointer over it.

WLITERAL (---)

is used to compile **SLIT** and the desired character string into the current dictionary definition. See the **fbForth 2.0** Glossary (Appendix D) for more detail.

To use **CLOAD** , there must always be a Forth block number on the stack. The word **CLOAD** must be followed by the word whose conditional presence in the dictionary will determine whether or not the Forth block number on the stack is loaded.

```
27 CLOAD FOO
```

This instruction, for example, will load **fbForth 2.0** block 27 only if a dictionary search via **(FIND)** fails to find **FOO** . **FOO** should be the last word loaded by the command **27 LOAD** to insure all the code dependencies were loaded.

It is also possible to use **CLOAD** to abort the loading of the currently loading **fbForth 2.0** block. This is done by using the command:

```
0 CLOAD TESTWORD
```

If this line of code were located on **fbForth 2.0** block 50, and the word **TESTWORD** were in the present dictionary, the load would abort just as if a **;S** had been encountered.

Caution must be exercised when using **BASE->R** and **R->BASE** with **CLOAD** as these will cause the return stack to be polluted if a **LOAD** is aborted and the **BASE->R** is not balanced by an **R->BASE** at execution time.

11.3 CRU Words

The five words below have been included to assist in performing CRU (Communications Register Unit) related functions. They allow the **fbForth 2.0** programmer to perform the **LDCR**, **STCR**, **TB**, **SBO** and **SBZ** operations of the TMS9900 without using the Assembler. See CRU documentation in the *Editor/Assembler Manual* for more information. These words are not part of the resident dictionary. They must be loaded from block 5 of FBLOCKS (01SEP2014 or later). You can always type **MENU** to view the loadable options for **fbForth 2.0**.

Please note that the CRU base address used here is the CRU bit number, not the "CRU Address" in § 24.3.3 "CRU Allocation" of the *Editor/Assembler Manual*. Each of the instructions below doubles the CRU bit number *addr* before putting it in R12. If you are accustomed to using the already-shifted CRU base address for a device, you will need to shift it right 1 bit (divide by 2) for *addr* in all of these words such that it is the actual CRU base bit number. For **TB** , **SBO** and **SBZ** , you will need to compose the CRU bit number from the base + the bit to be tested, set or reset because each of these words operates on bit 0 of the address (*addr*) passed to it, *i.e.*, they do not operate like their namesakes in TMS9900 Assembler. In the author's opinion, these words should emulate the behavior of their TMS9900 Assembler counterparts, but rather than break old TI Forth code by changing their definitions, the author offers the following comparison of **fbForth 2.0** code and TMS9900 Assembler code for the same operation:

Scenario: You wish to set CRU bit 9 of the disk controller's CRU address space, **1100h** – **11FEh** (CRU bits **880h** – **8FFh**).

TMS9900 Assembler: Load R12 with **1100h** followed by **SBO 9**:

```
LI     R12,>1100
SBO    9
```

fbForth 2.0: Convert the CRU base address (**1100h**) to the CRU bit number (**880h**) it represents, add the bit number (**9**) to be set and push the result to the stack before executing **SBO** :

```
HEX 889 SBO  ok:0
```

which actually executes the following TMS9900 Assembler code:

```
MOV    *SP+,R12       <--pop 889h from the stack to R12
A      R12,R12        <--double the CRU bit number
SBO    0              <--set the bit pointed to by R12
```

LDCR (n_1 n_2 *addr* ---)

Performs a TMS9900 **LDCR** instruction. The CRU base address *addr* will be shifted left one bit and stored in workspace register R12 prior to executing the TMS9900 **LDCR** instruction. The low-order n_2 bits of value n_1 are transferred to the CRU, where the following condition, $n_2 \leq 15$, is enforced by n_2 AND **0Fh**. If $n_2 = 0$, 16 bits are transferred. For program clarity, you may certainly use $n_2 = 16$ to transfer 16 bits because $n_2 = 0$ will be the value actually used by the final machine code.

STCR (n_1 *addr* --- n_2)

Performs the TMS9900 **STCR** instruction. The CRU base address *addr* will be shifted left one bit and stored in workspace register R12 prior to executing the TMS9900 **STCR** instruction. There will be n_1 bits transferred from the CRU to the stack as n_2, where the following condition, $n_1 \leq 15$, is enforced by n_1 AND **0Fh**. If $n_1 = 0$, 16 bits will be transferred. For program clarity, you may certainly use $n_1 = 16$ to transfer 16 bits because $n_1 = 0$ will be the value actually used by the final machine code.

TB (*addr* --- *flag*)

TB performs the TMS9900 **TB** instruction. The bit at CRU address *addr* is tested by this instruction. Its value (*flag* = 1|0) is returned to the stack. The CRU base address *addr* will be shifted left one bit and stored in workspace register R12 prior to executing the TMS9900 instruction, **TB 0**, to effect testing the bit.

SBO (*addr* ---)

This word expects to find on the stack the CRU address *addr* of the bit to be set to 1. **SBO** will put this address into workspace register R12, shift it left (double it) and execute TMS9900 instruction, **SBO 0**, to effect setting the bit.

SBZ (*addr* ---)

This word expects to find on the stack the CRU address *addr* of the bit to be reset to 0. **SBZ** will put this address into workspace register R12, shift it left (double it) and execute TMS9900 instruction, **SBZ 0**, to effect resetting the bit.

11.4 Useful Additional Stack Words

The words in this section were, for the most part, required by the new Stack-based String Library (see Chapter 14). The author added a few complementary words to round out the set. They are loaded from block 41 of FBLOCKS (21NOV2014 or later).

2DUP (n_1 n_2 --- n_1 n_2 n_1 n_2)

Duplicate the top two numbers on the stack.

2DROP (n_1 n_2 ---)

Drop the top two numbers from the stack.

NIP (n_1 n_2 --- n_2)

Remove from the stack the number that is under the top number.

TUCK (n_1 n_2 --- n_2 n_1 n_2)

Put a copy of the top number under the top two numbers on the stack.

CELLS (*n* --- 2*n*)

Replace *n* (a number of cells) with 2*n* (the number of bytes in *n* cells).

-ROT (n_1 n_2 n_3 --- n_3 n_1 n_2)

Rotate right the top three numbers on the stack, resulting in the top number on the bottom.

PICK (+*n* --- [*n*])

Copy to the top of the stack the nth number down. The 0th number is the top number. [*n*] means "the contents of cell *n* from the top of the stack". The number *n* must be positive.

0 PICK is equivalent to **DUP** .
1 PICK is equivalent to **OVER** .

ROLL ([*n*] … [0] +*n* --- [*n*-1] … [0] [*n*])

Rotate left the top n+1 numbers on the stack, resulting in the nth number down moving to the top of the stack. The number *n* must be positive. The source for **ROLL** was Marshall Linker via George Smyth's "Forth Forum" column in the *MANNERS Newsletter* (1985) Vol. 4(5), pp. 12 – 16.

0 ROLL is a null operation.
1 ROLL is equivalent to **SWAP** .
2 ROLL is equivalent to **ROT** .

WITHIN (n_1 n_2 n_3 --- *flag*)

Result *flag* is true (1) if $n_2 \leq n_1 < n_3$ and false (0) otherwise.

<> (n_1 n_2 --- *flag*)

Result *flag* is true (1) if $n_1 \neq n_2$ and false (0) otherwise.

$. (*n* ---)

Display the top number on the stack as an unsigned hexadecimal number.

EXIT (---) *[immediate word]*

EXIT is a synonym for **;S** , which stops interpretation of a Forth block or ends the current word's execution and returns to the calling procedure.

12 fbForth 2.0 Dictionary Entry Structure

The structure of an entry (a Forth *word*) in the **fbForth 2.0** dictionary is briefly described in this chapter to give the reader a better understanding of **fbForth 2.0** and how its dictionary may differ from other Forth implementations.

The dictionary entries are shown here schematically as a stack of single cells of 16 bits each:

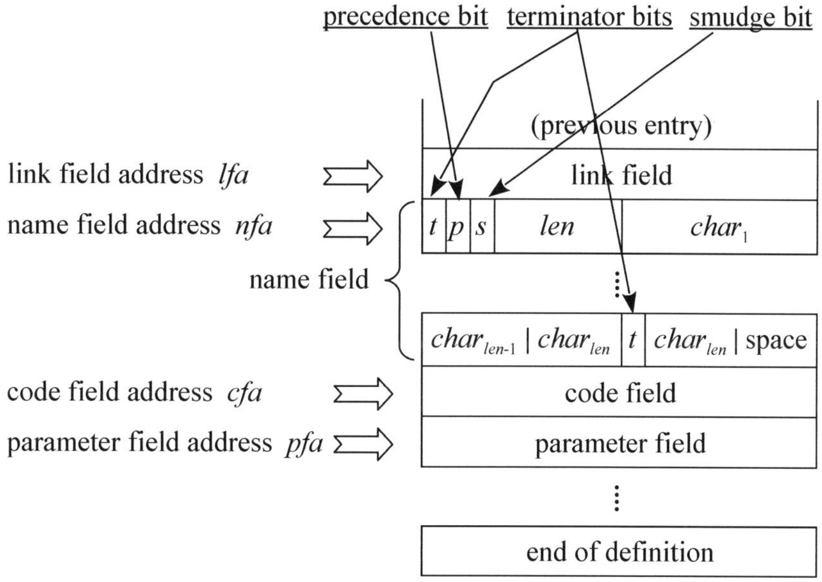

At the least, each entry contains a link field (1 cell), a name field (1 – 16 cells), a code field (1 cell) and a parameter field ($n \geq 1$ cells).

12.1 Link Field

The link field is the first field in a definition. It contains the address of the name field of the immediately preceding word in the vocabulary list to which the word belongs in the dictionary. The address of this field is termed the link field address *lfa* and may be retrieved by pushing the *pfa* (see § 12.4) onto the stack and executing **LFA** .

12.2 Name Field

The name field follows the link field and may be as long as 16 cells (32 bytes). The name field address *nfa* points to this field and may be retrieved by pushing the *pfa* (see § 12.4) onto the stack and executing **NFA** .

The name field is a packed character string (see footnote 5 on page 22) in that the first byte is the length byte followed by the character string that represents the name. The three highest bits of the length byte are the beginning terminator bit (**80h**), the precedence bit (**40h**) and the smudge bit (`20h`). These are shown in the above figure as *t*, *p* and *s*, respectively. That leaves 5 bits for the character-length *len* of the name, which is the reason that **fbForth 2.0** words have a maximum length of 31 characters. The name field in **fbForth 2.0** always occupies an even number of bytes, *i.e.*, it begins and ends on a cell boundary. The last byte of the name field will be either the last character of the name or a space and will have the highest bit (`80h`) set as the ending terminator bit.

To clarify the above diagram a bit, when the name is only one character long, the first character is obviously the last character and the ending terminator bit will be set in that byte, which results in a name field occupying just one cell.

The terminator bits are flags used by **TRAVERSE** (*q.v.*) to find the beginning or end of the name field, given the address of one end and the direction (+1|-1) to search.

The precedence bit is used to indicate that a word should be executed rather than compiled during compilation. It is set by **IMMEDIATE**, which sets the precedence bit for the most recently completed definition.

The smudge bit is used to hide|unhide a word from a dictionary search during compilation. If the smudge bit is set (`20h`), **'** , **-FIND** and **(FIND)** will not find the word. During compilation, the smudge bit is toggled by **SMUDGE** or similar code and toggled again by **;** or similar termination code.

12.3 Code Field

The code field immediately follows the last cell of the name field. The code field address *cfa* points to this field and may be retrieved by pushing the *pfa* (see § 12.4) onto the stack and executing **CFA** . The code field contains the address of the machine-code routine that **fbForth 2.0** will run when it executes this word and depends on the nature of the word's definition. The following table shows common situations:

Word Defined by	Code Field Contains Address of	What the Runtime Code Does
VARIABLE	Runtime code of **VARIABLE**	Pushes word's *pfa* onto stack
CONSTANT	Runtime code of **CONSTANT**	Pushes contents of word's *pfa* onto stack
:	Runtime code of **:**	Executes the list of previously defined words, the addresses of which are stored beginning at this word's *pfa*
CODE:	*pfa* of word	Executes machine code stored beginning at this word's *pfa*
ASM:	*pfa* of word	Executes machine code stored beginning at this word's *pfa*

12.4 Parameter Field

The parameter field follows the code field. The parameter field address *pfa* points to this address, which can be retrieved by using **'** :

```
' cccc
```

where **cccc** is the name of the Forth word for which you desire the *pfa*.. If the word is not found, however, you will get an error message. If the error occurred during a **LOAD**, two values will be left on the stack that indicate the character offset and block number of the error, allowing you to use **WHERE** to open the editor at the bad code. **-FIND** (*q.v.*) will also return the *pfa* along with the length byte of the name field and *true* if the word is found in the dictionary or just *false* if it is not found. It is used the same way as **'** , but more work is required if all you want is the *pfa*, so it is more suited to colon definitions:

```
-FIND cccc DROP DROP
```

If you know only the *nfa*, you can retrieve the *pfa* by executing **PFA** .

The contents of the parameter field depend on the type of word defined. The following table shows common situations:

Word Defined by	Parameter Field Contains
VARIABLE	Value of variable
CONSTANT	Value of constant
:	Mostly a list of the addresses (usually their *cfa*s) of previously defined words that comprise this word's definition
CODE:	Machine code comprising this word's runtime code
ASM:	Machine code comprising this word's runtime code

12.5 Notes on Resident Dictionary Words

The structure of a Forth word described above is strictly true only for words defined in CPU RAM space. For words in the resident dictionary, the various fields are split into two ROM banks in the 32 KiB cartridge, with the link and name fields in bank 2 and the code and parameter fields in bank 0. There are three additional fields following the name field of each word in bank 2. The first contains the *cfa;* the second, the *pfa;* the third, the address of the previous word's *pfa* pointer.

The resident dictionary structure is only searchable in bank 2, where two linked lists reside. The first is the normal link-field-to-name-field chain and the second is a *pfa*-pointer-pointer-to-*pfa*-pointer chain, mentioned in the previous paragraph. The only way to find the *nfa*, given a *pfa* in ROM, is for **NFA** to search the latter chain from the last ROM definition to the first until the *pfa*'s pointer is found, back up three bytes to the last byte of the name field and traverse the name field to its first byte. The address of that byte is the *nfa*.

To find the *lfa*, **LFA** first finds the *nfa* via **NFA** and then backs up two bytes, *i.e.*, *lfa* = *nfa* – 2.

Finally, **CFA** finds the *cfa* from the *pfa* in the same way for both ROM and RAM: *cfa* = *pfa* – 2.

13 Screen Fonts and the Font Editor

Words introduced in this chapter:

FONTED **FNT** **SCRFNT** **USEFFL**

13.1 Screen Font Changes as of **fbForth 2.0:8**

The default Screen Font File with descenders for ASCII character values 0 – 127 (1024 bytes) is no longer in ROM. Now, it is to be found in DSK1.FBFONT unless the default disk has been changed at bootup. The boot DSK #, *n*, is saved as the 5th byte of the packed string for the default blocks filename, "DSK*n*.FBLOCKS", the 1st byte of which is the string length.

At powerup,

- **SCRFNT** is set to its new default value of -1;
- The default font is loaded from DSK*n*.FBFONT by **FNT** .

At non-powerup **COLD** , the font file, loaded before **COLD** was invoked, is reloaded, unless the user changed the default value of **SCRFNT** to 0. The default value of **SCRFNT** can be changed to 0 to force loading the console font, with its small caps for lowercase, with the following code:

```
0 UCONS$ @ 68 + !
```

UCONS$ is the address of the default-value table of User Variables and 68 (**44h**) is **SCRFNT** 's position in the table.

If the default font file cannot be found,

- **SCRFNT** and its default value are set to 0;
- The console font, with small caps for lowercase, is loaded.

If **SCRFNT** ≠ 0, **FNT** loads the default font file, the PAB for which follows the **fbForth 2.0** disk buffer, **DISK_BUF** , in VRAM.

The user can change the default font to come from a binary font file of the user's choosing with **USEFFL** . **USEFFL** will set up the font-file PAB (immediately follows **DISK_BUF** in VRAM). The default font filename will be copied to the font PAB in VRAM.

The **fbForth 2.0** word **FNT** loads either the default font file (can be changed by user) or the console font into the Pattern Descriptor Table (PDT) depending on the value of the user variable **SCRFNT** . The default font is loaded from DSK1.FBFONT by **FNT** (or from DSK*n*.FBFONT if key *n* is held down) at **fbForth 2.0** startup because **SCRFNT** = -1 at startup. The **fbForth 2.0** system default font contains the patterns for ASCII character codes 0 – 127. The font pattern for each character is 8 bytes, which means that 1 KiB of pattern code is loaded into the PDT. This font contains true lowercase characters with true descenders.

It should be noted that each time the VDP mode is changed (except for Graphics2 [bitmap]), the current screen font is reloaded. The user can always change the value of **SCRFNT** to 0 to force (re)loading the console screen font. Changing **SCRFNT** back to a non-zero value will switch font loading to the currently stored font-file name, be it the system or user font file.

13.2 User Fonts

fbForth 2.0 allows users to load their own fonts instead of the default font from cartridge ROM as long as a few rules are followed:

- The font file should not be larger than 2 KiB, *i.e.*, it should not code for more than 256 characters. Attempting to load font files larger than 2 KiB will result in a file I/O error.
- The first character is assumed to code for ASCII 0 and must start at the first byte of the file. *TI Writer* CHARA1-style font files will not work because the font code begins at byte 6, not byte 0, of the file. The Font Editor (see next section) can be used to correct the file's pattern registration so that it will load properly.
- Font files larger than 1 KiB (ASCII 0 – 127) will cause a problem in SPLIT2 mode in that characters 128 – 255 will appear in the top of the bitmap graphics part of the screen. This can be corrected with the following code after **SPLIT2** has been invoked:

```
PDT 1024 + 1024 0 VFILL
```

To install a user font file that will be loaded the next time **FNT** is executed, the word **USEFFL** must be followed by the full pathname of the font file as in the following example:

```
USEFFL DSK1.MYFONT
```

Once **USEFFL** executes without an error, the user's font file will be installed at the next execution of **FNT** , unless **SCRFNT** = 0.

13.3 Using the Font Editor

Typing **FONTED** opens the font editor with 2 KiB of the current font loaded from the PDT and with the uppercase 'A' (ASCII 65) in the edit box. A full 2 KiB is always loaded into the edit buffer from the PDT regardless of the actual size of the screen font loaded by the last execution of **FNT** :

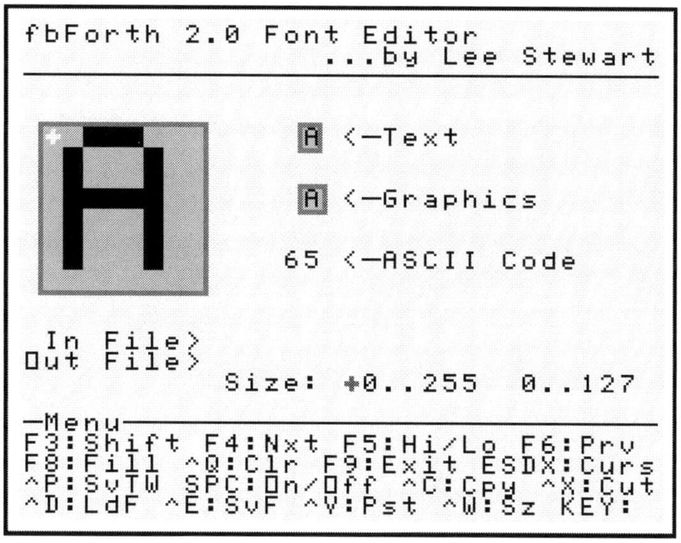

Editing the font will not affect the current font because the working buffer is not the PDT. Though all the menu keys are shown at the bottom of the screen, they are rather cryptic, so here is a brief description:

Function	Keystroke
<FCTN+4>	Next character pattern
<FCTN+6>	Previous pattern
<FCTN+S>	Move edit cursor left
<FCTN+D>	Move edit cursor right
<FCTN+X>	Move edit cursor down
<FCTN+E>	Move edit cursor up
<FCTN+5>	Select character pattern 128 characters up/down
<CTRL+Q>	Turn off all pixels of character pattern block
<FCTN+8>	Turn on all pixels of character pattern block
<CTRL+C>	Copy character pattern to clipboard
<CTRL+X>	Cut character pattern to clipboard
<CTRL+V>	Paste character pattern from clipboard
<SPACE>	Toggle current character pattern pixel on/off
Key	Select any character key to edit its pattern
<CTRL+D>	Load font file
<FCTN+3>	Toggle 6-byte font pattern offset
<CTRL+W>	Toggle output file size between 1 KiB (ASCII 1 – 127) and 2 KiB (ASCII 0 – 255)
<CTRL+E>	Save font in fbForth 2.0 format
<CTRL+P>	Save font in TI Writer format
<FCTN-9>	Exit font editor

To aid in editing, the current pattern is shown actual size in a 6x8-pixel, text-mode character box and an 8x8-pixel, graphics-mode character box. The ASCII value of the current character is also shown. The edit cursor is a white '+' and can be moved around with the arrow keys. The pixel under the cursor can be toggled on/off with the space bar. You will see any changes appearing in all three display boxes.

You can load *TI-Writer*-format font files and toggle the font offset with ***<FCTN+3>*** so the patterns are properly registered for editing. Saving the font as an **fbForth-2.0**-style font will write the font starting at the first byte of the file. Saving it as a *TI-Writer*-style font will write six bytes of zeroes before writing the font to the file. The only other output variation is choosing whether to save only patterns 0 – 127 (1 KiB file) or all patterns 0 – 255 (2 KiB file). The blue '+' character marks which of these occurs with the next file save and is toggled with ***<CTRL+W>***.

13.4 Modifying the 64-Column Editor's Font

The 64-column editor does not use the normal screen fonts described above, so modifying it will be a bit more of a challenge. The following graphic shows the complete character set, with the true lowercase letters and the '@' designed by the author, for bitmap mode:

This character set is used principally by the 64-column editor via the word **SMASH** defined in block 13 of FBLOCKS. Designing the characters for a 3×7 matrix was quite a challenge. The '&' should probably be re-designed.

To design your own 3×7 font, use a 4×8-pixel grid for each character. Each row of the character pattern is one nybble of the pattern code, so each character is four bytes. You then need only overwrite the character codes for the tiny character set in block 15, lines 3 – 9 of FBLOCKS. Loading the following three blocks from a blocks file of your design, with contiguous block numbers, would accomplish this. As with any modification of FBLOCKS, be sure you have a backup copy before making any changes! [*Note:* The comment, `( ^0)` (Shift+0), on line 5 below is a substitute for `( ))`, a syntax error]:

```
BLOCK #10
  0 ( DEFINITIONS FOR true lowercase TINY CHARACTERS) BASE->R HEX
  1 0EEE  VARIABLE TCHAR  DATA[ EEEE
  2 0000 0000 (  )  0444 4404 ( !)  0AA0 0000 ( ")  08AE AEA2 ( #)
  3 04EC 46E4 ( $)  0A24 448A ( %)  06AC 4A86 ( &)  0480 0000 ( ')
  4 0248 8842 ( ()  0842 2248 ( ^0) 04EE 4000 ( *)  0044 E440 ( +)
  5 0000 0048 ( ,)  0000 E000 ( -)  0000 0004 ( .)  0224 4488 ( /)
  6 04AA EAA4 ( 0)  04C4 4444 ( 1)  04A2 488E ( 2)  0C22 C22C ( 3)
  7 02AA AE22 ( 4)  0E8C 222C ( 5)  0688 CAA4 ( 6)  0E22 4488 ( 7)
  8 04AA 4AA4 ( 8)  04AA 622C ( 9)  0004 0040 ( :)  0004 0048 ( ;)
  9 0024 8420 ( <)  000E 0E00 ( =)  0084 2480 ( >)  04A2 4404 ( ?)
 10 04AE AE86 ( @)  04AA EAAA ( A)  0CAA CAAC ( B)  0688 8886 ( C)
 11 0CAA AAAC ( D)  0E88 C88E ( E)  0E88 C888 ( F)  04A8 8AA6 ( G)
 12 0AAA EAAA ( H)  0E44 444E ( I)  0222 22A4 ( J)  0AAC CAAA ( K)
 13 0888 888E ( L)  0AEE AAAA ( M)  0AAE EEAA ( N)  0EAA AAAE ( O)
 14 0CAA C888 ( P)  0EAA AAEC ( Q)  0CAA CAAA ( R)  0688 422C ( S)
 15 -->
```

```
BLOCK #11
( DEFINITIONS FOR true lowercase TINY CHARACTERS continued)
0E44 4444 ( T)  0AAA AAAE ( U)  0AAA AA44 ( V)  0AAA AEEA ( W)
0AA4 44AA ( X)  0AAA E444 ( Y)  0E24 488E ( Z)  0644 4446 ( [)
0884 4422 ( \)  0C44 444C ( ])  044A A000 ( $)  0000 000F ( _)
0420 0000 ( `)  000E 2EAE ( a)  088C AAAC ( b)  0006 8886 ( c)
0226 AAA6 ( d)  0004 AE86 ( e)  0688 E888 ( f)  0006 A62C ( g)
088C AAAA ( h)  0404 4442 ( i)  0202 22A4 ( j)  088A ACAA ( k)
0444 4444 ( l)  000A EEAA ( m)  0008 EAAA ( n)  0004 AAA4 ( o)
000C AC88 ( p)  0006 A622 ( q)  0008 E888 ( r)  0006 842C ( s)
044E 4442 ( t)  000A AAA6 ( u)  000A AAA4 ( v)  000A AEEA ( w)
000A A4AA ( x)  000A A62C ( y)  000E 248E ( z)  0644 8446 ( {)
0444 0444 ( |)  0C44 244C ( })  02E8 0000 ( ~)  0EEE EEEE ( DEL)
 ]DATA  DROP DROP    R->BASE   -->

BLOCK #12
( DEFINITIONS FOR true lowercase TINY CHARACTERS concluded)
 BASE->R  DECIMAL
: TCOPY TCHAR 15 BLOCK 192 + 194 MOVE UPDATE FLUSH  ;

 CR ." Make FBLOCKS current, execute TCOPY and FORGET TCHAR . If
FBLOCKS is on DSK1:" CR CR
."    USEBFL DSK1.FBLOCKS" CR
."    TCOPY" CR
."    FORGET TCHAR" CR CR    R->BASE  ;S
```

After loading the above blocks, follow the directions on the screen. The instructions you will be prompted to type are explained below:

USEBFL DSK1.FBLOCKS	Make DSK1.FBLOCKS the current blocks file.
TCOPY	Copy new tiny-character patterns to correct location in block 15 of DSK1.FBLOCKS.
FORGET TCHAR	Reclaim dictionary space used by **TCHAR** array and **TCOPY** word.

14 The Stack-based String Library

This chapter describes the stack-based string library package ported by Mark Wills to **fbForth 2.0** from code he wrote for his own **TurboForth 1.2** (see his website: *turboforth.net*). The string library simplifies string handling through the use of a string stack. To accommodate users of the string library in **fbForth 2.0** and with permission, the author has freely edited Mark's documentation written 2/27/2014 for **TurboForth 1.2** (*cf.* his website) for this chapter. In addition, the author rendered some minor assistance in this **fbForth-2.0** port.

[Mark Wills' Note for his PDF documentation: This paper is adapted from a paper that I wrote describing a string library that I developed for ANS Forth systems. The code[21] presented at the end of this paper has been modified where appropriate for compatibility with the Forth-83[22] standard, and, specifically, TurboForth V1.2. The original ANS paper can be downloaded as a PDF:
turboforth.net/downloads/docs/ANS_String_Lib.pdf.]

Mark Wills' abstract for **TurboForth 1.2**:

> String handling is not one of Forth's strong points. Out-of-the-box support for strings is all but non-existent in standard Forth. Whilst the concept of strings does exist in the language, relatively few words are provided to allow effective string manipulation. The normal approach for Forth programmers is to roll one's own string functions as required. Issues such as heap allocation and de-allocation, and memory fragmentation are thorny issues which are often passed over in preference for a 'quick-and-dirty' solution that solves the problem at hand. This paper presents a Forth-83[22] Forth compliant library which affords the Forth programmer such facilities as string constants, transient strings, and a wide range of string manipulation words. Issues such as memory allocation, memory de-allocation and memory fragmentation are rendered irrelevant through the provision of a string stack, which is used to host and manipulate transient strings.

14.1 Introduction—The Concepts behind the Library

The String Library offers two types of strings:

- Transient strings—these exist on a string stack, which is separate from the data and return stacks. Their size is variable, and may be increased and decreased in size as necessary.
- String constants—declared with a maximum size, string constants are generally initialized to a constant string value throughout the life of the application. It is possible to change the string assigned to a string constant, but its maximum size cannot be changed.

14.1.1 Coding Conventions

The following coding-style conventions are employed in the library:

21 The code for the **fbForth 2.0** version of the String Stack Library is located in Appendix J starting at block 42.

22 **fbForth 2.0** is not Forth-83 compliant. It is based on fig-Forth , with some features of Forth-79 thrown in, both of which predate the Forth-83 standard. Most of the modifications necessary to port the string library to **fbForth 2.0** were due to this disparity.

- Words intended to be called by a user of the library all end with a dollar sign. The dollar sign should be read as the word "string". For example, **DROP$** would be pronounced "drop string".
- Low-level words internal to the library for housekeeping, or general factors of code are surrounded with parentheses. For example: **(lenOf$)** .

14.1.2 Stack Notation

Normal Forth stack notation conventions are used. Where words have an effect on the string stack, the string stack effects are shown alongside the normal data stack effects. For example,

VAL$ (--- *ud*) (SS: *str* ---)

The above example indicates that the word **VAL$** takes a string from the string stack and results in an unsigned double being pushed to the data stack.

The suggested pronunciation of the word is also given in quotes following the stack signature(s).

If a word expects additional characters from the input stream (the terminal input buffer or a block buffer), "IS:" is shown on the "before execution" side of the stack effects followed by a descriptor in italics and, possibly, a terminator (usually a double quote) in the font used for Forth words in this document.

For example,

$CONST (*max_len* IS:*name*" ---)

14.1.3 Loading the String Stack Library

The String Stack Library is supplied in the FBLOCKS file, ready to **LOAD** . Typing **MENU** will provide you with instructions for **LOAD**ing the library. Currently, it is **LOAD**ed by typing **42 LOAD** .

The string stack must be initialized to some convenient size by executing **INIT$** once the library is **LOAD**ed:

512 INIT$ ok:0[23]

will initialize the string stack to 512 bytes. **INIT$** should only be executed once because initializing the string stack a second time will orphan the previous instance and waste memory.

14.2 String Constant Words

Since only a handful of words are associated with string constants, they will be documented first:

$CONST (*max_len* IS:*name* ---) RUNTIME: (--- *$Caddr*) "string constant"

The word **$CONST** declares a string constant. Declared at compile time, string constants require a maximum length and a name. For example,

50 $CONST WELCOME ok:0

23 Note that computer responses are underlined as is the case here for ok:0 .

The above example declares a string with a maximum size of 50 characters. It shall be referenced in code using the name **WELCOME** .

Note the runtime stack effect. It can be seen that at runtime, when the name of the string is referenced, it shall push its address to the data stack. The label *$Caddr* indicates that it is the address of a string constant. A string constant pushes the address of its maximum length field which can be read with the word **MAXLEN$** .

**MAXLEN$** (*$Caddr* --- *max_len*) "maximum length of string"

Given the address of a string constant on the data stack the word **MAXLEN$** returns the maximum allowed string length for that string constant. For example,

```
50 $CONST WELCOME  ok:0
WELCOME MAXLEN$ . 50  ok:0
```

The above code fragment shall display the value 50.

:=" (*$Caddr* IS:*string*" ---) "assign string constant"

Given the address of a string constant on the data stack, the word **:="** initializes the string constant with the string from the input stream. For example,

```
50 $CONST WELCOME  ok:0
WELCOME :=" Hello and welcome!"  ok:0
```

.$CONST (*$Caddr* ---) "display string constant"

Given the address of a string constant on the data stack the word **.$CONST** shall display the string. For example,

```
50 $CONST WELCOME  ok:0
WELCOME :=" Hello and welcome!"  ok:0
WELCOME .$CONST CR
Hello and welcome!  ok:0
```

**CLEN$** (*$Caddr* --- *len*) "string constant length"

Given the address of a string constant on the data stack the word **CLEN$** returns its actual length on the data stack. For example,

```
50 $CONST WELCOME  ok:0
WELCOME :=" Hello and welcome!"  ok:0
WELCOME CLEN$ . 18  ok:0
```

The above code displays 18—the length of the string **WELCOME** .

**>$** (*$Caddr* ---) (SS: --- *str*) "to string stack"

Given the address of a string constant on the data stack the word **>$** copies the contents of the string to the string stack where it can be manipulated. For example,

```
50 $CONST WELCOME  ok:0
WELCOME :=" Hello and welcome!"  ok:0
WELCOME >$  ok:0
```

Note that the string stack has received a copy of the string contained within **WELCOME** . The string **WELCOME** still exists as a string constant.

14.3 String Stack Words

The convention within this document is to refer to words that exist on the string stack as transient strings. They are referred to as transient strings because they generally only exist for a short time on the string stack. Strings are placed on the string stack (which is separate from the data and returns stacks) and then manipulated in some way before being consumed. Memory allocation and de-allocation is managed by virtue of the strings being on the stack in the same way that the size of the data stack is managed by simply adding or removing values on the data stack.

$" (IS:*string*" ---) (SS: --- *str*) "string to string stack"

The word **$"** takes a string from the input stream and pushes it to the string stack. The end of the string is indicated by a quotation mark. For example,

```
$" Hello, World!"  ok:0
```

In this example the string "Hello, world!" is pushed directly to the string stack, thus becoming the top item on the string stack.

Note that **$"** is a state-smart word. It can be used in both colon definitions and also directly at the command line. The correct action will be taken in either case.

In order that the runtime actions of **$"** may be compiled into a definition if so desired, the runtime action of this word is encapsulated within the word **($")** . Therefore, if the runtime behavior of this word is to be compiled into another word, one must compile the word **($")** .

DUP$ (---) (SS: str_1 --- str_1 str_1) "duplicate string"

The word **DUP$** duplicates the top item on the string stack. For example,

```
$" Hello, World!" DUP$  ok:0
```

The string stack now contains two copies of the string.

DROP$ (---) (SS: *str* ---) "drop string"

The word **DROP$** removes the topmost string item from the string stack. For example,

```
$" Hello, World!"  ok:0
$" How are you?"  ok:0
DROP$  ok:0
```

At this point the string "Hello, World!" is the topmost string the string stack. "How are you?" was pushed onto the string stack, but it was immediately dropped.

SWAP$ (---) (SS: str_1 str_2 --- str_2 str_1) "swap string"

The word **SWAP$** swaps the topmost two strings on the string stack. For example,

```
$" Hello, World!"  ok:0
$" How are you?"  ok:0
SWAP$  ok:0
```

At this point, the string "Hello, World!" is the topmost string on the string stack.

NIP$ (---) (SS: str_1 str_2 --- str_2) "nip string"

The word **NIP$** removes the string underneath the topmost string from the string stack. For example,

```
$" red"  ok:0
$" blue"  ok:0
```

At this point, "blue" is on the top of the string stack, with "red" underneath it.

```
NIP$
```

At this point, "red" has been removed from the string stack, leaving "blue" as the topmost string.

OVER$ (---) (SS: str_1 str_2 --- str_1 str_2 str_1) "over string"

The word **OVER$** pushes a copy of the string str_1 to the top of the string stack, above str_2. For example,

```
$" red"  ok:0
$" green"  ok:0
OVER$  ok:0
```

At this point, the string stack contains the following strings:

"red" (the topmost string)
"green"
"red"

ROT$ (---) (SS: str_1 str_2 str_3 --- str_2 str_3 str_1) "rotate strings"

The word **ROT$** rotates the top three strings to the left. The third string down (prior to the execution of **ROT$**) moves to the top of the string stack.

Note that, for ease of implementation, this routine copies (using **PICK$**) the strings to the top of the string stack in their correct final order, then removes the 3 original strings underneath. Consequently, it is possible to run out of string stack space. If this happens, the condition will be correctly trapped in **(set$SP)** .

-ROT$ (---) (SS: str_1 str_2 str_3 --- str_3 str_1 str_2) "rotate strings"

The word **–ROT$** rotates the top three strings to the right. The top string (prior to the execution of **–ROT$**) moves to the third position. Note that, for ease of implementation, this routine copies (using **PICK$**) the strings to the top of the string stack in their correct final order, then removes the 3 original strings underneath. Consequently, it is possible to run out of string stack space. If this happens, the condition will be correctly caught in **(set$SP)** .

>$CONST (*$Caddr* ---) (SS: *str* ---) "to string constant"

The word **>$CONST** takes the topmost string from the string stack and moves it into the string constant whose address is on the data stack. For example,

```
4 $CONST COLOR  ok:0
$" red" COLOR >$CONST  ok:0
```

At this point, the string constant **COLOR** has the value "red". To verify, display the string using **.$CONST** as follows:

COLOR .$CONST red ok:0

+$ (---) (SS: str_1 str_2 – str_1& str_2) "concatenate strings"

The word **+$** replaces the top two strings on the string stack with their concatenated equivalent. For example,

$" red" $" blue" +$ ok:0

At this point, "red" and "blue" have been removed from the string stack. The topmost string on the string stack has the value "redblue". Note that the topmost string goes to the right of the newly concatenated string.

LEN$ (--- *len*) (SS: ---) "length of string"

The word **LEN$** returns the length of the topmost string on the string stack. For example,

$" Hello world!" len$. 12 ok:0

displays the value 12.

MID$ (*start end* ---) (SS: str_1 --- str_1 str_2) "mid-string"

The word **MID$** produces a sub-string on the string stack, consisting of the characters from the topmost string starting at character *start* and ending at character *end.* For example,

$" redgreenblue" 3 7 mid$ ok:0

At this point, the topmost two strings on the string stack are as follows:

"green" (the topmost item)
"redgreenblue"

Note, as indicated in the string stack signature, the original string (str_1) is retained. Note also that the first character in the string (the leftmost character) is character number 0.

LEFT$ (*len* ---) (SS: str_1 --- str_1 str_2) "left of string"

The word **LEFT$** pushes the leftmost *len* characters to the string stack as a new string. The original string is retained. For example,

$" redgreenblue" 3 LEFT$ ok:0

The above causes the string "red" to be pushed to the string stack.

RIGHT$ (*len* ---) (SS: str_1 --- str_1 str_2) "right of string"

The word **RIGHT$** causes the rightmost *len* characters to be pushed to the string stack as a new string. The original string is retained. For example,

$" redgreenblue" 4 RIGHT$ ok:0

The above causes the string "blue" to be pushed to the string stack.

FINDC$ (*char* --- *pos*|-1) (SS: ---) "find character in string"

The word **FINDC$** returns the position of the first occurrence of the character char, beginning at the left side of the topmost string, with the search proceeding towards the right. If the character is not found, -1 is returned. For example,

$" redgreenblue" 98 FINDC$. 8 ok:0

Displays the value 8, as the character 'b' (ASCII 98) is found in the 8th character position (where the first character is character 0).

FIND$ (*start* --- *pos* | -1) (SS: ---) "find string in string"

The word **FIND$** searches the second string on the string stack, starting from position *start*, for the first occurrence of the topmost string and pushes its starting position to the data stack. As a convenience, to make subsequent searches for the same substring easier, both strings are retained on the string stack. For example,

$" redgreenbluegreen" $" green" 0 FIND$. 3 ok:0

displays the value 3, as the substring is found at character position 3 (the leftmost character being character 0). The strings "redgreenbluegreen" and "green" remain on the stack. Thus, the second instance of "green" could be found if desired.

REPLACE$ (--- *pos* | -1) (SS: str_1 str_2 str_3 --- str_4 | [str_1 str_2]) "replace string"

The word **REPLACE$** searches string str_2 for the first occurrence of string str_3. If it is found, it is replaced with the string str_1, the position of str_3 within str_2 is pushed to the data stack, str_1 and str_3 are removed from the string stack and the new string str_4 is left on the string stack. For example,

```
512 INIT$  ok:0
$" PURPLE"  ok:0
$" redgreenblue"  ok:0
$" green"  ok:0
REPLACE$ . 3  ok:0
$.S
 Index|Length|String
------+------+------
     0|    13|redPURPLEblue

Allocated stack space:  16 bytes
    Total stack space: 512 bytes
Stack space remaining: 496 bytes
 ok:0
```

If the search string str_3 is not found, -1 is pushed to the data stack, str_1 and str_2 are left on the string stack, ready for another search if desired.

.$ (---) (SS: *str* ---) "display string"

The word **.$** pops the topmost string from the string stack and displays it. For example,

$" Hello, World!" .$ Hello, World! oK:0

The above code displays the string "Hello, World!" on the output device.

REV$ (---) (SS: str_1 --- str_2) "reverse string"

The word **REV$** replaces the topmost string on the string stack with its reversed equivalent. For example,

```
$" green" REV$ .$ neerg ok:0
```

The above displays "neerg".

LTRIM$ (---) (SS: str_1 --- str_2) "trim left of string"

The word **LTRIM$** removes leading spaces from the topmost string. For example,

```
$"          hello!" LTRIM$ .$ hello! ok:0
```

Displays "hello!" with the leading spaces removed.

RTRIM$ (---) (SS: str_1 --- str_2) "trim right of string"

The word **RTRIM$** removes leading spaces from the topmost string. For example,

```
$" hello!      " RTRIM$ .$ hello! ok:0
```

Displays "hello!" with the trailing spaces removed.

TRIM$ (---) (SS: str_1 --- str_2) "trim string"

The word **TRIM$** removes both leading and trailing spaces from the topmost string. For example,

```
$"          hello!      " TRIM$ .$ hello! ok:0
```

The above code removes leading *and* trailing spaces and displays the string.

UCASE$ (---) (SS: str_1 --- str_2) "convert to upper case"

The word **UCASE$** converts all lower case characters in the topmost string to upper case. For example,

```
$" hello world! 1234" UCASE$ .$ HELLO WORLD! 1234 ok:0
```

The above displays "HELLO WORLD! 1234"

LCASE$ (---) (SS: str_1 --- str_2) "convert to lower case"

The word **LCASE$** converts all upper case characters in the topmost string to lower case. For example,

```
$" HELLO WORLD! 1234" LCASE$ .$  hello world! 1234 ok:0
```

The above displays "hello world! 1234".

CMP$ (--- -1|0|+1) (SS: str_1 str_2 --- str_1 str_2) "compare strings"

The word **CMP$** performs a case-sensitive comparison of the topmost two strings on the string stack and returns -1 if $str_1 < str_2$, 0 if $str_1 = str_2$ and +1 if $str_1 > str_2$. The strings are retained. For example,

```
$" hello" $" HELLO" CMP$ . 1  ok:0
```

Displays "1" since the first string is greater than the second (the comparison is case sensitive).

```
$" hello" $" hello" CMP$ . 0  ok:0
```

Displays "0" since the strings are identical.

```
$" hell" $" hello" CMP$ . -1  ok:0
```

Displays "-1" since the first string is less than the second.

A case in-sensitive comparison can easily be built as follows:

: CMPCI$ (--- *flag*) (SS: str_1 str_2 --- str_1 str_2)
OVER$ OVER$ UCASE$ SWAP$ UCASE$ CMP$ DROP$ DROP$; ok:0

The above code creates copies of str_1 and str_2 (using **OVER$**) then converts them both to upper case. **CMP$** then compares the strings placing the appropriate flag on the data stack. Finally, the uppercase versions of str_1 and str_2 are removed from the string stack. Thus, str_1 and str_2 are retained, unchanged.

PICK$ (*index* ---) (SS: --- *str*) "pick string"

Given the index of a string on the string stack, copy the indexed string to the top of the string stack. **0 PICK$** is equivalent to **DUP$**, **1 PICK$** is equivalent to **OVER$** *etc.* For example,

```
$" blue"  ok:0
$" green"  ok:0
$" red"  ok:0
2 PICK$  ok:0
```

The above causes the string "blue" to be copied to the top of the string stack.

VAL$ (--- *d*) (SS: *str* ---)

The word **VAL$** uses **NUMBER** to convert the topmost string on the string stack to a double number *d* (2-cell, 32-bit integer) on the data stack. An error occurs if the string cannot be represented as a double number. An erroneous value (but, without an error report) will result if a convertible number is outside the signed, 32-bit range: -2147483648 – 2147483647.

The same interpretation rules apply to the putative number string that apply to a number typed at the terminal or loaded from a blocks file:

- '-' and '.' are the only non-numeric characters allowed.
- '-' must be the first character in negative-number strings.
- '.' can occur anywhere in the number string any number of times. It is ignored except that the position of the last '.' relative to the right end of the number is stored in **DPL** .
- The number string is converted to a number in the current radix.

A number that is known to be a 16-bit number can be managed by dropping the leading 0 cell from the stack. A better procedure would be to **DUP** the top cell, test it and deal with the possibility that it may not be 0, which it must be for the double number to be successfully converted to a 16-bit number.

Note, in the following examples, that the decimal point only affects output—the double number on the stack is a 32-bit integer. **DPL** is updated every time **NUMBER** successfully converts a string to a double number.

Examples:

```
$" 9900" VAL$ D. 9900  ok:0
$" 9900" VAL$ DROP . 9900  ok:0
$" 1234567890" VAL$ D.  1234567890  ok:0
$" 9.900" VAL$ D. 9.900  ok:0
$" 9.945" $" 1234.0" D. D. 1234.0 994.5  ok:0
```

$.S (---) (SS: ---)

The word **$.S** displays a non-destructive string stack dump to the output device. The length of each string is given, along with the total number of strings on the string stack. The amount of space allocated to the string stack, the amount of space in use, and the amount of free space is also reported. An example appears above under the description of **REPLACE$** .

DEPTH$ (--- *n*) (SS: ---)

Returns the current depth of the string stack, with 0 meaning the string stack is empty.

RESET$ (---) (SS: ---)

Resets, *i.e.*, empties, the string stack.

14.4 The String Stack

The string stack is **ALLOT**ed from dictionary space by **INIT$** , which *must* be executed before the String Stack Library can be used. The constant **($sSize)** determines the amount of space reserved and is set by **INIT$** by the user after the library is loaded.

14.5 Error Checking

Error checking is included in all words that could cause a string stack underflow or overflow condition. In the event that an underflow or overflow is detected, the code aborts with an error message.

Other words such as **DUP$** also perform checks. For example, **DUP$** checks that there is at least one item on the string stack. **SWAP$** checks that there are at least two items on the string stack, *etc.*

14.6 String Stack Format

The string stack grows from higher memory addresses to lower memory addresses.

The format of the strings on the string stack is very simple, as follows:

Actual length (1 cell)	String payload (1 char=1 byte)

14.7 String Constant Format

String Constants have the same format, but are preceded by a maximum length cell in order to check that a requested string can be accommodated within the string constant:

Maximum length (1 cell)	Actual length (1 cell)	String payload (1 char=1 byte)

14.8 Throw Codes

The words in the library perform sanity checks on input parameters where necessary. In particular, the string stack, being statically **ALLOT**ed from dictionary space, is carefully guarded, since the string stack is very likely to have code and/or data on either side of it, resulting in catastrophic software failure in the event of a string stack underflow or overflow. Where errors are detected, the library throws the following THROW codes:

Throw Code	Nature of Error	Thrown By
9900	String stack underflow	**(set$SP)**
9901	String too large to assign	**:="**
9902	String stack is empty	**PICK$ DUP$ LEN$ >$CONST MID$ LEFT$ RIGHT$ FINDC$.$ REV$ LTRIM$ RTRIM$ UCASE$ LCASE$ DROP$**
9903	Need at least 2 strings on string stack	**SWAP$ NIP$ OVER$ FIND$ CMP$ +$**
9904	String too large for string constant	**>$CONST**
9905	Illegal LEN value	**MID$ LEFT$ RIGHT$**
9906	Need at least 3 strings on string stack	**ROT$ -ROT$ REPLACE$**
9907	String is not a legal number	**VAL$**
9999	String stack not initialized	any THROW if **($sSize)** = 0

It should be noted that the author of this library has not checked that the THROW codes listed here are used in other systems or libraries elsewhere.

14.9 Author Information

The library was developed by Mark Wills in February, 2014. The code was released to the public domain. He can be contacted by email via: *markwills1970@gmail.com*.

15 TI Forth Block Utilities

Words introduced in this chapter:

TIF2FBF **TIFBLK** **TIFIDX** **TIFVU**

The TI Forth Block Utilities are not part of the resident dictionary so must be loaded from FBLOCKS (see current FBLOCKS file **MENU** for TI Forth Block Utilities). They are provided to make it easy to view TI Forth blocks (called "screens" in TI Forth), index lines of a range of blocks and copy a range of blocks to an **fbForth 2.0** blocks file. The utilities listed in the first three sections below perform these functions individually. The last section presents a browser/copier that is patterned after the **fbForth 2.0** block editors.

Remember that TI Forth disks start at block 0 and that TI Forth system disks are mixed format.

Note that "IS:" is short for "Input Stream:".

15.1 *TIFBLK: Display TI Forth Block*

TIFBLK (IS:*blk DSKn*)

TIFBLK displays block *blk* from disk *DSKn*. The display may be paused/resumed by tapping any key except *<BREAK>*, which will abort the display. The display is automatically paused if the block cannot be displayed all at once.

The following shows the first screen of a Text mode example displayed with the Forth code just before the screen shot:

TIFBLK 11 DSK3

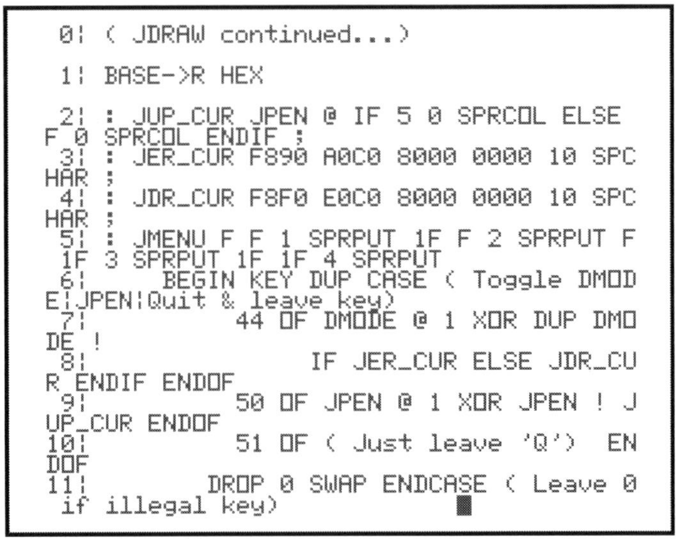

```
 0| ( JDRAW continued...)
 1| BASE->R HEX
 2| : JUP_CUR JPEN @ IF 5 0 SPRCOL ELSE
F 0 SPRCOL ENDIF ;
 3| : JER_CUR F890 A0C0 8000 0000 10 SPC
HAR ;
 4| : JDR_CUR F8F0 E0C0 8000 0000 10 SPC
HAR ;
 5| : JMENU F F 1 SPRPUT 1F F 2 SPRPUT F
 1F 3 SPRPUT 1F 1F 4 SPRPUT
 6|     BEGIN KEY DUP CASE ( Toggle DMOD
E|JPEN|Quit & leave key)
 7|            44 OF DMODE @ 1 XOR DUP DMO
DE !
 8|                IF JER_CUR ELSE JDR_CU
R ENDIF ENDOF
 9|            50 OF JPEN @ 1 XOR JPEN ! J
UP_CUR ENDOF
10|            51 OF ( Just leave 'Q') EN
DOF
11|          DROP 0 SWAP ENDCASE ( Leave 0
 if illegal key)
```

The display was paused after twelve lines were displayed due to wrapping of 64-character lines on the 40-character display. Tapping a key will continue the display of the remaining four lines.

The following is the same example in Text80 mode using the same Forth code as above:

```
 0| ( JDRAW continued...)
 1| BASE->R HEX
 2| : JUP_CUR JPEN @ IF 5 0 SPRCOL ELSE F 0 SPRCOL ENDIF ;
 3| : JER_CUR F890 A0C0 8000 0000 10 SPCHAR ;
 4| : JDR_CUR F8F0 E0C0 8000 0000 10 SPCHAR ;
 5| : JMENU F F 1 SPRPUT 1F F 2 SPRPUT F 1F 3 SPRPUT 1F 1F 4 SPRPUT
 6|      BEGIN KEY DUP CASE ( Toggle DMODE|JPEN|Quit & leave key)
 7|           44 OF DMODE @ 1 XOR DUP DMODE !
 8|                IF JER_CUR ELSE JDR_CUR ENDIF ENDOF
 9|           50 OF JPEN @ 1 XOR JPEN ! JUP_CUR ENDOF
10|           51 OF ( Just leave 'Q')  ENDOF
11|         DROP 0 SWAP ENDCASE ( Leave 0 if illegal key)
12|      -DUP UNTIL ( Leave value if legal key)
13|      5 1 DO 10 0D0 I SPRPUT LOOP ( Hide menu)    ;  R->BASE -->
14|
15|                                                                ok:0
█
```

15.2 TIFIDX: Display TI Forth Index Lines

TIFIDX (IS:*strtBlk endBlk DSKn*)

TIFIDX displays the index lines (first lines) of a range of TI Forth blocks (*strtBlk* to *endBlk*) from disk *DSKn*. The display may be paused/resumed by tapping any key except ***<BREAK>***, which will abort the display. The display is automatically paused if the block cannot be displayed all at once.

The following shows the first screen of a Text mode example:

TIFIDX 10 15 DSK3

```
 10| CR ." LOADing JDRAW---" CR ."    Joy
stick drawing program..."
 11| ( JDRAW continued...)

 12| ( JDRAW continued...)

 13| ( JDRAW continued...)

 14|

 15|

...done ok:0
```

The index line, (line #0) of each block from block #10 – #15 is listed above. Had more than 12 blocks (64 characters each index line) been selected, the display would have paused as for **TIFBLK** in the previous section.

The following is the same example in Text80 mode:

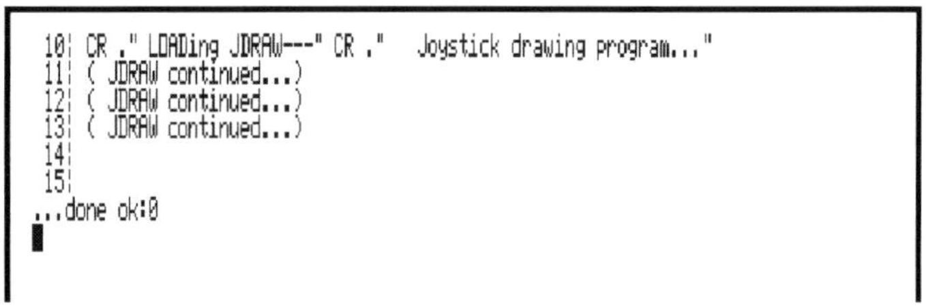
10¦ CR ." LOADing JDRAW---" CR ."   Joystick drawing program..."
11¦ (JDRAW continued...)
12¦ (JDRAW continued...)
13¦ (JDRAW continued...)
14¦
15¦
...done ok:0

15.3 TIF2FBF: Copy TI Forth Blocks to *fbForth* Blocks

TIF2FBF (IS:*srcStrtBlk srcEndBlk DSKn dstStrtBlk dstFile*)

TIF2FBF functions in much the same way as **CPYBLK** . The format of the command is the same except that the source is *DSKn*, not a filename. The *n* of *DSKn* is the disk number of the TI Forth disk. The destination *dstFile* must be the name of an existing blocks file (see **MKBFL** to create one). The following command will copy blocks 4 – 7 from TI Forth DSK3 to blocks 10 – 13 of DSK1.MYBLOCKS:

```
TIF2FBF 4 7 DSK3 10 DSK1.MYBLOCKS
```

15.4 TIFVU: TI Forth Browser/Copier

TIFVU (IS:*blk DSKn*)

Browse TI Forth blocks and, optionally, copy a range of blocks to an **fbForth** blocks file. The browser is interactive with the following functions:

Key	Function
<FCTN+4>	View next block.
<FCTN+6>	View previous block.
<FCTN+D>	View the next panel for Text mode—ignored in Text80 mode.
<FCTN+S>	View the previous panel for Text mode—ignored in Text80 mode.
<FCTN+T>	View a specific TI Forth block number.
<FCTN+F>	Specify a destination **fbForth** block number for next copy.
<CTRL+F>	Specify a destination **fbForth** blocks file, which must already exist.
<CTRL+S>	Copy a range of blocks starting from the displayed TI Forth block to the displayed destination **fbForth** block. You are prompted for the number of blocks to copy after selecting this command.
<FCTN+9>	Exit the browser.

Following is an example of the browser/copier in Text mode, which shows three panels of the same block:

```
TIFVU 12 DSK3
```

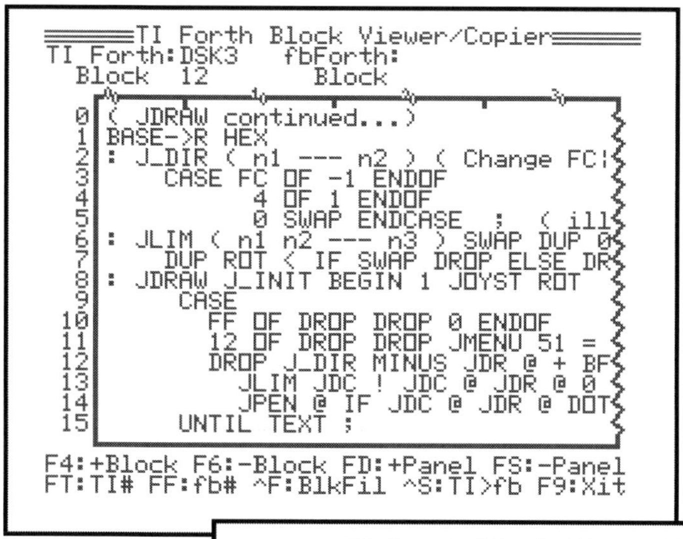
TI Forth Block Viewer/Copier
TI Forth:DSK3 fbForth:
Block 12 Block
0 (JDRAW continued...)
1 BASE->R HEX
2 : J_DIR (n1 --- n2) (Change FC!
3 CASE FC OF -1 ENDOF
4 4 OF 1 ENDOF
5 0 SWAP ENDCASE ; (ill
6 : JLIM (n1 n2 --- n3) SWAP DUP 0
7 DUP ROT < IF SWAP DROP ELSE DR
8 : JDRAW J_INIT BEGIN 1 JOYST ROT
9 CASE
10 FF OF DROP DROP 0 ENDOF
11 12 OF DROP DROP JMENU 51 =
12 DROP J_DIR MINUS JDR @ + BF
13 JLIM JDC ! JDC @ JDR @ 0
14 JPEN @ IF JDC @ JDR @ DOT
15 UNTIL TEXT ;
F4:+Block F6:-Block FD:+Panel FS:-Panel
FT:TI# FF:fb# ^F:BlkFil ^S:TI>fb F9:Xit

Left panel showing columns 0 – 33.

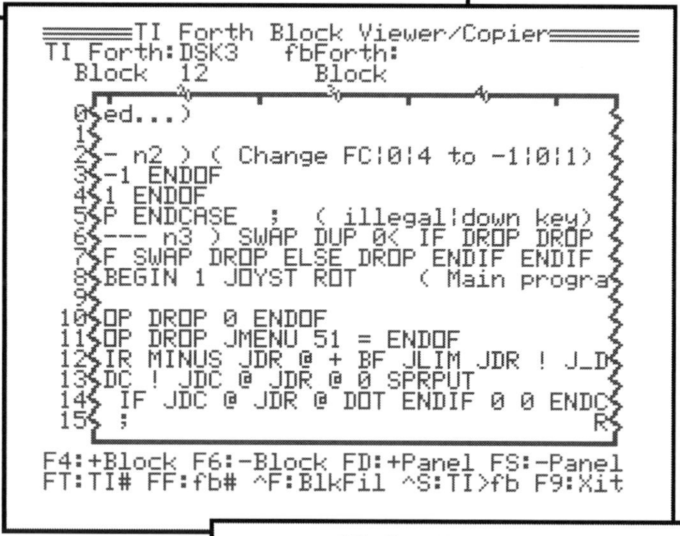
TI Forth Block Viewer/Copier
TI Forth:DSK3 fbForth:
Block 12 Block
0 ed...)
1
2 - n2) (Change FC!0!4 to -1!0!1)
3 -1 ENDOF
4 1 ENDOF
5 P ENDCASE ; (illegal!down key)
6 --- n3) SWAP DUP 0< IF DROP DROP
7 F SWAP DROP ELSE DROP ENDIF ENDIF
8 BEGIN 1 JOYST ROT (Main progra
9
10 OP DROP 0 ENDOF
11 OP DROP JMENU 51 = ENDOF
12 IR MINUS JDR @ + BF JLIM JDR ! J_D
13 DC ! JDC @ JDR @ 0 SPRPUT
14 IF JDC @ JDR @ DOT ENDIF 0 0 ENDC
15 ; R
F4:+Block F6:-Block FD:+Panel FS:-Panel
FT:TI# FF:fb# ^F:BlkFil ^S:TI>fb F9:Xit

Middle panel showing columns 15 – 48.

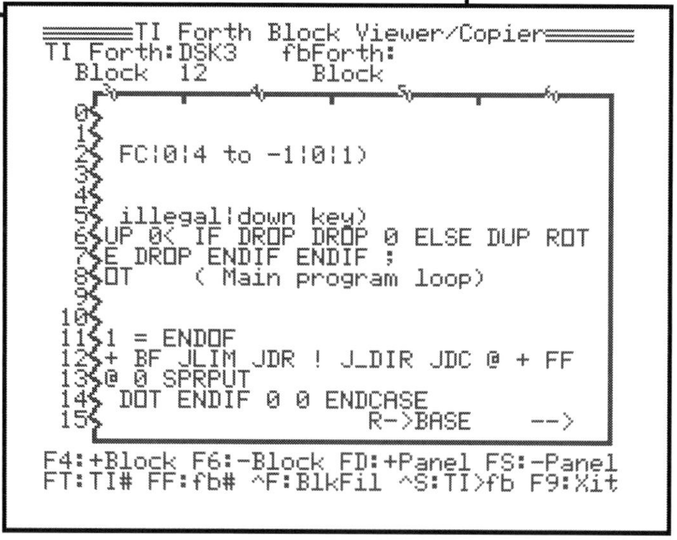
TI Forth Block Viewer/Copier
TI Forth:DSK3 fbForth:
Block 12 Block
0
1
2 FC!0!4 to -1!0!1)
3
4
5 illegal!down key)
6 UP 0< IF DROP DROP 0 ELSE DUP ROT
7 E DROP ENDIF ENDIF ;
8 OT (Main program loop)
9
10
11 1 = ENDOF
12 + BF JLIM JDR ! J_DIR JDC @ + FF
13 @ 0 SPRPUT
14 DOT ENDIF 0 0 ENDCASE
15 R->BASE -->
F4:+Block F6:-Block FD:+Panel FS:-Panel
FT:TI# FF:fb# ^F:BlkFil ^S:TI>fb F9:Xit

Right panel showing columns 30 – 63.

And, here is the same example in Text80 mode:

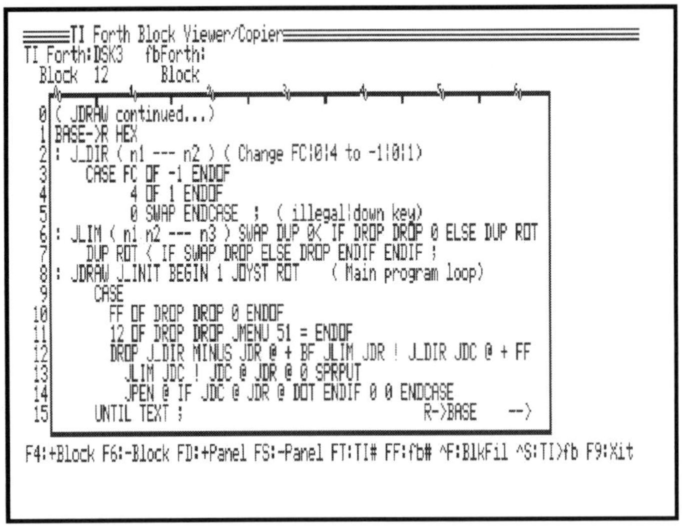

16 Speech Words

Words introduced in this chapter:

SAY **STREAM** **TALKING?**

The words **SAY** , **STREAM** and **TALKING?** in this chapter were ported from **TurboForth**[1] code courtesy of Mark Wills.

A TI-99/4A equipped with a TI Speech Synthesizer module can be made to talk by sending the Speech Synthesizer commands that include

- Word data addresses of words in the Speech Synthesizer's resident vocabulary or
- Raw speech data.

The **fbForth 2.0** speech words require the system ISR to be active, which is the default. See Chapter 10 "Interrupt Service Routines (ISRs)" for how this works.

Consult § 22 of the *Editor/Assembler Manual* for a detailed discussion of speech processing.

16.1 Testing the State of the Speech Synthesizer

Use **TALKING?** to test whether the Speech Synthesizer is busy before using **SAY** or **STREAM** in following sections.

TALKING? (--- *flag*)

> **TALKING?** returns *flag* = 0 if the Speech Synthesizer is idle, otherwise, *flag* = 1.

16.2 Using the Speech Synthesizer's Resident Vocabulary

To have the Speech Synthesizer speak words from its resident vocabulary (see table below), it is sufficient to use **SAY** , described here:

SAY (*addr n* ---)

> **SAY** needs on the stack the address *addr* of a block of Speech Synthesizer ROM speech addresses and the number *n* of those addresses. This can be accomplished with **DATA[…]DATA** .

This example uses addresses from the table below to say, "Do not be so negative.":

```
HEX DATA[ 2480 4AAB 1A42 6153 48DC ]DATA SAY  ok:0
```

It is a good idea to use **TALKING?** before using **SAY** in word definitions to insure the Speech Synthesizer is not busy.

16.3 The Speech Synthesizer's Resident Vocabulary

The following table of phrases and addresses from § 24.6 "Speech Synthesizer Resident Vocabulary" in the *Editor/Assembler Manual* is included here for your convenience:

Phrase	Address	Phrase	Address	Phrase	Address
- (negative)	48DC	2	145C	6	15A8
+ (positive)	51B3	3	149A	7	15E8
. (point)	50EC	4	14E7	8	1637
0	13C3	5	1531	9	1664
1	1409				
A (ay)	16E4	ALL	1807	ANY	1962
A1 (uh)	1700	AM	1830	ARE	556E
ABOUT	1714	AN	1876	AS	19A7
AFTER	1769	AND	18AC	ASSUME	19E8
AGAIN	17A5	ANSWER	1913	AT	1A25
B	1A42	BLACK	1B47	BUT	1C20
BACK	1A64	BLUE	1B8A	BUY	1C48
BASE	1A8F	BOTH	1BB6	BY	1C48
BE	1A42	BOTTOM	1BEA	BYE	1C48
BETWEEN	1ADE				
C	1C86	COLOR	1E20	COMPUTER	2034
CAN	1CD9	COME	1E54	CONNECTED	208B
CASSETTE	1D10	COMES	1E87	CONSOLE	20F3
CENTER	1D47	COMMA	1EDE	CORRECT	213C
CHECK	1D82	COMMAND	1F1A	COURSE	2182
CHOICE	1DA2	COMPLETE	1F71	CYAN	21C0
CLEAR	1DE6	COMPLETED	1FCD		
D	2203	DIFFERENT	23C4	DONE	253E
DATA	223C	DISKETTE	242D	DOUBLE	2599
DECIDE	2294	DO	2480	DOWN	25D3
DEVICE	22FD	DOES	24B3	DRAW	2612
DID	2366	DOING	24EA	DRAWING	2668
E	26CB	ELEVEN	2579	ENTER	28AD
EACH	26F0	ELSE	27B6	ERROR	28EF
EIGHT	1637	END	27F5	EXACTLY	2937
EIGHTY	2723	ENDS	2866	EYE	3793

Phrase	Address	Phrase	Address	Phrase	Address
F	299F	FINISH	2B5B	FORTY	2C3E
FIFTEEN	29C2	FINISHED	2B94	FOUR	14E7
FIFTY	2A1D	FIRST	2BD7	FOURTEEN	2C7F
FIGURE	2A60	FIT	2C14	FOURTH	2D19
FIND	2AD7	FIVE	1531	FROM	2D74
FINE	2B1E	FOR	14E7	FRONT	2DBC
G	2DEB	GO	2FFC	GOODBYE	3148
GAMES	2E28	GOES	3031	GOT	31A0
GET	2E8C	GOING	3079	GRAY	31D1
GETTING	2EBA	GOOD	30D6	GREEN	321D
GIVE	2F38	GOOD WORK	30FA	GUESS	327E
GIVES	2F8D				
H	32C0	HEAD	348C	HIT	360A
HAD	32EF	HEAR	34E5	HOME	363E
HAND	3339	HELLO	351A	HOW	3689
HANDHELD UNIT	337F	HELP	3571	HUNDRED	36EF
HAS	3405	HERE	34E5	HURRY	3757
HAVE	344A	HIGHER	35AE		
I	3793	INCH	38B5	INSTRUCTIONS	39BD
I WIN	37CF	INCHES	38FA	IS	3A32
IF	3850	INSTRUCTION	394B	IT	3A7A
IN	3872				
J	3AAE	JOYSTICK	3AED	JUST	3B4C
K	3B8A	KEYBOARD	3BE9	KNOW	3C4F
KEY	3BB9				
L	3C8F	LEFT	3E78	LOAD	404B
LARGE	3CD0	LESS	3EB2	LONG	40D3
LARGER	3D19	LET	3F08	LOOK	413D
LARGEST	3D67	LIKE	3F2F	LOOKS	4191
LAST	3DDE	LIKES	3F6A	LOWER	41E7
LEARN	3E1E	LINE	3FD5		

Phrase	Address	Phrase	Address	Phrase	Address
M	4233	MEMORY	4405	MODULE	45DF
MADE	4267	MESSAGE	446C	MORE	4642
MAGENTA	42AE	MESSAGES	44D7	MOST	4693
MAKE	432E	MIDDLE	4551	MOVE	46DF
ME	437D	MIGHT	4593	MUST	473D
MEAN	43BD				
N	4789	NEXT	4959	NO	3C4F
NAME	47C0	NICE TRY	49A5	NOT	4AAB
NEAR	4833	NINE	1664	NOW	4ADA
NEED	4880	NINETY	4A4E	NUMBER	4B20
NEGATIVE	48DC				
O	4B7D	ON	4C41	ORDER	4D34
OF	4BBA	ONE	1409	OTHER	4D8A
OFF	4C13	ONLY	4C8B	OUT	4DD4
OH	4B7D	OR	4CDC	OVER	4E0A
P	4E66	PLEASE	5093	PRINTER	52AA
PART	4E9F	POINT	50EC	PROBLEM	52F9
PARTNER	4EE0	POSITION	5148	PROBLEMS	5360
PARTS	4F31	POSITIVE	51B3	PROGRAM	53EE
PERIOD	4F81	PRESS	5231	PUT	5477
PLAY	4FE5	PRINT	526D	PUTTING	54AA
PLAYS	502D				
Q	5520				
R	556E	RECORDER	5745	RETURN	58CF
RANDOMLY	55A0	RED	57C1	REWIND	593A
READ (read)	5652	REFER	5801	RIGHT	7C38
READ1 (red)	57C1	REMEMBER	5861	ROUND	59C2
READY TO START	56B3				
S	5A5A	SHAPES	5DDE	SOME	6197
SAID	5AA1	SHIFT	5E27	SORRY	61C6
SAVE	5AEF	SHORT	5E5C	SPACE	6226

Phrase	Address	Phrase	Address	Phrase	Address
SAY	5B65	SHORTER	5EA5	SPACES	625D
SAYS	3BA2	SHOULD	5F24	SPELL	62CC
SCREEN	5BFB	SIDE	5F6D	SQUARE	6333
SECOND	5C5B	SIDES	5FC8	START	637C
SEE	1C86	SIX	15A8	STEP	63C5
SEES	5CBF	SIXTY	601A	STOP	63F7
SET	5D1B	SMALL	6070	SUM	6197
SEVEN	15E8	SMALLER	60AE	SUPPOSED	6423
SEVENTY	5D50	SMALLEST	60F1	SUPPOSED TO	6489
SHAPE	5DA5	SO	6153	SURE	64F4
T	6551	THERE	6A72	TIME	6E69
TAKE	658B	THESE	6ADE	TO	145C
TEEN	65BF	THEY	6B47	TOGETHER	6EB0
TELL	6603	THING	6BA0	TONE	6F1F
TEN	664E	THINGS	6C0F	TOO	145C
TEXAS INSTRUMENTS	6696	THINK	6C73	TOP	6F8D
THAN	675B	THIRD	6CBC	TRY	6FBB
THAT	67B6	THIRTEEN	6D11	TRY AGAIN	700F
THAT IS INCORRECT	6816	THIRTY	6DA2	TURN	7092
THAT IS RIGHT	68FE	THIS	6DDE	TWELVE	70CE
THE (thee)	6974	THREE	149A	TWENTY	7119
THE1 (the)	69B6	THREW	6E26	TWO	145C
THEIR	6A72	THROUGH	6E26	TYPE	7170
THEN	69E1				
U	71BE	UNDERSTAND	729D	UPPER	73C3
UHOH	71F4	UNTIL	732F	USE	7403
UNDER	7245	UP	739F		
V	7449	VARY	7487	VERY	74DA
W	7520	WERE	775D	WILL	7A11
WAIT	759D	WHAT	77BC	WITH	7A6B
WANT	75DF	WHAT WAS THAT	77E9	WON	1409
WANTS	7621	WHEN	7875	WORD	7AAB
WAY	76B0	WHERE	78AB	WORDS	7B0A

Phrase	Address	Phrase	Address	Phrase	Address
WE	767D	WHICH	78F4	WORK	7B75
WEIGH	76B0	WHITE	7924	WORKING	7BBC
WEIGHT	759D	WHO	7969	WRITE	7C38
WELL	7717	WHY	79B4		
X	7C8D				
Y	7CB2	YET	7D99	YOU WIN	7DDB
YELLOW	7CF8	YOU	71BE	YOUR	7E4D
YES	7D58				
Z	7E99	ZERO	13C3		

16.4 Streaming Raw Speech Data

You can stream raw speech data to the Speech Synthesizer with the following word:

STREAM (*addr n* ---)

> **STREAM** needs on the stack the address *addr* of a block of raw speech data to be spoken and the number of cells *n* in the buffer. This can be accomplished with **DATA[…]DATA** . **STREAM** will feed the raw speech data to the Speech Synthesizer.

You should use **TALKING?** (see § 16.1 "Testing the State of the Speech Synthesizer" above) in word definitions to insure the Speech Synthesizer is not busy.

17 Sound Words

Words introduced in this chapter:

PLAY **PLAYING?** **SOUND**

The words **PLAY** , **SOUND** and **PLAYING?** in this chapter were ported from **TurboForth**[1] code courtesy of Mark Wills.

The TI-99/4A uses the TMS9919 Sound Generator Controller to generate sound. There are three tone generators and one noise generator available. For more detailed information about generating sound with the TMS9919, consult § 20 "Sound" in the *Editor/Assembler Manual*.

17.1 Generating Individual Sounds

The three tone generators and the noise generator may be managed directly by the programmer with the **SOUND** word:

SOUND (*pitch vol ch#* ---)

Pitch *pitch*, volume *vol* and channel *ch#* are as described in the *Editor/Assembler Manual* in § 20. Pitch values range from 0 – 1023, 0 representing the highest pitch. Volume values range from 0 – 15, 15 representing silence. Channels 0 – 2 represent the corresponding tone generators and channel 3 is the noise generator.

SOUND uses the pitch value for setting the type of noise for the noise generator (channel 3). Shift rates are 0 – 3. Noise type can be white noise (0) or periodic noise (4). The pitch value to pass to **SOUND** is the sum of shift rate and noise type and ranges from 0 – 7.

Once a tone or noise generator is started, the sound/noise continues until silenced by executing **SOUND** with a volume of 15. The pitch must be supplied, but is irrelevant. The following Forth code will silence channel 2:

```
0 15 2 SOUND  ok:0
```

17.2 Playing Sound Lists

Playing sound lists involves setting up a sound table with one or more contiguous sound lists and providing a flag and the address of the sound table to **PLAY** (see description below).

fbForth 2.0 does *not* use the console's keyscan routine for the interrupt-driven playing of sound lists as described in § 20 of the *Editor/Assembler Manual*, but rather processes them in its own ISR (see Chapter 10 "Interrupt Service Routines (ISRs)"). A sound table is, however, set up in the same manner as described in the *Editor/Assembler Manual*.

A second, presumably shorter, sound table can also be played while muting the first until the second table is finished. This should make it easy to periodically interrupt a game theme with short event-driven sounds such as crashes, beeps and warnings.

Each sound list consists of a list of sound commands starting with a byte count and ending with a duration count byte (sixtieths of a second) that is not included in the byte count. The last sound list should silence all four sound generators (or, at least, the ones you used) and end with a duration of 0. After setting up a sound table, it may be played with **PLAY** and monitored with **PLAYING?** :

PLAY (*addr flag* ---)

Starts playing sound lists in the sound table set up at address *addr* depending on *flag* and continues until a sound list begins with a count of 0 or ends with a duration of 0. The value of *flag* can be positive, negative or zero with the following effect:

Flag	Action
0	Do not play if either sound table is active.
1	Unconditionally play, killing all previous sound tables.
-1	Plays as sound table #2, muting sound table #1 for the duration of sound table #2.

PLAYING? (--- *flag*)

PLAYING? checks both **fbForth 2.0** sound status registers, ORs them and leaves that value on the stack as *flag*. If *flag* = 0, no sound table is active.

It should be noted that **PLAYING?** doe not work for sounds initiated with **SOUND** because **SOUND** communicates with the TMS9919 directly, bypassing the **fbForth 2.0** sound status registers.

A sound table may be prepared for **PLAY** with **DATA[…]DATA** by dropping the cell count. Here is such a sound table set up as the word **CHIME** , which was taken from the chime sound example of § 20.4.2 of the *Editor/Assembler Manual*. For convenience, every other sound list in the **CHIME** sound table is shaded:

```
HEX
: CHIME  ( -- addr )
    DATA[
      059F BFDF FFE3 0109 8E01 A402 C501 90B6 D306 0391 B7D4 0503
      92B8 D504 05A7 0493 B0D6 0503 94B1 D706 0395 B2D8 0705 CA02
      96B3 D006 0397 B4D1 0503 98B5 D204 0585 0390 B6D3 0503 91B7
      D406 0392 B8D5 0705 A402 93B0 D606 0394 B1D7 0503 95B2 D804
      05C5 0196 B3D0 0503 97B4 D106 0398 B5D2 0703 9FBF DF00
    ]DATA  DROP  ;
```

The **CHIME** sound table may now be played unconditionally with

```
CHIME 1 PLAY  ok:0
```

18 Signed Integer Division

When performing integer division, we usually think no further than the fact that there is a quotient and a remainder. This is often all there is. This is the case when both dividend and divisor are positive and, usually, when they have the same sign, positive or negative. But, what do we do when the signs differ? In what direction do we round the quotient? Toward zero (truncation)? Toward positive infinity (ceiling)? Negative infinity (floor)? Greatest integer less than or equal to the quotient (rounded)? What should be the sign of the remainder? The same as the dividend? The divisor? Always positive (Euclidean)? Always negative? Whatever we choose must satisfy the equation,

$$n = q\,d + r$$

where n = numerator (dividend), q = quotient, d = denominator (divisor) and r = remainder.

Among the many possible definitions for signed integer division [1] [2] are

1. Truncation: $q = \text{trunc}(n/d)$ (T-division),[24]
2. Floor: $q = \lfloor n/d \rfloor$ (F-division),
3. Ceiling: $q = \lceil n/d \rceil$ (C-division),
4. Rounding $q = \text{round}(n/d)$ (R-division) and
5. Euclidean $0 \leqslant r < |d|$ (r always positive). (E-division)

The following table shows most of the possible results for each of the above-described divisions for both $|n| > |d|$ and $|n| < |d|$. The capital-letter subscripts (after Leijen [1]) correspond to the above division types and their order:

(n,d)	(q_T,r_T)	(q_F,r_F)	(q_C,r_C)	(q_R,r_R)	(q_E,r_E)
(+10,+4)	(+2,+2)	(+2,+2)	(+3,–2)	(+2,+2)	(+2,+2)
(+10,–4)	(–2,+2)	(-3,–2)	(–2,+2)	(–2,+2)	(–2,+2)
(–10,+4)	(–2,–2)	(-3,+2)	(–2,–2)	(–2,–2)	(-3,+2)
(–10,–4)	(+2,–2)	(+2,–2)	(+3,+2)	(+2,–2)	(+3,+2)
(+2,+3)	(0,+2)	(0,+2)	(+1,–1)	(+1,–1)	(0,+2)
(+2,–3)	(0,+2)	(–1,–1)	(0,+2)	(–1,–1)	(0,+2)
(–2,+3)	(0,–2)	(–1,+1)	(0,–2)	(–1,+1)	(–1,+1)
(–2,–3)	(0,–2)	(0,–2)	(+1,+1)	(+1,+1)	(+1,+1)

When discussing "Integer Functions and Elementary Number Theory", Knuth defines the quotient q of two real numbers, x and y, as $q = \lfloor x/y \rfloor$ [3]. This is the F-division meant in this discussion.

Boute compares more than just the five definitions of signed integer division listed above. E-division and F-division are shown to be superior, with E-division edging out F-division. E-division

24 I have adopted Leijen's [1] use of the first letter of each division type's definitive operation followed by "-division" to identify each type of division.

has only positive *r*, no matter the signs of *n* and *d* [2]. Leijen considers E-division "rare, but mathematically elegant" [1]. Both are considered more suitable for various technical applications like raster scan display generation, time division multiplexing and communications [2].

There may be good reasons for choosing any one of several of the above-described types of division, but we are only considering two, (1) T-division, the so-called "symmetric integer division", which involves rounding toward zero or truncation and (2) F-division, "floored integer division", which involves rounding toward negative infinity. The reason for limiting the rest of this discussion to these two, if not obvious, is that the default for TI Forth and **fbForth 2.0** is T-division and the Forth-83 standard's superior F-division. Probably the only reason (and, probably, not a good reason!) to choose T-division is that most of us expect the answers it gives and T-division is what many CPUs employ. Developers often do not deign to change the underlying function of the CPU. Notably, the TMS9900 is not such a CPU by virtue of the fact that it does not have any instruction for signed integer division. It remains for the developer of higher-level languages based on the TMS9900 to decide how to implement signed integer division. TI Forth, and hence **fbForth**, followed fig-Forth's use of T-division.

T-division is considered symmetric due to its rounding the quotient towards zero, *i.e.*, truncation, which produces a "symmetric"[25] distribution of the integer quotient around zero. This results in a disconcerting discontinuity near zero for the quotient, when it changes sign, and for the cyclic nature of the remainder, which changes sign because it retains the sign of the dividend [4]. For the remainder to be cyclic for any given *d*, $r = \text{rem}(n/d) = \text{rem}((n+d)/d)$ should hold for all *n*. The following table shows what happens to the remainder for T- and F-divisions, with $d = 3$:

$d = 3$	**T-division**		**F-division**	
n	rem(*n*/*d*)	rem((*n*+*d*)/*d*)	rem(*n*/*d*)	rem((*n*+*d*)/*d*)
4	1	1	1	1
3	0	0	0	0
2	2	2	2	2
1	1	1	1	1
0	0	0	0	0
-1	-1	2	2	2
-2	-2	1	1	1
-3	0	0	0	0
-4	-1	-1	2	2

The breakdown in the cycling of the remainder for T-division can be seen in the shaded cells above. F-division, on the other hand, provides continuity of the integer quotient near zero as well as a cyclic remainder (see above table) that maintains the sign of the divisor.

This suggests very sound reasons for choosing floored integer division, especially when calculating position for electromechanical devices such as plotters and robots so that motions will

25 The use of "symmetric" here is to point out that only the absolute values of the quotient are truly symmetric about zero. The actual values are anti-symmetric mathematically [4]. The quotes will be dropped elsewhere because of common usage and to avoid distraction.

be as nearly continuous as possible [4]. It was for this reason that floored integer division was adopted for Forth-83 [5]. Because of the turmoil and consternation this caused many Forth programmers, Forth standards since then have made it optional by providing a way to do either T-division or F-division:

> By introducing the requirement for "floored" division, Forth 83 produced much controversy and concern on the part of those who preferred the more common practice followed in other languages of implementing division according to the behavior of the host CPU, which is most often symmetric (rounded toward zero). In attempting to find a compromise position, this standard provides primitives for both common varieties, floored and symmetric (see **SM/REM**). **FM/MOD** is the floored version [6].

Smith [4] summarizes, "Floored division is simply more useful in the majority of applications programs."

18.1 M/

T-division (symmetric integer division) is the default for **fbforth 2.0**, but can easily be changed to F-division (floored integer division) by changing the user variable **S|F** .

S|F (--- *addr*) (read "S or F" for "Symmetric or Floored")

User variable that determines whether **M/** uses T-division or F-division. A value of zero (the default) specifies T-division and a non-zero value, F-division.

M/ (*d n* --- *rem quot*)

A mixed magnitude math operator that leaves the signed, single-number (16 bits) remainder *rem* and signed, single-number quotient *quot* from a signed, double-number (32 bits) dividend *d* and single-number divisor *n*. **M/** acts like one of the ANS Forth words, **SM/REM** (symmetric **M/**) or **FM/MOD** (floored **M/**) depending on the value in **S|F** .

SM/REM and **FM/MOD** (see next section) have the same stack signature as **M/** . Where they differ is whether the division is symmetric or floored when the signs of divisor and dividend differ.

Currently, **M/** uses T-division since **fbForth** is based on fig-Forth, which uses T-division. It will continue to be the default to support expectations of TI Forth programmers. However, **S|F** will make it easy for the user to change the behavior of **M/** at will to accommodate floored integer division. Doing so will change all of the following words to use floored integer division because they are all based on **M/** :

/MOD / MOD */MOD */

Mark Wills' **TurboForth**[1] uses floored integer division by default because it complies with the Forth-83 Standard, which, as noted by Smith [4], was the first standard to make that move. The author would actually prefer to make floored integer division the **fbForth** default, but has chosen not to do so for the reasons in the last paragraph.

M/ does not test for overflow (an error). It simply passes back to the user the result of the TMS9900 **DIV** instruction. **DIV** tests for overflow before actually performing the division by checking that the MSW (high-order 16 bits) of the 32-bit dividend is smaller than the 16-bit divisor. **DIV**, by the way, is unsigned, for which reason **M/** presumes the supplied dividend and divisor are signed, *i.e.*, that the leftmost bits are sign bits, and only calls **DIV** with their absolute values. If the dividend's MSW ≥ the divisor, **DIV** does not perform the division. This has the effect of setting the remainder to the dividend's LSW and the quotient to the dividend's MSW, which are both passed to the user as the results of **M/** without throwing an error. This was carried over from TI Forth's behavior.

18.2 SM/REM and FM/MOD

SM/REM performs T-division on a signed 32-bit numerator by a signed 16-bit denominator, yielding a signed 16-bit remainder and a signed 16-bit quotient. The quotient is rounded toward zero, *i.e.*, truncated, while the remainder takes the sign of the dividend. The code for **SM/REM** in **fbForth 2.0** is written in ALC, so here it is were it written in high-level Forth:

Word Definition	Comment
`: SM/REM`	*(d n --- rem quot) <== stack signature*
`OVER >R >R`	*copy MSB of numerator to and move denominator to return stack*
`DABS R ABS`	*make numerator and denominator both positive*
`U/`	*divide to get remainder and quotient*
`R> R XOR`	*get sign of quotient by XOR of numerator & MSB of denominator*
`+- SWAP`	*give quotient proper sign*
`R> +- SWAP`	*give any remainder sign of numerator*
`;`	

FM/MOD performs floored integer division of a signed 32-bit numerator by a signed 16-bit denominator, yielding a signed 16-bit remainder and a signed 16-bit quotient. The quotient is rounded toward negative infinity, *i.e.*, floored, while the remainder takes the sign of the divisor. The code for **FM/MOD** in **fbForth 2.0** is written in ALC, so here it is were it written in high-level Forth:

Word Definition	Comment
`: FM/MOD`	*(d n --- rem quot) <== stack signature*
`OVER OVER XOR 0<`	*denominator and numerator signs differ?*
`IF`	*signs differ*
`>R R SM/REM OVER`	*do symmetric division*
`IF`	*deal with remainder*
`1- SWAP R> + SWAP`	*floor quotient;rem = rem + denominator*
`ELSE`	*no remainder*
`R> DROP`	*clean up return stack*
`THEN`	
`ELSE`	*denominator and numerator signs same*
`SM/REM`	*do symmetric division (same as floored here)*
`THEN`	
`;`	

The code for **FM/MOD** is written in terms of **SM/REM** and is very similar to the Forth code for **/MOD** at the end of Smith's article [4].

18.3 S|F Programming Considerations

S|F changes how **M/** works, which changes all of the other words (**/MOD / MOD */MOD */**) that use signed integer division except **SM/REM** and **FM/MOD** , which unconditionally perform T-division and F-division, respectively. If you change the value of **S|F** , you will change how signed integer division works from that point on in **fbForth 2.0**, regardless of when words using such division were defined, unless those words explicitly set **S|F** themselves.

Only two words in the resident dictionary use signed integer division but are not affected by changes to **S|F** . FBLOCKS is likely quite another story and is left as an exercise for the reader.

Any words requiring the use of one specific type of signed integer division should save the current value of **S|F** before changing it and restoring it when done. This is especially important for development of software packages for other users of **fbForth 2.0** to avoid surprises.

Changes to **S|F** do not survive **COLD** , but can be made to do so by also changing the initial value of **S|F** in the initial value table for User Variables. That table starts at the address in **UCONS$** . The offset for **S|F** is **4Ah**. Both of these are listed in Appendix F "User Variables in fbForth 2.0". The following code will set the initial value of **S|F** to 1 for F-division:

```
HEX 1 UCONS$ @ 04A + !
```

To insure that **S|F** has a particular value, *e.g.*, 1 for F-division, you might set **S|F**

1. As the first order of business in any project.
2. In block #1 of FBLOCKS: **1 S|F !**
3. (2) plus the initial value in block #1 so **S|F** will survive **COLD** :

```
HEX 1 S|F ! 1 UCONS$ @ 04A + !
```

References

1. Daan Leijen, Division and Modulus for Computer Scientists, 2001, *www.microsoft.com/en-us/research/wp-content/uploads/2016/02/divmodnote-letter.pdf*.
2. Raymond T. Boute, The Euclidean Definition of the Functions div and mod, *ACM Transactions on Programming Languages and Systems*, Vol. 14, No. 2, April 1992.
3. Donald E. Knuth, *The Art of Computer Programming: Volume I, Fundamental Algorithms*, Third Edition, Boston: Addison-Wesley, 1997, p. 39.
4. Robert L. Smith, Signed Integer Division, *Dr. Dobb's Journal*, Vol. 8, No. 9, September 1983.
5. Forth Standards Team, Forth-83 Standard, 1983, *http://forth.sourceforge.net/standard/fst83/*.
6. Forth 200x Standardisation Committee, Forth 2012 Standard, 2013, *https://forth-standard.org/standard/words*.

This page left intentionally blank

Appendix A ASCII Keycodes (Sequential Order)

Character			ASCII Code hex	ASCII Code decimal	Character			ASCII Code hex	ASCII Code decimal
NUL	<CTRL+,>		00h	0	SP			20h	32
SOH	<CTRL+A>	<FCTN+7>	01h	1	!			21h	33
STX	<CTRL+B>	<FCTN+4>	02h	2	"	<FCTN+P>		22h	34
ETX	<CTRL+C>	<FCTN+1>	03h	3	#			23h	35
EOT	<CTRL+D>	<FCTN+2>	04h	4	$			24h	36
ENQ	<CTRL+E>	<FCTN+=>	05h	5	%			25h	37
ACK	<CTRL+F>	<FCTN+8>	06h	6	&			26h	38
BEL	<CTRL+G>	<FCTN+3>	07h	7	'	<FCTN+O>		27h	39
BS	<CTRL+H>	<FCTN+S>	08h	8	(			28h	40
HT	<CTRL+I>	<FCTN+D>	09h	9	)			29h	41
LF	<CTRL+J>	<FCTN+X>	0Ah	10	*			2Ah	42
VT	<CTRL+K>	<FCTN+E>	0Bh	11	+			2Bh	43
FF	<CTRL+L>	<FCTN+6>	0Ch	12	,			2Ch	44
CR	<CTRL+M>		0Dh	13	-			2Dh	45
SO	<CTRL+N>	<FCTN+5>	0Eh	14	.			2Eh	46
SI	<CTRL+O>	<FCTN+9>	0Fh	15	/			2Fh	47
DLE	<CTRL+P>		10h	16	0	<CTRL+0>		30h	48
DC1	<CTRL+Q>		11h	17	1	<CTRL+1>		31h	49
DC2	<CTRL+R>		12h	18	2	<CTRL+2>		32h	50
DC3	<CTRL+S>		13h	19	3	<CTRL+3>		33h	51
DC4	<CTRL+T>		14h	20	4	<CTRL+4>		34h	52
NAK	<CTRL+U>		15h	21	5	<CTRL+5>		35h	53
SYN	<CTRL+V>		16h	22	6	<CTRL+6>		36h	54
ETB	<CTRL+W>		17h	23	7	<CTRL+7>		37h	55
CAN	<CTRL+X>		18h	24	8			38h	56
EM	<CTRL+Y>		19h	25	9	<FCTN+Q>	<FCTN+.>	39h	57
SUB	<CTRL+Z>		1Ah	26	:	<FCTN+/>		3Ah	58
ESC	<CTRL+.>		1Bh	27	;	<CTRL+/>		3Bh	59
FS	<CTRL+;>		1Ch	28	<	<FCTN+0>		3Ch	60
GS	<CTRL+=>		1Dh	29	=	<FCTN+;>		3Dh	61
RS	<CTRL+8>		1Eh	30	>	<FCTN+B>		3Eh	62
US	<CTRL+9>		1Fh	31	?	<FCTN+H>	<FCTN+I>	3Fh	63

…continued from previous page—

Character		**ASCII Code**		**Character**		**ASCII Code**	
		hex	**decimal**			**hex**	**decimal**
@	***<FCTN+J>***	**40h**	64	`	***<FCTN+C>***	**60h**	96
A	***<FCTN+K>***	**41h**	65	a		**61h**	97
B	***<FCTN+L>***	**42h**	66	b		**62h**	98
C	***<FCTN+M>***	**43h**	67	c		**63h**	99
D	***<FCTN+N>***	**44h**	68	d		**64h**	100
E		**45h**	69	e		**65h**	101
F	***<FCTN+Y>***	**46h**	70	f		**66h**	102
G		**47h**	71	g		**67h**	103
H		**48h**	72	h		**68h**	104
I		**49h**	73	i		**69h**	105
J		**4Ah**	74	j		**6Ah**	106
K		**4Bh**	75	k		**6Bh**	107
L		**4Ch**	76	l		**6Ch**	108
M		**4Dh**	77	m		**6Dh**	109
N		**4Eh**	78	n		**6Eh**	110
O		**4Fh**	79	o		**6Fh**	111
P		**50h**	80	p		**70h**	112
Q		**51h**	81	q		**71h**	113
R		**52h**	82	r		**72h**	114
S		**53h**	83	s		**73h**	115
T		**54h**	84	t		**74h**	116
U		**55h**	85	u		**75h**	117
V		**56h**	86	v		**76h**	118
W		**57h**	87	w		**77h**	119
X		**58h**	88	x		**78h**	120
Y		**59h**	89	y		**79h**	121
Z		**5Ah**	90	z		**7Ah**	122
[	***<FCTN+R>***	**5Bh**	91	{	***<FCTN+F>***	**7Bh**	123
\	***<FCTN+Z>***	**5Ch**	92	|	***<FCTN+A>***	**7Ch**	124
]	***<FCTN+T>***	**5Dh**	93	}	***<FCTN+G>***	**7Dh**	125
^		**5Eh**	94	~	***<FCTN+W>***	**7Eh**	126
_	***<FCTN+U>***	**5Fh**	95	DEL	***<FCTN+V>***	**7Fh**	127

Appendix B ASCII Keycodes (Keyboard Order)

	ASCII Code			ASCII Code	
Control Key	hex	decimal	Function Key	hex	decimal
<CTRL+1>	31h	49	<FCTN+1>	03h	3
<CTRL+2>	32h	50	<FCTN+2>	04h	4
<CTRL+3>	33h	51	<FCTN+3>	07h	7
<CTRL+4>	34h	52	<FCTN+4>	02h	2
<CTRL+5>	35h	53	<FCTN+5>	0Eh	14
<CTRL+6>	36h	54	<FCTN+6>	0Ch	12
<CTRL+7>	37h	55	<FCTN+7>	01h	1
<CTRL+8>	1Eh	30	<FCTN+8>	06h	6
<CTRL+9>	1Fh	31	<FCTN+9>	0Fh	15
<CTRL+0>	30h	48	<FCTN+0>	3Ch	60
<CTRL+=>	1Dh	29	<FCTN+=>	05h	5
<CTRL+Q>	11h	11	<FCTN+Q>	39h	57
<CTRL+W>	17h	23	<FCTN+W>	7Eh	126
<CTRL+E>	05h	5	<FCTN+E>	0Bh	11
<CTRL+R>	12h	18	<FCTN+R>	5Bh	91
<CTRL+T>	14h	20	<FCTN+T>	5Dh	93
<CTRL+Y>	19h	25	<FCTN+Y>	46h	70
<CTRL+U>	15h	21	<FCTN+U>	5Fh	95
<CTRL+I>	09h	9	<FCTN+I>	3Fh	63
<CTRL+O>	0Fh	15	<FCTN+O>	27h	39
<CTRL+P>	10h	16	<FCTN+P>	22h	34
<CTRL+/>	3Bh	59	<FCTN+/>	3Ah	58

…continued from previous page—

	ASCII Code			ASCII Code	
Control Key	**hex**	**decimal**	**Function Key**	**hex**	**decimal**
<CTRL+A>	01h	1	<FCTN+A>	7Ch	124
<CTRL+S>	13h	19	<FCTN+S>	08h	8
<CTRL+D>	04h	4	<FCTN+D>	09h	9
<CTRL+F>	06h	6	<FCTN+F>	7Bh	123
<CTRL+G>	07h	7	<FCTN+G>	7Dh	125
<CTRL+H>	08h	8	<FCTN+H>	3Fh	63
<CTRL+J>	0Ah	10	<FCTN+J>	40h	64
<CTRL+K>	0Bh	11	<FCTN+K>	41h	65
<CTRL+L>	0Ch	12	<FCTN+L>	42h	66
<CTRL+;>	1Ch	28	<FCTN+;>	3Dh	61
<CTRL+Z>	1Ah	26	<FCTN+Z>	5Ch	92
<CTRL+X>	18h	24	<FCTN+X>	0Ah	10
<CTRL+C>	03h	3	<FCTN+C>	60h	96
<CTRL+V>	16h	22	<FCTN+V>	7Fh	127
<CTRL+B>	02h	2	<FCTN+B>	3Eh	62
<CTRL+N>	0Eh	14	<FCTN+N>	44h	68
<CTRL+M>	0Dh	13	<FCTN+M>	43h	67
<CTRL+,>	00h	0	<FCTN+,>	38h	56
<CTRL+.>	1Bh	27	<FCTN+.>	39h	57

Appendix C How fbForth 2.0 differs from *Starting FORTH* (1st Ed.)

Page	Word	Changes Required
10	`BACKSPACE`	*<FCTN+S>* produces a backspace on the TI 99/4A.
10	`ok`	**fbForth 2.0** automatically prints a space before " `ok:n` ".
16		The **fbForth 2.0** dictionary can store names up to 31 characters in length.
18	`^`	Not a special character in **fbForth 2.0**.
18	`."`	Will execute inside or outside a colon definition in **fbForth 2.0**.
42	`/MOD`	Uses signed numbers in **fbForth 2.0**. Remainder has sign of dividend.
42	`MOD`	Uses signed numbers in **fbForth 2.0**. Remainder has sign of dividend.
50	`.S`	The resident **fbForth 2.0** version prints a vertical bar '|' instead of '0' followed by the stack contents. The stack contents will be printed as unsigned numbers. The definition shown does not work in **fbForth 2.0**, even changing `'S` to `SP@ 2-` to account for vocabulary differences, because of the expectation that the bottom stack location contains '0' for an empty stack. It also does not print the extra number at the left to mark the bottom of the stack when the stack is not empty.
52	`2SWAP`	This word is not in **fbForth 2.0** but can be created with the following definition: `: 2SWAP ROT >R ROT R> ;`
52	`2DUP`	This word is not in **fbForth 2.0** but can be created with the following definition: `: 2DUP OVER OVER ;`
52	`2OVER`	This word is not in **fbForth 2.0** but can be created with the following definition: `: 2OVER SP@ 6 + @ SP@ 6 + @ ;`
52	`2DROP`	This word is not in **fbForth 2.0** but can be created with the following definition: `: 2DROP DROP DROP ;`
57		When you redefine a word that is already in the dictionary, **fbForth 2.0** will issue a message saying " `WORD isn't unique.` ". In the example, a message saying " `GREET isn't unique.` " would appear.
60		In **fbForth 2.0**, there is no unique limit to the number of blocks (screens) in a blocks file except the number of blocks included when the file was created.

Page	Word	Changes Required
63-82		The **fbForth 2.0** Editor is different (much better) than the editor described in this section. Read the section of this **fbForth 2.0** *Manual* describing the Editor.
83	**DEPTH**	**DEPTH** is defined in the resident **fbForth 2.0** dictionary.
84	**COPY**	**fbForth 2.0** has **CPYBLK** for this purpose, *q.v.*
84-5		Ignore Editor words.
89*ff*	**THEN**	**THEN** is in the **fbForth 2.0** vocabulary and is a synonym for the word **ENDIF** . Many people find **ENDIF** less confusing than **THEN** .
91	**NOT**	This word is not in **fbForth 2.0**, but can be created with the following definition: `: NOT 0= ;`
101	**?DUP**	This word is identical to **-DUP** in **fbForth 2.0**. Use the following definition if necessary: `: ?DUP -DUP ;`
101*ff*	**ABORT"**	As with the Forth-79 Standard, **fbForth 2.0** provides **ABORT** instead of **ABORT"** .
102	**?STACK**	In **fbForth 2.0** this word automatically calls **ABORT** and prints the appropriate error message.
107	**2***	This word is not in **fbForth 2.0**, but can be created with the following definition: `: 2* DUP + ;`
107	**2/**	This word is not in **fbForth 2.0**, but can be created with the following definition: `: 2/ 1 SRA ;`
108	**NEGATE**	This word is not in **fbForth 2.0**, but can be created with the following definition: `: NEGATE MINUS ;`
110	**I**	This word exists in **fbForth 2.0** but also has a duplicate definition, **R** . **I** and **R** are identical in function. They both get a copy of the return stack top.
110	**I'**	This word is not in **fbForth 2.0**, but can be created with the following definition: (*Note*: **R** is a synonym for **I** .) `: I' R> R SWAP >R ;`
112		If you will notice, there is a **.** (print) missing in the **QUADRATIC** definition. You must add a **.** after the last **+** to make **QUADRATIC** work correctly.
112		Ignore the last two paragraphs. They do not apply.

Page	Word	Changes Required
131		Just a reminder! You must define **2DUP** and **2DROP** before the **COMPOUND** example may be used.
132		There is a mistake in the second definition of **TABLE**. It should look like this: **: TABLE CR 11 1 DO** **11 1 DO I J * 5 U.R LOOP CR LOOP ;**
134		When you execute the **DOUBLING** example, an extra number will be printed after 16384. This is because **+LOOP** behaves a little differently in **fbForth 2.0**.
136		In the definition of **COMPOUND**, the **CR** should precede **SWAP** instead of **LOOP**.
137	**XX**	When **fbForth 2.0** detects an error, the stack is cleared, but then the contents of **BLK** and **IN** are saved on the stack, if **LOAD**ing, to assist in locating the error. The stack may be completely cleared with the word **SP!** .
161	**U/MOD**	This word is not in **fbForth 2.0**, but is the same as **U/** and can be created with the following definition: **: U/MOD U/ ;**
161	**/LOOP**	This word is not in **fbForth 2.0**.
162	**OCTAL**	**OCTAL** does not exist in **fbForth 2.0**. See p. 163 for definition.
164-5		Numbers in **fbForth 2.0** may only be punctuated with periods. Commas, slashes and other marks are not permitted. Any number containing a period (**.**) is considered double-length. In later examples using **D.** and **UD.** , replace all punctuation in the inputs with decimal points. It is recommended that you not place more than one decimal place in each number if you want valid output.
166	**UD.**	This word is already defined in **fbForth 2.0**.
173	**D-**	This word is not in **fbForth 2.0**, but can be created with the following definition: **: D- DMINUS D+ ;**
173	**DNEGATE**	This word is not in **fbForth 2.0**, but can be created with the following definition: **: DENEGATE DMINUS ;**
173	**DMAX**	This word is not in **fbForth 2.0**, but can be created with the following definition: **: DMAX 2OVER 2OVER D- SWAP DROP 0<** **IF 2SWAP ENDIF** **2DROP ;**

Page	Word	Changes Required

173	`DMIN`	This word is not in **fbForth 2.0**, but can be created with the following definition:
		`: DMIN 2OVER 2OVER 2SWAP D- SWAP DROP 0<`
		`IF 2SWAP ENDIF`
		`2DROP ;`

173	`D=`	This word is not in **fbForth 2.0**, but can be created with the following definition: `: D= D- 0= SWAP 0= AND ;`
173	`D0=`	This word is not in **fbForth 2.0**, but can be created with the following definition: `: D0= 0. D= ;`
173	`D<`	This word is not in **fbForth 2.0**, but can be created with the following definition: `: D< D- SWAP DROP 0<;`

173	`DU<`	This word is not in **fbForth 2.0**, but can be created with the following definition:
		`: DU< ROT SWAP OVER OVER`
		`U<`
		`IF` *(determined less using high order halves)*
		`DROP DROP DROP DROP 1`
		`ELSE` *(test if high halves equal)*
		`=`
		`IF` *(equal so just test low halves)*
		`U<`
		`ELSE` *(test fails)*
		`DROP DROP 0`
		`ENDIF`
		`ENDIF ;`

174	`M+`	This word is not in **fbForth 2.0**, but can be created with the following definition: `: M+ 0 D+ ;`
174	`M/`	This word is different in **fbForth 2.0** and can be changed with the following definition: `: M/ M/ SWAP DROP ;`
174	`M*/`	Not available in **fbForth 2.0** because no triple precision arithmetic has been included. This could be created using either a relatively complicated colon definition or by using the Assembler included with **fbForth 2.0**.

Page	Word	Changes Required
183*ff*		Variables in **fbForth 2.0** are required to be initialized at creation, thus the word **VARIABLE** takes the top item on the stack and places it into the variable as its initial value. For example, **12 VARIABLE DATE** both creates the variable **DATE** and initializes it to 12. If desired, the advanced user can use the words **<BUILDS** and **DOES>** to create a new defining word, **VARIABLE** , which has exactly the behavior of **VARIABLE** as used in this section. The code to do this is: `: VARIABLE <BUILDS 0 , DOES> ;`
193	**2VARIABLE**	This word is not in **fbForth 2.0**, but can be created with the following definition: `: 2VARIABLE <BUILDS 0. , , DOES> ;` This definition does not require a number to be on the stack when it is executed.
193	**2!**	This word is not in **fbForth 2.0**, but can be created with the following definition: `: 2! >R R ! R> 2+ ! ;`
193	**2@**	This word is not in **fbForth 2.0**, but can be created with the following definition: `: 2@ >R R 2+ @ R> @ ;`
193	**2CONSTANT**	This word is not in **fbForth 2.0**, but can be created with the following definition: `: 2CONSTANT <BUILDS , , DOES> 2@ ;` This definition does *not* require a number on the stack.
199		You must place a 0 on the stack before executing **VARIABLE COUNTS 10 ALLOT** . This, however, initializes only the first element of the array **COUNTS** to 0. You must execute either the **FILL** or **ERASE** instruction at the bottom of the page to properly initialize the array.
204	**DUMP**	**fbForth 2.0** already has a dump instruction which must be loaded from the disk. Dumps are always printed in hexadecimal. See Appendix D for location of **DUMP** .
207	**CREATE**	The **CREATE** word of **fbForth 2.0** behaves somewhat differently. Hackers should consult fig-Forth documentation.
216	**EXECUTE**	Because this word operates a little differently in **fbForth 2.0**, it must be preceded by the word **CFA** . The example should read: `' GREET CFA EXECUTE`
217		The example illustrating indirect execution must be modified to work in **fbForth 2.0**: `' GREET CFA POINTER ! POINTER @ EXECUTE`

Page	Word	Changes Required
218	`[']`	In **fbForth 2.0**, this word is unnecessary as the word **'** will take the following word of a definition when used in a definition.
219	`NUMBER`	In **fbForth 2.0**, **NUMBER** is always able to convert double precision numbers.
219	`'NUMBER`	**fbForth 2.0** does not use **'NUMBER** to locate the **NUMBER** routine.
220		In **fbForth 2.0**, the name field is variable length and contains up to 31 characters. Also, the link field precedes the name field in **fbForth 2.0**.
225	`EXIT`	This word is **;S** in **fbForth 2.0**. **;S** is the word compiled by **;** so to create **EXIT** we might use: `: EXIT [COMPILE] ;S ; IMMEDIATE`
225	`I`	In **fbForth 2.0**, the interpreter pointer is called **IP** , not **I** .
232		See Chapter 1 in this **fbForth 2.0** *Instruction Manual* for instructions for loading elective blocks.
232	`RELOAD`	This instruction is not available in **fbForth 2.0**.
233	`H`	This word is **DP** (dictionary pointer) in **fbForth 2.0**.
235	`'S`	In **fbForth 2.0**, **SP@** is used instead of **'S** .
240		See Appendix F in this **fbForth 2.0** *Instruction Manual* for a complete list of user variables.
240	`>IN`	This word is **IN** in **fbForth 2.0**.
245	`LOCATE`	**fbForth 2.0** does not support **LOCATE** .
256	`COPY`	In **fbForth 2.0**, use the word **CPYBLK** . **CPYBLK** is disk resident. See Appendix D for location and usage.
259	`[']`	Change the **[']** to **'** in the bottom example. In **fbForth 2.0**, **'** will compile the address of the next word in the colon definition.
261	`>TYPE`	Unnecessary in non-multiprogramming systems. Not present in **fbForth 2.0**.
265	`RND`	**fbForth 2.0** has two random number generators: **RND** and **RNDW** . See Appendix D for descriptions. See also definitions for **SEED** and **RANDOMIZE** .
266	`MOVE`	In **fbForth 2.0**, **MOVE** moves *u* words in memory, not *u* bytes. Use **CMOVE** instead. If you must conform to *Starting FORTH (1st Ed.),* **MOVE** can be redefined: `: MOVE 2/ MOVE ;`
266	`<CMOVE`	Not present in **fbForth 2.0**. Must be created with the Assembler if required. This word is used only when the source and destination regions of a move overlap and the destination is higher than the source.

Page	Word	Changes Required
270	**WORD**	In **fbForth 2.0**, the word **WORD** does not leave an address on the stack.

270	**TEXT**	This word's name conflicts with **fbForth 2.0**'s Graphics mode word of the same name. The definition that follows will work, but has a different name to avoid conflict. It does not check for a 72-character limit:
		`: TXT PAD 72 BLANKS PAD HERE - 1-`
		`DUP ALLOT MINUS SWAP WORD ALLOT ;`
		If you want the count to also be stored at PAD, remove the **1-** from the definition. See also, **TOKEN** and **S"** .

277	**>BINARY**	This is named **(NUMBER)** in **fbForth 2.0**.
277		Because **WORD** does not leave an address on the stack, it is necessary to redefine **PLUS** as follows: `: PLUS 32 WORD HERE NUMBER DROP + ." = " . ;`
279	**NUMBER**	This definition of **NUMBER** is not compatible with **fbForth 2.0**.
281	**-TEXT**	Not in **fbForth 2.0**. Use the definition on page 282.
292		**fbForth 2.0** uses the word pair **<BUILDS … DOES>** to define a new defining word. **<BUILDS** calls **CREATE** as part of its function.

297		To create a byte **ARRAY** in **fbForth 2.0**:
		`: ARRAY <BUILDS OVER , * ALLOT`
		`DOES> DUP @ ROT * + + 2+ ;`

298		Just a reminder! Don't forget to define **2*** *before* trying the example at the bottom of the page. Also, replace the word **CREATE** with **<BUILDS** .
301	**(DO)**	This is the runtime behavior of **DO** just as listed. **2>R** is not used, however.
301	**DO**	The given definition of **DO** is not compatible with **fbForth 2.0**. **fbForth 2.0**'s definition of **DO** is much more complex because of compile-time error checking.
303	**(LITERAL)**	The **fbForth 2.0** name for this word is **LIT** .
306		**fbForth 2.0** remains in compilation mode until a **;** is typed.

This page left intentionally blank.

Appendix D The fbForth 2.0 Glossary

fbForth 2.0 words appear in this glossary on the left of the word's entry line and ordered in the ASCII collating sequence, displayed as a handy reference at the bottom of each page of this appendix. If the word is an immediate word, that fact is shown in the middle of the entry line as "*[immediate word]*". The block in FBLOCKS that needs to be loaded to load the word's definition is enclosed in "[ ]" and right-justified on the entry line preceded by some or all of the description given by executing **MENU** . The word's definition can be found in or following that block. If the word is part of the core system, it is listed as "Resident". *Note:* With the exception of **;ASM** and **NEXT,** , words in the Assembler vocabulary are only referenced in Chapter 9 "The fbForth 2.0 TMS9900 Assembler".

The state of the top of the parameter stack (usually referred to simply as "the stack") before and after execution of an **fbForth 2.0** word is shown schematically as "(*before* --- *after*)", where "*before*" and "*after*" represent 0 or more cells relevant to the **fbForth 2.0** word being described and "---" represents the execution of the word. The topmost, *i.e.*, most accessible, item on the stack is on the right. These stack effects are usually listed on the second line. However, when an **fbForth 2.0** word is a compiler word, *i.e.*, it can only appear within the definition of another word, the compilation and runtime stack effects will be shown on the lines beginning the relevant descriptions.

The stack effects of the return stack will also be shown when the return stack is affected by the execution of the **fbForth 2.0** word. These will be indicated by "R:" following the '(' as in the following: "(R: *n* ---)", which would mean that a 16-bit number *n* is removed from the top of the return stack after the word being described is executed.

For the Stack-based String Library, the String Stack effects will be shown similarly as the return stack effects with "(SS: *before* --- *after*)". See Chapter 14 "The Stack-based String Library" for details.

A few words expect information from the input stream following the Forth word, which will be shown after stack effects with "(IS: *input*)".

D.1 Explanation of Some Terms and Abbreviations

When the following terms and abbreviations are part of the stack effects schematic, each *before* and *after* token in the schematic represents 1 cell (16-bits or 2 bytes) on the stack unless otherwise noted under "Meaning".

Term/Abbreviation	Meaning
$Caddr	string constant address
addr, $addr_1$, ...	memory address
b	byte
col	column position
cccc , **nnnn** , **xxxx**	string representations
cfa	code field address

Term/Abbreviation	Meaning
char	ASCII character code
count	count (length)
$d, d_1, d_2, \ldots$	signed double-precision numbers (2 cells each)
$dotcol, dotcol_1, dotcol_2, \ldots$	dot column position
$dotrow, dotrow_1, dotrow_2, \ldots$	dot row position
flag	Boolean flag
false	Boolean false flag (value = 0)
$f, f_1, f_2, \ldots$	floating point numbers (4 cells each)
lfa	link field address
$n, n_1, n_2, \ldots$	signed single-precision numbers
nfa	name field address
pfa	parameter field address
row	row position
rem	remainder
blk	block number
spr	sprite number
str	string address
true	Boolean true flag (value $\neq$ 0)
tol	tolerance limit
u	unsigned single-precision number
ud	unsigned double-precision number (2 cells)
vaddr	VDP address

D.2 Naming Conventions for Forth Words

This section is an effort to aid you in navigating this glossary, as well as to assist you in contriving names for your own Forth words.

A few, core Forth words are very short and cryptic because they are used so often:

Word	Function
:	Begin definition
;	End definition
@	Fetch
!	Store
,	Compile
'	Look up
.	Print

Words that begin or end with the above word symbols are usually expected to have a similar function. Here are a few examples:

Word	Function
C@	Character fetch
C!	Character store
C,	Character compile
.BASE	Print value in **BASE**
.S	Print stack
D.	Double-number print
ASM:	Assembly Language Code, begin definition
;ASM	End definition, Assembly Language Code

‘ **( )** ’ and ‘ **< >** ’ surround runtime versions of similarly named words. Here are a few examples:

High-level Word	Runtime Version
DO	(DO)
LOOP	(LOOP)
+LOOP	(+LOOP)
-FIND	(FIND)
NUMBER	(NUMBER)
USEBFL	(UB)
CLOAD	<CLOAD>
."	(.")

‘ **>** ’, may also mean “greater?”, “to” (sometimes preceded by ‘ **-** ’ in words inherited from TI Forth) or “this”. Here are some examples with implied locations in brackets:

Word	Function
>R	[Parameter stack] **to** return stack
R>	Return stack **to** [parameter stack]
F->S	Floating point (FP) number **to** parameter stack
DOES>	Does **this** (high-level Forth code that follows this word)
>	**Greater?** ($n_1 > n_2$?)
>F	**To** FP number (converts FP number text in input stream and pushes it to the stack)
>DEG	[Parameter stack value (radians)] **to** degrees

Word	Function
ASM>CODE	Assembly language code **to** hexadecimal machine code
BASE->R	Value in **BASE to** return stack
R->BASE	Return stack value **to BASE**
F>	FP **greater?** ($f_1 > f_2$?)
F>R	FP number on parameter stack **to** return stack

‘ **<** ’, may also mean “less?” or “that”. Here are some examples with implied locations in brackets:

Word	Function
<	**Less?** ($n_1 < n_2$?)
<BUILDS	**That** (the word pointed to) builds new words
0<	0 **less?** ($n < 0$?)

At the beginning of a word, ‘ **?** ’ usually means “query” and may or may not leave a flag on the parameter stack. Most of the words below are querying for error conditions and will abort with an error message when such an error condition exists. At the end of a word, you may think of it as making the word a question.

Word	Function
?	**Query** address on stack and print contents
?COMP	**Query STATE** for compilation—abort with error message if not
?CSP	**Query** stack position for same level as start of definition—abort with error message if not
?ERROR	**Query** *flag* on stack and issue error number *n* if false
?EXEC	**Query STATE** for execution—abort with error message if not
?FLERR	**Query** for FP calculation error—abort with error message if so
?KEY	**Query** keyboard for any key—leave 7-bit ASCII value of key or 0 if none
?KEY8	**Query** keyboard for any key—leave 8-bit value of key or 0 if none
?LOADING	**Query BLK** for whether we are **LOAD**ing—abort with error message if not
?PAIRS	**Query** the two numbers on the stack for identity—abort with error message if not
?STACK	**Query** stack for overflow or underflow—abort with error message if either
?TERMINAL	**Query** keyboard for break key—leave *true* if so; *false* if not

Word	Function
PLAYING?	Are we playing a soundlist?—leave a flag on the stack to indicate whether a soundlist is active
TALKING?	Is the Speech Synthesizer talking?—leave a flag on the stack to indicate whether speech is active

A very good reference for explaining and recommending naming conventions is *THINKING FORTH: A Language and Philosophy for Solving Problems* by Leo Brodie (1984, 1994, 2004), available free online from SourceForge at *http://thinking-forth.sourceforge.net/*. Of particular note are:

- Chapter 5 "Implementation: Elements of Forth Style", p.135—especially, the sections on
  - "Choosing Names: The Art", p. 163, and
  - "Naming Standards: The Science", p. 167
- Appendix E "Summary of Style Conventions", p. 283

D.3 fbForth 2.0 *Word Descriptions*

! Resident

(*n addr* ---)

Stores 16 bit-number *n* at address. Pronounced "store".

!CSP Resident

(---)

Saves the stack position in user variable **CSP** . Used as part of compiler security.

Resident

(d_1 --- d_2)

Converts the rightmost digit of a double number d_1 to an ASCII character, which is placed in a pictured numeric output string built downward from **PAD** to **HERE** . The digit to convert is the remainder from division of d_1 by the current radix contained in **BASE** . The quotient d_2 is maintained for further processing. Used between **<#** and **#>** . See **#S** , **<#** and **#>** . The details of pictured numeric output are shown at **<#** .

#> Resident

(*d* --- *addr count*)

Terminates pictured numeric output conversion by dropping *d* and leaving the text address and character count suitable for **TYPE** , *q.v.* The details of pictured numeric output are shown at **<#** .

#MOTION Resident

(*n* ---)

Sets sprite numbers 0 to $n - 1$ in automotion.

#S Resident

(d_1 --- d_2)

Generates pictured numeric output as ASCII text at **PAD** from d_1 by executing **#** until a zero double number d_2 results. Used between **<#** and **#>** , *q.v.* The details of pictured numeric output are shown at **<#** .

$" Stack-based String Library [42]

(---) (SS: --- *str*) (IS: *string*") "string to string stack"

The word **$"** takes a string from the input stream and pushes it to the string stack. The end of the string is indicated by a quotation mark. For example,

```
$" Hello, World!"  ok:0
```

In this example the string "Hello, world!" is pushed directly to the string stack, thus becoming the top item on the string stack.

$" is a state-smart word. It can be used in both colon definitions and also directly at the command line. The correct action will be taken in either case.

In order that the runtime actions of **$"** may be compiled into a definition if so desired, the runtime action of this word is encapsulated within the word **($")** . Therefore, if the runtime behavior of this word is to be compiled into another word, one must compile the word **($")** .

$. More Useful Stack Words etc. [41]

(*n* ---)

Display the top number on the stack as an unsigned hexadecimal number.

$.S Stack-based String Library [42]

(---) (SS: ---)

The word **$.S** displays a non-destructive string stack dump to the output device. The length of each string is given, along with the total number of strings on the string stack. The amount of space allocated to the string stack, the amount of space in use and the amount of free space is also reported. An example appears above under the description of **REPLACE$** .

$CONST Stack-based String Library [42]

(*max_len* ---) (IS:*name*) "string constant"

RUNTIME: (--- *$Caddr*)

The word **$CONST** declares a string constant. Declared at compile time, string constants require a maximum length and a name. For example,

```
50 $CONST WELCOME  ok:0
```

The above example declares a string with a maximum size of 50 characters. It shall be referenced in code using the name **WELCOME** .

A string constant pushes the address of its maximum length field which can be read with the word **MAXLEN$** .

' *[immediate word]* Resident

(--- *pfa*) (IS: *word*)

Used in the form:

```
' nnnn
```

Searches the dictionary for **nnnn** and, if found, leaves the parameter field address *pfa* of the word. As a compiler directive, **'** , because it is an immediate word, executes in a colon definition to compile the address of a literal, *viz.*, the *pfa* of the found word. If the word is not found after a search of **CONTEXT** and **CURRENT** , it is echoed followed by '?' to indicate the error. The stack is then cleared, the contents of **IN** and **BLK** are left on the stack, if **LOAD**ing, and **QUIT** is called. Pronounced "tick".

(*[immediate word]* Resident

(---) (IS: *comment*))

(is used in the form:

```
( cccc)
```

It starts a comment that will not be compiled if it occurs in a definition. It causes the interpreter to consume characters from the input stream until a ')' is found or the end of the input stream (block or TIB) is reached. May occur during execution or in a colon definition. A blank after the leading parenthesis is required. This is most useful for commenting Forth source code in blocks.

(+LOOP) Resident

(*n* ---)

The runtime procedure compiled by **+LOOP** , which adds *n* to the loop index and then tests for loop completion. See **+LOOP** .

(.") Resident

(---)

The runtime procedure, compiled by **."** ,which transmits the in-line text that follows it to the selected output device. See **."** .

(;CODE) Resident

(---)

The runtime procedure, compiled by **DOES>ASM:** , **DOES>CODE:** and **;CODE** (execution mode, for TI Forth compatibility), that rewrites the code field of the most recently defined word to point to the machine code sequence following **DOES>ASM:** , **DOES>CODE:** or **;CODE** . See **DOES>ASM:** , **DOES>CODE:** and **;CODE** for more details.

(ABORT) Resident

(---)

Executes after an error when **WARNING** < 0. Normally, **WARNING** = 1. **(ABORT)** normally executes **ABORT** , but may be redirected (with care!) to execute a user's alternative procedure. It is defined as

```
: (ABORT) ABORT ;
```

If you wished to have **(ABORT)** execute your error procedure, say **MY_ERROR_PROC** , you would need to replace the *cfa* of **ABORT** in the definition of **(ABORT)** with the *cfa* of **MY_ERROR_PROC** . Fortunately, this is easy to do! The *cfa* of **ABORT** sits in the parameter field of **(ABORT)** , the address *pfa* of which is what ticking **(ABORT)** gives you. You can verify this with the following code:

```
HEX  ok:0
' (ABORT) @ U. 6AAC  ok:0
' ABORT CFA U. 6AAC  ok:0
```

The second line above ticks **(ABORT)** , fetches the resulting *pfa*'s contents and prints what should be the *cfa* of **ABORT** . The third line above ticks **ABORT** , gets its *cfa* and prints it. As you can see, they are, indeed, the same address.

Now, to install your error procedure, simply get its *cfa* and stash it in the parameter field of **(ABORT)** as follows:

```
' MY_ERROR_PROC CFA  ok:1
' (ABORT) !  ok:0
```

To get your error procedure to run at the next error, set **WARNING** to a negative number as below:

```
-1 WARNING !  ok:0
```

To re-instate normal **fbForth 2.0** error handling, you only need to store a positive number in **WARNING** . You can restore the default action of **(ABORT)** with the following Forth code:

```
' ABORT CFA  ok:1
' (ABORT) !  ok:0
```

(DO) Resident

(---)

The runtime procedure compiled by **DO** , which moves the loop control parameters to the return stack. See **DO** .

(DOES>) Resident

(---)

The runtime procedure compiled by **DOES>** .

(FIND) Resident

(*addr nfa --- false | pfa b true*)

Searches the dictionary starting at the name field address *nfa*, looking for a match to the text at *addr*. The addresses, *addr* and *nfa*, both point to the length byte of packed character strings (see footnote 5 on page 22). Returns the parameter field address *pfa*, length byte *b* of name field, and *true* for a match. If no match is found, only *false* is left. [*Note:* See Chapter 12 about the length byte of a name field.]

(LINE) Resident

(*n blk* --- *addr count*)

Converts the line number *n* and the Forth block number *blk* to the disk buffer address *addr* containing the data and the number *count* of characters. If the block is not in a block buffer, it is loaded from the current blocks file. If *count* is 64, the full-line text length of the block is indicated.

(LOOP) Resident

(---)

The runtime procedure compiled by **LOOP** , which increments the loop index and tests for loop completion. See **LOOP** .

(NUMBER) Resident

(d_1 $addr_1$ --- d_2 $addr_2$)

The double number d_1 should be 0, *i.e.*, the stack should contain two 16-bit zeroes. The address $addr_1$ must point to the packed character string of the ASCII text to be converted to a double number, which will be left as d_2. The conversion begins at $addr_1 + 1$ with respect to the current radix in **BASE** . The new value is accumulated with double number $d_1 = 0$ as the initial value. If a decimal point is encountered in the string, **DPL** is updated with the number of digits to the right of the decimal point. The address of the first unconvertible digit is $addr_2$. **(NUMBER)** is used by **NUMBER** .

(OF) Resident

(---)

The run time procedure compiled by **OF** .

(UB) Resident

(*addr* ---)

Runtime routine compiled or executed by **USEBFL** that changes the current blocks file to the filename as a packed character string (see footnote 5 on page 22) pointed to by *addr*.

***** Resident

(n_1 n_2 --- n_3)

Leaves the signed product of two signed numbers.

***/** Resident

(n_1 n_2 n_3 --- *quot*)

Leaves the quotient *quot* of $(n_1 * n_2) / n_3$, where all are signed numbers. Retention of an intermediate signed 32-bit product permits greater accuracy than would be available with the sequence :

n_1 n_2 * n_3 /

***/** is based on **M/** , which uses user variable **S|F** , *q.v.*, to determine whether symmetric (the default) or floored division is used. See Chapter 18 "Signed Integer Division" for more details.

***/MOD** Resident

(n_1 n_2 n_3 --- *rem quot*)

Leaves the quotient *quot* and remainder *rem* of the operation $(n_1 * n_2) / n_3$. An intermediate signed 32-bit product is used just as for ***/** . In fact, ***/MOD** is used by ***/** . ***/MOD** is based on **M/** , which uses user variable **S|F** , *q.v.*, to determine whether symmetric (the default) or floored division is used. See Chapter 18 "Signed Integer Division" for more details.

+ Resident

(n_1 n_2 --- n_3)

Leaves the sum of $n_1 + n_2$ as n_3.

+! Resident

(*n addr* ---)

Adds *n* to the value at the address. Pronounced "plus store".

+$ Stack-based String Library [42]

(---) (SS: str_1 str_2 – str_1& str_2) "concatenate strings"

The word **+$** replaces the top two strings on the string stack with their concatenated equivalent. For example,

```
$" red"  $" blue"  +$  ok:0
```

At this point, "red" and "blue" have been removed from the string stack. The topmost string on the string stack now has the value "redblue". Note that the topmost string goes to the right of the newly concatenated string.

+- Resident

(n_1 n_2 --- n_3)

Apply the sign of n_2 to n_1, which is left as n_3.

+BUF Resident

($addr_1$ --- $addr_2$ *flag*)

Advance the disk buffer address $addr_1$ to the address of the next buffer $addr_2$. Boolean flag is false when $addr_2$ is the buffer presently pointed to by user variable **PREV** .

+LOOP *[immediate word]* Resident

Used in a colon definition in the form:

DO … *n* +LOOP

COMPILE TIME: (*addr* 3 ---)

+LOOP compiles the runtime word **(+LOOP)** and the branch offset computed from **HERE** to the address *addr* left on the stack by **DO** . The value 3 is used for compile-time error checking.

RUNTIME: (*n* ---)

+LOOP selectively controls branching back to the corresponding **DO** based on *n*, the loop index and the loop limit. The signed increment *n* is added to the index and the total compared to the limit. The branch back to **DO** occurs until the new index is equal to or greater than the limit ($n > 0$), or until the new index is equal to or less than the limit ($n < 0$). Upon exiting the loop, the parameters are discarded and execution continues ahead.

, Resident

(*n* ---)

Store *n* into the next available dictionary memory cell, advancing the dictionary pointer. Pronounced "comma".

- Resident

(n_1 n_2 --- n_3)

Leave the difference n_3 of $n_1 - n_2$.

--> *[immediate word]* Resident

(---)

Continues interpretation with the next Forth block in the current blocks file. **-->** can only be used while loading blocks. Pronounced "next block".

-DUP Resident

(n_1 --- n_1 | n_1 n_1)

Duplicate n_1 only if it is non-zero. This is usually used to copy a value just before **IF** , to eliminate the need for an **ELSE** clause to drop a **DUP**ed 0.

-FIND Resident

(--- *false* | *pfa len true*) (IS: *word*)

Accepts the next text word (delimited by blanks) in the input stream to **HERE** as a packed character string (see footnote 5 on page 22), searches the **CONTEXT** and then **CURRENT** vocabularies for a matching entry. If found, the dictionary entry's parameter field address *pfa*, its length byte *len* and *true* are left. Otherwise, only *false* is left. [*Note:* See Chapter 12 about the length byte.]

-ROT More Useful Stack Words etc. [41]

(n_1 n_2 n_3 --- n_3 n_1 n_2)

Rotate right the top three numbers on the stack, resulting in the top number on the bottom.

-ROT$ Stack-based String Library [42]

(---) (SS: *str*$_1$ *str*$_2$ *str*$_3$ --- *str*$_3$ *str*$_1$ *str*$_2$) "rotate strings"

The word **–ROT$** rotates the top three strings to the right. The top string prior to the execution of **–ROT$** moves to the third position. See Chapter14 for implementation details regarding stack space limitations.

-TRAILING Resident

(*addr* n_1 --- *addr* n_2)

Adjusts the character count n_1 of a character string at *addr* to suppress the output of trailing blanks by **TYPE** , *i.e.*, the characters at *addr* + n_2 to *addr* + n_1 are blanks. If the character string is a packed character string (see footnote on page), *addr* points to the first character after the length byte. **-TRAILING** starts at the last character and steps to the beginning of the string as it looks for trailing blanks, decrementing n_1 until a non-blank character is encountered. At that point, n_1 is replaced with n_2. The output parameters of **COUNT** are suitable input parameters for **-TRAILING** .

. Resident

(*n* ---)

Prints a number from a signed 16-bit two's complement value *n*, converted according to the numeric base stored in **BASE** . A trailing blank follows. Pronounced "dot".

." *[immediate word]* Resident

(---) (IS: *string*")

Used in the form:

```
." cccc"
```

Compiles an in-line string **cccc** (delimited by the trailing **"**) with an execution procedure to transmit the text to the selected output device. If executed outside a definition, **."** will immediately print the text until the final **"** . See (**."**) .

.$ Stack-based String Library [42]

(---) (SS: *str* ---) "display string"

The word **.$** pops the topmost string from the string stack and displays it. For example,

```
$" Hello, World!" .$ Hello, World! oK:0
```

.$CONST Stack-based String Library [42]

(*$Caddr* ---) "display string constant"

Given the address of a string constant on the data stack the word **.$CONST** shall display the string. For example,

```
50 $CONST WELCOME  ok:0
WELCOME :=" Hello and welcome!"  ok:0
WELCOME .$CONST CR
Hello and welcome!  ok:0
```

.BASE Resident

(--- *n*)

Print the decimal value *n* of the current radix (number base).

.LINE Resident

(*n blk* ---)

Print on the terminal device a line of text from the current blocks file corresponding to the line number *n* of block number *blk*. Trailing blanks are suppressed.

.R Resident

(n_1 n_2 ---)

Prints the number n_1 right aligned in a field whose width is n_2. No following blank is printed.

.S Resident

(---)

Prints the entire contents of the parameter stack as unsigned numbers in the current **BASE** . The bottom of the stack is shown by an initial '|'.

/ Resident

(n_1 n_2 --- n_3)

Leaves the quotient n_3 of n_1 / n_2. **/** is based on **M/** , which uses user variable **S|F** , *q.v.*, to determine whether symmetric (the default) or floored division is used. See Chapter 18 "Signed Integer Division" for more details.

/MOD Resident

(n_1 n_2 --- *rem quot*)

Leaves the remainder *rem* and signed quotient *quot* of n_1 / n_2. The remainder has the sign of the dividend. **/MOD** is based on **M/** , which uses user variable **S|F** , *q.v.*, to determine whether symmetric (the default) or floored division is used. See Chapter 18 "Signed Integer Division" for more details.

0 1 2 3 Resident

(--- *n*)

These small numbers are used so often that it is useful to define them by name in the dictionary as constants. Doing so saves compile time because the interpreter searches the dictionary for a match before it decides whether it is a number. Also, numbers, otherwise, require two extra bytes of dictionary storage when used in definitions.

0< Resident

(*n* --- *flag*)

Leaves a true flag if the number *n* is less than zero (negative). Otherwise, **0<** leaves a false flag.

0= Resident

(*n* --- *flag*)

Leaves a true flag if the number is equal to zero. Otherwise, **0=** leaves a false flag.

0> Resident

(*n* --- *flag*)

Leaves a true flag if the number is greater than zero (positive). Otherwise, **0>** leaves a false flag.

0BRANCH Resident

(*flag* ---)

The runtime procedure to conditionally branch. If *flag* is *false* (zero), the following in-line parameter is added to the interpretive pointer to branch ahead or back. Compiled by **IF** , **UNTIL** , **END** and **WHILE** .

1+ Resident

(n_1 --- n_2)

Increments n_1 by 1.

1– Resident

(n_1 --- n_2)

Decrements n_1 by 1.

2+ Resident

(n_1 --- n_2)

Leaves n_1 incremented by 2 as n_2.

2– Resident

(n_1 --- n_2)

Leaves n_1 decremented by 2 as n_2.

2DROP More Useful Stack Words etc. [41]

(n_1 n_2 ---)

Drop the top two numbers from the stack.

2DUP More Useful Stack Words etc. [41]

(n_1 n_2 --- n_1 n_2 n_1 n_2)

Duplicate the top two numbers on the stack.

: *[immediate word]* Resident

(---) (IS: *<new name>* *<Forth code>* **;**)

Used in the form, called a colon definition:

```
: cccc … ;
```

Creates a dictionary entry defining **cccc** as equivalent to the sequence of Forth word definitions in '...' until the next **;** , **DOES>ASM:** or **DOES>CODE:** . The compiling process is done by the text interpreter as long as **STATE** is non-zero. Other details are that the **CONTEXT** vocabulary is set to the **CURRENT** vocabulary and that words with the precedence bit (see § 12.2 "Name Field") set are executed rather than being compiled.

If you wish to **FORGET** an unfinished definition, the word likely will not be found. If it is the last definition attempted, you can make it findable by executing **SMUDGE** and then **FORGET**ting it.

: (*traceable*) *[immediate word]* TRACE — Colon Definition Tracing [23]

(---) (IS: *<new name> <Forth code>* **;**)

This is an alternate definition of **:** that adds the capability to colon definitions of being traced when they are executed. When a colon definition is compiled under the **TRACE** option, tracing output may be turned on with **TRON** and off with **TROFF** prior to executing the word so defined. After **TRON** is executed, each time the word is executed its name will be output along with the contents of the stack. See **TRACE** , **UNTRACE** , **TRON** and **TROFF** .

:=" Stack-based String Library [42]

(*$Caddr* ---) (IS:*string*") "assign string constant"

Given the address of a string constant on the data stack, the word **:="** initializes the string constant with the string from the input stream. For example,

```
50 $CONST WELCOME  ok:0
WELCOME :=" Hello and welcome!"  ok:0
```

; *[immediate word]* Resident

(---)

Terminates a colon definition and stops further compilation. Compiles the runtime **;S** .

;ASM Resident

(---)

;ASM should be paired with **ASM:** to clearly surround assembly code:

ASM: *<new word> <assembly mnemonics>* **;ASM**

;ASM puts **045Fh** at **HERE** and advances **HERE** . This machine code for ALC, **B *NEXT** or **B *R15**, branches to the inner interpreter to fetch the next word to be executed. See Chapter 9 "The fbForth 2.0 TMS9900 Assembler" for more information. See also **ASM:** .

;CODE *[immediate word]* Resident

([ ] | **C0DEh** ---)

Only if compiling: (IS: [*<alc>*|*<mc>* **,** [*<mc>* **,**] ...] **NEXT,**) to maintain compatibility with TI Forth.

;CODE is the terminator for **CODE:** and for **DOES>CODE:** . **CODE:** defines a new word **cccc** with machine code contents that do not use **,** to compile them. The following ALC quadruples the value on the stack by double addition:

```
ASM: QUAD  ( n -- 4n )
   *SP *SP A,
   *SP *SP A,
;ASM
```

The above code can be re-stated in machine code without requiring the TMS9900 Assembler:

```
HEX CODE: QUAD A659 A659 ;CODE
```

With a very long definition, using **CODE: cccc … ;CODE** is significantly faster and is much clearer to read regardless of the code's length.

The same situation obtains for **DOES>CODE:** , *q.v.* for more details. The following code

: cccc <BUILDS … DOES>CODE: *<MC only>* **;CODE**

is the machine-code equivalent of

: cccc <BUILDS … DOES>ASM: *<ALC only>* **;ASM**

;S Resident

(---)

Stops interpretation of a Forth block. **;S** is also the runtime word compiled at the end of a colon definition, which returns execution to the calling procedure.

< Resident

(n_1 n_2 --- *flag*)

Leaves a true flag if n_1 is less than n_2. Otherwise, **<** leaves a false flag.

<# Resident

(---)

Sets up for pictured numeric output formatting using the words, **<#** , **#** , **HOLD** , **#S** , **SIGN** and **#>** . **<#** initializes **HLD** with **PAD** . **HLD** is decremented by **#** via **HOLD** for each successive digit converted. A few format examples follow:

<# #S #>	converts all digits.
<# #S SIGN #>	converts all digits with a preceding sign.
<# # # #S #>	converts at least 3 digits with leading zeroes.
<# # # 46 HOLD #S #>	converts all digits with a dot before last 2 digits.

Though **<#** requires no input parameters, you should provide the parameters on the stack that are required by all of the formatting words between **<#** and **#>** . At the very least, this is the double number you wish to convert. **DABS** should usually be executed prior to **<#** because **<# … #>** will not properly convert negative numbers. If you wish to include a sign in the output, a signed number should be pushed to the stack before the double number to be converted.

The conversion is done on a 31-bit (positive) double number producing text at **PAD** (working downward toward **HERE**), eventually suitable for output by **TYPE** . The picture template between **<#** and **#>** represents the output picture from right to left, *i.e.*, the rightmost digit is processed first. The following is an example of generalized output from a double number on the stack that may be positive or negative:

```
SWAP OVER DABS <# #S SIGN #> TYPE
```

In the example above, **SWAP** puts the high-order cell, which contains the sign bit, on the bottom; **OVER** copies it back to its proper place on top, leaving 3 cells (*n d*) on the stack; and **DABS** forces *d* positive. This arrangement is what is expected by **SIGN** .

Important note: You should not execute words that change **HERE** or **PAD** until after you have finished formatting the number and retrieving the converted output. See **#** , **#S** , **SIGN** , **#>** , **HLD** and **HOLD** for more information.

<> More Useful Stack Words etc. [41]

(n_1 n_2 --- *flag*)

Result *flag* is true (1) if $n_1 \neq n_2$ and false (0) otherwise.

<BUILDS Resident

(---)

It is used within a colon-definition to build a new defining word:

```
: cccc <BUILDS … DOES> … ;            or
: cccc <BUILDS … DOES>ASM: … ;ASM     or
: cccc <BUILDS … DOES>CODE: … ;CODE
```

Each time **cccc** is executed, **<BUILDS** defines a new word with a high-level (**DOES>**) or machine-code (**DOES>ASM:** or **DOES>CODE:**) execution procedure. Executing **cccc** in the form:

```
cccc  nnnn
```

uses **<BUILDS** to create a dictionary entry for **nnnn** . For the definition with **DOES>** , when **nnnn** is later executed, it has the parameter field address *pfa* on the stack and executes the words after **DOES>** in **cccc** . For the definition with **DOES>ASM:** or **DOES>CODE:** , when **nnnn** is later executed, it only executes the words after **DOES>ASM: or DOES>CODE:** in **cccc** , but *without* the *pfa* of **nnnn** on the stack. **<BUILDS** allows runtime procedures to be written in high-level code with **DOES>** , in assembler with **DOES>ASM:** or in machine code with **DOES>CODE:** .

<BUILDS is simply defined as

```
: <BUILDS CREATE SMUDGE ;
```

<CLOAD> Resident

(---)

The runtime procedure compiled by **CLOAD** .

= Resident

(n_1 n_2 --- *flag*)

Leaves a true flag if $n_1 = n_2$. Otherwise, it leaves a false flag.

=CELLS Resident

($addr_1$ --- $addr_1$ | $addr_2$)

This instruction expects an address or an offset to be on the stack. If this number is odd, it is incremented by 1 to put it on the next even word boundary. Otherwise, it remains unchanged.

> Resident

(n_1 n_2 --- *flag*)

Leaves a true flag if $n_1 > n_2$. Otherwise, it leaves a false flag.

>$ Stack-based String Library [42]

(*$Caddr* ---) (SS: --- *str*) "to string stack"

Given the address of a string constant on the data stack, the word **>$** copies the contents of the string to the string stack where it can be manipulated. For example,

```
50 $CONST WELCOME  ok:0
WELCOME :=" Hello and welcome!"  ok:0
WELCOME >$  ok:0
```

>$CONST Stack-based String Library [42]

(*$Caddr* ---) (SS: *str* ---) "to string constant"

The word **>$CONST** takes the topmost string from the string stack and moves it into the string constant whose address is on the data stack. For example,

```
4 $CONST COLOR  ok:0
$" red" COLOR >$CONST  ok:0
```

At this point, the string constant **COLOR** has the value "red". To verify, display the string using **.$CONST** as follows:

```
COLOR .$CONST red ok:0
```

>DEG Resident

(f_1 --- f_2)

Converts an 8-byte floating point number f_1 from radians to f_2 degrees.

>F *[immediate word]* Resident

(--- *f*) (IS: *<fp number string>*)

This instruction expects to be followed by a string representing a legitimate floating point number terminated by a space. This string is converted into floating point and placed on the stack. This instruction can be used in colon definitions or directly from the keyboard.

>MAP Resident

(*bank addr* ---)

This word is ported from **TurboForth**[1] code courtesy of Mark Wills.

If a SAMS card is present, **>MAP** maps memory bank *bank* to address *addr*.

Address *addr* should be a valid address on a 4 KiB boundary, *viz.*, **2000h**, **3000h**, **A000h**, **B000h**, **C000h**, **D000h**, **E000h** or **F000h**. Bank *bank* should be a number between 0 and **FFh**.

S0&TIB! , *q.v.*, should be used to change **S0** and **TIB** both to **EFA0h** or **DFA0h** (exactly 4 KiB or 8 KiB [1 or 2 SAMS page(s)] lower than the default **FFA0h**), thus allowing the use of **F000h** and/or **E000h** with impunity!

When a SAMS memory expansion card is installed, the 32 KiB of CPU RAM is actually taken from the SAMS memory. At startup, **fbForth 2.0** reserves the following banks of SAMS memory for the "standard" 32 KiB RAM:

Bank	4 KiB Boundary
F8h	2000h
F9h	3000h
FAh	A000h
FBh	B000h
FCh	C000h
FDh	D000h
FEh	E000h
FFh	F000h

As can be seen from the above table, fbForth assumes a 1024 KiB SAMS memory card, so **fbForth 2.0** is not compatible with 256 KiB AMS cards.

Lower RAM **2000h** – **3FFFh** is reserved by **fbForth 2.0** for four block buffers, low-level support, system variables and the return stack. Therefore, extreme care should be taken when paging banks **F8h** and **F9h** out of **2000h** and **3000h**, respectively. The same care should be taken with upper RAM when paging banks **FAh** and **FFh** out of **A000h** (start of User Dictionary) and **F000h** (TIB and base of parameter stack), respectively.

Because the RAM portion of the dictionary grows up from **A030h** and the parameter stack grows down from **FFA0h**, extreme care must be taken mapping SAMS memory if not using **S0&TIB!** . It is probably advisable to limit SAMS mapping to one or two 4 KiB window(s) at **F000h** and/or **E000h**. If **E000h** is used, the space available for the stack and user dictionary is ~16 KiB, down from the ~24 KiB available before moving the stack base.

>R Resident

(*n* ---) (R: --- *n*)

Removes a number from the parameter stack and place as the most accessible number on the return stack. Use should be balanced with **R>** in the same definition.

>RAD Resident

(f_1 --- f_2)

Converts an 8-byte floating point number f_1 from degrees to f_2 radians.

? Resident

(*addr* ---)

Prints the value contained at address *addr* in free format according to the current radix stored in **BASE** . This word is short for the two words, **@ .** .

?COMP Resident

(---)

This word is typically used in the definitions of compile-only words to insure the word containing it is being used in a definition. When **?COMP** is executed in other than compile mode, it displays the word just interpreted with a '?', issues the error message, "compilation only", clears the stack, echoes the word causing the error, leaves the contents of **IN** and **BLK** on the stack, if **LOAD**ing, and executes **QUIT** , *e.g.*,

```
9 0 DO I . LOOP  DO ? compilation only
```

Though **LOOP** is also a compile-only word, **DO** is the first one encountered and the one that triggers the above error.

?CSP Resident

(---)

This word is used in the definitions of **;** , **DOES>ASM:** and **DOES>CODE:** to insure that the stack position at the end of the definition is at the same height as when it was started with **:** , which stores the stack pointer in **CSP** . The error condition typically occurs with unbalanced conditionals. Whichever terminating word tested the stack height will be displayed followed by a '?' and "definition not finished", *e.g.*,

```
: XXXX IF ;  ; ? definition not finished
```

?ERROR Resident

(*flag n* ---)

Issues an error message corresponding to error number *n* if the Boolean flag is true. **?ERROR** is the word that all the error-checking words in **fbForth 2.0** execute to actually check for an error and to display the error message. It is defined as

```
: ?ERROR SWAP IF ERROR ELSE DROP THEN ;
```

?EXEC Resident

(---)

This word is used in the definitions of **:** , **CODE:** , **ASM:** and most of the words in the **ASSEMBLER** vocabulary to insure those words are executing and not being used in a definition. **?EXEC** issues the error message, "execution only", as in

: XXXX : … ; _: ?_ _execution only_

?FLERR Resident

(---)

Determines if the most recently executed floating-point (FP) operation resulted in an error. This word will give valid information any time before executing another FP operation clears the FP error location at **8354h**. **?FLERR** issues the error message, "floating point error", upon finding an error. The nature of the floating-point error may be ascertained by executing **FLERR** , *q.v.*, to get the FP error number and cross-referencing the code in the error table in § 7.14 "Floating Point Error Codes".

?KEY Resident

(--- *char*)

Scans the keyboard for input. If no key is pressed, a 0 is left on the stack. Otherwise, the 7-bit ASCII code of the key pressed is left on the stack.

?KEY8 Resident

(--- *n*)

Scans the keyboard for input. If no key is pressed, a 0 is left on the stack. Otherwise, the 8-bit code of the key pressed is left on the stack.

?LOADING Resident

(---)

This word is used in the definition of **-->** to insure that **fbForth 2.0** is loading from the current blocks file rather than executing on the command line. **?LOADING** issues error message, "use only when loading", if not loading as in

--> _--> ?_ _use only when loading_

?PAIRS Resident

(n_1 n_2 ---)

Issue the error message, "conditionals not paired", if n_1 does not equal n_2. The message indicates that compiled conditionals do not match, such as when a **DO** has been left without a **LOOP** , an **IF** has no corresponding **ENDIF** or **THEN** , *etc.*

?STACK Resident

(---)

INTERPRET uses **?STACK** to check whether the parameter stack is out of bounds after processing a word or number. If the top of the stack is lower than its base, "empty stack" will be displayed. If the stack has run into the output buffer at **PAD** in the other direction, "full stack" will be displayed. **?STACK** is defined as

```
: ?STACK
     SP@ S0 @ SWAP U< 1 ?ERROR
     SP@ HERE 128 + U< 7 ?ERROR ;
```

?TERMINAL Resident

(--- *flag*)

Scans the terminal keyboard for actuation of the break key (***<BREAK>***). A true flag indicates actuation. On the TI-99/4A, ***<FCTN+4>***, ***<BREAK>*** and ***<CLEAR>*** are all the same key.

@ Resident

(*addr* --- *n*)

Leave the 16-bit contents *n* of *addr*.

A$$M TMS9900 Assembler [21]

(---)

This word is compiled into the **FORTH** vocabulary and marks the end of the **ASSEMBLER** vocabulary. It is used by **CLOAD** to determine whether the TMS9900 Assembler has been loaded.

ABORT Resident

(---)

ABORT is **fbForth 2.0**'s warm start. It clears the stacks, sets both **CONTEXT** and **CURRENT** to the **FORTH** vocabulary, enters the execution state and, after printing "**fbForth 2.0**", executes **INTERPRET** to get user input from the terminal.

ABS Resident

(n_1 --- n_2)

Leaves the absolute value of n_1 as n_2.

AGAIN *[immediate word]* Resident

Used in a colon definition in the form:

BEGIN … AGAIN

COMPILE TIME: (*addr* 1 ---)

AGAIN compiles **BRANCH** with an offset from **HERE** to *addr*, which it copies to the space reserved for it at *addr*. The value 1 is used for compile-time error checking.

RUNTIME: (---)

AGAIN forces execution to return to the corresponding **BEGIN** . There is no effect on the stack. Execution cannot leave the loop unless **R> DROP** is executed one level below by some word in the loop.

ALIGN Resident

(---)

ALIGN insures that **HERE** is on an even address boundary. Use of **C,** is one way **HERE** can land on an odd address boundary. **CREATE** uses **ALIGN** before installing the header for a new word definition. Align is very similar to **=CELLS** except that it neither expects nor leaves anything on the stack.

ALLOT Resident

(*n* ---)

Adds the signed number *n* to the dictionary pointer **DP** , which moves **HERE** by *n* bytes. It has the effect of reserving *n* bytes of dictionary space if it is positive and moving **HERE** backwards to reclaim memory if it is negative (*be careful!*).

ALTIN Resident

(--- *addr*)

A user variable whose value is 0 if input is coming from the keyboard or a pointer to the VDP address where the PAB (Peripheral Access Block) for the alternate input device is located if its value is non-zero.

ALTOUT Resident

(--- *addr*)

A user variable whose value is 0, if output is going to the monitor, or a pointer to the VDP address where the PAB (Peripheral Access Block) for the alternate output device is located if its value is non-zero.

AND Resident

(n_1 n_2 --- n_3)

Leave the bitwise logical AND of n_1 and n_2 as n_3.

APPND Resident

(---)

Assigns the APPEND attribute to the file whose PAB (Peripheral Access Block) is pointed to by **PAB-ADDR** .

ASCII *[immediate word]* Resident

(--- *ascii*) (IS:*token*)

Leaves on the stack the ASCII value of the first character of the next token in the input stream:

ASCII G . <u>**71**</u> <u>**ok:0**</u>

ASM: Resident

(---) (IS: *<new word>* *<alc>* **;ASM**)

ASM: opens an **ASM: cccc … ;ASM** word definition that allows the programmer to write the body of the word in Assembly Language. To do so, requires the **fbForth 2.0** TMS9900 Assembler first be loaded from FBLOCKS. Typing **MENU** will reveal the block number to load the Assembler. It is used as follows:

ASM: *<new word>* *<assembly mnemonics>* **;ASM**

See Chapter 9 "The fbForth 2.0 TMS9900 Assembler" for more information. See also **;ASM** .

ASM>CODE ASM>CODE -- Code Output Utility

(---) (IS:*word DSKn.file*)

ASM>CODE appends to *DSKn.file* the hexadecimal machine code of a Forth word written in ALC (Assembly Language Code) in **CODE: *newword* … ;CODE** format, where '…' represents the machine code in text. This is useful for loading words defined in ALC without the need for loading the **fbForth** TMS9900 Assembler from FBLOCKS. *Please note that* **ASM>CODE** *should* not *be used for words in the resident dictionary because word entries in the resident dictionary are in an unconventional, non-contiguous format.*

ASM>CODE first checks to insure that *word* is a word defined in ALC. If it is not or it does not exist, **ASM>CODE** quits with an error message to that effect. If it is an ALC word, **ASM>CODE** attempts to open the file *DSKn.file* in Append mode. Failing that, *DSKn.file* is created and opened in Output mode.

As an example you might assemble the word **LDCR** , the ALC for which is listed in Appendix H "Assembly Source for CODEd Words", and then run the following code:

```
ASM>CODE LDCR DSK1.CRUWORDS
```

Examining the contents of DSK1.CRUWORDS would reveal the same code as shown in Block #5 of FBLOCKS (17JUN2016 and later).

If you are using the TI-99/4A emulator, *Classic99* (*www.HarmlessLion.com*), in Microsoft Windows, you can use the Windows clipboard as the file **CLIP** as follows:

```
ASM>CODE LDCR CLIP
```

See Chapter 9 "The fbForth 2.0 TMS9900 Assembler" in the manual for additional information.

ASSEMBLER *[immediate word]* Resident

(---)

The name of the **fbForth 2.0** Assembler vocabulary. Execution makes **ASSEMBLER** the **CONTEXT** vocabulary. Because **ASSEMBLER** is immediate, it will execute during the creation of a colon definition to select this vocabulary at compile time. See **VOCABULARY** .

ATN Resident

(f_1 --- f_2)

Calculates the arctangent in radians of f_1 leaving the floating point result f_2 on the stack.

B/BUF Resident

(--- 1024)

This constant leaves the number of bytes *n* per disk buffer (always 1024 in **fbForth 2.0**), the byte count read from the current blocks file by **BLOCK** . It is included for backward compatibility with TI Forth

B/SCR Resident

(--- 1)

This constant always leaves 1 on the stack. It is included for backward compatibility with TI Forth, where it is the number of blocks per editing screen. By convention, an editing screen is 1024 bytes organized as 16 lines of 64 characters each.

BACK Resident

(*addr* ---)

Calculates the backward branch offset from **HERE** to *addr* and compile into the next available dictionary memory address. Used by **LOOP** , **+LOOP** , **UNTIL** and **AGAIN** to calculate the distance back to the beginning of the loop.

BANK@ Resident

(*addr* n_1 --- n_2)

Returns on the stack the contents n_2 of the cell at address *addr* in bank n_1. If the bank number does not exist, the returned value will be from bank 0. If the address is in CPU RAM space, the returned value will be from there.

BANKC@ Resident

(*addr n* --- *b*)

Returns on the stack the contents *b* of the byte at address *addr* in bank *n*. See **BANK@** .

BASE Resident

(--- *addr*)

A user variable containing the current radix or number base used for input and output conversion.

BASE->R Resident

(---)

Places the current radix on the return stack. Caution must be exercised when using **BASE->R** and **R->BASE** with **CLOAD** as these will cause the return stack to be polluted if a **LOAD** is aborted and the **BASE->R** is not balanced by a **R->BASE** at execution time. See **R->BASE** .

BEEP Resident

(---)

Produces the sound associated with correct input or prompting.

BEGIN *[immediate word]* Resident

Occurs in a colon-definition in the form:

```
BEGIN … UNTIL or BEGIN … END
BEGIN … AGAIN
BEGIN … WHILE … REPEAT
```

COMPILE TIME: (--- *addr* 1)

BEGIN leaves its return address *addr* for branching calculation and storage by **UNTIL** , **END** , **AGAIN** and **REPEAT** and a 1 for compiler error checking.

RUNTIME: (---)

BEGIN marks the start of a sequence that may be repetitively executed. It serves as a return point from the corresponding **UNTIL** , **AGAIN** or **REPEAT** . When executing **UNTIL** , a return to **BEGIN** will occur if the top of the stack is false; for **AGAIN** and **REPEAT** a return to **BEGIN** always occurs.

BFLNAM Resident

(*flag* --- [ ] | *addr*)

Helper routine that gets a blocks filename from the input stream into PAD or HERE and passes a name pointer (*addr*) if *flag* is true (used on command line), but passes nothing if *flag* is false (*addr* is compiled by **SLIT** in a colon definition).

BL Resident

(--- *char*)

A constant that leaves the ASCII value 32 (**20h**) for "blank".

BLANKS Resident

(*addr count* ---)

Fills an area of memory beginning at *addr* with *count* blanks.

BLK Resident

(--- *addr*)

A user variable containing the block number being interpreted. If zero, input is being taken from the terminal input buffer.

BLKRW Resident

([*bfnaddr* | *#blks bfnaddr* | *bufaddr blk#*] *opcode* --- *flag*)

Blocks I/O utility routine called by **DO_BRW** . Addresses passed point to blocks file name (*bfnaddr*) and block RAM buffer (*bufaddr*). The number of items required on the stack depends on the opcode (passed by the corresponding command) as follows:

(*bfnaddr* -14 --- *flag*)	passed by **USEBFL**
(*#blks bfnaddr* -16 --- *flag*)	passed by **MKBFL**
(*bufaddr blk#* -18 --- *flag*)	passed by **RBLK**
(*bufaddr blk#* -20 --- *flag*)	passed by **WBLK**

BLOAD Resident

(*blk* --- *flag*)

Loads the binary image at *blk* which was created by **BSAVE** . **BLOAD** returns a true flag (1) if the load was not successful and a false flag (0) if the load was successful.

BLOCK Resident

(*n* --- *addr*)

Leaves the memory address of the block buffer containing block *n*. If the block is not already in memory, it is transferred from the current blocks file to whichever buffer was least recently written. If the block occupying that buffer has been marked as updated, it is written to the current blocks file before block *n* is read into the buffer. See also **BUFFER** , **R/W** , **UPDATE** and **FLUSH** .

BOOT Resident

(*n* | [ ]---)

This word's functionality has been changed from the original TI Forth functionality, which essentially was a continuation of **COLD** . It now simply restarts the system as though the user had just chosen the second or third option on the cartridge menu screen. It expects the default text mode *n* on the stack. The value *n* is forced to 0 or 1 for **TEXT80** or **TEXT** , respectively. **BOOT** may be executed with nothing on the stack, in which case **TEXT** is used.

A key may be held down to select the boot disk number or ***<ENTER>*** may be held down to prevent loading of FBLOCKS.

BPB Resident

(--- v*addr*)

Gets the offset in VRAM from the **fbForth 2.0** record buffer (in **DISK_BUF**) for blocks file PABs from user variable **3Eh**, adds the offset to the contents of **DISK_BUF** and pushes it to the stack.

BPOFF Resident

(--- v*addr*)

Pushes to stack the VRAM address v*addr* containing the offset of the current blocks file's PAB. This offset is used to manage blocks file PABs space, which has room for two PABs. This offset is toggled between 0 and 70 each time a new blocks file is made current.

BRANCH Resident

(---)

The runtime procedure to unconditionally branch. An in-line offset is added to the interpretive pointer (IP) to branch ahead or back. **BRANCH** is compiled by **ELSE** , **AGAIN** , **REPEAT** , and **ENDOF** .

BSAVE Resident

(*addr* blk_1 --- blk_2)

Places a binary image (starting at blk_1 and going as far as necessary) of all dictionary contents between *addr* and **HERE** . The next available Forth block number blk_2 is returned on the stack. **BSAVE** empties all block buffers before saving the image because the current blocks file may have changed. It is the user's responsibility to flush any dirty buffers before executing this command. Note that this is different behavior from TI Forth's **BSAVE** , which first flushes any dirty buffers. See **BLOAD** .

BUFFER Resident

(*n* --- *addr*)

Obtains the next memory buffer, assigning it to block *n*. If the contents of the buffer is marked as updated, it is written to the disk. The block is not read from the disk. The address left is the first cell within the buffer for data storage.

C! Resident

(*b addr* ---)

Stores the low-order byte (8 bits) of *b* (16-bit number on the stack) at *addr*.

C, Resident

(*b* ---)

Stores the low-order byte (8 bits) of *b* (16-bit number on the stack) into the next available dictionary byte (**HERE**), advancing the dictionary pointer one byte. This instruction should be used with caution on computers with byte-addressing, word-oriented CPUs such as the TMS9900. If **HERE** is left at an odd address and the next operation stores a cell at **HERE** , the last byte will be overwritten. See **=CELLS** .

C/L Resident

(--- *n*)

Returns on the stack the number of characters per line (stored in **C/L$**). The default value is 64 and usually represents the number of characters per line of a Forth block as it is edited (16 lines per 1024-byte block).

C/L$ Resident

(--- *addr*)

A user variable whose value is the number of characters per line. See **C/L** .

C@ Resident

(*addr* --- *b*)

Leaves the 8-bit contents *b* of memory address *addr* on the stack.

CASE *[immediate word]* Resident

Used in a colon definition to initiate the construct:

```
CASE
      n1 OF … ENDOF
      n2 OF … ENDOF
      …
      ELSEOF … ENDOF    <==This clause is optional.  See below.
ENDCASE
```

Compile time: (--- *csp* 4)

CASE gets the value *csp* of **CSP** to the stack for later restoration at the end of

ENDCASE 's compile-time activity. It stores the current stack position in **CSP** to help **ENDCASE** track how many **OF** clause branch distances to process. It finally pushes 4 to the stack for compile-time error checking by **OF** and **ENDCASE** .

RUNTIME: (*n* --- *n*)

CASE itself does nothing with the number *n* on the stack, but it must be there for **OF** , **ELSEOF** or **ENDCASE** to consume. If $n = n_1$, the code between the immediately following **OF** and **ENDOF** is executed. Execution then continues after **ENDCASE** . If *n* does not match any of the values preceding any **OF** , the code between the last **ENDOF** and **ENDCASE** is executed and may use *n*, but one cell *must* be left for **ENDCASE** to consume or a stack underflow will result. Execution then continues after **ENDCASE** .

Use of the optional **ELSEOF** obviates the necessity of putting any difficult-to-design default action between the last **ENDOF** and **ENDCASE** .

CAT CAT -- Disk Catalog Utility [58]

(*n* ---)

CAT catalogs to the output device the disk number *n* on the stack for the current DSR. **CAT** reads the VIB, FDIR and each file's FDR to get its information (see Appendix K "Diskette Format Details"). **CAT** will not load if **DIR** is loaded.

Usage: **2 CAT** to catalog DSK2.

CEIL Resident

(f_1 --- f_2)

Finds the least integer f_2 (in floating point format) not less than the floating point number f_1.

CELLS More Useful Stack Words etc. [41]

(*n* --- 2*n*)

Replace *n* (a number of cells) with 2*n* (the number of bytes in *n* cells).

CF? Compact Flash Utilities [69]

(--- *flag*)

Checks for the magic number, **AA03h**, at VRAM address, **3FF8h**, where the nanoPEB or CF7+ DSR places it. It leaves a true flag (1) if found and a false flag (0) if not.

CFA Resident

(*pfa* --- *cfa*)

Converts the parameter field address *pfa* of a definition to its code field address *cfa* .

CFMOUNT Compact Flash Utilities [69]

(*vol#* *dsk#* ---)

Mounts the volume *vol#* in the virtual disk *dsk#*. The following entry will mount volume #234 in DSK2:

```
234 2 CFMOUNT
```

The volumes mounted by **CFMOUNT** will persist only through the current session of **fbForth 2.0**. This includes cycling through **COLD** and **BOOT** . A reset to the TI-99/4A title screen will mount the three volumes stored in the CF card before **fbForth 2.0** was started. As you can see, you will need to use some other means to write the volume mounts to the CF card. The following permanent mounting methods are available:

- CALL MOUNT(*vol# dsk#*)—TI Basic command, available when a nanoPEB or CF7+ is attached to the TI-99/4A;
- CFMGR—TI-99/4A program supplied with the nanoPEB or CF7+;
- CF2K—TI-99/4A program by Fred Kaal (*www.ti99-geek.nl*);
- TI99Dir.exe—PC program by Fred Kaal (*www.ti99-geek.nl*).

CFVOLS Compact Flash Utilities [69]

(--- *volDSK1 volDSK2 volDSK3*)

Leaves on the stack the volume numbers associated with DSK1, DSK2 and DSK3.

CHAR Resident

(n_1 n_2 n_3 n_4 *char* ---)

Defines character # *char* to have the pattern specified by the 4 numbers (n_1, n_2, n_3, n_4) on the stack. The definition for character #0 by default resides at **800h**. Each character definition is 8 bytes long with each number on the stack representing two bytes.

CHARPAT Resident

(*char* --- n_1 n_2 n_3 n_4)

Places the 4-cell (8-byte) pattern of a specified character *char* on the stack. By default, the definition for character #0 resides at **800h**.

CLEAR Resident

(*blk* ---)

Gets a block buffer for block# *blk*, fills it with blanks and marks it as updated.

CLEN$ Stack-based String Library [42]

(*$Caddr* --- *len*) "string constant length"

Given the address of a string constant on the data stack the word **CLEN$** returns its actual length on the data stack. For example,

```
50 $CONST WELCOME  ok:0
WELCOME :=" Hello and welcome!"  ok:0
WELCOME CLEN$ . 18  ok:0
```

CLINE 64-Column Editor [6] Compact List [13]

(*addr count n* ---)

Prints one line of tiny characters on the display screen. **CLINE** expects on the stack the address *addr* of the line to be written in memory, the number of characters *count* in that line, and the line number *n* on which it is to be written on the display screen. **CLINE** calls **SMASH** to do the actual work. See **SMASH** and **CLIST** .

CLIST 64-Column Editor [6] Compact List [13]

(*blk* ---)

Lists the specified Forth block in tiny characters to the monitor. **CLIST** executes 16 calls to **CLINE** for the requisite 16 lines. See **CLINE** and **TCHAR** .

CLOAD *[immediate word]* Resident

(*blk* ---) (IS: <*check word*>)

Used in the form:

```
blk CLOAD WWWW
```

CLOAD will load Forth block *blk* only if the word **WWWW** is not in the **CONTEXT** vocabulary. **WWWW** should be the last word loaded when the series of blocks beginning with *blk* is loaded. A block number of 0 (*blk* = 0) will suppress loading of the current Forth block if the specified word has already been compiled.

CLR_BLKS Resident

(blk_1 blk_2 ---)

CLR_BLKS will **CLEAR** a range of blocks to blanks in the current blocks file. The blocks will be marked as updated (see **CLEAR**).

CLS Resident

(---)

Clears the display screen by filling the screen image table with blanks. The screen image table runs from **SCRN_START** to **SCRN_END** .

CLSE Resident

(---)

Closes the file whose PAB (Peripheral Access Block) is pointed to by **PAB-ADDR** .

CMOVE Resident

($addr_1$ $addr_2$ *count* ---)

Moves *count* number of bytes from $addr_1$ to $addr_2$. The contents of $addr_1$ is moved first, proceeding toward high memory. This is ***not*** overlap safe for $addr_1 < addr_2$.

CMP$ Stack-based String Library [42]

(--- -1|0|+1) (SS: str_1 str_2 --- str_1 str_2) "compare strings"

The word **CMP$** performs a case-sensitive comparison of the topmost two strings on the string stack and returns -1 if $str_1 < str_2$, 0 if $str_1 = str_2$ and +1 if $str_1 > str_2$. The strings are retained. For example,

```
$" hello" $" HELLO" CMP$ . 1  ok:0
$" hello" $" hello" CMP$ . 0  ok:0
$" hell" $" hello" CMP$ . -1  ok:0
```

A case insensitive comparison can easily be built as follows:

: CMPCI$ (--- *flag*) (SS: str_1 str_2 --- str_1 str_2)
OVER$ OVER$ UCASE$ SWAP$
UCASE$ CMP$ DROP$ DROP$;

The above code creates copies of str_1 and str_2 (using **OVER$**) then converts them both to upper case. **CMP$** then compares the strings placing the appropriate flag on the data stack. Finally, the uppercase versions of str_1 and str_2 are removed from the string stack. Thus, str_1 and str_2 are retained, unchanged.

CODE *(deprecated TI Forth word)* Resident

(---)

CODE has been maintained for TI Forth compatibility. It has been deprecated in favor of **ASM:** and **CODE:** , *q.v.* See Chapter 9 "The fbForth 2.0 TMS9900 Assembler" for details.

CODE: *[immediate word]* Resident

(---) (IS: *<newword>* [*<mc>* ...] **;CODE**)

CODE: opens a **CODE: cccc … ;CODE** word definition that converts numbers in the IS and compiles them before the interpreter sees them, obviating the necessity of using the **,** required by **CODE** in TI Forth. It is also faster. **N>S** , *q.v.*, has been provided to push numbers from the IS to the stack for necessary calculations. See Chapter 9 "The fbForth 2.0 TMS9900 Assembler" for more information.

COINC Resident

(spr_1 spr_2 *tol* --- *flag*)

Detects a coincidence between two given sprites within a specified tolerance of *tol* dot positions. A true flag indicates a coincidence.

COINCALL Resident

(--- *flag*)

Detects a coincidence between the visible portions of any two sprites on the display screen. A true flag indicates a coincidence, but not which sprites.

COINCXY Resident

(*dotcol dotrow spr tol* --- *flag*)

Detects a coincidence between a specified sprite and a given point (*dotcol*,*dotrow*) within a given tolerance of *tol* dot positions. A true flag indicates a coincidence.

COLD Resident

(---)

COLD is the cold-start procedure that may be called from the terminal to remove application programs and to restart **fbForth 2.0**. It is also the last routine executed by the **fbForth 2.0** startup code. Formerly, it was a high-level Forth word that called another high-level Forth word (**BOOT**) at its conclusion. They have both been combined into a single ALC routine that (re-)sets the Forth environment to the default startup conditions.

In restarting **fbForth 2.0**, **COLD** resets user variables to their startup values, including the dictionary pointer (to point to just after the resident dictionary), resets the current blocks file to the default DSK*n*.FBLOCKS (*n* is the boot disk number), loads block #1 and executes **ABORT** , *q.v.*

COLD may be called from the terminal to remove application programs and to restart **fbForth 2.0**.

See § 1.7.4 "Changes to COLD" for more detail.

COLOR Resident

(n_1 n_2 n_3 ---)

Causes a specified character set n_3 to have the given foreground color n_1 and background color n_2.

COLTAB Resident

(--- *vaddr*)

A constant whose value is the beginning VDP address of the color table. The default value is **380h**. This constant can only be changed via user variable number **22h**.

COMPILE Resident

(---) (IS: <*word*>)

COMPILE is a compile-only word that will execute when its containing word executes, which means that its containing word must be a compile-only word that executes during compilation, *i.e.*, an immediate word. This effectively defers compilation of the word following **COMPILE** until the word containing them is executed within the definition of yet another word.

When the word containing **COMPILE** executes during the compilation of a new word, the execution address *cfa* of the word following **COMPILE** is copied (compiled) into the dictionary entry for the new word's definition. For example,

```
: WORD1 … COMPILE WORD0 … ;   IMMEDIATE
: WORD2 WORD1 … ;
```

When **WORD2** is compiled, **WORD1** executes, which executes **COMPILE** to place the *cfa* of **WORD0** into the definition of **WORD2** .

CONSTANT Resident

(*n* ---) (IS: <*new name*>)

A defining word used in the form:

***n* CONSTANT cccc**

to create word **cccc** , with its parameter field containing *n*. When **cccc** is later executed, it will invoke **CONSTANT** 's execution procedure to push the value of *n* to the stack.

CONTEXT Resident

(--- *addr*)

A user variable containing a pointer to the vocabulary within which dictionary searches will first begin.

COS Resident

(f_1 --- f_2)

Calculates the cosine of f_1 radians and leaves the floating point result f_2 on the stack.

COUNT Resident

($addr_1$ --- $addr_2$ b)

Leave the byte address $addr_2$ and byte count *b* of the packed character string (see footnote 5 on page 22) beginning at $addr_1$. It is presumed that the first byte at $addr_1$ contains the character count *b* and that the actual text starts with the second byte. Typically, **COUNT** is followed by **TYPE** .

CPYBLK CPYBLK -- Block Copying Utility [4]

(---)

Copy a range of blocks from one blocks file to the same or a different blocks file. The destination file must already exist. The copy is overlap safe for same file copies. The source blocks copied are enumerated during the copy.

Usage:

CPYBLK ***src_start src_end src-file dst_start dst-file*** ,

where ***src_start*** and ***src_end*** are source start and end block numbers, ***src-file*** is the source blocks file, ***dst_start*** is the destination start block number and ***dst-file*** is the destination blocks file.

Example:

```
CPYBLK 4 10 DSK1.FBLOCKS 25 DSK2.MYBLOCKS
4 5 6 7 8 9 10  ok:0
```

will copy blocks 4 – 10 from DSK1.FBLOCKS to DSK2.MYBLOCKS, starting at block 25.

CR Resident

(---)

Transmit a carriage return and a line feed to the current output device.

CREATE Resident

(---)

A defining word used in the form:

CREATE cccc

by such words as **:** , **<BUILDS** , **ASM:** and **CODE:** to create a dictionary header for a Forth definition. The code field contains the address of the word's parameter field.

Space for the parameter field is ***not*** reserved by **CREATE** . The new word is created in the **CURRENT** vocabulary. **CREATE** limits new word names to 31 characters in length in **fbForth 2.0** by ANDing the count byte with 31. The reason for this is that the three leftmost bits of the count byte are control bits (see Chapter 12 "fbForth 2.0 Dictionary Entry Structure"), which leaves only 5 bits for the character count.

CSP Resident

(--- *addr*)

A user variable temporarily storing the stack pointer position for compilation error checking.

CURPOS Resident

(--- *addr*)

A user variable that stores the current VDP (Visual Display Processor) screen cursor position.

CURRENT Resident

(--- *addr*)

A user variable pointing to the vocabulary into which new definitions will be compiled. **DEFINITIONS** will store the contents of **CONTEXT** into **CURRENT** . At system startup, **CURRENT** points to the **FORTH** vocabulary.

D+ Resident

(d_1 d_2 --- d_3)

Leave the double number sum of two double numbers ($d_3 = d_1 + d_2$).

D+- Resident

(d_1 *n* --- d_2)

Negate double number d_1 if the sign of *n* is negative, leaving the result as d_2.

D. Resident

(*d* ---)

Print a signed double number from a 32-bit two's complement value *d*. The high-order 16 bits are most accessible on the stack. Conversion is performed according to the current radix in **BASE** . A blank follows. Pronounced "d dot".

D.R Resident

(*d n* ---)

Print a signed double number *d* right-aligned in a field *n* characters wide.

DABS Resident

(d_1 --- d_2)

Leave the absolute value d_2 of a double number d_1.

DATA[*[immediate word]* Resident

(--- *addr n*) (IS:n_1 ... n_n)

DATA[opens a **DATA[…]DATA** construct that compiles numbers and leaves their beginning address *addr* and cell count *n* on the stack. If compiling within another definition, **DATA[** compiles **DATA[]** and cell count *n* in front of the array.

DATA[] Resident

(--- *addr n*)

Runtime routine compiled by **DATA[** to push to the stack the address *addr* and number of cells *n* of the number array that follows it in a word definition.

DCHAR Resident

(*addr cnt chr* ---)

DCHAR is similar to "CALL CHAR" in TI Extended Basic, but is not limited to 4 characters. It is similar to **CHAR** , but uses an array of numbers instead of the stack for pattern definition. It is used to define one or more characters starting at the pattern address of character *chr.* **DCHAR** moves *cnt* cells from address *addr* to the pattern address of character *chr* in VRAM.

DCOLOR Resident

(--- *addr*)

A variable which contains the dot-color information used by **DOT** . Its value may be a two-digit hexadecimal number that will be used to set the foreground and background color or -1 to signal that no color information is to be changed.

DCT Resident

(--- *addr*)

A constant that pushes to the stack the address *addr* of the Default Colors Table for all VDP modes. It also gives the user access to the default text mode because it immediately follows the table.

VDP Mode	Table Offset (bytes)	Screen/ Text Colors	Color Table Colors
TEXT80	0	4Fh	00h
TEXT	2	4Fh	00h
GRAPHICS	4	F4h	F4h
MULTI	6	11h	F4h
GRAPHICS2	8	FEh	10h
SPLIT	10	FEh	F4h
SPLIT2	12	FEh	F4h

Default Text Mode	Table Offset (bytes)	VDP Mode
TEXT	14	0001h

All changes to the above values will survive execution of **COLD** .

DECIMAL Resident

(---)

Set the radix in **BASE** for decimal input/output.

DEFBF Resident

(--- *addr*)

Gets the address *addr* of the default blocks filename (DSK1.FBLOCKS) in low RAM to the stack. This address points to the string-length byte and can be displayed by

```
COUNT TYPE
```

If the boot disk is other than DSK1, that will be reflected in the name displayed by the above Forth code.

DEFINITIONS Resident

(---)

Sets the **CURRENT** vocabulary to the **CONTEXT** vocabulary by copying the contents of **CONTEXT** to **CURRENT**. Executing a vocabulary name makes it the **CONTEXT** vocabulary and executing **DEFINITIONS** makes both specify the same vocabulary. The following example will make both **CONTEXT** and **CURRENT** point to the **FORTH** vocabulary, which is the system default:

```
FORTH DEFINITIONS  ok:0
```

DEG/RAD Resident

(--- *f*)

Constant in floating point format representing degrees/radian = 57.295779513082.

DELALL Resident

(---)

Delete all sprites. **DELALL** stops sprite motion, fills the sprite motion table with zeroes and stores **D0h** in the *y* position of all 32 sprites to leave them in an undefined state. **DELALL** does nothing to the sprite descriptor table. See § 6.6.2 for details.

DELALL must be used to initialize sprites after changing to the desired VDP mode.

DELSPR Resident

(*spr* ---)

Delete the specified sprite by positioning it off-screen at $x = 1$, $y = 192$; setting it to sprite pattern #0; and clearing its motion table entries.

DEPTH Resident

(--- *n*)

Return the number of cells on the parameter stack. This word is used by the new command-line (**ok:*n***) response, where ***n*** indicates stack depth.

DEPTH$ Stack-based String Library [42]

(--- *n*) (SS: ---)

Returns the current depth *n* of the string stack, with 0 meaning the string stack is empty.

DIGIT Resident

(*char* n_1 --- *false* | n_2 *true*)

Convert the ASCII character *char* (using number base n_1) to its binary equivalent n_2, accompanied by a true flag. If the conversion is invalid, leave only a false flag. For example, " **DECIMAL 53 10 DIGIT** " will leave " **5 1** " on the stack because 53 is the ASCII code for '5' and is a legitimate digit in base 10. On the other hand, " **DECIMAL 74 16 DIGIT** " will leave only " **0** "on the stack because 74 is the ASCII code for 'J' and is *not* a legitimate digit in base 16. However, **" DECIMAL 74 20 DIGIT "** will leave **" 19 1 "** on the stack because 'J' *is* a legitimate digit in base 20.

DIR DIR--Disk Catalog Utility [36]

(---)

DIR catalogs to the output device the disk device name that follows it in the input stream. The disk device name must be terminated with a period. **DIR** gets its information from the DSR's catalog "file". **DIR** will not load if **CAT** is loaded.

Usage: **DIR DSK1.**

DISK_BUF Resident

(--- *addr*)

A user variable that points to the first byte in VDP RAM of the 128-byte **fbForth 2.0** record buffer.

DKB+ Resident

(*n* ---)

Defining word used to create words that calculate addresses from user variables containing offsets from **fbForth 2.0**'s VRAM record buffer. Execution of the defined word pushes to the stack an address calculated by adding the record buffer address to the offset passed in the user variable, the user-variable-table offset of which is the parameter field value *n* passed to **DKB+** .

Usage: ***userVarOffset*** **DKB+** ***new_word***

DLITERAL *[immediate word]* Resident

Compile time: (*d* ---) Runtime: (--- *d*) Interpreting: (---)

Same behavior as **LITERAL**, *q.v.*, except for a double number *d*

DLT Resident

(---)

The file I/O routine that deletes the file whose PAB (Peripheral Access Block) is pointed to by **PAB-ADDR** .

DMINUS Resident

(d_1 --- d_2)

Convert d_1 to its double number two's complement d_2, *i.e.*, $d_2 = -d_1$.

DMODE Resident

(--- *addr*)

A variable that determines which dot mode is currently in effect. A **DMODE** value of 0 indicates DRAW mode, a value of 1 indicates UNDRAW mode and a value of 2 indicates DOT-TOGGLE mode. This variable is set by the **DRAW** , **UNDRAW** and **DTOG** words.

DO *[immediate word]* Resident

Occurs in a colon-definition in the form:

```
DO … LOOP
DO … +LOOP
```

COMPILE TIME: (--- *addr* 3)

When compiling within the colon-definition, **DO** compiles **(DO)** , leaving the following address *addr* and the value 3 for later error checking by the compile-time action of **LOOP** or **+LOOP** .

RUNTIME: (*lim strt* ---)

DO begins a sequence with repetitive execution controlled by a loop limit *lim* and an index with initial value *strt*. **DO** removes these from the stack and puts them on the return stack, with the index on top. Upon reaching **LOOP** , the index is incremented by one. Until the new index equals or exceeds the limit, execution loops back to just after **DO** , otherwise the loop parameters are discarded and execution continues ahead. Both *lim* and *strt* are determined at runtime and may be the result of other operations. Within a loop, **I** will copy the current value of the index to the stack. See **I** , **LOOP** , **+LOOP** and **LEAVE** .

DOES> *[immediate word]* Resident

(---)

A word which defines the runtime action within a high-level defining word. **DOES>** alters the code field and first parameter of the new word to execute the sequence of compiled word addresses following **DOES>** . It is always used in combination with **<BUILDS** . When the **DOES>** part executes it begins with the address of the first parameter of the new word on the stack. This allows interpretation using this area or its contents. Typical uses include the Forth assembler, multidimensional arrays and compiler generation.

DOES>ASM: *[immediate word]* Resident

(---) (IS: [<*alc*>] **;ASM**)

DOES>ASM: has the same function as **DOES>** , *q.v.*, for defining the runtime action within a high-level defining word, except that its runtime action is defined using Assembly Language Code (ALC) rather than high-level Forth code. **DOES>ASM:** must be paired with **;ASM** to enclose the ALC:

```
: cccc <BUILDS … DOES>ASM: … ;ASM
```

See Chapter 9 “The fbForth 2.0 TMS9900 Assembler” for more information.

DOES>CODE: *[immediate word]* Resident

(---) (IS: [<*mc*>] **;CODE**)

This is the machine-code (MC) version of **DOES>ASM:** , *q.v.* It must be paired with **;CODE** to enclose the MC:

```
: cccc <BUILDS … DOES>CODE: … ;CODE
```

DOES>CODE: compiles any numbers it finds in the IS by jumping into **CODE:** , *q.v.*, to compile the MC. Just as with **CODE:** , use **N>S** , *q.v.*, to push numbers to the stack for necessary calculations. See Chapter 9 "The fbForth 2.0 TMS9900 Assembler" for more information.

DOT Resident

(*dotcol dotrow* ---)

In bitmap graphics, plots a dot at (*dotcol,dotrow*) in whatever mode is selected by **DMODE** and in whatever color is selected by **DCOLOR** .

DO_BRW Resident

([*bfnaddr* | *#blks bfnaddr* | *bufaddr blk#*] *opcode* ---)

Helper routine that executes **BLKRW** and processes returned flag. See **BLKRW** for items required on stack for each opcode and for an explanation of the stack effects abbreviations.

DP Resident

(--- *addr*)

A user variable, the dictionary pointer, which contains the address of the next free memory above the dictionary. The value may be read by **HERE** and altered by **,** and **ALLOT** , among other words.

DPL Resident

(--- *addr*)

A user variable containing the number of digits to the right of the decimal point on double integer input. It may also be used to hold output column location of a decimal point in user-generated formatting. The default value on single number input is -1 for no decimal point. **DPL** is updated for every double number input.

DRAW Resident

(---)

Sets **DMODE** equal to 0. This means that dots are plotted in the 'on' state.

DROP Resident

(*n* ---)

Drop the top number from the stack.

DROP$ Stack-based String Library [42]

(---) (SS: *str* ---) "drop string"

The word **DROP$** removes the topmost string item from the string stack. For example,

```
$" Hello, World!"  ok:0
$" How are you?"  ok:0
DROP$  ok:0
```

At this point the string "Hello, World!" is the topmost string the string stack. "How are you?" was pushed onto the string stack, but it was immediately dropped.

DSPLY Resident

(---)

Assigns the attribute DISPLAY to the file pointed to by **PAB-ADDR** .

DSRLNK Resident

(---)

Links an **fbForth 2.0** program to any Device Service Routine (DSR) in ROM. Before this instruction may be used, a PAB must be set up in VDP RAM and a pointer to PAB + 9 stored at **8356h**. See the *Editor/Assembler Manual* and Chapter 8 of this manual for additional setup information. This word automatically passes 8 to the DSR to execute DSR routines. It cannot execute DSR subprograms that require passing 10.

DTOG Resident

(---)

Sets **DMODE** equal to 2. This means that each dot plotted takes on the opposite state as the dot currently at that location.

DUMP Memory Dump Utility [16]

(*addr n* ---)

Print the contents of *n* memory locations beginning at *addr*. Both addresses and contents are shown in hexadecimal notation. **DUMP** is 80-column-text-mode aware if your computer is so equipped. See **PAUSE** .

DUP Resident

(*n* --- *n n*)

Duplicates the value on top of the stack.

DUP$ Stack-based String Library [42]

(---) (SS: str_1 --- str_1 str_1) "duplicate string"

The word **DUP$** duplicates the top item on the string stack. For example,

```
$" Hello, World!" DUP$  ok:0
```

DXY Resident

($dotcol_1$ $dotrow_1$ $dotcol_2$ $dotrow_2$ --- n_1 n_2)

Places on the stack the square of the ***x*** distance n_1 and the square of the ***y*** distance n_2 between the points ($dotcol_1$,$dotrow_1$) and ($dotcol_2$,$dotrow_2$).

ECOUNT Resident

(--- *addr*)

A user variable that contains an error count. This is used to prevent error recursion.

ED@ Resident

(---)

Brings you back into the 40/80-column editor on the last **fbForth 2.0** block you edited. This block is pointed to by **SCR** . Must be in Text or Text80 mode.

ED@ (*EDITOR2 Vocabulary*) 64-Column Editor [6]

(---)

Brings you back into the 64-column editor on the last **fbForth 2.0** block you edited. This block is pointed to by **SCR** .

EDIT Resident

(*blk* ---)

Brings you into the 40/80-column editor on the specified **fbForth 2.0** block, loading it from the current blocks file if necessary. Must be in Text or Text80 mode.

EDIT (*EDITOR2 Vocabulary*) 64-Column Editor [6]

(*blk* ---)

Brings you into the 64-column editor on the specified **fbForth 2.0** block, loading it from the current blocks file if necessary.

ELSE *[immediate word]* Resident

Occurs within a colon-definition in the form:

IF … ELSE … ENDIF

COMPILE TIME: ($addr_1$ 2 --- $addr_2$ 2)

ELSE emplaces **BRANCH** , reserving a branch offset and leaves the address $addr_2$ and 2 for error testing because the incoming '2' is consumed for error checking. **ELSE** also resolves the pending forward branch from **IF** by calculating the offset from $addr_1$ to **HERE** and storing it at $addr_1$.

RUNTIME: (---)

ELSE executes after the true part following **IF** . **ELSE** forces execution to skip over the following false part and resume execution after **ENDIF** . It has no stack effect.

ELSEOF *[immediate word]* Resident

ELSEOF is the start of the catchall default **ELSEOF … ENDOF** clause that occurs inside a colon definition as the optional default clause within the **CASE … ENDCASE** construct, just before **ENDCASE** . If execution reaches **ELSEOF** , the words between **ELSEOF** and **ENDOF** will always be executed. There should be no value preceding **ELSEOF** because the runtime stack value will be duplicated in its place to force a match by the compiled **(OF)** .

Use of the **ELSEOF** clause guarantees that **ENDCASE** will never execute. It is a lot easier to use an **ELSEOF** clause instead of trying to contrive a default action ahead of **ENDCASE** . Compare with a description of just such a default action at **CASE** .

COMPILE TIME: (4 --- *addr* 5)

Checks for the value 4 on the stack left there by **CASE** or a previous **ENDOF** , compiles **DUP** to force runtime comparison of the value on the stack with itself (guaranteeing a match), compiles **(OF)** , leaves its address *addr* for branching resolution by **ENDOF** and leaves a 5 for its matching **ENDOF** to check.

RUNTIME: (*n n* ---)

Duplicates the value *n*, which was on top of the stack when **CASE** 's runtime action occurred. Comparison of the two identical numbers forces execution of the words between **ELSEOF** and **ENDOF** . See **CASE** and **ENDOF** .

EMIT Resident

(*char* ---)

Transmit 7-bit ASCII character *char* to the current output device. **OUT** , *q.v.*, is incremented for each character output.

EMIT8 Resident

(*char* ---)

Transmit an 8-bit character *char* to the current output device. **OUT** , *q.v.*, is incremented for each character output.

EMPTY-BUFFERS Resident

(---)

Mark all block buffers as empty, not necessarily affecting the contents. Updated blocks are not written to the current blocks file. This is also an initialization procedure executed by **COLD** , *q.v.*, before first use of the default blocks file.

ENCLOSE Resident

($addr_1$ *char* --- $addr_1$ n_1 n_2 n_3)

The text scanning primitive used by **WORD** . From the text address $addr_1$ and an ASCII-delimiting character *char*, is determined the byte offset n_1 to the first non-delimiter character, the offset n_2 to the delimiter after the text and the offset n_3 to the first character not included, *i.e.*, the character about to be read. This procedure will not process past an ASCII NUL (0), treating it as an unconditional parsing terminator.

WORD uses the output from **ENCLOSE** to advance **IN** by n_3 and calculate the parsed word's length as $n_2 - n_1$ for use in constructing the packed character string (see footnote 5 on page 22) for the word, which **WORD** copies to **HERE** .

If we let each '{}' represent one character; each character is either a non-delimiter character, 'chr', a delimiter character, 'delim', or the null character, '0', **ENCLOSE** allows three possible parsing scenarios after leading delimiter characters are skipped:

1) $n_1 n_3 \{0\} n_2$

2) $n_1 \{chr\} \ldots \{chr\} n_2 n_3 \{0\}$

3) $n_1 \{chr\} \ldots \{chr\} n_2 \{delim\} n_3 \{chr \mid 0\} \ldots$

The offsets, n_1, n_2 and n_3 are shown above in the positions they indicate when returned on the stack by **ENCLOSE** . Where they are shown next to each other, they, in fact, have the same value. One thing to keep in mind is that n_3 will never point to the position after an ASCII 0.

Scenario (1) above is important because it is the only way that **INTERPRET** , otherwise an infinite loop, can be forced to exit. The null character will be parsed as a single-character word that will be found in the dictionary and executed by **INTERPRET** , causing **INTERPRET** 's demise.

END *[immediate word]* Resident

COMPILE TIME: (*addr* 1 ---) RUNTIME: (*flag* ---)

This is an alias or duplicate definition for **UNTIL** . See **UNTIL** for details.

ENDCASE *[immediate word]* Resident

Occurs in a colon definition as the termination of the **CASE … ENDCASE** construct.

COMPILE TIME: (*csp* $addr_1$ … $addr_n$ 4 ---)

It uses the 4 for compile-time error checking. It uses the value in **CSP** put there by **CASE** to track the number of **OF** clauses for which it must calculate branch distances from the addresses ($addr_1$ … $addr_n$) that each **ENDOF** left on the stack.

RUNTIME: (*n* ---)

If all **OF** clauses fail, any code after the last **ENDOF** , including **ENDCASE** , will execute. **ENDCASE** will remove the number *n* left on the stack by the failure of the last **OF** clause.

If you include code between the last **ENDOF** and **ENDCASE** , it must leave at least one number on the stack for **ENDCASE** to consume to prevent stack underflow. See **CASE** .

A better default action is to use an **ELSEOF** clause (with no preceding value) as the last clause before **ENDCASE** . See **ELSEOF** for more information.

ENDIF *[immediate word]* Resident

Occurs in a colon-definition in the form:

IF … ENDIF (also **IF … THEN**)
IF … ELSE … ENDIF (also **IF … ELSE … THEN**)

COMPILE TIME: (*addr* 2 ---)

ENDIF computes the forward branch offset from *addr* to **HERE** and stores it at the spot reserved for it at *addr*. The value 2 is used for error testing.

RUNTIME: (---)

ENDIF serves only as the destination of a forward branch from **IF** or **ELSE** . It marks the conclusion of the conditional structure. **THEN** is another name for **ENDIF** . Both names are supported in fig-Forth. See also **IF** and **ELSE** .

ENDOF *[immediate word]* Resident

Occurs in a colon definition as the termination of the **OF ... ENDOF** construct within the **CASE ... ENDCASE** construct.

COMPILE TIME: ($addr_1$ 5 --- $addr_2$ 4)

ENDOF checks for a 5 on the stack. It then compiles **BRANCH** , leaves its address $addr_2$ for processing by **ENDCASE** . It next leaves 4 on the stack for compile-time error checking by the next **OF** or **ENDCASE** . It finally calculates the forward branch offset from $addr_1$ to **HERE** for its matching **OF** and stores the value at the spot reserved for it at $addr_1$.

RUNTIME: (---)

ENDOF causes execution to proceed after **ENDCASE** . See **OF** .

ERASE Resident

(*addr n* ---)

Clear *n* bytes of memory to zero starting at *addr*.

ERROR Resident

(n_1 --- n_2 n_3 | [ ])

ERROR processes error notification and restarts the interpreter. **WARNING** is first examined. If **WARNING** < 0, **(ABORT)** , *q.v.*, is executed. The sole action of **(ABORT)** is to execute **ABORT** . This allows the user to (*cautiously*!) modify this behavior by replacing the *cfa* of **(ABORT)** with the *cfa* of the user's error procedure. **ABORT** clears the stacks and executes **QUIT** , which stops compilation and restarts the interpreter.

If **WARNING** ≥ 0, **ERROR** clears **ECOUNT** and the parameter stack. Then, if the input stream is coming from the loading of blocks and not the terminal, **ERROR** leaves the contents of **IN** n_2 and **BLK** n_3 on the stack to assist in determining the location of the error. Execution of **WHERE** , at this point, will open the offending block in the editor and place the cursor at the text immediately following the token that caused the error.

If **WARNING** > 0, **ERROR** prints the error text of system message number n_1. If **WARNING** = 0, **ERROR** prints n_1 as an error number (This was used in TI Forth in a non-disk installation, but this is unnecessary in **fbForth 2.0** because the system messages are always present in cartridge ROM). The last thing **ERROR** does is to execute **QUIT** , which, as above, stops compilation and restarts the interpreter.

EXECUTE Resident

(*cfa* ---)

Execute the definition whose code field address is on the stack. The code field address is also called the compilation address.

EXIT *[immediate word]* More Useful Stack Words etc. [41]

(---)

EXIT is a synonym for **;S** , which stops interpretation of a Forth block or ends the current word's execution and returns to the calling procedure.

EXP Resident

(f_1 --- f_2)

Raises ***e*** to the power specified by the floating point number f_1 on the stack and leaves the result f_2 on the stack.

EXPECT Resident

(*addr count* ---)

Transfer characters from the terminal to *addr* until ***<ENTER>*** or *count* characters have been received. The character count is not stored with the string. One or more nulls are added at the end of the text.

F! Resident

(*f addr* ---)

Stores a floating point number *f* into the 4 words (cells) beginning with the specified address.

F* Resident

($f_1 f_2$ --- f_3)

Multiplies the top two floating point numbers on the stack and leaves the result on the stack. $f_1 * f_2 = f_3$.

F+ Resident

($f_1 f_2$ --- f_3)

Adds the top two floating point numbers on the stack and places the result on the stack. $f_1 * f_2 = f_3$.

F– Resident

($f_1 f_2$ --- f_3)

Subtracts f_2 from f_1 and places the result on the stack ($f_1 - f_2 = f_3$).

F->S Resident

(*f* --- *n*)

Converts a floating point number *f* on the parameter stack into a single precision number *n*.

F-D" *[immediate word]* Resident

(---) (IS: *filename*")

Expects a file descriptor ending with a " to follow. This instruction places the file descriptor in the PAB (Peripheral Access Block) pointed to by **PAB-ADDR** .

F. Resident

(*f* ---)

Prints a floating point number *f* in TI Basic format to the output device.

F/ Resident

($f_1 f_2$ --- f_3)

Divides f_1 by f_2 and leaves the floating point quotient f_3 on the stack. $f_1 / f_2 = f_3$.

F0< Resident

(*f* --- *flag*)

Compares the floating point number *f* on the stack to 0. If it is less than 0, a true flag is left on the stack, else a false flag is left.

F0= Resident

(*f* --- *flag*)

Compares the floating point number *f* on the stack to 0. If it is equal to 0, a true flag is left on the stack, else a false flag is left.

F< Resident

($f_1 f_2$ --- *flag*)

Leaves a true flag if $f_1 < f_2$, else leaves a false flag.

F= Resident

($f_1 f_2$ --- *flag*)

Leaves a true flag if $f_1 = f_2$, else leaves a false flag.

F> Resident

($f_1 f_2$ --- *flag*)

Leaves a flag if $f_1 > f_2$, else leaves a false flag.

F>R Resident

(*f* ---) (R: --- *f*)

Moves the 8-byte floating point number *f* from the parameter stack to the return stack. See **R>F** .

F@ Resident

(*addr* --- *f*)

Retrieves the floating point contents *f* of the given address (4 words) and places it on the stack.

FABS Resident

(f_1 --- f_2)

Converts the floating point number f_1 to its absolute value f_2.

FCONSTANT Resident

(*f* ---) (IS: const*Name*)

A defining word used in the form:

f FCONSTANT cccc

to create word **cccc** , with its parameter field containing the initial value *f*. When **cccc** is later executed, it will invoke **FCONSTANT** 's execution procedure to push the 8-byte floating point value in **cccc**'s parameter field to the stack.

FDROP Resident

(*f* ---)

Drops the top floating point number *f* from the stack.

FDUP Resident

(*f* --- *f f*)

Duplicates the top floating point number *f* on the stack.

FENCE Resident

(--- *addr*)

A user variable containing an address (usually the nfa of a Forth word) below which **FORGET**ting is trapped. To **FORGET** below this point the user must alter the contents of **FENCE** . It *is* possible to set the value of **FENCE** to a value that is actually less than the address of the end of the last word in the core dictionary (**TASK**) such that **UNFORGETABLE** [*sic*] will report false. However, **FORGET** will still trap that error.

FFMT. Resident

(*f* [*intLen fracLen*] *optMask* ---)

This word can handle free-format, TI Basic-style output of floating point numbers as well as fixed-format output that includes F-, E- and extended E-type formats. For free-format output, only the floating point number and *optMask* = 0 is required on the stack.

optMask is composed of the following bits:

- bit 0: 0 = free form TI Basic style
  - no other bits should be set
  - *intLen* and *fracLen* should not be on the stack
  - 1 = fixed format
- bit 1: 2 = explicit sign
- bit 2: 4 = show '+' for positive number instead of space
  - bit 1 must also be set
- bit 3: 8 = E-notation (2 exponent digits)
- bit 4: 16 = extended E-notation (3 exponent digits)
  - bit 3 must also be set

If *optMask* is not 0, *intLen* and *fracLen* must be on the stack, as well. If the sum of *intLen* and *fracLen* exceeds 16, an error message will be displayed:

- *intLen*: number of places before decimal point, including sign position
- *fracLen*: number of places after decimal point, including decimal point and excluding E-notation

Various examples, using floating point numbers defined with **>F** and **FPCON** , *q.v.*, follow:

```
>F 1.234567890123E-7  ok:4
0 FFMT.  1.23457E-07  ok:0
>F 1.234567890123E-102 FCONSTANT FPCON  ok:0
FPCON  ok:4
0 FFMT.  1.23457E-**  ok:0
FPCON FDUP FDUP FDUP FDUP  ok:20
2 14 1 FFMT.   .0000000000000  ok:16
2 10 9 FFMT.  1.234567890E-**  ok:12
2 12 25 FFMT.  1.23456789012E-102  ok:8
2 14 31 FFMT. +1.2345678901230E-102  ok:4
2 15 9 FFMT. field too big!  ok:0
```

FILE Resident

(*vaddr*$_1$ *addr* *vaddr*$_2$ ---) (IS: <*file word*>)

A defining word which permits you to create a word by which a file will be known. You must place on the stack the **PAB-ADDR** , **PAB-BUF** and **PAB-VBUF** addresses you wish to be associated with the file.

Used in the form:

vaddr$_1$ ***addr vaddr***$_2$ **FILE cccc**

When **cccc** executes, **PAB-ADDR** , **PAB-BUF** and **PAB-VBUF** are set to *vaddr*$_1$, *addr* and *vaddr*$_2$, respectively.

FILES Resident

(*n* ---)

Change the number of files **fbForth 2.0** can have open simultaneously. The number of files can be 1 – 16. Each additional file requires an additional 518 bytes of upper VRAM, reducing the available VRAM for your program. Location **8370h** holds the highest available address in VRAM.

FILL Resident

(*addr count b* ---)

Fill memory beginning at *addr* with *count* bytes of byte *b*.

FIND$ Stack-based String Library [42]

(*start* --- *pos* | -1) (SS: ---) "find string in string"

The word **FIND$** searches the second string on the string stack, starting from position *start*, for the first occurrence of the topmost string and pushes its starting position to the data stack. As a convenience to making subsequent searches for the same substring easier, both strings are retained on the string stack. For example,

```
$" redgreenbluegreen" $" green" 0 FIND$ . 3  ok:0
```

displays the value 3, as the substring is found at character position 3, the leftmost character being character 0. The strings "redgreenbluegreen" and "green" remain on the stack. Thus, the second instance of "green" could be found with a second search.

FINDC$ Stack-based String Library [42]

(*char* --- *pos*|-1) (SS: ---) "find character in string"

The word **FINDC$** returns the position of the first occurrence of the character char, beginning at the left side of the topmost string, with the search proceeding towards the right. If the character is not found, -1 is returned. For example,

```
$" redgreenblue" 98  FINDC$ . 8  ok:0
```

Displays the value 8, as the character 'b' (ASCII 98) is found in the 8th character position, where the first character is character 0.

FIRST Resident

(--- *addr*)

A constant that leaves the address of the first (lowest) block buffer.

FIRST$ Resident

(--- *addr*)

A user variable which contains the first byte of the disk buffer area.

FLERR Resident

(--- *n*)

Returns on the stack the contents *n*, reported by the floating point library in its floating point error variable.

FLOOR Resident

(f_1 --- f_2)

Finds the greatest integer f_2 (in floating point format) not less than the floating point number f_1.

FLUSH Resident

(---)

Writes to disk all disk buffers that have been marked as updated.

FM/MOD Resident

(*d n* --- *rem quot*)

A mixed magnitude math operator that performs floored division to leave the signed remainder *rem* and signed quotient *quot* from a double-number dividend *d* and single-number divisor *n*. The quotient is rounded toward negative infinity and the remainder given the sign of the divisor. See Chapter 18 "Signed Integer Division" for more details.

FMINUS Resident

(f_1 --- f_2)

Negates f_1 by taking the two's complement of the cell on top of the stack, *i.e.*, $f_2 = -f_1$.

The top cell on the stack is the most significant cell (2 bytes) of a floating point number.

FNT Resident

(---)

FNT loads either the default font file (can be changed by user with **USEFFL**, *q.v.*) or the console font into the Pattern Descriptor Table (PDT) depending on the value of the user variable **SCRFNT** . The default font is loaded from DSK1.FBFONT by **FNT** (or from DSK*n*.FBFONT if key *n* is held down) at **fbForth 2.0** startup because **SCRFNT** = -1 at startup. The **fbForth 2.0** system default font contains the patterns for ASCII character codes 0 – 127. The font pattern for each character is 8 bytes, which means that 1 KiB of pattern code is loaded into the PDT. This font contains true lowercase characters with true descenders.

Executing **COLD** will maintain the currently selected font as the default. Restarting the system with **BOOT** , **MON** or a power cycle will restore loading of the system font from DSK1.FBFONT.

See Chapter 13 "Screen Fonts and the Font Editor" for more detail.

FONTED Resident

(---)

Typing **FONTED** opens the font editor with the current font loaded from the PDT. Editing the font will not affect the current font because the working buffer is not the PDT. See Chapter 13 "Screen Fonts and the Font Editor" for details.

FORGET Resident

(---)

Executed in the form:

FORGET cccc

Deletes the definition named **cccc** from the dictionary along with all dictionary entries physically following it.

FORGET first checks the *lfa* of **cccc** to see if it is lower than the address in **FENCE** . If it is not, **FORGET** then checks whether it is lower than the address of the last byte of the core dictionary. If it is not lower than either of these addresses, **FORGET** updates **HERE** to the *lfa* of **cccc** , effectively deleting the desired part of the dictionary. Otherwise, an appropriate error message is displayed.

If you wish to **FORGET** an unfinished definition, the word likely will not be found. If it is the last definition attempted, you can make it findable by executing **SMUDGE** and then **FORGET**ting it.

FORTH *[immediate word]* Resident

(---)

The name of the primary vocabulary. Execution makes **FORTH** the **CONTEXT** vocabulary. Until additional user vocabularies are defined, new user definitions become a part of **FORTH** because it is at that point also the **CURRENT** vocabulary.

Because **FORTH** is immediate, it will execute during the creation of a colon definition to select this vocabulary at compile time.

FOVER Resident

(f_1 f_2 --- f_1 f_2 f_1)

Copies the second floating point number on the stack to the top of the stack.

FP1 Resident

(--- *f*)

Pushes a floating point 1 *f* to the stack.

FP10 Resident

(--- *f*)

Pushes a floating point 10 *f* to the stack.

FPB Resident

(--- v*addr*)

Pushes VRAM address v*addr* of user screen font file PAB to stack.

FRAC Resident

(f_1 --- f_2)

Truncates f_1, leaving the fractional portion f_2 on the stack.

This word has a bug that causes a system crash. It will be fixed in the next revision of **fbForth 2.0**. In the meantime, you can redefine **FRAC** as follows:

```
: FRAC FDUP TRUNC F- ;
```

FRND Resident

(--- *f*)

Generates a pseudo-random floating point number *f* greater than or equal to 0 and less than 1.

FROT Resident

(f_1 f_2 f_3 --- f_2 f_3 f_1)

Moves the third floating point number f_1 down from the top of the stack to the top of the stack.

FSWAP Resident

(f_1 f_2 --- f_2 f_1)

Swaps the top two floating point numbers on the stack.

FVARIABLE Resident

(*f* ---) (IS: *varName*)

A defining word used in the form:

```
f FVARIABLE cccc
```

to create word **cccc**, with its parameter field containing ***f***. When **cccc** is later executed, it will invoke **FVARIABLE**'s execution procedure to push to the stack

cccc 's parameter field address, from which the current value may be fetched with **F@** or to which a new value may be stored with **F!** .

FXD Resident

(---)

Assigns the attribute FIXED to the file whose PAB (Peripheral Access Block) is pointed to by **PAB-ADDR** .

GCHAR Resident

(*col row* --- *char*)

Returns on the stack the ASCII code *char* of the character currently at (*col,row*). *Note:* Rows and columns are numbered from 0.

GOTOXY Resident

(*col row* ---)

Places the cursor at the designated column *col* and row *row* position. *Note:* Rows and columns are numbered from 0.

GPLLNK Resident

(*addr* ---)

Links a Forth program to the Graphics Programming Language (GPL) routine located at the given address.

GRAPHICS Resident

(---)

Converts from present display screen mode into standard Graphics mode configurations.

GRAPHICS2 Resident

(---)

Converts from present display screen mode into standard Graphics2 (Bitmap) mode configuration.

HCHAR Resident

(*col row count char* ---)

Prints a horizontal stream of a specified character *char* beginning at (*col,row*) and having a length *count*. *Note:* Rows and columns are numbered from 0. **HCHAR** does *not* check to see whether (*col,row*) is within the screen buffer or whether count will overrun VRAM after the screen buffer. This is the same behavior as in TI Forth. This behavior will be changed in the next build of **fbForth 2.0** to conform to how TI Basic and TI Extended Basic implement this function, *i.e.*, in the next build, **HCHAR** will throw an error if it would start outside the screen buffer and it will wrap to the start of the screen buffer upon reaching the end of the screen buffer.

HERE Resident

(--- *addr*)

Leave the address of the next available dictionary location.

HEX Resident

(---)

Set the numeric conversion base to sixteen (hexadecimal).

HLD Resident

(--- *addr*)

A user variable that holds the address of the latest character of text during numeric output conversion.

HOLD Resident

(*char* ---)

Used between **<#** and **#>** to insert an ASCII character into a pictured numeric output string, *e.g.*, **2E HOLD** will place a decimal point.

HONK Resident

(---)

Produces the sound associated with incorrect input.

I Resident

(--- *n*)

Used within a **DO** loop to copy the loop index to the stack. **I** is a synonym for **R** .

ID. Resident

(*nfa* ---)

Print a definition's name from its name field address *nfa*.

IF *[immediate word]* Resident

Occurs in a colon definition in form:

```
IF (true part) … THEN
IF (true part) … ENDIF
IF (true part) … ELSE (false part) … THEN
IF (true part) … ELSE (false part) … ENDIF
```

Compile time: (--- *addr* 2)

IF compiles **0BRANCH** and reserves space for an offset at *addr*; *addr* and 2 are used later for resolution of the offset and error testing.

Runtime: (*flag* ---)

IF selects execution based on a Boolean flag. If *flag* is *true* (non-zero), execution continues ahead through the true part. If *flag* is *false* (zero), execution skips to just after **ELSE** to execute the false part when an **ELSE** clause is present. After either part, execution resumes after **THEN** (or **ENDIF**). **ELSE** and its false part are optional. With no **ELSE** clause, false execution skips to just after **THEN** (or **ENDIF**).

IMMEDIATE Resident

(---)

Mark the most recently made definition so that when encountered at compile time, it will be executed rather than being compiled. *i.e.*, the precedence bit in its header is set. This method allows definitions to handle unusual compiling situations rather than build them into the fundamental compiler. The user may force compilation of an immediate definition by preceding it with **[COMPILE]** .

IN Resident

(--- *addr*)

A user variable containing the byte offset within the current input text buffer (terminal or disk) from which the next text will be accepted. **WORD** uses and moves the value of **IN** .

INDEX Printing Routines [19]

(n_1 n_2 ---)

Prints to the terminal a list of the line #0 comments from Forth block n_1 through Forth block n_2. See **PAUSE** .

INIT$ Stack-based String Library [42]

(*size* ---) (SS: ---) "initialize string stack"

The string stack must be initialized to some convenient size by executing **INIT$** once the library is **LOAD**ed:

```
512 INIT$  ok:0
```

will initialize the string stack to 512 bytes. **INIT$** should only be executed once because initializing the string stack a second time will orphan the previous instance and waste memory.

INPT Resident

(---)

Assigns the attribute INPUT to the file whose PAB is pointed to by **PAB-ADDR** .

INT Resident

(f_1 --- f_2)

Returns the greatest integer f_2 not greater than the input value f_1.

INTERPRET Resident

(---)

The outer text interpreter, which sequentially executes or compiles text from the input stream (terminal or disk) depending on **STATE** . If the word name cannot be found after a search of **CONTEXT** and then **CURRENT** , **INTERPRET** attempts to convert it into a number according to the current radix in **BASE** . That also failing, an error message echoing the name with a "?" will be given. Text input will be taken according to the convention for **WORD** . If a decimal point is found as part of a number, a double number value will be left. The decimal point has no other purpose than to force this action. See **NUMBER** .

INTLNK Resident

(--- *addr*)

A user variable which is a pointer to the Interrupt Service linkage.

INTRNL Resident

(---)

Assigns the attribute INTERNAL to the file whose PAB is pointed to by **PAB-ADDR** .

ISR Resident

(--- *addr*)

A user variable that initially contains 0 to indicate that no user Interrupt Service Routine (ISR) has been installed. The user must modify **ISR** to contain the *cfa* of the Forth routine to be executed each 1/60 second. Next, the contents of the console ISR hook, **83C4h**, must contain the address of the **fbForth 2.0** ISR, which it does at startup. Note that the interrupt service linkage code address is always available in **INTLNK** .

The console ISR hook, **83C4h**, should be zeroed before changing **ISR** and restored with the value in **INTLNK** after changing it.

See Chapter 10"Interrupt Service Routines (ISRs)" for much more detail.

J Resident

(--- *n*)

Used within an inner **DO** loop to copy the loop index of the next outer **DO** loop to the stack.

JCRU Resident

(n_1 --- n_2)

Executed by **JOYST** when **JMODE** $\neq 0$, **JCRU** allows input from joystick #1 ($n_1 = 1$) or #2 ($n_1 = 2$). The value n_2 returned will have 0 or more of the 5 least significant bits set for direction and fire-button status. Bit values are 1 = Fire, 2 = W, 4 = E, 8 = S and 16 = N. Two-bit directional combinations are 18 = NW (N + W or 16 + 2), 20 = NE, 10 = SW and 12 = SE. See § 6.8 "Using Joysticks" for more information.

JKBD Resident

(n_1 --- *char* n_2 n_3)

Executed by **JOYST** when **JMODE** = 0, **JKBD** allows input from joystick #1 and the left side of the keyboard ($n_1 = 1$) or from joystick #2 and the right side of the keyboard ($n_1 = 2$). Values returned are the character code *char* of the key pressed, the ***x*** status n_2 and the ***y*** status n_3. See § 6.8 "Using Joysticks" for more information.

JMODE Resident

(--- *addr*)

A user variable that uses offset **26h** of the user variable table. It is used by **JOYST** to determine whether to execute **JKBD** (= 0) or **JCRU** ($\neq 0$). The default value is 0. See **JOYST** , **JKBD** and **JCRU** .

JOYST Resident

(n_1 --- [*char* n_2 n_3] | n_2)

Allows input from joystick #1 and the left side of the keyboard ($n_1 = 1$) or from joystick #2 and the right side of the keyboard ($n_1 = 2$). Return values depend on the value in **JMODE** . If **JMODE** = 0 (default), **JOYST** executes **JKBD** , which returns the character code *char* of the key pressed, the *x* status n_2 and the *y* status n_3. If **JMODE** ≠ 0, **JOYST** executes **JCRU** , which reads only the joysticks and returns a single value with 0 or more of the 5 least significant bits set. See **JCRU** and § 6.8 "Using Joysticks" for their meaning.

KEY Resident

(--- *char*)

Wait for the next terminal keystroke. Leave its ASCII (7-bit) value on the stack.

KEY8 Resident

(--- *char*)

Wait for the next terminal keystroke. Leave its full 8-bit value on the stack.

L/SCR Resident

(--- *n*)

Returns on the stack the number of lines per Forth block.

LATEST Resident

(--- *nfa*)

Leave the name field address *nfa* of the most recently defined word in the **CURRENT** vocabulary. At compile time, this "latest" word will be the most recently compiled word.

LCASE$ Stack-based String Library [42]

(---) (SS: str_1 --- str_2) "convert to lower case"

The word **LCASE$** converts all upper case characters in the topmost string to lower case. For example,

```
$" HELLO WORLD! 1234" LCASE$ .$ hello world! 1234 ok:0
```

LD Resident

(*n* ---)

The file I/0 process to load a program file from a disk into VDP RAM. The parameter *n* specifies the maximum number of bytes to be loaded and is usually the size of the file on disk. The file's PAB must be set up and be the current PAB, to which **PAB-ADDR** points, before executing this word.

LDCR CRU Words [5]

(n_1 n_2 *addr* ---)

Performs a TMS9900 LDCR instruction. The CRU base address *addr* will be shifted left one bit and stored in workspace register R12 prior to executing the TMS9900 LDCR instruction. The low-order n_2 bits of value n_1 are transferred to the CRU, where the following condition, $n_2 \leq 15$, is enforced by n_2 AND **0Fh**. If $n_2 = 0$, 16 bits are transferred. For program clarity, you may certainly use $n_2 = 16$ to transfer 16 bits because $n_2 = 0$ will be the value actually used by the final machine code. See § 11.3 and CRU documentation in the *Editor/Assembler Manual* for more information.

LEAVE Resident

(---)

Force termination of a **DO** loop at the next opportunity by setting the loop limit equal to the current value of the index. The index itself remains unchanged, and the execution proceeds normally until **LOOP** or **+LOOP** is encountered.

LEFT$ Stack-based String Library [42]

(*len* ---) (SS: str_1 --- str_1 str_2) "left of string"

The word **LEFT$** pushes the leftmost *len* characters to the string stack as a new string. The original string is retained. For example,

```
$" redgreenblue" 3 LEFT$  ok:0
```

The above causes the string "red" to be pushed to the string stack.

LEN$ Stack-based String Library [42]

(--- *len*) (SS: ---) "length of string"

The word **LEN$** returns the length of the topmost string on the string stack. For example,

```
$" Hello world!"  len$ . 12  ok:0
```

LFA Resident

(*pfa* --- *lfa*)

Convert the parameter field address *pfa* of a dictionary definition to its link field address *lfa*.

LIMIT Resident

(--- *addr*)

A constant which leaves the address *addr* just above the highest memory available for a disk buffer.

LIMIT$ Resident

(--- *addr*)

A user variable that contains the address just above the highest memory available for a disk buffer. The address of **LIMIT$** is left on the stack.

LINE Resident

($dotcol_1$ $dotrow_1$ $dotcol_2$ $dotrow_2$ ---)

The high resolution graphics routine which plots a line from ($dotcol_1$,$dotrow_1$) to

($dotcol_2$,$dotrow_2$). **DCOLOR** and **DMODE** must be set before this instruction is used.

LIST Resident

(*blk* ---)

Lists the specified Forth block to the output device. See **PAUSE** .

LIT Resident

(--- *n*)

Within a colon-definition, **LIT** is automatically compiled before each 16-bit literal number encountered in input text. Later execution of **LIT** causes the contents of the next dictionary address to be pushed to the stack.

LITERAL *[immediate word]* Resident

INTERPRETATION: (---)

Interpretation of **LITERAL** does nothing, unlike almost all other compiling words.

COMPILE TIME: (*n* ---)

Compiles the stack value *n* as a 16-bit literal. This will execute during a colon definition. The intended use is:

```
: xxx [ calculation ] LITERAL ;
```

Compilation is suspended for the compile-time calculation of a value. Compilation is resumed and **LITERAL** compiles this value.

RUNTIME: (--- *n*)

Pushes *n* to the stack.

LN10INV Resident

(--- *f*)

Leaves the floating point number $f = 0.43429448190325$, which is the inverse of $\ln(10) = 2.302585092994$.

LOAD Resident

(*n* ---)

Begin interpretation of Forth block *n*. Loading will terminate at the end of the Forth block or at **;S** . See **;S** and **-->** .

LOG Resident

(f_1 --- f_2 | f_1)

The floating point operation that returns the natural logarithm f_2 of the floating point number f_1. If f_1 is 0 or negative, the original number f_1 is returned instead.

LOG10 Resident

(f_1 --- f_2 | f_1)

The floating point operation that returns the decimal logarithm f_2 of the floating point number f_1. If f_1 is 0 or negative, the original number f_1 is returned instead.

LOOP *[immediate word]* Resident

Occurs in a colon definition in the form:

DO … LOOP

COMPILE TIME: (*addr* 3 ---)

LOOP compiles **(LOOP)** and uses *addr* to calculate an offset to **DO** . The value 3 is used for compile-time error testing.

RUNTIME: (---)

LOOP selectively controls branching back to the corresponding **DO** based on the loop index and limit. The loop index is incremented by one and compared to the limit. The branch back to **DO** occurs until the index equals or exceeds the limit. At that time, the parameters are discarded and execution continues ahead.

LTRIM$ Stack-based String Library [42]

(---) (SS: str_1 --- str_2) "trim left of string"

The word **LTRIM$** removes leading spaces from the topmost string. For example,

$"   hello!" LTRIM$.$ <u>**hello!**</u> <u>**ok:0**</u>

M* Resident

(n_1 n_2 --- *d*)

A mixed magnitude math operation that leaves the double-number signed product *d* of two signed numbers, n_1 and n_2.

M/ Resident

(*d n* --- *rem quot*)

A mixed magnitude math operator that leaves the signed remainder *rem* and signed quotient *quot* from a double-number dividend *d* and single-number divisor *n*. **M/** uses user variable **S|F** , *q.v.*, to determine whether to use **SM/REM** , *q.v.*, for symmetric division (the default) or **FM/MOD** , *q.v.*, for floored division. See Chapter 18 "Signed Integer Division" for more details.

M/MOD Resident

(*ud u* --- *urem udquot*)

An unsigned mixed-magnitude math operation that leaves an unsigned double-number quotient *udquot* and an unsigned single-number remainder *urem* from an unsigned double-number dividend *ud* and an unsigned single-number divisor *u*.

MAGNIFY Resident

(n_1 ---)

Alters the sprite magnification factor to be n_1. The value of n_1 must be 0, 1, 2 or 3.

MAX Resident

(n_1 n_2 --- n_3)

Leave the greater n_3 of the two numbers, n_1 and n_2.

MAXLEN$ Stack-based String Library [42]

(*$Caddr* --- *max_len*) "maximum length of string"

Given the address of a string constant on the data stack the word **MAXLEN$** returns the maximum allowed string length for that string constant. For example,

```
50 $CONST WELCOME  ok:0
WELCOME MAXLEN$ . 50  ok:0
```

MCHAR Resident

(*n col row* ---)

Places a square of color *n* at (*col,row*). Used in multicolor mode.

MENU Welcome Block [1]

(---)

Displays the available Load Options.

MESSAGE Resident

(*n* ---)

Print on the selected output device the text of system error number *n*. If **WARNING** = 0, the message will simply be printed as a number (**msg** ***#n***). When **WARNING** = 0 in TI Forth, it means the disk is unavailable, but this is not necessary in **fbForth 2.0** because error messages are always memory resident.

The word **MESSAGE** now only works for predefined error messages and should not be used to display user-defined messages as was possible with TI Forth. The reason for this is that system messages in **fbForth 2.0** now reside in cartridge ROM. The word **.LINE** , *q.v.*, can be used for this purpose.

MID$ Stack-based String Library [42]

(*start end* ---) (SS: str_1 --- str_1 str_2) "mid-string"

The word **MID$** produces a sub-string on the string stack, consisting of the characters from the topmost string starting at character *start* and ending at character *end*. For example,

```
$" redgreenblue"  3 7 mid$  ok:0
```

At this point, the topmost two strings on the string stack are as follows:

"green" (the topmost item)

"redgreenblue"

Note, as indicated in the string stack signature, the original string (str_1) is retained. Note also that the first character in the string (the leftmost character) is character number 0.

MIN Resident

(n_1 n_2 --- n_3)

Leave the smaller n_3 of the two numbers (n_1 and n_2).

MINIT Resident

(---)

Initializes the monitor screen for use with **MCHAR** .

MINUS Resident

(n_1 --- n_2)

Leaves the two's complement n_2 of a number n_1, *i.e.*, negates n_1.

MKBFL Resident

(---) (IS: *DSKn.<blocks filename> n*)

Create a blocks file from the string and number in the input stream. To create a file named MYBLOCKS on DSK1 with room for 80 blocks, type

```
MKBFL DSK1.MYBLOCKS 80  ok:0
```

MOD Resident

(n_1 n_2 --- *rem*)

Leave the remainder *rem* of n_1/n_2, with the same sign as n_1. **MOD** is based on **M/** , which uses user variable **S|F** , *q.v.*, to determine whether symmetric (the default) or floored division is used. See Chapter 18 "Signed Integer Division" for more details.

MON Resident

(---)

Exit to the TI 99/4A color bar display screen and the system monitor program.

MOTION Resident

(n_1 n_2 *spr* ---)

Assigns a horizontal n_1 and vertical n_2 velocity to the specified sprite *spr*.

MOVE Resident

($addr_1$ $addr_2$ *n* ---)

Moves the contents of *n* cells (16-bit contents) beginning at $addr_1$ into *n* cells beginning at $addr_2$. The contents of $addr_1$ is moved first, proceeding toward high memory. This is ***not*** overlap safe for $addr_1 < addr_2$.

MULTI Resident

(---)

Converts from present display screen mode into standard Multicolor mode configuration.

MYSELF *[immediate word]* Resident

(---)

Used in a colon definition. Places the code field address (*cfa*) of a word into its own definition. This permits recursion.

N>S Resident

(--- *n*) (IS: *token*) "number to stack"

N>S attempts to convert the next blank-delimited token in the input stream to a number in the current radix (number base). If successful, **N>S** pushes the number to the stack. Otherwise, an error message is issued and the stack is cleared:

```
.BASE 10  ok:0
N>S 123  ok:1
N>S 12X 12X ?
```

N>S is the only way to get numbers from the input stream to the stack while using **CODE:** and **DOES>CODE:** because those words compile numbers into the dictionary instead of pushing them to the stack as the interpreter does.

NEXT, Resident

(---)

NEXT, is one of only two words in the Assembler vocabulary that are part of the resident dictionary. The other is **;ASM** . **NEXT,** puts **045Fh** at **HERE** and advances **HERE** . This machine code for ALC, **B *NEXT** or **B *R15**, branches to the inner interpreter to fetch the next word to be executed. See **ASM:** , **;ASM** and Chapter 9 "The fbForth 2.0 TMS9900 Assembler" for more information.

NFA Resident

(*pfa* --- *nfa*)

Convert the parameter field address *pfa* of a definition to its name field address *nfa*.

NIP More Useful Stack Words etc. [41]

(n_1 n_2 --- n_2)

Remove from the stack the number that is under the top number.

NIP$ Stack-based String Library [42]

(---) (SS: str_1 str_2 --- str_2) "nip string"

The word **NIP$** removes the string underneath the topmost string from the string stack. For example,

```
$" red"  ok:0
$" blue"  ok:0
```

At this point, "blue" is on the top of the string stack, with "red" underneath it.

```
NIP$
```

At this point, "red" has been removed from the string stack, leaving "blue" as the topmost string.

NOP Resident

(---)

A do-nothing instruction. **NOP** is useful for patching as in assembly code.

NULL *[Literally* NUL *(ASCII 0)]* *[immediate word]* Resident

(---)

There is actually no word in **fbForth 2.0** with the name, ‘ **NULL** ’. The name field for **NULL** contains an ASCII 0. Every **fbForth 2.0** buffer, including the terminal input buffer, must end with an ASCII 0. When **INTERPRET** reaches it, it will search for it in the dictionary and will find what we are here calling **NULL** . **NULL** is the only way to exit the endless loop in **INTERPRET** . When **NULL** executes, it drops the top value on the return stack and thus returns, not to **INTERPRET**, but to the word that executed **INTERPRET** (usually **QUIT** or **LOAD**). Here is its definition, keeping in mind that ‘ **NULL** ’ represents an actual NUL (ASCII 0):

```
: NULL BLK @ IF ?EXEC THEN R> DROP ;  IMMEDIATE
```

NUMBER Resident

(*addr* --- *d*)

Convert a packed character string (see footnote 5 on page 22) left at *addr* with the character count in the first byte, to a signed double number *d* , using the current numeric base. If a decimal point is encountered in the text, its position will be given in **DPL** , but no other effect occurs. If numeric conversion is not possible, an error message will be given.

OF *[immediate word]* Resident

Occurs inside a colon definition as part of the **OF ... ENDOF** construct inside of the **CASE ... ENDCASE** construct.

COMPILE TIME: (4 --- *addr* 5)

Checks for the value 4 on the stack left there by **CASE** or a previous **ENDOF** , compiles **(OF)** , leaves its address *addr* for branching resolution by **ENDOF** and leaves a 5 for its matching **ENDOF** to check.

RUNTIME: (*n* --- [ ] | *n*)

The value *n* is compared to the value which was on top of the stack when **CASE** ’s runtime action occurred. If the numbers are identical, the words between **OF** and **ENDOF** will be executed. Otherwise, *n* is put back on the stack for execution to continue after **ENDOF** . See **CASE** and **ENDOF** .

OPN Resident

(---)

Opens the file whose PAB is pointed to by **PAB-ADDR** .

OR Resident

(n_1 n_2 --- n_3)

Leave the bit-wise logical OR n_3 of two 16-bit values, n_1 and n_2.

OUT Resident

(--- *addr*)

A user variable that contains a value incremented by **EMIT** and **EMIT8** . The user may alter and examine **OUT** to control display formatting.

OUTPT Resident

(---)

Assigns the attribute OUTPUT to the file whose PAB is pointed to by **PAB-ADDR** .

OVER Resident

(n_1 n_2 --- n_1 n_2 n_1)

Copy the second stack value n_1 to the top of the stack.

OVER$ Stack-based String Library [42]

(---) (SS: str_1 str_2 --- str_1 str_2 str_1) "over string"

The word **OVER$** pushes a copy of the string str_1 to the top of the string stack, above str_2. For example,

```
$" red"  ok:0
$" green"  ok:0
OVER$  ok:0
```

At this point, the string stack contains the following strings:

"red" (the topmost string)
"green"
"red"

PAB-ADDR Resident

(--- *addr*)

A variable containing the VDP address of the first byte of the current PAB (Peripheral Access Block).

PAB-BUF Resident

(--- *addr*)

A variable which holds the address of the area in CPU RAM used as the source or destination of the data to be transferred to/from a file. This is a file I/O word.

PAB-VBUF Resident

(--- *addr*)

A variable pointing to a VDP RAM buffer which serves as a temporary buffer when transferring data to/from a file. The VDP address stored in **PAB-VBUF** is also stored in the file's PAB.

PABS Resident

(--- *addr*)

A user variable which points to a region in VDP RAM, which has been set aside for creating PABs.

PAD Resident

(--- *addr*)

Leave the address of the text output buffer, which is a fixed offset (68 bytes in **fbForth 2.0**) above **HERE** . Every time **HERE** changes, **PAD** is updated.

PAGE Resident

(---)

Clears the display screen and places the cursor at the top, left corner. It is a shortcut for

```
CLS
0 0 GOTOXY
```

PANEL Resident

(*x y w h* ---)

Sets up a panel within the video display for **SCROLL** to scroll in any orthogonal direction with or without wrapping, depending on the value of **WRAP** . The panel will be *w* characters wide, *h* characters high with its upper, left corner at column *x* and row *y*.

PAUSE Resident

(--- *flag*)

Checks for a keystroke and issues *false* if none, *true* if ***<BREAK>*** (***<CLEAR>*** or ***<FCTN+4>***) or idles until a second keystroke before issuing *false* (or *true* if second keystroke is ***<BREAK>***). The words **LIST** , **INDEX** , **DUMP** and **VLIST** all call the word **PAUSE** . These routines exit when *flag* = *true*. **PAUSE** allows the user to temporarily halt the output by pressing any key. Pressing another key will allow continuation. To exit one of these routines prematurely, press ***<BREAK>*** .

PDT Resident

(--- *vaddr*)

A constant which contains the VDP address of the Pattern Descriptor Table. Default value is **800h**. This constant can only be changed via user variable number **28h**.

PFA Resident

(*nfa* --- *pfa*)

Convert the name field address *nfa* of a compiled definition to its parameter field address *pfa*.

PI Resident

(--- *f*)

A floating point approximation of π to 13 significant figures. (3.141592653590)

PICK More Useful Stack Words etc. [41]

(+*n* --- [*n*])

Copy to the top of the stack the nth number down. The 0th number is the top number. [*n*] means "the contents of cell *n* from the top of the stack". The number *n* must be positive.

0 PICK is equivalent to **DUP** .

1 PICK is equivalent to **OVER** .

PICK$ Stack-based String Library [42]

(*index* ---) (SS: --- *str*) "pick string"

Given the index of a string on the string stack, copy the indexed string to the top of the string stack. **0 PICK$** is equivalent to **DUP$**, **1 PICK$** is equivalent to **OVER$** *etc*. For example,

```
$" blue"  ok:0
$" green"  ok:0
$" red"  ok:0
2 PICK$  ok:0
```

The above causes the string "blue" to be copied to the top of the string stack.

PLAY Resident

(*addr flag* ---)

This word is ported from **TurboForth**[1] code courtesy of Mark Wills.

PLAY starts the table of sound lists at address *addr*, depending on *flag*:

Flag	Action
0	Do not play if either sound table is active.
1	Unconditionally play, killing all previous sound tables.
-1	Plays as sound table #2, muting sound table #1 for the duration of sound table #2.

Sound lists consist of a list of sound commands starting with a byte count and ending with a duration count byte (sixtieths of a second) that is not included in the byte count. The last sound list should silence all four sound generators and end with a duration of 0. See § 20 of the *Editor/Assembler Manual* for details on sound lists.

A sound table may be prepared for **PLAY** with **DATA[…]DATA** by dropping the cell count:

DATA[*<sound list>* **]DATA**

DROP 1 PLAY

PLAYING? Resident

(--- *flag*)

This word is ported from **TurboForth**[1] code courtesy of Mark Wills.

PLAYING? checks both **fbForth 2.0** sound status registers, ORs them and leaves that value on the stack as *flag*. If *flag* = 0, no sound table is active.

PLAYING? is intended for use with **PLAY** , not **SOUND** . **SOUND** does not use the **fbForth 2.0** sound status registers.

PREV Resident

(--- *addr*)

A user variable containing the address of the disk buffer most recently referenced. The **UPDATE** command marks this buffer to be later written to disk.

QUERY Resident

(---)

Input 80 characters of text (or until ***<ENTER>*** is pressed) from the operator's terminal. Text is positioned at the address contained in **TIB** with **IN** set to 0.

QUIT Resident

(---)

Clear the return stack, stop compilation and return control to the operator's terminal. No message is given, including the usual **ok:*n*** .

R Resident

(--- *n*) (R: *n* --- *n*)

Copy the top of the return stack to the parameter stack.

R# Resident

(--- *addr*)

A user variable which may contain the location of an editing cursor or other file-related function.

R->BASE Resident

(---) (R: *n* ---)

Restore the current base from the return stack. See **BASE->R** .

R/W Resident

(*addr* n_1 *flag* ---)

The fig-Forth standard disk read/write linkage. The only modification to **R/W** for **fbForth 2.0** is that it now calls **RBLK** and **WBLK** instead of the replaced **RDISK** and **WDISK** . The source or destination block buffer address is *addr*, n_1 is the sequential number of the referenced block and *flag* indicates whether the operation is write (*flag* = 0) or read (*flag* = 1). **R/W** determines the location on mass storage, performs the read/write and error checking.

R0 Resident

(--- *addr*)

A user variable containing the initial location of the return stack. Pronounced "r zero". See **RP!** .

R> Resident

(--- *n*) (R: *n* ---)

Remove the top value from the return stack and leave it on the parameter stack. See **>R** and **R** .

R>F Resident

(--- *f*) (R: *f* ---)

Moves the 8-byte floating point number *f* from the return stack to the parameter stack. See **F>R** .

RAD/DEG Resident

(--- *f*)

Constant in floating point format representing degrees/radian = 0.01745329251994.

RANDOMIZE Resident

(---)

Creates an unpredictable seed for the random number generator. See details in § 5.5 .

RBLK Resident

(*addr blk* ---)

Read a block from the current blocks file.

RD Resident

(--- *count*)

The file I/O instruction that reads from the current PAB. This instruction uses **PAB-BUF** and **PAB-VBUF** .

REC-LEN Resident

(*b* ---)

Stores the length *b* of the record for the upcoming write into the appropriate byte in the current PAB.

REC-NO Resident

(*n* ---)

Writes a zero-based record number *n* into the appropriate location in the current PAB.

REPEAT *[immediate word]* Resident

Used within a colon-definition in the form:

BEGIN … WHILE … REPEAT

COMPILE TIME: ($addr_1$ 1 $addr_2$ 4 ---)

At compile-time, **REPEAT** processes the **0BRANCH** offset $addr_2$ and the offset from **HERE** to the loop-back address $addr_1$, which it stores at the space reserved for it at $addr_1$ by **BEGIN** , *q.v.* The values 1 and 4 are used for error testing.

RUNTIME: (---)

At runtime, **REPEAT** forces an unconditional branch back to just after the corresponding **BEGIN** . See **WHILE** and **BEGIN** .

REPLACE$ Stack-based String Library [42]

(--- *pos* | -1) (SS: str_1 str_2 str_3 --- str_4 | [str_1 str_2]) "replace string"

The word **REPLACE$** searches string str_2 for the first occurrence of string str_3. If it is found, it is replaced with the string str_1, the position of str_3 within str_2 is pushed to the data stack, str_1 and str_3 are removed from the string stack and the new string str_4 is left on the string stack. For example,

```
512 INIT$  ok:0
$" PURPLE"  ok:0
$" redgreenblue"  ok:0
$" green"  ok:0
REPLACE$ . 3  ok:0
$.S
 Index|Length|String
------+------+------
     0|    13|redPURPLEblue

Allocated stack space:  16 bytes
    Total stack space: 512 bytes
Stack space remaining: 496 bytes
 ok:0
```

If the search string str_3 is not found, -1 is pushed to the data stack, str_1 and str_2 are left on the string stack, ready for another search.

RESET$ Stack-based String Library [42]

(---) (SS: ---)

Resets, *i.e.*, empties, the string stack.

REV$ Stack-based String Library [42]

(---) (SS: str_1 --- str_2) "reverse string"

The word **REV$** replaces the topmost string on the string stack with its reversed equivalent. For example,

$" green" REV$.$ <u>neerg</u> <u>ok:0</u>

RIGHT$ Stack-based String Library [42]

(*len* ---) (SS: str_1 --- str_1 str_2) "right of string"

The word **RIGHT$** causes the rightmost *len* characters to be pushed to the string stack as a new string. The original string is retained. For example,

$" redgreenblue" 4 RIGHT$ <u>ok:0</u>

The above causes the string "blue" to be pushed to the string stack.

RLTV Resident

(---)

Assigns the attribute RELATIVE to the file whose PAB is pointed to by **PAB-ADDR** .

RND Resident

(n_1 --- n_2)

Generates a positive random integer n_2, such that $0 \leq n_2 < n_1$. See details in § 5.5 .

RNDW Resident

(--- *u*)

Generates a random unsigned integer *u*, such that $0 \leq u \leq$ **FFFFh**. See details in § 5.5 .

ROLL More Useful Stack Words etc. [41]

([*n*] … [0] +*n* --- [*n*-1] … [0] [*n*])

Rotate left the top *n*+1 numbers on the stack, resulting in the nth number down moving to the top of the stack. The number *n* must be positive. The source for **ROLL** was Marshall Linker via George Smyth's "Forth Forum" column in the *MANNERS Newsletter* (1985) Vol. 4(5), pp. 12 – 16.

0 ROLL is a null operation.
1 ROLL is equivalent to **SWAP** .
2 ROLL is equivalent to **ROT** .

ROT Resident

(n_1 n_2 n_3 --- n_2 n_3 n_1)

Rotate the top three values on the stack, bringing the third n_1 to the top.

ROT$ Stack-based String Library [42]

(---) (SS: str_1 str_2 str_3 --- str_2 str_3 str_1) "rotate strings"

The word **ROT$** rotates the top three strings to the left. The third string down (prior to the execution of **ROT$**) moves to the top of the string stack. See Chapter 14 for implementation details regarding stack space limitations.

RP! Resident

(---)

A procedure to initialize the return stack pointer from user variable **R0** .

RP@ Resident

(--- *addr*)

Returns the address *addr* of the current top of the return stack.

RSTR Resident

(*n* ---)

Restores the file whose PAB is pointed to by the current PAB to the specified record number *n*.

RTRIM$ Stack-based String Library [42]

(---) (SS: str_1 --- str_2) "trim right of string"

The word **RTRIM$** removes leading spaces from the topmost string. For example,

```
$" hello!       " RTRIM$ .$ hello! ok:0
```

S" *[immediate word]* Resident

(--- *addr* | [ ]) (IS: *string*")

Accepts a string from the input stream (IS) until '"' is encountered. When executing, the packed string is stored at **PAD** and the address *addr* of the length byte is left on the stack.

When compiling a word definition, **SLIT** is first compiled into the definition, then the packed string. Later, when the word is executed, **SLIT** will push the address of the string's length byte to the stack and skip over the string to the word following it in the definition.

S->D Resident

(*n* --- *d*)

Sign-extend a single number *n* to form a double number *d*.

S->F Resident

(*n* --- *f*)

Converts a single-precision number *n* on the stack to a floating point number *f*.

S0 Resident

(--- *addr*)

User variable that points to the base of the parameter stack. Pronounced "s zero". See **SP!** .

S0&TIB! Resident

($addr_1$ --- $addr_2$)

This word is primarily for use in a 1024 KiB SAMS environment, where it is or may be necessary to move the stack base (in **S0**) and the Terminal Input Buffer (in **TIB**), both of which start up at the same address, *viz.*, **FFA0h**. **S0&TIB!** forces $addr_1$ to **AFA0h**, **BFA0h**, **CFA0h**, **DFA0h**, **EFA0h** or **FFA0h**; copies it to the user variables, **S0** and **TIB** , in the table of default values so the settings will survive **COLD** ; and leaves the new address on the stack as $addr_2$. The lower limit is forced above **HERE** so as not to destroy the user's dictionary.

SAMS! Resident

(---)

This word is ported from **TurboForth**[1] code courtesy of Mark Wills.

This calls the SAMS initialization in the startup code in bank 1 to restore SAMS mapping to initial conditions.

SAMS? Resident

(--- *flag*)

This word is ported from **TurboForth**[1] code courtesy of Mark Wills.

Leaves a copy of the SAMS flag from startup as *flag*.

SATR Resident

(--- *vaddr*)

A constant whose value *vaddr* is the VDP address of the Sprite Attribute List. Default value is **300h**. This constant can only be changed via user variable number **24h**.

SAY Resident

(*addr n* ---)

This word is ported from **TurboForth**[1] code courtesy of Mark Wills.

SAY needs on the stack the address *addr* of a block of Speech Synthesizer ROM speech addresses and the number *n* of those addresses. This can be accomplished with **DATA[…]DATA** . Consult Section 22 of the *Editor/Assembler Manual* for details.

SBO CRU Words [5]

(*addr* ---)

This word expects to find on the stack the CRU address *addr* of the bit to be set to 1. **SBO** will put this address into workspace register R12, shift it left (double it) and execute TMS9900 instruction, **SBO 0**, to effect setting the bit. See § 11.3 and CRU documentation in the *Editor/Assembler Manual* for more information.

SBZ CRU Words [5]

(*addr* ---)

This word expects to find on the stack the CRU address *addr* of the bit to be reset to 0. **SBZ** will put this address into workspace register R12, shift it left (double it) and execute TMS9900 instruction, **SBZ 0**, to effect resetting the bit. See § 11.3 and CRU documentation in the *Editor/Assembler Manual* for more information.

SCMP CPYBLK -- Block Copying Utility [4]

(str_1 str_2 --- -1 | 0 | +1)

Compares two strings with leading byte counts pointed to by str_1 and str_2 and leaves the result on the stack: -1, if $str_1 < str_2$; 0, if $str_1 = str_2$; +1, if $str_1 > str_2$.

SCR Resident

(--- *addr*)

A user variable containing the Forth block number most recently referenced by **LIST** or **EDIT** .

SCRFNT Resident

(--- *addr*)

A user variable containing a flag indicating whether **FNT** should load the current default font (flag ≠ 0) or the console font (flag = 0). Changing the value in **SCRFNT** does not take effect until the next time **FNT** is executed.

See Chapter 13 "Screen Fonts and the Font Editor" for more detail.

SCREEN Resident

(*n* ---)

Changes the display screen color to the color specified *n*. The foreground (FG) and background (BG) screen colors must be placed in the low-order byte of *n*, with FG the high-order 4 bits and BG the low-order 4 bits, *e.g.*, *n* = 27 (**1Bh**) for black on light yellow. The FG color is only necessary in the text modes.

SCRN_END Resident

(--- *addr*)

A user variable containing the address *addr* of the byte immediately following the last byte of the display screen image table to be used as the logical display screen.

SCRN_START Resident

(--- *addr*)

A user variable containing the address *addr* of the first byte of the display screen image table to be used as the logical display screen.

SCRN_WIDTH Resident

(--- *addr*)

A user variable which contains the number of characters (32 or 40) that will fit across the display screen. Used by the display screen scroller.

SCROLL Resident

(*dir* ---)

Scrolls the display screen panel set up by **PANEL** in direction *dir*. **PANEL** must be executed at least once before **SCROLL** because its parameters are indeterminate after powerup. Acceptable values for *dir* are

Direction	Value
left	0
right	2
up	4
down	6

SEED Resident

(*n* ---)

Places a new seed *n* into the random number generator. See details in § 5.5 .

SET-PAB Resident

(---)

This instruction assumes that **PAB-ADDR** is set. It then zeroes out the PAB (Peripheral Access Block) pointed to by **PAB-ADDR** and places the contents of **PAB-VBUF** into the appropriate word of the PAB. This initializes the PAB.

SGN Resident

(*n* --- -1 | 0 | +1)

Returns the sign of *n* or 0.

SIGN Resident

(*n d* --- *d*)

Stores a minus sign (ASCII 45 or **2Dh**) at the current location in a converted numeric output string in the text output buffer if *n* is negative. At the time *n* is evaluated, it is discarded, but double number *d* is maintained for continued conversion until **#>** removes it from the stack. Must be used between **<#** and **#>** . Using **SIGN** implies that *d* can be negative, which means that *d* should be used to produce *n*. You should then replace *d* with its absolute value (|*d*|) on the stack by using **DABS** . This can be done by pushing *d* to the stack and executing **SWAP OVER DABS** : (*d* --- *n* |*d*|) prior to **<# … SIGN … #>** .

SIN Resident

(f_1 --- f_2)

Finds the sine f_2 of the floating point number f_1 on the stack and leaves the result f_2 on the stack.

SLA Resident

(n_1 *count* --- n_2)

Arithmetically shifts the number n_1 on the stack *count* bits to the left, leaving the result n_2 on the stack. Shifting by count will be modulo 16 except when *count* = 0, which causes 16 bits to be shifted. To create a word which does not perform a 16-bit shift when *count* is zero, use the following definition for the same stack contents:

```
: SLA0 -DUP IF SLA ENDIF ;
```

SLIT Resident

(--- *addr*)

SLIT is similar to **LIT** but acts on strings instead of numbers. **SLIT** places the address *addr* of the string following it on the stack. It modifies the top of the return stack to point to just after the string.

SM/REM Resident

(*d n* --- *rem quot*)

A mixed magnitude math operator that performs symmetric division to leave the signed remainder *rem* and signed quotient *quot* from a double-number dividend *d* and single-number divisor *n*. The quotient is rounded toward zero and the remainder given the sign of the dividend. See Chapter 18 “Signed Integer Division” for more details.

SMASH 64-Column Editor [6]

(*addr*$_1$ *count*$_1$ *n* --- *addr*$_2$ *vaddr* *count*$_2$)

The assembly code routine that formats a line of tiny characters. It expects the address *addr*$_1$ of the line in memory, the number *count*$_1$ of characters per line, and the line number *n* to which it is to be written. It returns on the stack the line buffer address *addr*$_2$, a VDP address *vaddr*, and a byte count *count*$_2$. See **CLIST** and **CLINE** .

SMTN Resident

(--- *vaddr*)

A constant whose value is the VDP address of the Sprite Motion Table. Default value is **780h**. This constant can only be changed via user variable number **26h**.

SMUDGE Resident

(---)

Used during word definition to toggle the smudge bit in the length byte of a definition's name field. This prevents an uncompleted definition from being found during dictionary searches until compilation is completed without error. **SMUDGE** is simply defined as

```
HEX  : SMUDGE LATEST 20 TOGGLE ;
```

SOUND Resident

(*pitch vol ch#* ---)

This word is ported from **TurboForth**[1] code courtesy of Mark Wills.

Pitch *pitch*, volume *vol* and channel *ch#* are as described in the *Editor/Assembler Manual* in Section 20. Pitch values range from 0 – 1023, 0 representing the highest pitch. Volume values range from 0 – 15, 15 representing silence. Channels 0 – 2 represent the corresponding tone generators and channel 3 is the noise generator.

SOUND uses the pitch value for setting the type of noise for the noise generator (channel 3). Shift rates are 0 – 3. Noise type can be white noise (0) or periodic noise (4). The pitch value to pass to **SOUND** is the sum of shift rate and noise type and ranges from 0 – 7.

Once a tone or noise generator is started, the sound/noise continues until silenced by executing **SOUND** with a volume of 15. The pitch must be supplied, but is irrelevant. The following Forth code will silence channel 2:

```
0 15 2 SOUND
```

SP! Resident

(---)

A procedure to initialize the parameter stack pointer from **S0** , the user variable that points to the base of the parameter stack.

SP@ Resident

(--- *addr*)

This word returns the address of the top of the stack as it was before **SP@** was executed, *e.g.*,

1 2 SP@ @ . . . 2 2 1 ok:0

SPACE Resident

(---)

Transmit a blank character (ASCII 32|**20h**) to the output device.

SPACES Resident

(*n* ---)

Transmit *n* blank characters (ASCII 32|**20h**) to the output device.

SPCHAR Resident

(n_1 n_2 n_3 n_4 *char* ---)

Defines a character *char* in the Sprite Descriptor Table to have the pattern composed of the 4 words (cells) on the stack.

SPDCHAR Resident

(*addr cnt chr* ---)

Same as **DCHAR** , but for sprite pattern definitions because SPDTAB does not always start at the same VRAM address as PDT.

SPDTAB Resident

(--- *vaddr*)

A constant whose value is the VDP address of the Sprite Descriptor Table. Default value is **800h**. Notice that this coincides with the Pattern Descriptor Table. This constant can only be changed via user variable number **42h**.

SPLIT Resident

(---)

Converts from present display screen mode into standard Split mode configuration.

SPLIT2 Resident

(---)

Converts from present display screen mode into standard Split2 mode configuration.

SPRCOL Resident

(*n spr* ---)

Changes color of the given sprite number *spr* to the color *n* specified.

SPRDIST Resident

(spr_1 spr_2 --- *n*)

Returns on the stack the square of the distance *n* between two specified sprites, spr_1

and spr_2. Distance is measured in pixels and the maximum distance that can be detected accurately is 181 pixels.

SPRDISTXY Resident

(*dotcol dotrow spr --- n*)

Places on the stack *n*, the square of the distance between the point (*dotcol,dotrow*) and a given sprite *spr*. Distance is measured in pixels and the maximum distance that can be detected accurately is 181 pixels.

SPRGET Resident

(*spr --- dotcol dotrow*)

Returns the dot column *dotcol* and dot row *dotrow* position of sprite *spr*.

SPRITE Resident

(*dotcol dotrow n char spr ---*)

Defines sprite number *spr* to have the specified location (*dotcol,dotrow*), color *n*, and character pattern *char*. The size of the sprite will depend on the magnification factor.

SPRPAT Resident

(*char spr ---*)

Changes the character pattern of a given sprite *spr* to *char*.

SPRPUT Resident

(*dotcol dotrow spr ---*)

Places a given sprite *spr* at location (*dotcol,dotrow*).

SQNTL Resident

(---)

Assigns the attribute SEQUENTIAL to the file whose PAB is pointed to by **PAB-ADDR** .

SQR Resident

(f_1 --- f_2)

Finds the square root of a floating point number f_1 and leaves the result f_2 on the stack.

SRA Resident

(n_1 *count* --- n_2)

Arithmetically shifts n_1 count bits to the right and leaves the result n_2 on the stack. Shifting by *count* will be modulo 16 except when *count* = 0, which causes 16 bits to be shifted. To create a word which does not perform a 16-bit shift when count is zero, use the following definition for the same stack contents:

```
: SRA0 -DUP IF SRA ENDIF ;
```

SRC Resident

(n_1 *count* --- n_2)

Performs a circular right shift of count bits on n_1 leaving the result n_2 on the stack. If *count* is 0, 16 bits are shifted. To create a word which does not perform a 16-bit shift when *count* is zero, use the following definition for the same stack contents:

```
: SRC0 -DUP IF SRC ENDIF ;
```

SRL Resident

(n_1 *count* --- n_2)

Performs a logical right shift of *count* bits on n_1 and leaves the result n_2 on the stack. If *count* is 0, 16 bits are shifted. To create a word which does not perform a 16-bit shift when count is zero, use the following definition for the same stack contents:

```
: SRL0 -DUP IF SRL ENDIF ;
```

SSDT Resident

(*vaddr* ---)

No longer required for initializing sprites. Use **DELALL** , *q.v.*, instead. **SSDT** places the Sprite Descriptor Table at the specified VDP address *vaddr* and initializes all sprite tables. The address given must be on an even 2K boundary. See § 6.6.2 "Sprite Initialization" for details.

STAT Resident

(--- *b*)

Reads the status of the current PAB and returns the status byte *b* to the stack. See the table in § 8.5 following the explanation of **STAT** for the meaning of each bit of the status byte.

STATE Resident

(--- *addr*)

A user variable containing the compilation state. Zero indicates execution and a non-zero value indicates compilation. The compilation-state value for **fbForth 2.0** (inherited from TI Forth) is **C0h**. The reason for this value is that the length byte of a found word, which is also immediate, has the high-order two bits set (see Chapter 12, "fbForth 2.0 Dictionary Entry Structure" for details). **INTERPRET** compares the value of **STATE** with the length byte to decide whether to execute a word during compilation.

STCR CRU Words [5]

(n_1 *addr* --- n_2)

Performs the TMS9900 STCR instruction. The CRU base address *addr* will be shifted left one bit and stored in workspace register R12 prior to executing the TMS9900 STCR instruction. There will be n_1 bits transferred from the CRU to the stack as n_2, where the following condition, $n_1 \leq 15$, is enforced by n_1 AND **0Fh**. If

n_1 = 0, 16 bits will be transferred. For program clarity, you may certainly use n_1 = 16 to transfer 16 bits because n_1 = 0 will be the value actually used by the final machine code. See § 11.3 and CRU documentation in the *Editor/Assembler Manual* for more information.

STREAM Resident

(*addr n* ---)

This word is ported from **TurboForth**[1] code courtesy of Mark Wills.

STREAM needs on the stack the address *addr* of a block of raw speech data to be spoken and the number of cells *n* in the buffer. This can be accomplished with **DATA[...]DATA** . **STREAM** will feed the raw speech data to the Speech Synthesizer.

SV Resident

(*count* ---)

Performs the file I/O save operation. The number of bytes *count* to be saved will be the size of the file on disk. The file's PAB must be set up and be the current PAB, to which **PAB-ADDR** points, before executing this word.

SWAP Resident

(n_1 n_2 --- n_2 n_1)

Exchange the top two values on the stack.

SWAP$ Stack-based String Library [42]

(---) (SS: str_1 str_2 --- str_2 str_1) "swap string"

The word **SWAP$** swaps the topmost two strings on the string stack. For example,

```
$" Hello, World!"  ok:0
$" How are you?"  ok:0
SWAP$  ok:0
```

At this point, the string "Hello, World!" is the topmost string on the string stack.

SWCH Printing Routines [19]

(---)

A special purpose word which permits **EMIT** to output characters to an RS232 device rather than to the screen. See **UNSWCH** .

SWPB Resident

(n_1 --- n_2)

Reverses the order of the two bytes in n_1 and leaves the new number as n_2.

SYS$ Resident

(--- *addr*)

A user variable that contains the address of the system support entry point.

SYSTEM Resident

(*n* ---)

Calls the system synonyms. You must specify an offset *n* into a jump table for the routine you wish to call. The offset *n* must be one of the predefined even numbers. See system Forth block 33 for offsets 0 – 26.

S|F Resident

(--- *addr*) "s or f"

User variable that determines whether **M/** uses symmetric or floored integer division. A value of zero (the default) specifies "symmetric" integer division (T-division) and a non-zero value, floored integer division (F-division). See Chapter 18 "Signed Integer Division" for more details.

TALKING? Resident

(--- *flag*)

This word is ported from **TurboForth**[1] code courtesy of Mark Wills.

TALKING? returns *flag* = 0 if the Speech Synthesizer is idle, otherwise, *flag* = 1.

It is a good idea to use **TALKING?** to insure the Speech Synthesizer is not busy before executing **SAY** or **STREAM** .

TAN Resident

(f_1 --- f_2)

Finds the tangent of the floating point number (f_1 = angle in radians) on the stack and leaves the result f_2.

TASK Resident

(---)

A no-operation word or null definition, **TASK** is the last word defined in the resident Forth vocabulary of **fbForth 2.0** and the last word that cannot be forgotten using **FORGET** . Its definition is simply **: TASK ;** . Its address can be used to **BSAVE** a personalized **fbForth 2.0** system disk (see Chapter 11): **' TASK 21 BSAVE** (*Be sure to back up the original disk before trying this!*). By redefining **TASK** at the beginning of an application, you can mark the boundary between applications. By **FORGET**ting **TASK** and re-compiling, an application can be discarded in its entirety. You will be able to **FORGET** each instance of the definition of **TASK** except the first one described above.

TB CRU Words [5]

(*addr* --- *flag*)

TB performs the TMS9900 **TB** instruction. The bit at CRU address *addr* is tested by this instruction. Its value (*flag* = 1|0) is returned to the stack. The CRU base address *addr* will be shifted left one bit and stored in workspace register R12 prior to executing the TMS9900 instruction, **TB 0**, to effect testing the bit. See § 11.3 and CRU documentation in the *Editor/Assembler Manual* for more information.

TCHAR 64-Column Editor [6]

(--- *addr*)

Points to the array that holds the tiny character definitions for the 64-column editor. See **CLIST** .

TEXT Resident

(---)

Converts from present display screen mode into standard Text mode configuration.

TEXT80 Resident

(---)

Converts from present display screen mode into Text80 mode configuration if your computer has that facility.

THEN *[immediate word]* Resident

(---)

An alias for **ENDIF** .

TIB Resident

(--- *addr*)

A user variable containing the address of the terminal input buffer.

TIF2FBF TI Forth Block Utilities

(---) (IS: *srcStrtBlk srcEndBlk DSKn dstStrtBlk dstFile*)

Copies the range of blocks (screens) *srcStrtBlk* – *srcEndBlk* from TI Forth disk *DSKn* to **fbForth** blocks file *dstFile*, starting at block *dstStrtBlk*.

TIFBLK TI Forth Block Utilities

(---) (IS: *blk DSKn*)

Lists block (screen) *blk* of TI Forth disk *DSKn* to the display. The display will pause for user intervention in Text mode due to wrapping 64-byte lines on a 40-column display.

TIFIDX TI Forth Block Utilities

(---) (IS: *strtBlk endBlk DSKn*)

Lists the index (line #0) lines of a range of blocks (screens) *strtBlk* – *endBlk* of TI Forth disk *DSKn* to the display. The display will pause for user intervention if the list requires scrolling.

TIFVU TI Forth Block Utilities

(IS: *blk DSKn*)

Starts the TI Forth disk browser/copier at block (screen) *blk* of TI Forth disk *DSKn*. The browser is patterned after the **fbForth** block editors, allowing scrolling left and right by panels and blocks. The user may also copy a range of TI Forth blocks to an **fbForth** blocks file, which must have been created prior to entering the browser/copier.

TOGGLE Resident

(*addr b* ---)

Complement (XOR) the contents of the byte at *addr* by the bit pattern of byte *b*.

TOKEN Resident

(*delim* --- *addr* | [ ]) (IS: *string<delim>*)

TOKEN gets a string ending with *delim* from the input stream (IS) into **PAD** as a packed string and passes the address *addr* of the string's length byte on the stack if interpreting (command line or loading), but compiles the packed string to **HERE** , with nothing to the stack, if compiling.

TOKEN is used by several words in the resident dictionary, including **MKBFL** , **USEBFL** , **S"** , **."** , **WLITERAL** and **USEFFL** .

TRACE TRACE -- Colon Definition Tracing [18]

(---)

Forces colon definitions that follow it to be compiled in such a way that their execution can be traced. Once a routine has been compiled with the **TRACE** option, it may be executed with or without a trace. To implement a trace, type **TRON** before execution. To execute without a trace, type **TROFF** . Colon definitions that have been compiled under the **TRACE** option must be recompiled under the **UNTRACE** option to remove the tracing capability. **TRACE** and **UNTRACE** can be used alternately to select words to be traced. See **TRON** , **TROFF** , **UNTRACE** and § 5.4 .

TRAVERSE Resident

($addr_1$ *n* --- $addr_2$)

Traverse the name field of a fig-Forth variable-length name field. The starting point $addr_1$ is the address of either the length byte or the last letter. If $n = 1$, the direction is toward high memory; if $n = -1$, the direction is toward low memory. The resulting address $addr_2$ points to the other end of the name.

TRIAD Printing Routines [19]

(*blk* ---)

Display on the RS232 device the three Forth blocks that include block number *blk*, beginning with a Forth block evenly divisible by three. Output is suitable for source text records and includes a reference line at the bottom, "fbForth --- a TI-Forth/fig-Forth extension".

TRIADS Printing Routines [19]

(blk_1 blk_2 ---)

May be thought of as a multiple **TRIAD** , *q.v.* You must specify a Forth block range. **TRIADS** will execute **TRIAD** as many times as necessary to cover that range.

TRIM$ Stack-based String Library [42]

(---) (SS: str_1 --- str_2) "trim string"

The word **TRIM$** removes both leading and trailing spaces from the topmost string. For example,

$"** **hello!** **" TRIM$.$ hello! ok:0

TROFF TRACE -- Colon Definition Tracing [18]

(---)

Turn off tracing of words compiled with the **TRACE** option. See **TRON** , **TRACE** , **UNTRACE** and § 5.4 .

TRON TRACE -- Colon Definition Tracing [18]

(---)

Turn on tracing of words compiled with the **TRACE** option. See **TROFF** , **TRACE** , **UNTRACE** and § 5.4 .

TRUNC Resident

(f_1 --- f_2)

Truncates f_1, leaving the integer portion f_2 on the stack.

TUCK More Useful Stack Words etc. [41]

(n_1 n_2 --- n_2 n_1 n_2)

Put a copy of the top number under the top two numbers on the stack.

TYPE Resident

(*addr* *count* ---)

Transmit *count* characters from *addr* to the selected output device.

U Resident

(--- *n*)

Places the contents *n* of workspace register UP (R8) on the stack. Register U contains the base address of the user variable area. This is quicker than executing **U0 @** , which accomplishes the same thing.

U* Resident

(u_1 u_2 --- *ud*)

Leave the unsigned double number product *ud* of two unsigned numbers, u_1 and u_2.

U. Resident

(*u* ---)

Prints an unsigned number *u* to the output device.

U.R Resident

(*u* *n* ---)

Prints an unsigned number *u* right justified in a field of width *n*.

U/ Resident

(*ud* *u* --- *urem* *uquot*)

Leave the unsigned remainder *urem* and unsigned quotient *uquot* from the unsigned double dividend *ud* and unsigned divisor *u*.

U0 Resident

(--- *addr*)

A user variable that points to the base of the user variable area.

U< Resident

(u_1 u_2 --- *flag*)

Leaves a true flag if u_1 is less than u_2, else leaves a false flag.

UCASE$ Stack-based String Library [42]

(---) (SS: str_1 --- str_2) "convert to upper case"

The word **UCASE$** converts all lower case characters in the topmost string to upper case. For example,

```
$" hello world! 1234" UCASE$ .$ HELLO WORLD! 1234 ok:0
```

UCONS$ Resident

(--- *addr*)

A user variable which contains the base address of the user variable initial value table, which is used to initialize the user variables at a **COLD** start.

UD. Resident

(*ud* ---)

Prints an unsigned double number *ud* to the output device.

UD.R Resident

(*ud* *n* ---)

Prints an unsigned double number *ud* right justified in a field of length *n*.

UM/MOD

(*ud* *u* --- *urem* *uquot*)

See **U/** . This word is not in **fbForth 2.0**, but is identical to **U/** and is referenced here because of the inclusion of ANS Forth words **SM/REM** and **FM/MOD** , *q.v.*

UNDRAW Resident

(---)

Sets **DMODE** to 1. This means that dots are plotted in the off mode.

UNFORGETABLE [*sic*] Resident

(*addr* --- *flag*)

Decides whether or not a word can be forgotten. A true flag is returned if the address is not located between **FENCE** and **HERE** . Otherwise, a false flag is left. See **FORGET** . It *is* possible to set the value of **FENCE** to a value that is actually less than the address of the end of the last word (**TASK**) in the core dictionary such that **UNFORGETABLE** [sic] will report false. However, **FORGET** will still trap that error.

UNSWCH Printing Routines [19]

(---)

Causes the computer to send output to the display screen instead of an RS232 device. See **SWCH** .

UNTIL *[immediate word]* Resident

Occurs within a colon-definition in the form:

BEGIN … UNTIL

COMPILE TIME: (*addr* 1 ---)

UNTIL compiles **(0BRANCH)** and an offset from **HERE** to *addr*, which it stores at the space reserved for it at *addr* by **BEGIN** , *q.v.* The value 1 is used for error testing.

RUNTIME: (*flag* ---)

UNTIL controls the conditional branch back to the corresponding **BEGIN** . If *flag* is *false*, execution returns to just after **BEGIN** ; if *true*, execution continues ahead.

UNTRACE TRACE -- Colon Definition Tracing [18]

(---)

Colon definitions that have been compiled under the **TRACE** option must be recompiled under the **UNTRACE** option to remove the tracing capability. **TRACE** and **UNTRACE** can be used alternately to select words to be traced.

UPDATE Resident

(---)

Marks the most recently referenced block pointed to by **PREV** as altered. The block will subsequently be transferred automatically to disk should its buffer be required for storage of a different block. See **FLUSH** .

UPDT Resident

(---)

Assigns the attribute UPDATE to the file whose PAB is pointed to by **PAB-ADDR** .

USE Resident

(--- *addr*)

A user variable containing the address of the block buffer to use next as the least recently written.

USEBFL *[immediate word]* Resident

(---) (IS: *DSKn.<blocks file>*)

Selects the blocks file from the input stream to be the current blocks file. **USEBFL** is a state-smart word that can be used in either execution or compilation mode.

Usage: **USEBFL DSK1.MYBLOCKS**

USEFFL *[immediate word]* Resident

(---) (IS: *DSKn.<font file>*)

Selects the user-defined font file from the input stream to be the current font file. **USEFFL** is a state-smart word that can be used in either execution or compilation mode. The font file should be 2048 bytes long and define 8-byte character patterns for ASCII characters 0 – 255. It can be shorter than 2048 bytes, but not longer. If the file is found, **SCRFNT** , *q.v*, will be set to -1 so that the user's font will be loaded the next time **FNT** is executed. If the file is not a "PROGRAM" file or is longer than 2048 bytes, **FNT** will issue an error message and reload the default font.

If the font patterns do not start at byte 0 of the file, as with *TI Writer*'s CHARA1 and CHARA2 (offset 6 bytes), the patterns will be illegible. The font editor **FONTED** , *q.v.*, can be used to change the font file's registration to load properly.

Usage: **USEFFL DSK1.MYFONT**

USER Resident

(*n* ---)

A defining word used in the form:

n **USER cccc**

which creates a user variable **cccc** . The parameter field of **cccc** contains *n* as a fixed offset relative to the user variable base address pointed to by workspace register UP (R8) for this user variable. When **cccc** is later executed, it places the sum of its offset and the user area base address on the stack as the storage address of that particular variable. You should only use the even numbers **6Eh** – **7Eh** for *n*—enough for 9 user variables.

Even if you use odd offsets, storage/retrieval is always on even-address boundaries one byte less. However, **USER** does not check that the definition is within the **80h** size allotted to the user variable table.

VAL$ Stack-based String Library [42]

(--- *d*) (SS: *str* ---)

The word **VAL$** uses **NUMBER** to convert the topmost string on the string stack to a double number *d* (2-cell, 32-bit integer) on the data stack. An error occurs if the string cannot be represented as a double number. An erroneous value (but, without an error report) will result if a convertible number is outside the signed, 32-bit range: -2147483648 – 2147483647. Examples:

```
$" 9900" VAL$ D. 9900  ok:0
$" 9900" VAL$ DROP . 9900  ok:0
$" 1234567890" VAL$ D.  1234567890  ok:0
$" 9.900" VAL$ D. 9.900  ok:0
$" 9.945" $" 1234.0" D. D. 1234.0 994.5  ok:0
```

VAND Resident

(*b vaddr* ---)

Performs a logical AND on the byte at the specified VDP location *vaddr* and the given byte *b*. The result byte is stored back into the VDP address.

VARIABLE Resident

(*n* ---) (IS: <*new name*>)

A defining word used in the form:

n **VARIABLE cccc**

When **VARIABLE** is executed, it creates the definition **cccc** with its parameter field initialized to *n*. When **cccc** is later executed, the address of its parameter field (containing *n*) is left on the stack, so that a fetch or store may access this location.

VCHAR Resident

(*col row count char* ---)

Prints on the display screen a vertical stream of length *count* of the specified character *char*. The first character of the stream is located at (*col,row*). Rows and columns are numbered from 0 beginning at the upper left of the display screen. **VCHAR** does *not* check to see whether (*col,row*) is within the screen buffer. Upon reaching the end of the screen buffer, it wraps to the top of the same column. This is different from TI Forth, which wraps to the next column and then to (0,0), filling the screen buffer if *count* is high enough. This behavior will be changed in the next build of **fbForth 2.0** to conform to how TI Basic and TI Extended Basic implement this function, *i.e.*, in the next build, **VCHAR** will throw an error if it would start outside the screen buffer and it will wrap to (0,0) upon reaching the end of the screen buffer, as it does now.

VDPMDE Resident

(--- *addr*)

A user variable used by the mode changing words **TEXT80** , **TEXT** , **GRAPHICS** , **MULTI** , **GRAPHICS2** , **SPLIT** and **SPLIT2** to hold 0 – 6, respectively. **VMODE** , *q.v.*, also changes **VDPMDE** .

VFILL Resident

(*vaddr count b* ---)

Fills *count* locations beginning at the given VDP address *vaddr* with the specified byte *b*.

VLIST Resident

(---)

Prints the names of all words defined in the **CONTEXT** vocabulary. Note that **VLIST** will display the names of even ill-defined words in the dictionary that cannot be found with **'** , **-FIND** or **(FIND)** , *q.v.*, because their smudge bits are set. See **SMUDGE** and **PAUSE** .

VMBR Resident

(*vaddr addr count* ---)

Reads *count* bytes beginning at the given VDP address *vaddr* and places them at *addr*.

VMBW Resident

(*addr vaddr count* ---)

Writes *count* bytes from *addr* into VDP beginning at the given VDP address *vaddr*.

VMODE Resident

(*n* ---)

Changes the VDP mode to mode *n*, corresponding to the values shown in the entry for **VDPMDE** above.

VMOVE Resident

($vaddr_1$ $vaddr_2$ *n* ---)

Move a block of *n* bytes of VRAM from $vaddr_1$ to $vaddr_2$, all in VRAM, proceeding toward high memory. This is ***not*** overlap safe for $vaddr_1 < vaddr_2$.

VOC-LINK Resident

(--- *addr*)

A user variable containing the address of a field in the definition of the most recently created vocabulary. All vocabulary names are linked by these fields to allow control for forgetting with **FORGET** through multiple vocabularies.

VOCABULARY Resident

(---)

A defining word used in the form:

VOCABULARY cccc

to create a vocabulary definition **cccc** . Subsequent use of **cccc** will make it the **CONTEXT** vocabulary which is searched first by **INTERPRET** . The sequence **cccc DEFINITIONS** will also make **cccc** the **CURRENT** vocabulary into which new definitions are placed.

cccc will be so chained as to include all definitions of the vocabulary in which **cccc** is itself defined. All vocabularies ultimately chain to Forth. By convention, vocabulary names are to be declared **IMMEDIATE** . See **VOC-LINK** .

VOR Resident

(*b vaddr* ---)

Performs a logical OR on the byte at the specified VDP address and the given byte *b*. The result byte is stored back into the VDP address.

VRBL Resident

(---)

Assigns the attribute VARIABLE to the file whose PAB is pointed to by **PAB-ADDR** .

VSBR Resident

(*vaddr* --- *b*)

Reads a single byte from the given VDP address *vaddr* and places its value *b* on the stack.

VSBW Resident

(*b vaddr* ---)

Writes a single byte *b* into the given VDP address *vaddr.*

VWTR Resident

(*b n* ---)

Writes the given byte *b* into the specified VDP write-only register *n*.

VXOR Resident

(*b vaddr* ---)

Performs a logical XOR on the byte at the specified VDP address *vaddr* and the given byte *b*. The result byte is stored back into the VDP address *vaddr.*

WARNING Resident

(--- *addr*)

A user variable (initialized by **COLD** to 1 at system startup), containing a value controlling messages.

If **WARNING** > 0, full-text system error messages are displayed by **MESSAGE** and **ERROR** , which executes **MESSAGE** .

If **WARNING** = 0, messages will be presented by number (**msg *#n***). In TI Forth, it means the disk is unavailable, but this is not necessary in **fbForth 2.0** because error messages are always memory resident.

If **WARNING** < 0 when **ERROR** executes, **ERROR** will execute **(ABORT)** , which can be redefined to execute a user-specified procedure instead of the default **ABORT** .

See **MESSAGE** , **(ABORT)** , **ERROR** and **?ERROR** for more detail.

WBLK Resident

(*addr blk* ---)

Write a block to the current blocks file.

WHERE Resident

(n_1 n_2 ---)

When an error occurs on a **LOAD** instruction, typing **WHERE** will bring you into the 40/80-column editor and place the cursor at the exact location of the error. **WHERE** consumes the two numbers, n_1 and n_2, left on the stack by the **LOAD** error.

WHERE (*EDITOR2 Vocabulary*) 64-Column Editor [6]

(n_1 n_2 ---)

When an error occurs on a **LOAD** instruction, typing **WHERE** will bring you into the 64-column editor and place the cursor at the exact location of the error. **WHERE** consumes the two numbers, n_1 and n_2, left on the stack by the **LOAD** error.

WHILE *[immediate word]* Resident

Occurs in a colon-definition in the form:

BEGIN … WHILE (true part) **… REPEAT**

COMPILE TIME: ($addr_1$ 1 --- $addr_1$ 1 $addr_2$ 4)

WHILE emplaces **(0BRANCH)** and leaves $addr_2$ of the reserved offset. The stack values will be resolved by **REPEAT** . The values 1 and 4 are used for error checking.

RUNTIME: (*flag* ---)

WHILE selects conditional execution based on *flag*. If *flag* is *true* (non-zero), **WHILE** continues execution of the true part through to **REPEAT** , which then branches back to **BEGIN** . If *flag* is *false* (zero), execution skips to just after **REPEAT** , exiting the structure.

WIDTH Resident

(--- *addr*)

A user variable containing the maximum number of letters saved in the compilation of a definition's name. It must be 1 – 31, with a default value of 31. The name character count and its natural characters are saved up to the value in **WIDTH** . The value may be changed at any time within the above limits.

WITHIN More Useful Stack Words etc. [41]

(n_1 n_2 n_3 --- *flag*)

Result *flag* is true (1) if $n_2 \leq n_1 < n_3$ and false (0) otherwise.

WLITERAL *[immediate word]* Resident

COMPILE TIME (---) RUNTIME (--- *addr*) INTERPRETING (--- *addr*)

(IS: *<space-delimited string>*)

During compilation, **WLITERAL** compiles **SLIT** and the space-delimited string, which follows **WLITERAL** in the input stream, into the dictionary. At runtime, **SLIT** will push to the stack the address of the string's length byte and change IP to point to the Forth word following the string.

During execution, **WLITERAL** simply pushes to the stack the address of the string's length byte.

Used in the form: **WLITERAL cccc**

WORD Resident

(*char* ---)

Read the text characters from the input stream being interpreted until a delimiter *char* is found, storing the packed character string (see footnote 5 on page 22) beginning at the dictionary buffer **HERE** . **WORD** leaves the character count in the first byte followed by the input characters and ends with two or more blanks. Leading occurrences of *char* are ignored. If **BLK** is zero, text is taken from the terminal input buffer, otherwise from the disk block stored in **BLK** . See **BLK** , **IN** .

WRAP Resident

(--- *addr*)

A user variable containing the wrapping flag for **SCROLL** . A non-zero value signals **SCROLL** to wrap the disappearing row or column of the panel set up by **PANEL** to the opposite side of the panel. The initial value of **WRAP** is 0.

WRT Resident

(*count* ---)

Performs the file I/O write operation. You must specify the number of bytes *count* to be written.

XMLLNK Resident

(*addr* ---)

Links a Forth program to a routine in ROM or to a routine located in the memory expansion unit. A ROM address *addr* or XML vector must be specified as in the *Editor/Assembler Manual.*

XOR Resident

(n_1 n_2 --- n_3)

Leave n_3, the bitwise logical exclusive OR (XOR) of n_1 and n_2.

[*[immediate word]* Resident

(---)

Used in a colon-definition in the form:

```
: xxxx [ words ] more ;
```

Suspend compilation. The words after **[** are executed, not compiled. This allows calculation or compilation exceptions before resuming compilation with **]** . See **LITERAL** and **]** .

[COMPILE] *[immediate word]* Resident

(---)

Used in a colon definition in the form: **: xxxx [COMPILE] FORTH ;**

[COMPILE] will force the compilation of an immediate definition that would otherwise execute during compilation. The above example will select the Forth vocabulary when **xxxx** executes rather than at compile time.

[DCHAR] Resident

(*addr cnt chr vaddr* ---)

Helper routine for **DCHAR** and **SPDCHAR**.

**** *[immediate word]* Resident

(---) (IS: *comment*)

\ is used in the form:

```
\ cccc
```

It starts a rest-of-line line comment that will not be compiled if it occurs in a definition. It causes the interpreter to ignore the rest of the line of the input stream (block or TIB). For blocks, a line is 64 characters, even though there are no actual terminator characters until the end of the block. \ may occur during execution or in a colon definition. As with all Forth words, a blank after \ is required. This is most useful for commenting Forth source code in blocks.

] Resident

(---)

Resume compilation to the completion of a colon definition. See **[** .

]DATA *[immediate word]* Resident

(---)

]DATA closes a **DATA[…]DATA** construct that compiles numbers and leaves their beginning address and cell count on the stack. If compiling within another definition, **]DATA** stores the cell count between the compiled **DATA[]** and the first number of the array.

^ Resident

(f_1 f_2 --- f_3)

Returns f_3 on the stack as f_1 raised to the f_2 power. The operands must be floating point numbers.

Appendix E Differences: fbForth 2.0, fbForth 1.0 and TI Forth

This appendix will detail **fbForth 2.0** changes from **fbForth 1.0** and TI Forth. This will include words that have been added, removed, re-purposed, deprecated and whose descriptions have changed (usually means "clarified"). All of those words, except those removed, will also be discussed elsewhere in the manual where appropriate, including the **fbForth 2.0** Glossary. Even some of the removed words will be discussed elsewhere as necessary. Words that have been hoisted into the kernel (resident dictionary) will also be discussed.

E.1 TI Forth Words not in fbForth 2.0

Descriptions of words appearing in the comments here that are part of **fbForth 2.0** may be found in Appendix D "The fbForth 2.0 Glossary".

!"	
(!")	
-64SUPPORT	Now type **MENU** for options: **6 LOAD**
-ASSEMBLER	Now type **MENU** for options: **21 LOAD**
-BSAVE	Words loaded are now part of resident dictionary.
-CODE	Words loaded are now part of resident dictionary.
-COPY	**CPYBLK** replaces contents. Now type **MENU** for options: **4 LOAD**
-CRU	Now type **MENU** for options: **5 LOAD**
-DUMP	Now type **MENU** for options: **16 LOAD**
-EDITOR	Words loaded are now part of resident dictionary.
-FILE	Words loaded are now part of resident dictionary.
-FLOAT	Words loaded are now part of resident dictionary.
-GRAPH	Words loaded are now part of resident dictionary.
-GRAPH1	Words loaded are now part of resident dictionary.
-GRAPH2	Words loaded are now part of resident dictionary.
-MULTI	Words loaded are now part of resident dictionary.
-PRINT	Now type **MENU** for options: **19 LOAD**
-SPLIT	Words loaded are now part of resident dictionary.
-SYNONYMS	Words loaded are now part of resident dictionary except **FORMAT-DISK**, which has been removed.

-TEXT	Words loaded are now part of resident dictionary.
-TRACE	Now type **MENU** for options: **18 LOAD**
-VDPMODES	Words loaded are now part of resident dictionary.
>ARG	No longer a high-level Forth word
>FAC	No longer a high-level Forth word
ARG	No longer a high-level Forth word
B/BUF$	User variable no longer used.
B/SCR$	User variable no longer used.
CHAR-CNT!	No longer a high-level Forth word
CHAR-CNT@	No longer a high-level Forth word
CHK-STAT	No longer a high-level Forth word
CLR-STAT	No longer a high-level Forth word
DDOT	No longer a high-level Forth word
DISK-HEAD	
DISK_HI	User variable no longer used.
DISK_LO	User variable no longer used.
DISK_SIZE	User variable no longer used.
DR0	
DR1	
DR2	
DRIVE	
DTEST	
EDITOR1	No EDITOR1 vocabulary any longer
F.R	Use **F.** or **FFMT.** to compose a replacement definition if needed.
FAC	No longer a high-level Forth word
FAC->S	No longer a high-level Forth word
FAC>	No longer a high-level Forth word
FAC>ARG	No longer a high-level Forth word
FADD	No longer a high-level Forth word
FDIV	No longer a high-level Forth word
FF.	Use **FFMT.**
FF.R	Use **FFMT.** to compose a replacement definition if needed.

FLD	Unused user variable removed.
FMUL	No longer a high-level Forth word
FORMAT-DISK	
FORTH-COPY	
FORTH_LINK	User variable no longer used. Its function is part of **FORTH** (Forth vocabulary declaration word).
FSUB	No longer a high-level Forth word
GET-FLAG	No longer a high-level Forth word
OFFSET	User variable no longer used.
PUT-FLAG	No longer a high-level Forth word
RDISK	Replaced by **RBLK** .
S->FAC	No longer a high-level Forth word
SCOPY	Replaced by **CPYBLK** .
SCRTCH	Never should have been implemented!
SETFL	No longer a high-level Forth word
SMOVE	Replaced by **CPYBLK** .
STR	No longer a high-level Forth word
STR.	No longer a high-level Forth word
VAL	No longer a high-level Forth word
WDISK	Replaced by **WBLK** .

E.2 **fbForth 1.0** *Words not in* **fbForth 2.0**

Descriptions of words appearing in the comments here that are part of **fbForth 2.0** may be found in Appendix D "The fbForth 2.0 Glossary".

>ARG	No longer a high-level Forth word
>FAC	No longer a high-level Forth word
>ROA	No longer needed because the GPL/XML floating point routines that modified the rollout area have been replaced.
ARG	No longer a high-level Forth word
BPOFF	No longer needed
CHAR-CNT!	No longer a high-level Forth word
CHAR-CNT@	No longer a high-level Forth word
CHK-STAT	No longer a high-level Forth word
CLR-STAT	No longer a high-level Forth word
DBF	No longer needed
DDOT	No longer a high-level Forth word
EDITOR1	No EDITOR1 vocabulary any longer
F.R	Use **F.** or **FFMT.** to compose a replacement definition if needed.
FAC	No longer a high-level Forth word
FAC->S	No longer a high-level Forth word
FAC>	No longer a high-level Forth word
FAC>ARG	No longer a high-level Forth word
FADD	No longer a high-level Forth word
FDIV	No longer a high-level Forth word
FF.	Use **FFMT.**
FF.R	Use **FFMT.** to compose a replacement definition if needed.
FLD	Unused user variable removed.
FMUL	No longer a high-level Forth word
FSUB	No longer a high-level Forth word
GET-FLAG	No longer a high-level Forth word
LCT	No longer needed
MGT	No longer needed

PUT-FLAG	No longer a high-level Forth word
ROA	No longer needed because the GPL/XML floating point routines that modified the rollout area have been replaced.
ROA>	No longer needed because the GPL/XML floating point routines that modified the rollout area have been replaced.
S->FAC	No longer a high-level Forth word
SETFL	No longer a high-level Forth word
STR	No longer a high-level Forth word
STR.	No longer a high-level Forth word
TLC	No longer needed
VAL	No longer a high-level Forth word

E.3 New and Modified Words in fbForth 2.0

This list contains all the new words added since **fbForth 1.0** except for the String Stack Library (see Chapter 14 "The Stack-based String Library") and the additional words discussed in § 11.4 "Useful Additional Stack Words". New words have a light gray background and are indented. All of the words in this list are part of the resident dictionary. The words that are not highlighted have been modified by virtue of the fact that they are now part of the resident dictionary or their definitions and/or descriptions have changed. Detailed descriptions of words listed here may be found in Appendix D "The fbForth 2.0 Glossary".

#MOTION	
(ABORT)	
***/**	
***/MOD**	
.BASE	Display current radix in decimal.
/	
/MOD	
0>	Leaves true *flag* if number on stack is less than 0.
;CODE	Now, also terminates **CODE:** .
>DEG	Converts number on stack from radians to degrees.
>F	
>MAP	Map SAMS memory.
>RAD	Converts number on stack from degrees to radians.
?FLERR	
ALIGN	Insures that **HERE** is on an even address boundary.
APPND	
ASCII	Pushes to the stack the ASCII value of the next character in the input stream.
ATN	
BANK@	Returns the contents of the cell in the bank and address on the stack.
BANKC@	Returns the contents of the byte in the bank and address on the stack.
BEEP	
BOOT	
BSAVE	
CASE	

CEIL	Returns the floating point (FP) integer closest to but > the number on the stack.
CF?	Returns a flag indicating whether a nanoPEB or CF7+ is attached.
CFMOUNT	Mounts a CF volume in virtual DSK1, DSK2 or DSK3.
CFVOLS	Returns volumes mounted in virtual DSK1, DSK2 and DSK3.
CHAR	
CHARPAT	
CLSE	
CODE:	Defining word for new words with machine-code definitions.
COINC	
COINCALL	
COINCXY	
COLD	
COLOR	
COLTAB	Can only change this constant via user variable number **22h**.
COS	
DATA[	Begin compiling numbers, tracking the starting address and number count.
DATA[]	Runtime routine compiled by **DATA[** .
DCHAR	Copies an array of numbers to a character's location in the PDT.
DCT	A constant that is the address of the Default Colors Table.
DEFBF	Gets address of the default blocks filename.
DEG/RAD	FP constant for degrees/radian
DELALL	Use this word instead of **SSDT** to initialize sprites.
DELSPR	
DLT	
DOES>CODE:	Starts machine-code body of a defining word **cccc** created with " **: cccc <BUILDS …** ".
DOT	
DRAW	
DSPLY	
DTOG	
ED@	
EDIT	

ELSEOF	Catchall default **OF** for **CASE** .
ENDCASE	
ERROR	
EULER_E	FP constant for *e*.
EXP	
EXP10	Returns 10 raised to the power of the FP number on the stack.
F!	
F*	
F+	
F-	
F->S	
F-D"	
F.	
F/	
F0<	
F0=	
F<	
F=	
F>	
F>R	Transfers the FP number on the stack to the return stack.
F@	
FABS	Returns absolute value of FP number on stack.
FCONSTANT	Defines an FP constant.
FDROP	
FDUP	
FFMT.	Formats and displays/prints an FP number on the stack.
FILE	
FLERR	
FLOOR	Returns the floating point (FP) integer closest to but < the number on the stack.
FM/MOD	**M/** with floored integer division.
FMINUS	Negates the FP number on the stack.
FNT	Loads the current font (default in cartridge ROM or user-specified).

FONTED	Starts the new Font Editor.
FOVER	
FP1	FP constant for 1.
FP10	FP constant for 10.
FPB	Pushes VRAM address of user screen font file PAB to stack.
FRAC	Returns fractional part of FP number on the stack.
FROT	Rotates the third FP number on the stack to the top of the stack.
FSWAP	
FVARIABLE	Defines an FP variable.
FXD	
GCHAR	
GRAPHICS	
GRAPHICS2	
HCHAR	
HONK	
INPT	
INT	
INTRNL	
ISR	
JCRU	
JKBD	
JMODE	
JOYST	
LD	
LINE	
LN10INV	FP constant for 1/ln(10)
LOG	
LOG10	Returns the decimal logarithm of the FP number on the stack.
M/	Now, does either symmetric (default) or floored integer division, depending on S|F.
MAGNIFY	
MCHAR	

MINIT	
MOTION	
MULTI	
N>S	Converts a number from the input stream and pushes it to the stack.
OPN	
OUTPT	
PAB-ADDR	
PAB-BUF	
PAB-VBUF	
PABS	
PAGE	Clears display screen and puts cursor at (0,0).
PANEL	Sets up a scrollable text panel (window).
PDT	Can only change this constant via user variable number **28h**.
PI	
PLAY	Plays a sound list.
PLAYING?	Checks whether **fbForth 2.0** sound list #1 or #2 is active.
R>F	Transfers the FP number on the return stack to the stack.
RAD/DEG	FP constant for radians/degree.
RD	
REC-LEN	
REC-NO	
RLTV	
RP@	Returns address of top of return stack.
RSTR	
S"	Accepts a **"**-terminated string from the input stream, storing it as a packed (counted) string.
S->F	
S0&TIB!	Moves TIB (same as stack base) for SAMS use.
SAMS!	Initializes SAMS.
SAMS?	Leaves a copy of the SAMS flag.
SATR	Can only change this constant via user variable number **24h**.
SAY	Speaks a counted list of existing speech-synthesizer words .

SCREEN	
SCRFNT	User variable containing a flag indicating whether to load the default font (zero flag) or a user-defined font (nonzero flag).
SCROLL	Scrolls a display screen panel one row or column in a specified direction.
SET-PAB	
SIN	
SM/REM	**M/** with symmetric integer division (T-division).
SMTN	Can only change this constant via user variable number **26h**.
SOUND	Starts a sound on a given channel with a given pitch and volume.
SPCHAR	
SPDCHAR	Same as **DCHAR** but based on SPDTAB.
SPDTAB	Can only change this constant via user variable number **42h**.
SPLIT	
SPLIT2	
SPRCOL	
SPRDIST	
SPRDISTXY	
SPRGET	
SPRITE	
SPRPAT	
SPRPUT	
SQNTL	
SQR	
SSDT	This word is now optional. Use **DELALL** to initialize sprites.
STAT	
STREAM	Speaks a counted block of raw speech, given its RAM address.
SV	
S|F	"S or F": Signals M/ to perform Symmetric integer division (T-division) (= 0) or Floored integer division (F-division) ($\neq 0$)
TALKING?	Checks whether speech synthesizer is busy.
TAN	
TEXT	

TEXT80	
TOKEN	Accepts a string, terminated by a given code, from the input stream, storing it as a packed (counted) string.
TRUNC	Returns integer part of FP number on the stack.
USEFFL	Sets system to use a user-specified font file.
UNDRAW	
UPDT	
VCHAR	
VDPMDE	
VLIST	
VMODE	Sets the VDP mode to the mode of the number on the stack (0 – 6)
VRBL	
WARNING	
WHERE	
WRT	
WRAP	User variable containing wrapping flag for **SCROLL** .
[DCHAR]	Helper routine for **DCHAR** and **SPDCHAR** .
****	Line comment.
]DATA	Terminates a block of numbers begun with **DATA[** .
^	

Appendix F User Variables in fbForth 2.0

The purpose of this appendix is to detail the User Variables in **fbForth 2.0** to assist in their use and to provide the necessary information to change or add to this list as necessary. A more comprehensive description of each of these variables is provided in Appendix D . The table follows these comments in two layouts. The first is in address offset order and the second is in alphabetical order by variable name.

The user may use even numbers **6Eh** through **7Eh** to create his/her own user variables. See the definition of **USER** in Appendix D .

As of **fbForth 2.0:8**, there is one new word (**WRAP**) added to this table and one word (**FLD**) no longer part of this table. **S|F** was added in **fbForth 2.0:9**.

F.1 fbForth 2.0 *User Variables (Address Offset Order)*

Name	Offset	Initial Value	Description
UCONS$	06h	366Ch	Base of User Var initial value table
S0	08h	FFA0h	Base of Stack
R0	0Ah	3FFEh	Base of Return Stack
U0	0Ch	36B6h	Base of User Variables
TIB	0Eh	FFA0h	Terminal Input Buffer address
WIDTH	10h	31	Name length in dictionary
DP	12h	A000h	Dictionary Pointer
SYS$	14h	30DEh	Address of System Support
CURPOS	16h	0	Cursor location in VDP RAM
INTLNK	18h	3020h	Pointer to Interrupt Service Linkage
WARNING	1Ah	1	Message Control
C/L$	1Ch	64	Characters per Line
FIRST$	1Eh	2010h	Beginning of Disk Buffers
LIMIT$	20h	3020h	End of Disk Buffers
COLTAB	22h	380h	Color Table address in VRAM. **COLTAB** gets addr.
SATR	24h	300h	Sprite Attribute Table address in VRAM. **SATR** gets addr.
SMTN	26h	780h	Sprite Motion Table address in VRAM. **SMTN** gets addr.
PDT	28h	800h	Pattern Descriptor Table addr in VRAM. **PDT** gets addr.
FPB	2Ah	80h	User font file PAB offset from FRB. **FPB** gets addr.
DISK_BUF	2Ch	1000h	VDP location of 128B Forth Record Buffer (FRB)
PABS	2Eh	460h	VDP location for PABs
SCRN_WIDTH	30h	40	Display Screen Width in Characters
SCRN_START	32h	0	Display Screen Image Start in VDP
SCRN_END	34h	960	Display Screen Image End in VDP
ISR	36h	0	Interrupt Service Pointer
ALTIN	38h	0	Alternate Input Pointer
ALTOUT	3Ah	0	Alternate Output Pointer
VDPMDE	3Ch	1	VDP Mode
BPB	3Eh	C6h	Blocks PABs offset from FRB. **BPB** gets address.
BPOFF	40h	0	Current Blocks file offset from **BPB**. (**0** or **70h**)
SPDTAB	42h	800h	Sprite Descriptor Table addr in VRAM. **SPDTAB** gets addr.

Name	Offset	Initial Value	Description
SCRFNT	**44h**	-1	Flag for default/user font ($\neq 0$) or console font ($= 0$)
JMODE	**46h**	0	Flag for whether **JOYST** executes **JKBD** (=0) or **JCRU** ($\neq$0)
WRAP	**48h**	0	Flag for no wrap ($= 0$) or wrap ($\neq 0$); used by **SCROLL**
S|F	**4Ah**	0	Flag for Symmetric ($= 0$) or Floored Integer Division ($\neq 0$)
FENCE	**4Ch**		Dictionary Fence
BLK	**4Eh**		Block being interpreted
IN	**50h**		Byte offset in text buffer
OUT	**52h**		Incremented by **EMIT**
SCR	**54h**		Last Forth Block (Screen) referenced
CONTEXT	**56h**		Pointer to Context Vocabulary
CURRENT	**58h**		Pointer to Current Vocabulary
STATE	**5Ah**		Compilation State
BASE	**5Ch**		Number Base for Conversions
DPL	**5Eh**		Decimal Point Location
CSP	**60h**		Stack Pointer for error checking
R#	**62h**		Editing Cursor location
HLD	**64h**		Holds address during numeric conversion
USE	**66h**		Next Block Buffer to Use
PREV	**68h**		Most recently accessed disk buffer
ECOUNT	**6Ah**		Error control
VOC-LINK	**6Ch**		Vocabulary linkage
[*user to define*]	**6Eh**		—*available to user*—
[*user to define*]	**70h**		—*available to user*—
[*user to define*]	**72h**		—*available to user*—
[*user to define*]	**74h**		—*available to user*—
[*user to define*]	**76h**		—*available to user*—
[*user to define*]	**78h**		—*available to user*—
[*user to define*]	**7Ah**		—*available to user*—
[*user to define*]	**7Ch**		—*available to user*—
[*user to define*]	**7Eh**		—*available to user*—

F.2 fbForth 2.0 User Variables (Variable Name Order)

Name	Offset	Initial Value	Description
ALTIN	38h	0	Alternate Input Pointer
ALTOUT	3Ah	0	Alternate Output Pointer
BASE	5Ch		Number Base for Conversions
BLK	4Eh		Block being interpreted
BPB	3Eh	C6h	Blocks PABs offset from FRB. **BPB** gets address.
BPOFF	40h	0	Current Blocks file offset from **BPB**. (0 or 70h)
C/L$	1Ch	64	Characters per Line
COLTAB	22h	380h	Color Table address in VRAM. **COLTAB** gets addr.
CONTEXT	56h		Pointer to Context Vocabulary
CSP	60h		Stack Pointer for error checking
CURPOS	16h	0	Cursor location in VDP RAM
CURRENT	58h		Pointer to Current Vocabulary
DISK_BUF	2Ch	1000h	VDP location of 128B Forth Record Buffer (FRB)
DP	12h	A000h	Dictionary Pointer
DPL	5Eh		Decimal Point Location
ECOUNT	6Ah		Error control
FENCE	4Ch		Dictionary Fence
FIRST$	1Eh	2010h	Beginning of Disk Buffers
FPB	2Ah	80h	User font file PAB offset from FRB. **FPB** gets addr.
HLD	64h		Holds address during numeric conversion
IN	50h		Byte offset in text buffer
INTLNK	18h	3020h	Pointer to Interrupt Service Linkage
ISR	36h	0	Interrupt Service Pointer
JMODE	46h	0	Flag for whether **JOYST** executes **JKBD** (=0) or **JCRU** (≠0)
LIMIT$	20h	3020h	End of Disk Buffers
OUT	52h		Incremented by **EMIT**
PABS	2Eh	460h	VDP location for PABs
PDT	28h	800h	Pattern Descriptor Table addr in VRAM. **PDT** gets addr.
PREV	68h		Most recently accessed disk buffer
R#	62h		Editing Cursor location
R0	0Ah	3FFEh	Base of Return Stack
S0	08h	FFA0h	Base of Stack
SATR	24h	300h	Sprite Attribute Table address in VRAM. **SATR** gets addr.
SCR	54h		Last Forth Block (Screen) referenced
SCRFNT	44h	-1	Flag for default/user font (≠ 0) or console font (= 0)
SCRN_END	34h	960	Display Screen Image End in VDP
SCRN_START	32h	0	Display Screen Image Start in VDP
SCRN_WIDTH	30h	40	Display Screen Width in Characters
SMTN	26h	780h	Sprite Motion Table address in VRAM. **SMTN** gets addr.
SPDTAB	42h	800h	Sprite Descriptor Table addr in VRAM. **SPDTAB** gets addr.
STATE	5Ah		Compilation State
SYS$	14h	30DEh	Address of System Support
S|F	4Ah	0	Flag for Symmetric (= 0) or Floored Integer Division (≠ 0)
TIB	0Eh	FFA0h	Terminal Input Buffer address

Name	Offset	Initial Value	Description
U0	**0Ch**	**36B6h**	Base of User Variables
UCONS$	**06h**	**366Ch**	Base of User Var initial value table
USE	**66h**		Next Block Buffer to Use
VDPMDE	**3Ch**	1	VDP Mode
VOC-LINK	**6Ch**		Vocabulary linkage
WARNING	**1Ah**	1	Message Control
WIDTH	**10h**	31	Name length in dictionary
WRAP	**48h**	0	Flag for no wrap (= 0) or wrap (≠ 0); used by **SCROLL**
[*user to define*]	**6Eh**		*—available to user—*
[*user to define*]	**70h**		*—available to user—*
[*user to define*]	**72h**		*—available to user—*
[*user to define*]	**74h**		*—available to user—*
[*user to define*]	**76h**		*—available to user—*
[*user to define*]	**78h**		*—available to user—*
[*user to define*]	**7Ah**		*—available to user—*
[*user to define*]	**7Ch**		*—available to user—*
[*user to define*]	**7Eh**		*—available to user—*

Appendix G fbForth 2.0 Load Option Directory

The load options are displayed by typing **MENU** . The load options allow you to load only the Forth extensions you wish to use.

You will notice that some of the load options first load other Forth blocks upon which they depend. For example, option, 64-Column Editor, depends on the words loaded by block 13, which displays "loading compact list words" as block 13 starts to load. If, by chance, the prerequisite words were already in the dictionary at the time you type **6 LOAD** , they would not be loaded again. This is called a conditional load. *Note:* As of this writing, the 64-column editor and the "Stack-Based String Library" for **fbForth V2.0** " are the only options that do conditional loads of other blocks.

Though most load options load many more word definitions than are indicated below at "Words loaded:", only those of interest to the user and described in the glossary are listed.

G.1 Option: 64-Column Editor

Starting screen: 6

Words loaded:	**EDIT**	**ED@**	**WHERE**
	CLIST	**CLINE**	

G.2 Option: CPYBLK -- Block Copying Utility

Starting screen: 4

Words loaded: **SCMP** **CPYBLK**

G.3 Option: Memory Dump Utility

Starting screen: 16

Words loaded: **DUMP**

G.4 Option: TRACE -- Colon Definition Tracing

Starting screen: 18

Words loaded:	**TRACE**	**UNTRACE**	**TRON**
	TROFF	**:** *(alternate)*	

G.5 Option: Printing Routines

Starting screen: 19

Words loaded:

SWCH	UNSWCH	?ASCII
TRIAD	TRIADS	INDEX

G.6 Option: TMS9900 Assembler

Starting screen: 21

Words loaded: Entire Assembler vocabulary. See Chapter 9 of the manual.

G.7 Option: CRU Words

Starting screen: 5

Words loaded:

SBO	SBZ	TB
LDCR	STCR	

G.8 Option: More Useful Stack Words etc.

Starting screen: 41

Words loaded:

2DUP	2DROP	NIP	TUCK	CELLS	-ROT
PICK	ROLL	WITHIN	<>	$.	EXIT

G.9 Option: Stack-based String Library

Starting Screen: 42

Words loaded: Entire String Stack Library. See Chapter 14 of the manual.

G.10 Option: DIR -- Disk Catalog Utility

Starting screen: 36

Words loaded: DIR

G.11 Option: CAT -- Disk Catalog Utility

Starting screen: 58

Words loaded: CAT

G.12 Option: TI Forth Block Utilities

Starting screen: 61

Words loaded: **TIFBLK** **TIFIDX** **TIF2FBF** **TIFVU**

G.13 Option: ASM>CODE -- Code Output Utility

Starting screen: 39

Words loaded: **ASM>CODE**

G.14 Option: Compact Flash Utilities

Starting screen: 69

Words loaded: **CF?** **CFMOUNT** **CFVOLS**

Appendix H Assembly Source for CODEd Words

Several words in FBLOCKS have been written in TMS9900 code to increase their execution speeds and/or decrease their size. They include the words:

SBO	— a CRU instruction
SBZ	— a CRU instruction
TB	— a CRU instruction
LDCR	— a CRU instruction
STCR	— a CRU instruction
DDOT	— used by the dot plotting routine
SMASH	— used by **CLINE** and **CLIST**
TCHAR	— definitions for the tiny characters
JCRU	—joystick access via the CRU

These words have been coded in hexadecimal in FBLOCKS, thus they do not require that the **fbForth 2.0** Assembler be in memory before they can be loaded. Their Assembly source code (written in **fbForth 2.0** TMS9900 Assembler) is listed on the following pages.

Block 45 needs a little clarification:

1. It should be noted that the definition of **TCHAR** on line 1 is not actually Assembly source code. It is high-level Forth source code. If you wanted to change the character definitions and copy your new table to block 15 of FBLOCKS, you would need to first load the new character definitions. Let's say you have blocks 45 – 47 in a blocks file named MYBLOCKS on DSK1 with your new character definitions for **TCHAR** . This would require loading block 45 of MYBLOCKS to get the definition of **TCHAR** into memory and then copying the contents of **TCHAR** to lines 3 – 9 of block 15 of FBLOCKS. The following code will do the trick:

USEBFL DSK1.MYBLOCKS	<== Make MYBLOCKS current
45 LOAD	<== Load **TCHAR**
USEBFL DSK1.FBLOCKS	<== Make FBLOCKS current
TCHAR 15 BLOCK 192 + 194 MOVE	<== Copy **TCHAR** to block 15, line 3
FLUSH	<== Flush block to FBLOCKS
FORGET TCHAR	<== Recover space in dictionary used by **TCHAR**

2. The comment, `( ^0)` (Shift+0), on line 5 is a substitute for `( ))` , a syntax error.

For clarity of the code presentation, a few of the blocks below show the code of some of the numbered lines spanning multiple lines on the page:

```
BLOCK #40
  0 ( Source for CRU words...R12 is CRU register)   BASE->R  HEX
  1 ASM: SBO  ( addr --- )
  2    *SP+ R12 MOV,
       R12 R12 A,
  3    0 SBO,
    ;ASM

  4 ASM: SBZ  ( addr --- )
  5    *SP+ R12 MOV,
       R12 R12 A,
  6    0 SBZ,
    ;ASM

  7 ASM: TB  ( addr --- flag )
  8    *SP R12 MOV,
       R12 R12 A,
  9    *SP CLR,
       0 TB,
 10    EQ IF,
 11       *SP INC,
 12    THEN,
 13 ;ASM                      R->BASE -->
 14
 15
```

```
BLOCK #41
  0 ( Source for CRU words )   BASE->R  HEX
  1 ASM: LDCR  ( n1 n2 addr --- )
  2    *SP+ R12 MOV,
       R12 R12 A,
       *SP+ R1 MOV,
  3    *SP+ R0 MOV,
       R1 000F ANDI,
  4    NE IF,
  5       R1 0008 CI,
  6       LTE IF,
  7          R0 SWPB,
  8       THEN,
  9    THEN,
 10    R1 06 SLA,
       R1 3000 ORI,
       R1 X,
 11 ;ASM                  R->BASE -->
 12
 13
 14
 15
```

```
BLOCK #42
  0 ( Source for CRU words )   BASE->R  HEX
  1 ASM: STCR  ( n1 addr --- n2 )
  2    *SP+ R12 MOV,
       R12 R12 A,
       *SP R1 MOV,
  3    R0 CLR,
       R1 000F ANDI,
       R1 R2 MOV,
  4    R1 06 SLA,
       R1 3400 ORI,
       R1 X,
  5    R2 R2 MOV,
  6       NE IF,
  7          R02 0008 CI,
  8          LTE IF,
  9             R0 SWPB,
 10          THEN,
 11       THEN,
 12    R0 *SP MOV,
 13 ;ASM
 14
 15 R->BASE

BLOCK #43
  0 ( Source for DDOT )                                BASE->R HEX
  1  8040 VARIABLE DTAB 2010 , 0804 , 0201 , 7FBF , DFEF ,
  2                     F7FB , FDFE , 8040 , 2010 , 0804 , 0201 ,
  3 ASM: DDOT  ( dotcol dotrow --- b vaddr )
  4    *SP+ R1 MOV,
       *SP R3 MOV,
       R1 R2 MOV,
  5    R3 R4 MOV,
       R1 0007 ANDI,
       R3 0007 ANDI,
  6    R2 00F8 ANDI,
       R4 00F8 ANDI,
       R2 05 SLA,
  7    R2 R1 A,
       R4 R1 A,
       R1 2000 AI,
  8    R4 CLR,
       DTAB @(R3) R4 MOVB,
  9    R4 SWPB,
       R4 *SP MOV,
       SP DECT,
 10    R1 *SP MOV,
 11 ;ASM
 12
 13
 14
 15 R->BASE
```

```
BLOCK #44
  0 ( Source for SMASH )                              BASE->R HEX
  1 0 VARIABLE TCHAR 17E ALLOT 43 BLOCK TCHAR 180 CMOVE
  2 TCHAR 7C - CONSTANT TC 0 VARIABLE LB FE ALLOT
  3 ASM: SMASH ( addr #char line# --- lb vaddr cnt )
  4    *SP+ R1 MOV,
       *SP+ R2 MOV,
       *SP R3 MOV,
       R4 LB LI,
       R4 *SP MOV,
  5    SP DECT,
       R1 SWPB,
       R1 2000 AI,
       R1 *SP MOV,
       R2 R1 MOV,
       R1 INC,
  6    R1 FFFE ANDI,
       SP DECT,
       R1 2 SLA,
       R1 *SP MOV,
       R3 R2 A,
  7    BEGIN,
          R2 R3 C,
  8    GT WHILE,
          R5 CLR,
          R6 CLR,
          *R3+ R5 MOVB,
  9       *R3+ R6 MOVB,
          R5 6 SRL,
          R6 6 SRL,
 10       BEGIN,
             TC @(R5) R0 MOV,
             TC @(R6) R1 MOV,
             R1 4 SRC,
             R12 4 LI,
 11          BEGIN,
                R0 R11 MOV,
                R11 F000 ANDI,
                R1 R7 MOV,
                R7 F00 ANDI,
 12             R11 R7 SOC,
                R7 *R4+ MOVB,
                R0 C SRC,
                R1 C SRC,
                R12 DEC,
 13          EQ UNTIL,
             R5 INCT,
             R6 INCT,
             R5 R12 MOV,
             R12 2 ANDI,
 14       EQ UNTIL,
 15    REPEAT,
    ;ASM                                          R->BASE
```

BLOCK #45

```
( definitions of tiny chars with true lowercase) BASE->R HEX
0EEE  VARIABLE TCHAR  DATA[ EEEE
0000 0000 (  )  0444 4404 ( !)  0AA0 0000 ( ")  08AE AEA2 ( #)
04EC 46E4 ( $)  0A24 448A ( %)  06AC 4A86 ( &)  0480 0000 ( ')
0248 8842 ( ()  0842 2248 ( ^0) 04EE 4000 ( *)  0044 E440 ( +)
0000 0048 ( ,)  0000 E000 ( -)  0000 0004 ( .)  0224 4488 ( /)
04AA EAA4 ( 0)  04C4 4444 ( 1)  04A2 488E ( 2)  0C22 C22C ( 3)
02AA AE22 ( 4)  0E8C 222C ( 5)  0688 CAA4 ( 6)  0E22 4488 ( 7)
04AA 4AA4 ( 8)  04AA 622C ( 9)  0004 0040 ( :)  0004 0048 ( ;)
0024 8420 ( <)  000E 0E00 ( =)  0084 2480 ( >)  04A2 4404 ( ?)
04AE AE86 ( @)  04AA EAAA ( A)  0CAA CAAC ( B)  0688 8886 ( C)
0CAA AAAC ( D)  0E88 C88E ( E)  0E88 C888 ( F)  04A8 8AA6 ( G)
0AAA EAAA ( H)  0E44 444E ( I)  0222 22A4 ( J)  0AAC CAAA ( K)
0888 888E ( L)  0AEE AAAA ( M)  0AAE EEAA ( N)  0EAA AAAE ( O)
0CAA C888 ( P)  0EAA AAEC ( Q)  0CAA CAAA ( R)  0688 422C ( S)
-->
```

BLOCK #46

```
( definitions of tiny chars with true lowercase continued)
0E44 4444 ( T)  0AAA AAAE ( U)  0AAA AA44 ( V)  0AAA AEEA ( W)
0AA4 44AA ( X)  0AAA E444 ( Y)  0E24 488E ( Z)  0644 4446 ( [)
0884 4422 ( \)  0C44 444C ( ])  044A A000 ( $)  0000 000F ( _)
0420 0000 ( `)  000E 2EAE ( a)  088C AAAC ( b)  0006 8886 ( c)
0226 AAA6 ( d)  0004 AE86 ( e)  0688 E888 ( f)  0006 A62C ( g)
088C AAAA ( h)  0404 4442 ( i)  0202 22A4 ( j)  088A ACAA ( k)
0444 4444 ( l)  000A EEAA ( m)  0008 EAAA ( n)  0004 AAA4 ( o)
000C AC88 ( p)  0006 A622 ( q)  0008 E888 ( r)  0006 842C ( s)
044E 4442 ( t)  000A AAA6 ( u)  000A AAA4 ( v)  000A AEEA ( w)
000A A4AA ( x)  000A A62C ( y)  000E 248E ( z)  0644 8446 ( {)
0444 0444 ( |)  0C44 244C ( })  02E8 0000 ( ~)  0EEE EEEE ( DEL)
 ]DATA  DROP DROP    R->BASE ;S
```

BLOCK #48

```
( Source for JCRU used by JOYST for CRU access to joysticks)
BASE->R   HEX
ASM: JCRU  ( joystick# --- value )
   *SP R1 MOV,      ( get unit number)
   R1 5 AI,         ( use keyboard select 6 for #1, 7 for #2)
   R1 SWPB,
   R12 24 LI,
   R1 3 LDCR,
   R12 6 LI,
   R1 5 STCR,
   R1 SWPB,
   R1 INV,
   R1 001F ANDI,
   R1 *SP MOV,
   83D6 @() CLR,    ( defeat auto screen blanking without KSCAN)
;ASM                                      R->BASE
```

Appendix I Error Messages

Error#	Message	Probable Causes
1	empty stack	Procedure being executed attempts to pop a number off the parameter stack when there is no number on the parameter stack. The error may have occurred long before it is detected because Forth checks for this condition only when control returns to the outer interpreter.
2	dictionary full	The user dictionary space is full. Too many definitions have been compiled.
4	isn't unique	This message is more a warning than an error. It informs the user that a word with the same name as the one just compiled is already in the **CURRENT** or **CONTEXT** vocabulary.
5	FBLOCKS not current	This message is displayed when **fbForth 2.0** needs to read from the system blocks file, FBLOCKS, and the user has made another blocks file current with **USEBFL** . This is likely the result of executing **MENU** without FBLOCKS current.
6	disk error	This has several possible causes: No disk in disk drive, disk not initialized, disk drive or controller not connected properly, disk drive or controller not plugged in. The diskette may be damaged with some sector having a hard error.
7	full stack	The procedure being executed is leaving extra unwanted numbers on the parameter stack resulting in a stack overflow.
8	block # out of range	A block # has been requested from the current blocks file that is less than 1 or greater than the number of blocks in the file.
9	file I/O error	Any file I/O operation which results in an error will return this message. The high-order 3 bits of the flag/status byte (PAB + 1) contain the error code, which can be obtained with **HEX PAB-ADDR @ 1+ VSBR 0E0 AND 5 SRA** . An error code of 0 indicates no error only if the COND bit (bit 2) of the GPL status byte located at **837Ch** is ***not*** set.

code	meaning
00	Bad device name
01	Device is write protected
02	Bad open attribute

Error#	Message	Probable Causes
		03 Illegal operation
		04 Out of table or buffer space on the device
		05 Attempt to read past EOF
		06 Device error
		07 File error. Attempt to open nonexistent file, *etc.*
10	floating point error	This error message will be issued only when **?FLERR** is executed and a true flag is returned. **FLERR** may be executed to fetch the floating point status byte.
		code **meaning**
		01 Overflow
		02 Syntax
		03 Integer overflow on conversion
		04 Square root of negative
		05 Negative number to non-integer power
		06 Logarithm of a non-positive number
		07 Invalid argument in a trigonometric function
17	compilation only	Occurs when conditional constructs such as **DO … LOOP** or **IF … THEN** are executed outside a colon definition.
18	execution only	Occurs when you attempt to compile a compiling word into a colon definition.
19	conditionals not paired	A **DO** has been left without a **LOOP**, an **IF** has no corresponding **ENDIF** or **THEN**, *etc.*
20	definition not finished	A **;** was encountered and the parameter stack was not at the same height as when the preceding **:** was encountered. For example, an incomplete conditional construct such as **: xx IF ;** , will trigger this error message.
21	in protected dictionary	An attempt was made to **FORGET** a word with an address lower than or equal to that of **TASK** (last word in resident dictionary) or the contents of **FENCE** if that is higher.
22	use only when loading	This usually means an attempt was made to use **-->** on the command line.
25	bad jump token	Improper use of jump tokens or conditionals in the **fbForth 2.0** TMS9900 Assembler.

Appendix J Contents of FBLOCKS

The contents of the **fbForth 2.0** system blocks file, FBLOCKS, that follow are derived from TI Forth but are in different blocks. Much of this is due to the fact that the blocks are in a file rather than referenced as sectors on a disk. The blocks are also not necessarily in the same order as in TI Forth. However, the TI Forth block (screen) number is indicated as "(old TIF #...)" where applicable. There are also many changes from TI Forth. Many words have been moved to the resident dictionary and some TI Forth words have been removed. There are new words in **fbForth 2.0**, as well. (*cf.* Appendix E "Differences: fbForth 2.0, fbForth 1.0 and TI Forth")

Note that blocks are numbered from 1 in **fbForth 2.0** rather than 0 as in TI Forth. There are also 14 blank blocks (blocks 14, 57, 68, 70 – 80), which you can use as you wish.

Note, also, that the following file is dated 19APR2017:

```
BLOCK #1  ( old TIF #3)
( fbForth WELCOME SCREEN---LES 19APR2017)
BASE->R HEX
: MENU 1 BLOCK 2+ @ 6662 - 5 ?ERROR 2 LOAD ;
." FBLOCKS mod: 19APR2017"
CR CR ." Type MENU for load options." CR CR  R->BASE  ;S
```

```
BLOCK #2
PAGE  ." Load Options (19APR2017)  fbForth 2.0:"
( Type build #)  BASE->R HEX 6033 C@ EMIT R->BASE CR CR
 ." Description                  Load Block" CR
 ." ---------------------------------------" CR
 ." CPYBLK -- Block Copying Utility.......4" CR
 ." CRU Words.............................5" CR
 ." 64-Column Editor......................6" CR
 ." Memory Dump Utility..................16" CR
 ." TRACE -- Colon Definition Tracing....18" CR
 ." Printing Routines....................19" CR
 ." TMS9900 Assembler....................21" CR
 ." More Useful Stack Words etc..........41" CR
 ." Stack-based String Library...........42" CR
 ." DIR -- Disk Catalog Utility..........36" CR
 ." CAT -- Disk Catalog Utility..........58" CR
 ." TI Forth Block Utilities.............61" CR          -->
```

BLOCK #3

```
." ASM>CODE -- Code Output Utility......39" CR
." Compact Flash Utilities..............69" CR
." TMS9900 Assembler (v2.0:9 binary)....27" CR
." 64-Column Editor (v2.0:9 binary).....32" CR
." String Library (v2.0:9 binary).......52" CR CR
." Type <block> LOAD to load.  "   ;S
```

BLOCK #4 (old TIF #39)

```
( Block Copy   17JUN2016 LES )   CR CR ." CPYBLK copies a range
of blocks to the  same or another file, e.g.,"  CR CR ."    CPYB
LK 5 8 DSK1.F1 9 DSK2.F2" CR CR ." will copy blocks 5-8 from  DS
K1.F1  to  DSK2.F2 starting at block 9." CR CR 0 CLOAD CPYBLK
BASE->R DECIMAL 0 VARIABLE SFL 0 VARIABLE DFL 0 CONSTANT XD
: SCMP  OVER C@ OVER C@ OVER OVER - SGN >R MIN 1+ 0 SWAP 1 DO
DROP OVER I + C@ OVER I + C@ - SGN  DUP IF LEAVE THEN LOOP R>
OVER 0= IF OR ELSE DROP THEN SWAP  DROP SWAP DROP ;
: GBFL BL WORD HERE DUP C@ 1+ =CELLS
ALLOT SWAP !  ;  : CPYBLK EMPTY-BUFFERS 1 ' XD ! HERE BPB BPOFF
@ + 9 + DUP VSBR 1+ HERE SWAP DUP =CELLS ALLOT VMBR N>S N>S
OVER OVER > IF SWAP THEN OVER - 1+ >R SFL GBFL N>S DFL GBFL SFL
 @ DFL @ SCMP 0= IF OVER OVER - DUP 0< SWAP R MINUS > + 2 = IF
SWAP R + 1- SWAP R + 1- -1 ' XD ! THEN THEN CR R> 0 DO OVER DUP
. OVER SFL @ (UB) SWAP BLOCK 2- ! DFL @ (UB) UPDATE FLUSH XD +
SWAP XD + SWAP LOOP DROP DROP DUP (UB) DP ! ;    R->BASE
```

BLOCK #5 (old TIF #88)

```
( CRU WORDS   12OCT82 LAO )   0 CLOAD STCR
                           CR ." loading CRU words"
BASE->R  HEX
CODE: SBO  C339 A30C 1D00 ;CODE
CODE: SBZ  C339 A30C 1E00 ;CODE
CODE: TB   C319 A30C 04D9 1F00 1601 0599 ;CODE

CODE: LDCR C339 A30C C079 C039 0241 000F 1304 0281
           0008 1501 06C0 0A61 0261 3000 0481 ;CODE

CODE: STCR C339 A30C C059 04C0 0241 000F C081 0A61 0261 3400
           0481 C082 1304 0282 0008 1501 06C0 C640 ;CODE

  CR ." See Manual for usage." CR R->BASE
```

```
BLOCK #6  ( old TIF #22)
( 64 COLUMN EDITOR )
0 CLOAD  EDITOR2  ( ED@)
BASE->R DECIMAL 13 R->BASE CLOAD CLIST
BASE->R HEX                 CR ." loading 64-column editor"
VOCABULARY EDITOR2 IMMEDIATE EDITOR2 DEFINITIONS
  0 VARIABLE CUR
  : !CUR 0 MAX 3FF MIN CUR ! ;
  : +CUR CUR @ + !CUR ;
  : +LIN CUR @ C/L / + C/L * !CUR ;            DECIMAL
: LINE. DO I SCR @ (LINE) I CLINE LOOP ;
: PTR CUR @ SCR @ BLOCK + ;
: R/C CUR @ C/L /MOD ; ( --- col row )    R->BASE  -->

BLOCK #7  ( old TIF #23)
( 64 COLUMN EDITOR )  BASE->R HEX                   ." ."
: CINIT
  SATR 2 0 DO DUP >R D000 SP@ R> 2 VMBW DROP 4 + LOOP DROP
  0000 0000 0000 0000 5 SPCHAR  0 CUR !
  F090 9090 9090 90F0 6 SPCHAR 0 1 F 5 0 SPRITE ; DECIMAL
: PLACE CUR @ 64 /MOD 8 * 1+ SWAP 4 * 1- DUP 0< IF DROP 0 ENDIF
  SWAP 0 SPRPUT ;
: UP  -64 +CUR PLACE  ;
: DOWN  64 +CUR PLACE   ;
: LEFT  -1 +CUR PLACE  ;
: RIGHT  1 +CUR PLACE ;
: CGOTOXY ( col row --- ) 64 * + !CUR PLACE ;
R->BASE -->

BLOCK #8  ( old TIF #24)
( 64 COLUMN EDITOR ) BASE->R                            ." ."
DECIMAL
  : .CUR CUR @ C/L /MOD CGOTOXY ;
  : DELHALF PAD 64 BLANKS PTR PAD C/L R/C DROP - CMOVE ;
  : DELLIN R/C SWAP MINUS +CUR PTR PAD C/L CMOVE DUP L/SCR SWAP
    DO PTR 1 +LIN PTR SWAP C/L CMOVE LOOP
    0 +LIN PTR C/L 32 FILL C/L * !CUR ;
  : INSLIN R/C SWAP MINUS +CUR L/SCR +LIN DUP 1+ L/SCR 0 +LIN
    DO PTR -1 +LIN PTR SWAP C/L CMOVE -1 +LOOP
    PAD PTR C/L CMOVE C/L * !CUR ;
  : RELINE R/C SWAP DROP DUP  LINE. UPDATE .CUR ;
  : +.CUR +CUR .CUR ;
R->BASE -->
```

```
BLOCK #9  ( old TIF #25)
( 64 COLUMN EDITOR )  BASE->R  DECIMAL                        ." ."
: -TAB PTR DUP C@ BL >
  IF BEGIN 1- DUP -1 +CUR C@ BL =
     UNTIL
  ENDIF
  BEGIN CUR @ IF 1- DUP -1 +CUR C@ BL > ELSE .CUR 1 ENDIF UNTIL
  BEGIN CUR @ IF 1- DUP -1 +CUR C@ BL = DUP IF 1 +.CUR ENDIF
              ELSE .CUR 1 ENDIF
  UNTIL DROP ;
: TAB PTR DUP C@ BL = 0=
  IF BEGIN 1+ DUP 1 +CUR C@ BL =
     UNTIL
  ENDIF
  CUR @ 1023 = IF .CUR 1
               ELSE BEGIN 1+ DUP 1 +CUR C@ BL > UNTIL .CUR
               ENDIF DROP ;  R->BASE -->

BLOCK #10  ( old TIF #26)
( 64 COLUMN EDITOR )  BASE->R                                   ." ."
 DECIMAL
: !BLK PTR  C! UPDATE  ;
: BLNKS PTR R/C DROP C/L SWAP - 32 FILL ;
: HOME  0 0 CGOTOXY ;
: REDRAW SCR @ CLIST UPDATE .CUR ;
: SCRNO CLS 0 0 GOTOXY ." BLOCK #" SCR @ BASE->R DECIMAL U.
  R->BASE CR ;
: +SCR SCR @ 1+ DUP SCR ! SCRNO CLIST  ;
: -SCR SCR @ 1- 1 MAX DUP SCR ! SCRNO  CLIST ;
: DEL PTR DUP 1+ SWAP R/C DROP C/L SWAP - CMOVE 32
  PTR R/C DROP - C/L + 1- C! ;
: INS 32 PTR DUP R/C DROP C/L SWAP - + SWAP DO
  I C@ LOOP DROP PTR DUP R/C DROP C/L SWAP - + 1- SWAP 1- SWAP
  DO I C! -1 +LOOP ;   R->BASE  -->

BLOCK #11  ( old TIF #27)
( 64 COLUMN EDITOR  15JUL82 LAO )        BASE->R DECIMAL  ." ."
0 VARIABLE BLINK  0 VARIABLE OKEY
10 CONSTANT RL  150 CONSTANT RH  0 VARIABLE KC RH VARIABLE RLOG
: RKEY BEGIN ?KEY -DUP 1 BLINK +! BLINK @ DUP 60 < IF 6 0 SPRPAT
 ELSE 5 0 SPRPAT ENDIF    120 = IF 0 BLINK ! ENDIF
        IF ( SOME KEY IS PRESSED )    KC @   1 KC +!  0 BLINK !
          IF ( WAITING TO REPEAT )   RLOG @  KC @  <
             IF ( LONG ENOUGH ) RL RLOG ! 1 KC ! 1 ( FORCE EXT)
             ELSE OKEY @ OVER =
               IF DROP 0   ( NEED TO WAIT MORE )
               ELSE 1 ( FORCE EXIT )    DUP KC !   ENDIF
             ENDIF
          ELSE ( NEW KEY ) 1 ( FORCE LOOP EXIT )  ENDIF
        ELSE ( NO KEY PRESSED) RH RLOG ! 0 KC !   0
        ENDIF
UNTIL DUP OKEY !     ;                    R->BASE -->
```

BLOCK #12 (old TIF #28 & #29)

```
( 64 COLUMN EDITOR )                          BASE->R HEX      ." ."
: EDT   VDPMDE @ >R  SPLIT  ( 0 1000 040 VFILL)  ( 0F 7 VWTR)
  ( 1000 800 01B VFILL)  CINIT !CUR R/C CGOTOXY
  DUP DUP SCR ! SCRNO CLIST BEGIN RKEY  CASE 08 OF LEFT ENDOF
  0C OF -SCR ENDOF  0A OF DOWN ENDOF  03 OF DEL RELINE ENDOF
  0B OF UP ENDOF  04 OF INS RELINE ENDOF  09 OF RIGHT ENDOF
  07 OF DELLIN REDRAW ENDOF  06 OF INSLIN REDRAW ENDOF
  0E OF HOME  ENDOF  02 OF +SCR  ENDOF  16 OF TAB ENDOF
  0D OF 1 +LIN .CUR PLACE ENDOF 1E OF INSLIN BLNKS REDRAW ENDOF
  01 OF DELHALF BLNKS RELINE ENDOF  7F OF -TAB ENDOF
  0F OF 5 0 SPRPAT R> VMODE CLS SCRNO DROP QUIT ENDOF
 DUP 1F > OVER 7F < AND IF DUP !BLK R/C SWAP DROP DUP SCR @
 (LINE) ROT CLINE 1 +.CUR ELSE  7 EMIT  ENDIF ENDCASE AGAIN ;
FORTH DEFINITIONS     : EDIT EDITOR2 0 EDT ;
: WHERE EDITOR2 SWAP 2- EDT ;  : ED@ EDITOR2 SCR @ SCRNO EDIT ;
CR CR ." See Manual for usage." CR   R->BASE
```

BLOCK #13 (old TIF #65)

```
( COMPACT LIST )
0 CLOAD CLIST  BASE->R   CR ." loading compact list words"
DECIMAL  0 VARIABLE TCHAR 382 ALLOT
15 BLOCK 192 + TCHAR 384 CMOVE  HEX
TCHAR 7C - CONSTANT TC  0 VARIABLE BADDR  0 VARIABLE INDX
0 VARIABLE LB FE ALLOT
CODE: SMASH  ( ADDR #CHAR LINE# --- LB VADDR CNT )
  C079 C0B9 C0D9 0204 LB , C644 0649 06C1 0221 2000 C641 C042
  0581 0241 FFFE 0649 0A21 C641 A083 80C2 1501 1020 04C5 04C6
  D173 D1B3 0965 0966 C025 TC , C066 TC , 0B41 020C 0004 C2C0
  024B F000 C1C1 0247 0F00 E1CB DD07 0BC0 0BC1 060C 16F4 05C5
  05C6 C305 024C 0002 16E7 10DD ;CODE
DECIMAL
: CLINE LB 256 ERASE  SMASH   VMBW  ;
: CLOOP  DO I 64 * OVER + 64 I CLINE LOOP DROP  ;
: CLIST BLOCK 16 0 CLOOP ;     R->BASE
```

BLOCK #14

```
BLOCK #15  ( old TIF #67)
  0 ( Tiny character patterns for TCHAR array---compact list for
  1   64-column editor---388 bytes, lines 3:0-9:0 below )
  2
  3 * * * * * * * * * * * * * * * * * * * * * * * * * * * * * * * *
  4 * * * * * * * * * * * * * * * * * * * * * * * * * * * * * * * *
  5 * * *                                                     * * *
  6 * * *       B I N A R Y   C H A R A C T E R   D A T A     * * *
  7 * * *                                                     * * *
  8 * * * * * * * * * * * * * * * * * * * * * * * * * * * * * * * *
  9 * * * * * * * * * * * * * * * * * * * * * * * * * * * * * * * *
 10
 11
 12
 13
 14
 15

BLOCK #16  ( old TIF #42)
  0 ( DUMP ROUTINES 12JUL82 LCT...25OCT2015 LES mod)
  1 0 CLOAD DUMP    BASE->R HEX CR ." loading memory dump utility"
  2 : VM+ VDPMDE @ 0= IF + ELSE DROP THEN ;
  3 : DUMP8 -DUP
  4   IF
  5     BASE->R HEX 0 OUT ! OVER 4 U.R 3A EMIT
  6     OVER OVER 0 DO
  7       DUP @ 0 <# # # # # BL HOLD BL HOLD #> TYPE 2+ 2
  8     +LOOP DROP 1F 18 VM+ OUT @ - SPACES
  9   0 DO
 10     DUP C@ DUP 20 < OVER 7E > OR
 11     IF DROP 2E ENDIF
 12     EMIT 1+
 13   LOOP
 14   CR R->BASE ENDIF ;   -->
 15

BLOCK #17  ( old TIF #43)
  0 ( DUMP ROUTINES 12JUL82 LCT...25OCT2015 LES mod)        ." ."
  1 : DUMP CR 00 8 8 VM+ U/ >R SWAP R> -DUP
  2   IF 0
  3     DO 8 8 VM+ DUMP8 PAUSE IF SWAP DROP 0 SWAP LEAVE ENDIF LOOP
  4   ENDIF SWAP DUMP8 DROP ;
  5 ( .S and VLIST have been put in resident dictionary)
  6 R->BASE   ;S
  7
  8
  9
 10
 11
 12
 13
 14
 15
```

```
BLOCK #18  ( old TIF #44)
( TRACE COLON WORDS-FORTH DIMENSIONS III/2 P.58 26OCT82 LCT)
0 CLOAD (TRACE)     CR ." loading colon definition tracing "
FORTH DEFINITIONS
0 VARIABLE TRACF   ( CONTROLS INSERTION OF TRACE ROUTINE )
0 VARIABLE TFLAG   ( CONTROLS TRACE OUTPUT )
: TRACE 1 TRACF ! ;
: UNTRACE 0 TRACF ! ;
: TRON 1 TFLAG ! ;
: TROFF 0 TFLAG ! ;
: (TRACE) TFLAG @       ( GIVE TRACE OUTPUT? )
  IF  CR R 2- NFA ID.  ( BACK TO PFA NFA FOR NAME )
      .S ENDIF ;        ( PRINT STACK CONTENTS )
: :  ( REDEFINED TO INSERT TRACE WORD AFTER COLON )
  ?EXEC !CSP CURRENT @ CONTEXT ! CREATE [ ' : CFA @ ] LITERAL
 HERE 2- !   TRACF @ IF ' (TRACE) CFA DUP @ HERE 2- ! , ENDIF ]
  ; IMMEDIATE
```

```
BLOCK #19  ( old TIF #72)
( ALTERNATE I/O SUPPORT FOR RS232 PNTR 12JUL82 LCT...mod LES)
0 CLOAD INDEX                    CR ." loading printing routines"
0 0 0 FILE >RS232  BASE->R HEX
: SWCH >RS232 PABS @ 10 + DUP PAB-ADDR ! 1- PAB-VBUF !
  SET-PAB OUTPT F-D" RS232.BA=9600"              OPN 3
  PAB-ADDR @ VSBW 1 PAB-ADDR @ 5 + VSBW  PAB-ADDR @ ALTOUT ! ;
: UNSWCH 0 ALTOUT ! CLSE ;
: ?ASCII ( BLOCK# --- FLAG )
       BLOCK 0 SWAP DUP 400 + SWAP
       DO I C@ 20 > + I C@ DUP 20 < SWAP 7F > OR
          IF DROP 0 LEAVE ENDIF LOOP  ;
: TRIAD 0 SWAP SWCH 3 / 3 * 1+ DUP 3 + SWAP
  DO I ?ASCII IF 1+ I LIST CR ENDIF LOOP
  -DUP IF 3 SWAP - 14 * 0 DO CR LOOP
  ." fbForth --- a TI-Forth/fig-Forth extension" 0C EMIT
  ENDIF UNSWCH  ;                              R->BASE   -->
```

```
BLOCK #20  ( old TIF #73)
( SMART TRIADS AND INDEX 15SEP82 LAO...mod LES )
BASE->R DECIMAL                                         ." ."
: TRIADS ( from to --- )
  3 / 3 * 2+ SWAP 3 / 3 * 1+ DO I TRIAD 3 +LOOP ;
: INDEX  ( from to --- )  1+ SWAP
  DO I DUP ?ASCII IF CR 4 .R 2 SPACES I BLOCK 64 TYPE ELSE DROP
     ENDIF PAUSE IF LEAVE ENDIF LOOP  ;    R->BASE    ;S
```

```
BLOCK #21  ( old TIF #75)
( ASSEMBLER 12JUL82 LCT-LES12DEC2013)  0 CLOAD A$$M BASE->R HEX
ASSEMBLER DEFINITIONS CR ." loading TMS9900 Assembler" CR ."  "
: GOP' OVER DUP 1F > SWAP 30 < AND IF + , , ELSE + , ENDIF ;
: GOP <BUILDS , DOES> @ GOP' ;
0440 GOP B,      0680 GOP BL,      0400 GOP BLWP,
04C0 GOP CLR,   0700 GOP SETO,   0540 GOP INV,
0500 GOP NEG,   0740 GOP ABS,    06C0 GOP SWPB,
0580 GOP INC,   05C0 GOP INCT,   0600 GOP DEC,
0640 GOP DECT,  0480 GOP X,
: GROP <BUILDS , DOES> @ SWAP 40 * + GOP' ;
2000 GROP COC,  2400 GROP CZC,  2800 GROP XOR,
3800 GROP MPY,  3C00 GROP DIV,  2C00 GROP XOP,
: GGOP <BUILDS , DOES> @ SWAP DUP DUP 1F > SWAP 30 < AND
    IF 40 * + SWAP >R GOP' R> , ELSE 40 * + GOP' ENDIF ;
A000 GGOP A,  B000 GGOP AB,  8000 GGOP C,   9000 GGOP CB,
6000 GGOP S,  7000 GGOP SB,  E000 GGOP SOC, F000 GGOP SOCB, -->

BLOCK #22  ( old TIF #76)
( ASSEMBLER 12JUL82 LCT)                                ." ."
4000 GGOP SZC,  5000 GGOP SZCB,  C000 GGOP MOV,  D000 GGOP MOVB,
 : 0OP <BUILDS , DOES> @ , ;
0340 0OP IDLE,  0360 0OP RSET, 03C0 0OP CKOF,
03A0 0OP CKON,  03E0 0OP LREX, 0380 0OP RTWP,
: ROP <BUILDS , DOES> @ + , ;  02C0 ROP STST,  02A0 ROP STWP,
: IOP <BUILDS , DOES> @ , , ;  02E0 IOP LWPI,  0300 IOP LIMI,
: RIOP <BUILDS , DOES> @ ROT + , , ;   0220 RIOP AI,
0240 RIOP ANDI,  0280 RIOP CI,  0200 RIOP LI,  0260 RIOP ORI,
: RCOP <BUILDS , DOES> @ SWAP 10 * + + , ;
0A00 RCOP SLA,  0800 RCOP SRA,  0B00 RCOP SRC,  0900 RCOP SRL,
: DOP <BUILDS , DOES> @ SWAP 00FF AND OR , ;
1300 DOP JEQ,  1500 DOP JGT,  1B00 DOP JH,  1400 DOP JHE,
1A00 DOP JL,  1200 DOP JLE,  1100 DOP JLT,  1000 DOP JMP,
1700 DOP JNC,  1600 DOP JNE,  1900 DOP JNO,  1800 DOP JOC,
1C00 DOP JOP,  1D00 DOP SBO,  1E00 DOP SBZ,  1F00 DOP TB, -->

BLOCK #23  ( old TIF #77)
( ASSEMBLER 12JUL82 LCT)                    ." ." CR ."  "
: GCOP <BUILDS , DOES> @ SWAP 000F AND 040 * + GOP' ;
3000 GCOP LDCR,  3400 GCOP STCR,
00 CONSTANT R0  01 CONSTANT R1  02 CONSTANT R2  03 CONSTANT R3
04 CONSTANT R4  05 CONSTANT R5  06 CONSTANT R6  07 CONSTANT R7
08 CONSTANT R8  09 CONSTANT R9  0A CONSTANT R10  0B CONSTANT R11
 0C CONSTANT R12  0D CONSTANT R13  0E CONSTANT R14
0F CONSTANT R15  08 CONSTANT UP  09 CONSTANT SP  0A CONSTANT W
0D CONSTANT IP  0E CONSTANT RP  0F CONSTANT NEXT
: @() 020 ;  : *? 010 + ;  : *?+ 030 + ;  : @(?) 020 + ;
: @(R0) R0 @(?) ;  : *R0 R0 *? ;  : *R0+ R0 *?+ ;
: @(R1) R1 @(?) ;  : *R1 R1 *? ;  : *R1+ R1 *?+ ;
: @(R2) R2 @(?) ;  : *R2 R2 *? ;  : *R2+ R2 *?+ ;
: @(R3) R3 @(?) ;  : *R3 R3 *? ;  : *R3+ R3 *?+ ;
: @(R4) R4 @(?) ;  : *R4 R4 *? ;  : *R4+ R4 *?+ ;
: @(R5) R5 @(?) ;  : *R5 R5 *? ;  : *R5+ R5 *?+ ;      -->
```

BLOCK #24 (old TIF #78)

```
( ASSEMBLER 12JUL82 LCT)                                 ." ."
: @(R6) R6 @(?) ;  : *R6 R6 *? ;  : *R6+ R6 *?+ ;
: @(R7) R7 @(?) ;  : *R7 R7 *? ;  : *R7+ R7 *?+ ;
: @(R8) R8 @(?) ;  : *R8 R8 *? ;  : *R8+ R8 *?+ ;
: @(R9) R9 @(?) ;  : *R9 R9 *? ;  : *R9+ R9 *?+ ;
: @(R10) R10 @(?) ;  : *R10 R10 *? ;  : *R10+ R10 *?+ ;
: @(R11) R11 @(?) ;  : *R11 R11 *? ;  : *R11+ R11 *?+ ;
: @(R12) R12 @(?) ;  : *R12 R12 *? ;  : *R12+ R12 *?+ ;
: @(R13) R13 @(?) ;  : *R13 R13 *? ;  : *R13+ R13 *?+ ;
: @(R14) R14 @(?) ;  : *R14 R14 *? ;  : *R14+ R14 *?+ ;
: @(R15) R15 @(?) ;  : *R15 R15 *? ;  : *R15+ R15 *?+ ;
: @(UP) UP @(?) ;  : *UP UP *? ;  : *UP+ UP *?+ ;
: @(SP) SP @(?) ;  : *SP SP *? ;  : *SP+ SP *?+ ;
: @(W) W @(?) ;  : *W W *? ;   : *W+ W *?+ ;
: @(IP)  IP @(?) ;  : *IP  IP *? ;  : *IP+ IP *?+ ;
-->
```

BLOCK #25 (old TIF #79)

```
( ASSEMBLER 12JUL82 LCT)                                 ." ."
: @(RP) RP @(?) ;  : *RP RP *? ;  : *RP+ RP *?+ ;
: *NEXT+ NEXT *?+ ;  : *NEXT NEXT *? ;  : @(NEXT) NEXT @(?) ;
: @@ @() ; : ** *? ; : *+ *?+ ; : () @(?) ;  ( Wycove syntax)

( DEFINE JUMP TOKENS )
: GTE 1 ;  : H 2 ;  : NE 3 ;  : L 4 ;  : LTE 5 ;  : EQ 6 ;
: OC 7 ;  : NC  8 ;  : OO 9 ;  : HE 0A ;  : LE 0B ;  : NP 0C ;
: LT 0D ;  : GT 0E ;  : NO 0F ;  : OP 10 ;
: CJMP    ?EXEC
    CASE LT OF 1101 , 0 ENDOF    GT OF 1501 , 0 ENDOF
         NO OF 1901 , 0 ENDOF    OP OF 1C01 , 0 ENDOF
         DUP 0< OVER 10 > OR IF 19 ERROR ENDIF DUP
    ENDCASE 100 * 1000 + , ;
: IF,     ?EXEC [COMPILE] CJMP HERE 2- 42 ; IMMEDIATE
-->
```

BLOCK #26 (old TIF #80)

```
( ASSEMBLER 12JUL82 LCT)                                 ." ."
: ENDIF,  ?EXEC
    42 ?PAIRS HERE OVER - 2- 2 / SWAP 1+ C! ; IMMEDIATE
: ELSE,   ?EXEC 42 ?PAIRS 0 [COMPILE] CJMP HERE 2- SWAP 42
    [COMPILE] ENDIF, 42 ; IMMEDIATE
: BEGIN,  ?EXEC HERE 41 ; IMMEDIATE
: UNTIL,  ?EXEC SWAP 41 ?PAIRS [COMPILE] CJMP HERE - 2 / 00FF
    AND HERE 1- C! ; IMMEDIATE
: AGAIN,   ?EXEC  0 [COMPILE] UNTIL, ; IMMEDIATE
: REPEAT,   ?EXEC >R >R [COMPILE] AGAIN,
    R> R> 2- [COMPILE] ENDIF, ;   IMMEDIATE
: WHILE,   ?EXEC [COMPILE] IF, 2+ ; IMMEDIATE
( : NEXT, *NEXT B, ; ) ( <--now in kernel )
: RT, R11 ** B, ;  ( RT pseudo-instruction )
: THEN, [COMPILE] ENDIF, ; IMMEDIATE  ( ENDIF, synonym )
FORTH DEFINITIONS  : A$$M ;   R->BASE
```

BLOCK #27

```
\ TMS9900 Assembler BLOAD for fbForth 2.0:9
."  loading TMS9900 Assembler "
BASE->R DECIMAL 28 R->BASE BLOAD
: BLERR IF ." BLOAD error!" THEN ; BLERR FORGET BLERR
FORTH DEFINITIONS   ;S
```

BLOCK #28 – BLOCK #31 TMS9900 Assembler Binary

```
* * * * * * * * * * * * * * * * * * * * * * * * * * * * * * * *
* * * * * * * * * * * * * * * * * * * * * * * * * * * * * * * *
* * * * * * * * * * * * * * * * * * * * * * * * * * * * * * * *
* * *                                                     * * *
* * *                                                     * * *
* * *                    F O U R                          * * *
* * *                                                     * * *
* * *       B L O C K S  O F  B I N A R Y  C O D E        * * *
* * *                                                     * * *
* * *                    F O U R                          * * *
* * *                                                     * * *
* * *                                                     * * *
* * *                                                     * * *
* * * * * * * * * * * * * * * * * * * * * * * * * * * * * * * *
* * * * * * * * * * * * * * * * * * * * * * * * * * * * * * * *
* * * * * * * * * * * * * * * * * * * * * * * * * * * * * * * *
```

BLOCK #32

```
\ 64-Column Editor BLOAD for fbForth 2.0:9
."  loading 64-column editor "
BASE->R 33 R->BASE BLOAD
: BLERR IF ." BLOAD error!" THEN ; BLERR FORGET BLERR  ;S
```

BLOCK #33 – BLOCK #35 64-Column Editor Binary

```
* * * * * * * * * * * * * * * * * * * * * * * * * * * * * * * *
* * * * * * * * * * * * * * * * * * * * * * * * * * * * * * * *
* * * * * * * * * * * * * * * * * * * * * * * * * * * * * * * *
* * *                                                       * * *
* * *                                                       * * *
* * *                   T H R E E                           * * *
* * *                                                       * * *
* * *       B L O C K S   O F   B I N A R Y   C O D E       * * *
* * *                                                       * * *
* * *                   T H R E E                           * * *
* * *                                                       * * *
* * *                                                       * * *
* * *                                                       * * *
* * * * * * * * * * * * * * * * * * * * * * * * * * * * * * * *
* * * * * * * * * * * * * * * * * * * * * * * * * * * * * * * *
* * * * * * * * * * * * * * * * * * * * * * * * * * * * * * * *
```

BLOCK #36

```
( TurboForth [MRW] Disk Catalog Utility..mod 19JUN2015 LES)
0 CLOAD DIR 0 CLOAD CAT  CR ." loading DIR catalog utility"
BASE->R HEX 0 VARIABLE CatRec 24 ALLOT
1152 @ CatRec OVER 46 + FILE Cat  0 VARIABLE Total
0 VARIABLE FCount  0 VARIABLE LC  0 VARIABLE bpr
0 VARIABLE sect  0 VARIABLE prot  0B10 VARIABLE Tabs 1C00 ,
: Tab ( n --- ) Tabs + C@ CURPOS @ SCRN_WIDTH @ / GOTOXY ;
: @R100  9 * CatRec DUP C@ + 2+ + PAD 8 CMOVE PAD F@ F->S ;
: DskInfo  RD DROP CR CatRec COUNT ." Disk Name: " TYPE CR
 ." Total: " 1 @R100 DUP U.
 ." Free: " 2 @R100 DUP U.  ." Used: " - U. CR ;
: Ftype ( ftype --- ) 2 @R100 bpr !  CASE 1 OF ." DIS/FIX"
  ENDOF 2 OF ." DIS/VAR" ENDOF  3 OF ." INT/FIX" ENDOF 4 OF
  ." INT/VAR" ENDOF 5 OF ." PROGRAM" 0 bpr ! ENDOF
  ." ???????" 0 bpr !  ENDCASE
  bpr @ -DUP IF 4 U.R THEN ;             R->BASE  -->
```

BLOCK #37

```
BASE->R  DECIMAL                                          ." ."
: Head1 ( --- )  ." ---------- ---- ------- --- -" CR ;
: Head ( --- )   ." Name       Size Type    B/R P" CR  Head1 ;
: DoDIR   0 LC !  0 Total !  0 FCount !  Head   BEGIN
 LC @ 20 MOD 19 =  IF KEY DROP CR Head THEN  RD DROP
  CatRec COUNT DUP  WHILE  TYPE
  1 @R100 DUP 1- sect ! DUP  0 Tab 4 U.R  Total +! 0 @R100 DUP
  prot ! ABS 1 Tab Ftype prot @ 0< IF 2 Tab ." Y" THEN CR
  1 LC +!  1 FCount +! REPEAT
  DROP DROP  Head1
  FCount @ . ." files" 0 Tab Total @ 4 U.R ."  sectors" CR ;
                                                 R->BASE   -->
```

BLOCK #38

```
BASE->R                                                    ." ."
: DIR
   Cat SET-PAB         ( Initialize PAB skeleton)
   INTRNL  FXD  RLTV  INPT  38 REC-LEN
   ( Get directory name from input stream)
   PAB-ADDR @ 10 + 32 WORD HERE COUNT >R SWAP R VMBW R> N-LEN!
   ( Get the catalog and display it)
   OPN          ( open the catalog)
   DskInfo      ( display disk info)
   DoDIR        ( display file list)
   CLSE         ( close the catalog)  ;
R->BASE  CR
." DIR - Catalogs a disk." CR
." E.g., DIR DSK1." CR
```

BLOCK #39

```
( ASM>CODE [port of Mark Wills' code] LES20JUN2016)
CR ." Loading ASM>CODE"  0 CLOAD ASM>CODE  BASE @   HEX
0 VARIABLE pfa  0 VARIABLE STRPOS  0 VARIABLE FBUF 4E ALLOT
PABS @ FBUF 1200 FILE FileOut  FileOut  SET-PAB
: ClearBUF  FBUF 50 BLANKS ;  : SetFileName  ( IS:fileName )
  BL WORD HERE PAB-ADDR @ 9 + OVER C@ 1+ VMBW   ;
: ApdERR ( 0 msg# -- flag )  DROP PAB-ADDR @ 1+ VSBR 0E0 AND
  OR R> R> DROP >R  ;  : instApdERR   ' ApdERR CFA ' (ABORT) !
-1 WARNING !  ;  : uninstApdERR   ' ABORT CFA ' (ABORT) ! 1
WARNING !  ;  : OpenFile  ( -- ) FileOut DSPLY VRBL 50 REC-LEN
instApdERR 0 APPND OPN uninstApdERR IF OUTPT OPN THEN  ;
: Asm?  pfa @ DUP CFA @ = ;
: copyStr ( addr count -- )  STRPOS @ 5 * FBUF + SWAP CMOVE  ;
: SetName  ClearBUF S" CODE: " COUNT copyStr pfa @ NFA DUP C@
  01F AND SWAP 1+ SWAP FBUF 6 + SWAP 0 DO OVER C@ 07F AND
  OVER C! 1+ SWAP 1+ SWAP LOOP DROP DROP ;          -->
```

BLOCK #40

```
( ASM>CODE..continued  LES20JUN2016)        ." ."
: FlushLine  40 WRT ClearBUF 0 STRPOS ! ;  : PlaceCell  pfa @ @
0 <# # # # # #> copyStr 1 STRPOS +! 2 pfa +! ;
: &;  S" ;CODE" COUNT copyStr  ;
: ProcessWord SetName FlushLine BASE->R 10 BASE ! BEGIN pfa @ @
  045F = 0= WHILE PlaceCell STRPOS @ 0C = IF FlushLine THEN
  REPEAT &; FlushLine R->BASE ;
: ASM>CODE ( IS:wordName fileName) CR -FIND IF DROP ELSE 0 THEN
  pfa ! SetFileName pfa @ IF Asm? IF OpenFile ProcessWord CLSE
  ELSE ." Not an assembly language word" THEN
  ELSE ." Word not found" THEN ;
CR ." Usage: ASM>CODE <name> <file>"
CR ."  E.g.: ASM>CODE MYWORD DSK1.MYWORD" CR   BASE !   ;S
```

```
BLOCK #41
( Useful words--most are required by fbForth String Library)
( written by Mark Wills, Lee Stewart & Marshall Linker)
0 CLOAD $.     CR ." Loading useful additional words--" CR
." 2DUP 2DROP NIP TUCK CELLS -ROT PICK ROLL WITHIN <> $. EXIT"
: 2DUP ( a b -- a b a b ) OVER OVER ;
: 2DROP ( a b -- ) DROP DROP ;  : NIP ( a b -- b ) SWAP DROP ;
: TUCK ( a b -- b a b ) SWAP OVER ;  : CELLS ( n -- 2n ) 2 * ;
: -ROT ( a b c -- c a b ) ROT ROT ;
: PICK ( +n -- [n]) 1+ CELLS SP@ + @ ;
( The source for ROLL was Marshall Linker via
  George Smyth's Forth Forum)
: ROLL ( [n]..[0] +n -- [n-1]..[0][n] )
   -DUP  IF  1-  SWAP  >R  MYSELF  R>  SWAP  THEN  ;
: WITHIN ( n low high -- true|false ) OVER - >R - R> U< ;
: <> ( a b -- 1|0 ) = 0= ;   : $. BASE->R HEX U. R->BASE ;
: EXIT ( -- ) [COMPILE] ;S ; IMMEDIATE

BLOCK #42
( Portable, Stack Based String Library for fbForth V2.0   )
( V 1.0 - Mark Wills Sept 2014.)
( Ported from the original TurboForth code by Mark Wills  )
( Modified by Lee Stewart October 2014)
BASE->R DECIMAL 41 R->BASE CLOAD $.  0 CLOAD $.S
CR ." Loading String Library"
0 CONSTANT ($sSize)
HERE CONSTANT ($sEnd)
($sEnd) VARIABLE ($sp)
0 VARIABLE ($temp1)
0 VARIABLE ($depth)
0 VARIABLE ($temp0)
0 VARIABLE ($temp2)
0 VARIABLE ($temp3)      -->



BLOCK #43
( Throw codes for string library, mod: Lee Stewart)
BASE->R DECIMAL                                          ." ."
: (throw) ( code -- )
  CASE
     ($sSize) 0= IF DROP 9999 THEN
     9900 OF ." String stack underflow" ENDOF
     9901 OF ." String too large to assign" ENDOF
     9902 OF ." String stack is empty" ENDOF
     9903 OF ." Need at least 2 strings on string stack" ENDOF
     9904 OF ." String too large for string constant" ENDOF
     9905 OF ." Illegal LEN value" ENDOF
     9906 OF ." Need at least 3 strings on string stack" ENDOF
     9908 OF ." Illegal start value" ENDOF
     9999 OF ." String stack not initialized" ENDOF
  ENDCASE
  CR ABORT ;                              R->BASE   -->
```

BLOCK #44

```
( String stack words, mod: Lee Stewart [INIT$ added])
: ($depth+) ( -- )   1 ($depth) +! ;     BASE->R DECIMAL  ." ."
: ($sp@) ( -- addr )  ($sp) @ ;
: ($rUp) ( n -- n|n+1)   1+ -2 AND ;
: cell+ ( n -- n+2)  COMPILE 2+ ; IMMEDIATE
: (sizeOf$) ( $addr - $size)  @ ($rUp) cell+ ;
: (set$SP) ( $size -- )  MINUS DUP ($sp@) + ($sEnd)
    < IF 9900 (throw) THEN ($sp) +! ;
: (addrOf$) ( index -- addr )  ($sp@) SWAP DUP IF 0 DO
    DUP (sizeOf$) + LOOP ELSE DROP THEN ;
: (lenOf$) ( $addr -- len )
    STATE @ IF COMPILE @ ELSE @ THEN ; IMMEDIATE
: INIT$  ( stack_size -- )  ' ($sSize) !  HERE ' ($sEnd) !
    ($sEnd) ($sSize) + ($sp) !  ($sSize) ALLOT  ;
: RESET$ ( -- )  0 ($depth) !  ($sEnd) ($sSize) + ($sp) ! ;
: DEPTH$ ( -- $sDepth)  ($depth) @ ;          R->BASE   -->
```

BLOCK #45

```
( String constant words etc.)        BASE->R DECIMAL    ." ."
: $CONST ( max_len tib:"name" -- ) ( runtime: -- $Caddr)
   <BUILDS  ($rUp) DUP , 0 ,  ALLOT DOES> NOP ;
: CLEN$ ( $Caddr -- len )  cell+ @ ;
: MAXLEN$ ( $Caddr -- max_len )  (lenOf$) ;
: .$CONST ( $Caddr -- )   cell+ DUP (lenOf$)
    SWAP cell+ SWAP TYPE ;
: :=" ( $Caddr tib:"string" -- )   DUP @  34 WORD HERE COUNT
    SWAP >R  2DUP < IF 9901 (throw) THEN NIP 2DUP SWAP cell+
    ! >R [ 2 CELLS ] LITERAL + R> R> -ROT CMOVE ;
: ($") ( addr len -- ) ( ss: -- str ) DUP ($rUp) cell+ (set$SP)
    DUP ($sp@) !  ($sp@) cell+ SWAP CMOVE  ($depth+) ;
: (COMPILE$) ( addr len -- ) DUP >R PAD SWAP CMOVE HERE 6 CELLS
    COMPILE LIT  + ,  COMPILE LIT R ,  COMPILE BRANCH  HERE R
    ($rUp) +  HERE - 2+ , PAD 12 - R HERE SWAP CMOVE  R> ($rUp)
    ALLOT  COMPILE ($") ;                     R->BASE   -->
```

BLOCK #46

```
( String stack words)          BASE->R DECIMAL          ." ."
: $"  34 WORD HERE COUNT STATE @ IF (COMPILE$) ELSE ($") THEN ;
  IMMEDIATE   : >$  cell+ DUP (lenOf$) SWAP cell+ SWAP ($") ;
: PICK$  DEPTH$ 0= IF 9902 (throw) THEN
    (addrOf$) DUP (lenOf$) SWAP cell+ SWAP ($") ;
: DUP$  DEPTH$ 0= IF 9902 (throw) THEN  0 PICK$ ;
: DROP$  DEPTH$ 0= IF 9902 (throw) THEN
    ($sp@) (sizeOf$) MINUS (set$SP)  -1 ($depth) +! ;
: SWAP$  DEPTH$ 2 < IF 9903 (throw) THEN ($sp@) DUP (sizeOf$)
    HERE SWAP CMOVE 1 (addrOf$) DUP (sizeOf$) ($sp@) SWAP CMOVE
    HERE DUP (sizeOf$)  ($sp@) DUP (sizeOf$) + SWAP CMOVE ;
: NIP$  DEPTH$ 2 < IF 9903 (throw) THEN  SWAP$ DROP$ ;
: OVER$   DEPTH$ 2 < IF 9903 (throw) THEN  1 PICK$ ;
: (rot$)  ($sp@) 3 (addrOf$) ($sp@) (sizeOf$)
    1 (addrOf$) (sizeOf$) 2 (addrOf$) (sizeOf$) + + CMOVE
    3 (addrOf$) ($sp) !  -3 ($depth) +! ;      R->BASE   -->
```

BLOCK #47

```
( String stack words)           BASE->R DECIMAL         ." ."
: ROT$    DEPTH$ 3 < IF 9906 (throw) THEN
    1 PICK$  1 PICK$  4 PICK$ (rot$) ;
: -ROT$    DEPTH$ 3 < IF 9906 (throw) THEN
    0 PICK$  3 PICK$  3 PICK$ (rot$) ;
: LEN$   DEPTH$ 1 < IF 9902 (throw) THEN  ($sp@) @ ;
: >$CONST >R DEPTH$ 1 < IF 9902 (throw) THEN LEN$ R @ > IF 9904
  (throw) THEN ($sp@) DUP (sizeOf$) R> cell+ SWAP CMOVE DROP$ ;
: +$ DEPTH$ 2 < IF 9903 (throw) THEN 1 (addrOf$) cell+ HERE 1
(addrOf$) (lenOf$) CMOVE ($sp@) cell+ 1 (addrOf$) (lenOf$) HERE
+ LEN$ CMOVE HERE LEN$ 1 (addrOf$) (lenOf$) + DROP$ DROP$ ($") ;
 : MID$  DEPTH$ 1 < IF 9902 (throw) THEN DUP LEN$ > OVER 1 < OR
    IF 9905 (throw) THEN OVER DUP LEN$ > SWAP 0< OR IF 9908
    (throw) THEN SWAP ($sp@) cell+ +  SWAP  ($") ;
: LEFT$ DEPTH$ 1 < IF 9902 (throw) THEN DUP LEN$ > OVER 1 < OR
IF 9905 (throw) THEN 0 ($sp@) cell+ + SWAP ($") ;   R->BASE -->
```

BLOCK #48

```
( String stack words)           BASE->R DECIMAL         ." ."
: RIGHT$  DEPTH$ 1 < IF 9902 (throw) THEN DUP LEN$ > OVER 1 <
    OR IF 9905 (throw) THEN ($sp@) (lenOf$) OVER -
    ($sp@) cell+ + SWAP ($") ;
: FINDC$  DEPTH$ 1 < IF 9902 (throw) THEN -1 ($temp0) ! ($sp@)
    cell+  ($sp@) (lenOf$) 0 DO DUP C@ 2 PICK = IF I ($temp0) !
    LEAVE THEN 1+ LOOP DROP DROP ($temp0) @ ;
: FIND$  DEPTH$ 2 < IF 9903 (throw) THEN LEN$ ($temp1) ! 1
 (addrOf$) (lenOf$) ($temp0) ! DUP ($temp0) @ > IF DROP -1 EXIT
 THEN 1 (addrOf$) cell+ + ($temp2) ! ($sp@) cell+ ($temp3) !
 ($temp1) @ ($temp0) @ > IF DROP -1 EXIT THEN 0 ($temp0) @ 0 DO
 ($temp3) @ OVER + C@ ($temp2) @ I + C@ = IF 1+ DUP ($temp1) @
 = IF DROP I ($temp1) @ - 1+ -2 LEAVE THEN ELSE DROP 0 THEN
 LOOP DUP -2 = IF DROP ELSE DROP -1 THEN DROP$ ;
: .$ DEPTH$ 0= IF 9902 (throw) THEN
    ($sp@) cell+ ($sp@) (lenOf$) TYPE  DROP$ ;   R->BASE   -->
```

BLOCK #49

```
( String stack words)           BASE->R DECIMAL         ." ."
: REV$   DEPTH$ 0= IF 9902 (throw) THEN ($sp@) DUP cell+ >R
    (lenOf$)  R> SWAP HERE SWAP CMOVE ($sp@) (lenOf$) HERE 1- +
    ($sp@) cell+ DUP ($sp@) (lenOf$) +   SWAP DO
    DUP C@ I C!  1- LOOP  DROP ;
: LTRIM$  DEPTH$ 0= IF 9902 (throw) THEN ($sp@) DUP (lenOf$) >R
  HERE OVER (sizeOf$) CMOVE 0 R> HERE cell+ DUP >R + R> DO I C@
  BL = IF 1+ ELSE LEAVE THEN LOOP DUP 0 > IF >R ($sp@) (lenOf$)
  DROP$ HERE cell+ R + SWAP R> - ($") ELSE DROP THEN ;
: RTRIM$  DEPTH$ 0= IF 9902 (throw) THEN  REV$ LTRIM$ REV$ ;
: UCASE$  DEPTH$ 1 < IF 9902 (throw) THEN ($sp@) DUP (lenOf$) +
    cell+ ($sp@) cell+ DO I C@ DUP 97 123 WITHIN IF 32 -  I
    C! ELSE DROP THEN LOOP ;   : TRIM$  RTRIM$ LTRIM$ ;
: LCASE$  DEPTH$ 1 < IF 9902 (throw) THEN ($sp@) DUP (lenOf$) +
    cell+ ($sp@) cell+ DO I C@ DUP  65 91 WITHIN IF
    32 +  I C! ELSE DROP THEN LOOP ;             R->BASE   -->
```

BLOCK #50

```
( String stack words, mod: LES [CMP$ added])
 BASE->R DECIMAL                                            ." ."
: REPLACE$  DEPTH$ 3 < IF 9906 (throw) THEN LEN$ >R 0 FIND$ DUP
   ($temp0) ! -1 > IF ($sp@) cell+ HERE ($temp0) @ CMOVE 1
   (addrOf$) cell+ HERE ($temp0) @ + 1 (addrOf$) (lenOf$) CMOVE
   ($sp@) cell+ ($temp0) @ + R + HERE ($temp0) @ + 1 (addrOf$)
   (lenOf$) + LEN$ R> - ($temp0) @ -  DUP >R  CMOVE R> ($temp0)
   @ + 1 (addrOf$) (lenOf$) + DROP$ DROP$ HERE SWAP ($")
   ELSE R> DROP THEN ($temp0) @  ;
: CMP$ DEPTH$ 2 < IF 9903 (throw) THEN 1 (addrOf$) cell+ ($sp@)
    cell+ 1 (addrOf$) (lenOf$) LEN$ OVER OVER - SGN >R MIN 0
    SWAP 0 DO DROP OVER I + C@ OVER I + C@ - SGN DUP IF LEAVE
    THEN LOOP R> OVER 0= IF OR ELSE DROP THEN -ROT DROP DROP ;
: VAL$  ($sp@) DUP (lenOf$) >R cell+ PAD 1+ R CMOVE
    R PAD C! 32 PAD R> + 1+ C! PAD NUMBER DROP$ ;
                                                     R->BASE   -->
```

BLOCK #51

```
( String stack words)           BASE->R DECIMAL      ." ." CR
: $.S  CR  DEPTH$ 0 > IF ($sp@) DEPTH$ ."  Index|Length|String"
    CR ." ------+------+------" CR 0 BEGIN DEPTH$ 0 > WHILE DUP
    6 .R ." |" LEN$ 6 .R ." |" .$ 1+ CR  REPEAT DROP ($depth) !
    ($sp) ! CR ELSE ." String stack is empty." CR THEN
    ." Allocated stack space:" ($sEnd) ($sSize) + ($sp@) - 4 .R
    ."  bytes" CR ."     Total stack space:" ($sSize) 4 .R
    ."  bytes" CR ." Stack space remaining:" ($sp@) ($sEnd) - 4
    .R ."  bytes" CR ;           R->BASE
." You MUST initialize the string stack before you can use the
string library:" CR
."       512 INIT$" CR
." will create a string stack with 512 bytes available." CR
." Example: $" 34 EMIT ."  RED" 34 EMIT ."  $" 34 EMIT
 ."  GREEN" 34 EMIT ."  $" 34 EMIT ."  BLUE" 34 EMIT ."  $.S"
 CR
```

BLOCK #52

```
\ String Library BLOAD for fbForth 2.0:9
."  loading string library " CR
." You MUST initialize the string stack before you can use the
string library:" CR
."       512 INIT$" CR
." will create a string stack with 512 bytes available." CR
." Example: $" 34 EMIT ."  RED" 34 EMIT ."  $" 34 EMIT
 ."  GREEN" 34 EMIT ."  $" 34 EMIT ."  BLUE" 34 EMIT ."  $.S"
 CR
BASE->R DECIMAL 53 R->BASE BLOAD
: BLERR IF ." BLOAD error!" THEN ; BLERR FORGET BLERR
FORTH DEFINITIONS     ;S
```

BLOCK #53 – #56 String Library Binary

```
* * * * * * * * * * * * * * * * * * * * * * * * * * * * * * * *
* * * * * * * * * * * * * * * * * * * * * * * * * * * * * * * *
* * * * * * * * * * * * * * * * * * * * * * * * * * * * * * * *
* * *                                                     * * *
* * *                                                     * * *
* * *                      F O U R                        * * *
* * *                                                     * * *
* * *       B L O C K S  O F  B I N A R Y  C O D E        * * *
* * *                                                     * * *
* * *                      F O U R                        * * *
* * *                                                     * * *
* * *                                                     * * *
* * *                                                     * * *
* * * * * * * * * * * * * * * * * * * * * * * * * * * * * * * *
* * * * * * * * * * * * * * * * * * * * * * * * * * * * * * * *
* * * * * * * * * * * * * * * * * * * * * * * * * * * * * * * *
```

BLOCK #57

BLOCK #58

```
( Catalog program that uses VIB, FDIR and FDRs..LES 11NOV2015)
0 CLOAD CAT 0 CLOAD DIR
BASE->R  CR           ." loading CAT catalog program"
HEX 0 VARIABLE Buf1 0FE ALLOT   0 VARIABLE Buf2 12 ALLOT
0 VARIABLE Total   0 VARIABLE FCount  0 VARIABLE LC
0 VARIABLE bpr     0 VARIABLE sect    0 VARIABLE prot
1154 CONSTANT VBuf 0B10 VARIABLE Tabs 181E ,
0110 VARIABLE CATPAB
: RdErr?  ( err --- )  -DUP IF CR ." Disk I/O error "
  BASE->R [COMPILE] HEX . R->BASE ABORT THEN   ;
: DSRLNK10 0A 0E SYSTEM  8350 C@ RdErr?   ;
: getBuf ( bufadr count --- )  VBuf ROT ROT VMBR    ;
: getSect ( sect# --- )  8350 ! VBuf 834E ! VBuf 2- 8356 !
  DSRLNK10    ;
: Tab ( n --- )  Tabs + C@ CURPOS @ SCRN_WIDTH @ / GOTOXY  ;
                         R->BASE    -->
```

BLOCK #59

```
BASE->R DECIMAL                              ." ."
: getFree   ( --- n )  0 Buf2 !  Buf1 56 +  DUP 200 + SWAP DO
  I @ 65535 XOR  -DUP IF 16 0 DO DUP 1 AND Buf2 +! 1 SRL LOOP
  DROP THEN 2 +LOOP  Buf2 @  ;    : Head1 ( --- )
 ." ---------- ---- --- --- ----- -" CR ;   : Head ( --- )
 ." Name       Size Typ B/R Bytes P" CR Head1  ;    HEX
: DskInfo ( dsk# --- ) SWPB 1+ 834C ! 0 getSect Buf1 100 getBuf
  CR Buf1 0A ." Disk Name: " TYPE CR ." Total: " Buf1 0A + @ 2-
  DUP U. ." Free: "  getFree DUP U.
  ." Used: " - U. CR ;     DECIMAL
: Ftype ( --- )   Buf2 17 + C@ bpr !  Buf2 12 + C@ DUP 8 AND
  prot ! 247 AND    CASE 0 OF ." D/F" ENDOF  128 OF
  ." D/V" ENDOF  2 OF ." I/F" ENDOF  130 OF ." I/V"
  ENDOF  1 OF ." PGM" sect @ 256 *  Buf2 16 + C@ -DUP IF +
  256 - THEN 0 bpr ! 2 Tab 5 U.R ENDOF  ." ???" 0 bpr !
  ENDCASE   bpr @ -DUP IF 4 U.R THEN  ;         R->BASE -->
```

BLOCK #60

```
BASE->R DECIMAL                                      ." ."
: DoCAT ( --- ) 0 LC !  0 Total !  0 FCount !  Head 1 getSect
  Buf1 256 getBuf Buf1   BEGIN   LC @ 20 MOD 19 =  IF KEY DROP
  CR Head THEN  DUP @ -DUP WHILE getSect Buf2 20 getBuf Buf2 10
  TYPE Buf2 14 + @ DUP sect ! 1+ DUP 0 Tab 4 U.R Total +! 1 Tab
  Ftype prot @ IF 3 Tab ." Y" THEN CR 1 LC +!  1 FCount +!  2+
  REPEAT  DROP Head1 FCount @ .  ." files" 0 Tab Total @ 4 U.R
  ."  sectors" CR ;
: CAT ( dsk# --- )  BASE->R [COMPILE] DECIMAL
  CATPAB VBuf 2- 2 VMBW DskInfo DoCAT  R->BASE ;
CR ." n CAT - Catalogs a disk. n = disk #." CR
." E.g., 1 CAT catalogs DSK1." CR    R->BASE    ;S
```

BLOCK #61

```
( TI Forth disk browser/copier..LES 04DEC2015)   BASE->R HEX
CR ." loading TI Forth Viewer/Copier"
1154 CONSTANT VTIbuf  0110 VARIABLE TIPAB  1 VARIABLE Dsk
0 VARIABLE outBFL 10 ALLOT  0 VARIABLE curBFL 10 ALLOT
: GNUM BL WORD HERE NUMBER DROP ;  : getDOidx  ( -- lim idx )
 GNUM GNUM OVER OVER > IF SWAP THEN 1+ SWAP ;  : BlkBuf PREV @
 2+ ;  : getDsk ( IS:DSKn)  BL WORD HERE 4 + C@ 30 - Dsk ! ;
: RdErr? ( err -- ) -DUP IF CR ." Disk I/O error " BASE->R
 [COMPILE] HEX . R->BASE ABORT THEN ;  : DSRLNK10 0A 0E SYSTEM
 8350 C@ RdErr? ;  : getTIblock FLUSH TIPAB VTIbuf 2- 2 VMBW
 VTIbuf 834E ! Dsk @ SWPB 1+ 834C ! 2 SLA BlkBuf DUP 400 + SWAP
 DO DUP 8350 ! 1+ VTIbuf 2- 8356 ! DSRLNK10 VTIbuf I 100 VMBR
 100 +LOOP DROP ; : dnLeft CURPOS @ SCRN_WIDTH @ MOD IF CR THEN
;  : EMITG ( n -- ) CURPOS @ VSBW CURPOS @ 1+ DUP SCRN_END @ <
 IF CURPOS ! ELSE DROP CR THEN ;  : TYPEG ( addr cnt -- ) -DUP
 IF OVER + SWAP DO I C@ EMITG LOOP ELSE DROP THEN ; R->BASE -->
```

BLOCK #62

```
( TI Forth disk browser/copier..continued)   BASE->R HEX ." ."
: dspLine ( line# -- ) 40 * BlkBuf + 40 TYPEG  ;
: 64page? CURPOS @ 40 + SCRN_END @ > IF KEY DROP PAGE THEN  ;
: TIFBLK ( IS:blk# DSKn ) GNUM getDsk getTIblock PAGE 10 0 DO
 64page? dnLeft I 2 .R ." | " I dspLine PAUSE IF LEAVE THEN
 LOOP ;  : TIFIDX ( IS:startblk endblk DSKn) getDOidx getDsk
 PAGE DO I getTIblock 64page? dnLeft I 3 .R ." | " 0 dspLine
 PAUSE IF LEAVE THEN LOOP CR ." ...done" ;  : gBFL ( -- )  BL
 WORD HERE outBFL HERE C@ 1+ CMOVE ;  : saveCurBFL BPB BPOFF @
 + 9 + DUP VSBR curBFL SWAP 1+ VMBR ;  : getBFL TIB @ 0F EXPECT
 0 IN ! gBFL  ;  : cpyTI2FB ( dstBlk# lim idx -- ) CURPOS @ >R
 DO J CURPOS ! I 3 .R I getTIblock DUP PREV @ ! UPDATE FLUSH
 1+ LOOP DROP R> DROP  ;
: TIF2FBF ( IS:srcStrtBlk srcEndBlk DSKn dstStrtBlk dstBlksFil)
 saveCurBFL getDOidx getDsk GNUM gBFL outBFL (UB) ROT ROT
 cpyTI2FB curBFL (UB) ;     R->BASE                    -->
```

BLOCK #63

```
( TI Forth disk browser/copier..continued)   BASE->R HEX ." ."
: BOXCHRS DATA[  0000 003C 3C30 3030 0000 00F0 F030 3030 3030
  303C 3C00 0000 3030 30F0 F000 0000 0000 00FC FC00 0000 0000
  00FC FC30 3030 3030 3030 3030 3030 3060 C070 380C 1830 40A0
  A8B4 5414 0800 40C0 4854 F414 0800 40A0 2854 F414 0800 C020
  4834 D414 0800 2060 A8F4 3414 0800 E080 6834 D414 0800 4080
  C8B4 5414 0800 0000 FC00 FC00 FC00  ]DATA C9 DCHAR ;
D1CD VARIABLE TLDATA DATA[  CDCD CDCE CDCD CDCD D2CD CDCD CDCE
   CDCD CDCD D3CD CDCD CDCE CDCD CDCD D4CD CDCD CDCE CDCD CDCD
   D5CD CDCD CDCE CDCD CDCD D6CD CDCD CDCE CDCD CDCD D7CD CDCD
   ]DATA DROP DROP
0 VARIABLE TIFblk  0 VARIABLE fbFblk  0 CONSTANT OFFSET
: WINWID  ( -- winwid ) SCRN_WIDTH @ 28 = IF 22 ELSE 40 THEN ;
: CORNERS 3 3 1 0C9 HCHAR 3 14 1 0CB HCHAR 4 WINWID + DUP 3 1
 0CA HCHAR 14 1 0CC HCHAR ;  : TOPLN  ( -- )  OFFSET TLDATA + 4
 3 GOTOXY WINWID TYPEG ;     R->BASE                    -->
```

BLOCK #64

```
( TI Forth disk browser/copier..continued)   BASE->R HEX ." ."
: BOTLN  4 14 WINWID  0CD HCHAR ;  : SIDELN ( col chr -- ) 4 10
 ROT VCHAR ;  : SIDELNS 3 0CF SIDELN  WINWID 4 + 0CF SIDELN ;
: RPT ( chr cnt -- ) 0 DO DUP EMITG LOOP DROP ;  : drawScrn
 PAGE 0D8 6 RPT ." TI Forth Block Viewer/Copier" 0D8 6 RPT
 VDPMDE @ 0= IF 0D8 28 RPT THEN ." TI Forth:DSK    fbForth:" CR
 ."   Block            Block" 0 ' OFFSET ! CORNERS  TOPLN BOTLN
 SIDELNS SCRN_WIDTH @ DUP 4 * BASE->R DECIMAL 10 0 DO DUP
 CURPOS ! I 3 .R OVER + LOOP R->BASE DROP DROP CR CR
 ." F4:+Block F6:-Block FD:+Panel FS:-Panel "
 ." FT:TI# FF:fb# ^F:BlkFil ^S:TI>fb F9:Xit" ;  : dspLnSeg
 ( line# -- ) 40 * BlkBuf OFFSET + + WINWID TYPEG ;  : dspBlock
 SCRN_WIDTH @ 28 = IF 3 26 OFFSET CASE 00 OF 0CF 0D0 ENDOF 0F
 OF 0D0 0D0 ENDOF 1E OF 0D0 0CF ENDOF ELSEOF 0CF 0CF ENDOF
 ENDCASE ROT SWAP SIDELN SIDELN TOPLN THEN 10 0 DO SCRN_WIDTH @
 I 4 + * 4 + CURPOS ! I dspLnSeg LOOP ;  R->BASE          -->
```

```
BLOCK #65
( TI Forth disk browser/copier..continued)   BASE->R HEX ." ."
: calcOff ( -1|0|+1 -- ) DUP IF 0F * OFFSET + DUP 0< IF DROP 1E
 THEN DUP 1E > IF DROP 0 THEN THEN ' OFFSET ! ;  : dspPanel
 ( +1|-1 -- ) WINWID 22 = IF calcOff dspBlock ELSE DROP THEN ;
: getCmd ( -- key ) ?KEY DUP IF BEGIN ?KEY 0= UNTIL THEN ;
: dspBlk# ( n col row -- ) GOTOXY 3 .R ;  : get# ( -- n ) TIB @
 3 EXPECT 0 IN ! BL WORD HERE NUMBER DROP ;  : getBlk#
 ( min col row -- n ) ROT >R OVER OVER GOTOXY CURPOS @ DUP 3 20
 VFILL CURPOS ! get# DUP R < IF DROP R> ELSE R> DROP THEN DUP
 >R ROT ROT dspBlk# R> ;  : nxtTIblk ( +1|-1 -- ) TIFblk +!
 TIFblk @ DUP 8 2 dspBlk# getTIblock 0 calcOff dspBlock ;
: clrLstLn 0 17 SCRN_WIDTH @ 20 HCHAR 0 17 GOTOXY ;
: keyPrompt ."  ..tap key" KEY DROP clrLstLn ;  R->BASE    -->

BLOCK #66
( TI Forth disk browser/copier..continued)   BASE->R HEX ." ."
: cmd ( get command key) BEGIN getCmd CASE 02 OF 1 nxtTIblk 0
 ENDOF 0C OF TIFblk @ IF -1 nxtTIblk THEN 0 ENDOF 09 OF 1
 dspPanel 0 ENDOF 08 OF -1 dspPanel 0 ENDOF 5D OF 0 8 2 getBlk#
 DUP TIFblk ! getTIblock 0 calcOff dspBlock 0 ENDOF 7B OF 1 18
 2 getBlk# fbFblk ! 0 ENDOF 06 OF 18 1 GOTOXY CURPOS @ DUP 10
 20 VFILL CURPOS ! getBFL outBFL (UB) 0 ENDOF 13 OF fbFblk @
 DUP IF outBFL @ DUP IF SWAP TIFblk @ clrLstLn
 ." How many blocks? " get# OVER + SWAP clrLstLn cpyTI2FB
 ."  done" keyPrompt ELSE SWAP DROP THEN THEN 0= IF clrLstLn
 ." fbForth block#|file not set!" keyPrompt THEN 0 ENDOF 0F OF
 PAGE 1 ENDOF ELSEOF 0 ENDOF ENDCASE UNTIL ;
: TIFVU ( IS:blk# DSKn) GNUM DUP TIFblk ! getDsk getTIblock
 VDPMDE @ 2 < IF saveCurBFL BOXCHRS drawScrn 0C 1 GOTOXY Dsk @
 . TIFblk @ 8 2 dspBlk# dspBlock cmd curBFL (UB) ELSE CR
 ." TEXT or TEXT80 modes only!" THEN ;     R->BASE    -->

BLOCK #67
( TI Forth disk browser/copier..continued)   BASE->R HEX ." ."
CR CR ." USAGE:"
CR ."  TIFBLK <block#> DSKn"
CR ."    ex: TIFBLK 2 DSK2"
CR ."  TIFIDX <strtBlock#> <endBlock#> DSKn"
CR ."    ex: TIFIDX 9 40 dsk1"
CR ."  TIF2FBF <srcStrtBlk#> <srcEndBlk#>"
CR ."      DSKn <dstStrtBlk#> <dstFile>"
CR ."    ex: TIF2FBF 3 6 DSK3 9 DSK1.MYBLOCKS"
CR ."  TIFVU <block#> DSKn"
CR ."    ex: TIFVU 58 DSK2" CR CR  R->BASE ;S
```

BLOCK #68

BLOCK #69

```
\ Compact Flash Mount Utilities for nanoPEB/CF7+...
0 CLOAD CFMOUNT BASE->R  HEX    CR ." Loading CF Utilities..."
: CF?  ( -- flag )  3FF8 VSBR SWPB 3FF9 VSBR +  AA03 =  ;
: CFE  ( err# -- )  \ display selected error message and abort
   CASE
      1 OF ." No CF detected!" ENDOF
      2 OF ." DSK# must be 1-3!" ENDOF
   ENDCASE   ABORT  ;
: CFVOLS  ( -- volDSK1 volDSK2 volDSK3 )  \ get vol#s in DSKs
   CF? IF 3FFA PAD 6 VMBR PAD DUP 6 + SWAP DO I @ 2 +LOOP
   ELSE 1 CFE THEN  ;
: CFMOUNT  ( vol# dsk# -- )   \ mount CF vol# in DSK<dsk#>
   CF? IF 3FFB SWAP CASE  1 OF ENDOF  2 OF 2+ ENDOF
   3 OF 4 + ENDOF  ELSEOF 2 CFE ENDOF  ENDCASE
   OVER SWPB OVER 1- VSBW VSBW ELSE 1 CFE THEN   ;
                                          R->BASE  CR
```

BLOCK #70 – BLOCK #80

Appendix K Diskette Format Details

The information in this section is based on TI's *Software Specifications for the 99/4 Disk Peripheral (March 28, 1983)*.

The original disk drives supplied by TI supported only single-sided, single-density (SSSD), 90 KiB diskettes. The original TI Forth system was designed around and supplied in this disk format. Though the TI Forth system could not readily be moved to a disk of another size, **fbForth 2.0** consists of only one file, which can easily be moved to a disk of any size. Different disk formats are possible. However, we will consider the usual format of 256 bytes per sector and 40 tracks per side. The following table shows possible formats with 256 bytes/sector and 40 tracks/side:

Disk Type	Sides	Density	Sectors/ Track	Total Sectors	Capacity
SSSD	1	single	9	360	90 KiB
DSSD	2	single	9	720	180 KiB
SSDD	1	double	18	720	180 KiB
DSDD	2	double	18	1440	360 KiB
Compact Flash[26]	2	double	20	1600[27]	400 KiB

The information in the following sections accrues to all the above formats:

K.1 Volume Information Block (VIB)

Byte #	1st Byte	2nd Byte	Byte #
0 8	Disk Volume Name (10 characters padded on the right with blanks)		1 9
10	Total Number of Sectors		11
12	Sectors/Track	"D"	13
14	"S"	"K"	15
16	Protection ("P" or " ")	Tracks/Side	17
18	# of Sides	Density	19
20 54	Reserved		21 55
56 254	Allocation Bitmap (room for 1600 sectors)		57 255

26 This is a third-party peripheral expansion device with 400 KiB virtual disks using Compact Flash memory on devices named nanoPEB and CF7+ (see website: *http://webpages.charter.net/nanopeb/*)

27 1600 sectors is the maximum possible number of sectors that can be managed by the current specification.

Sector 0 contains the volume information block (VIB). The layout is shown in the above table.

K.2 File Descriptor Index Record (FDIR)

Sector 1 contains the file descriptor index record (FDIR). It can hold up to 127 2-byte entries, each pointing to a file descriptor record (FDR—see next section). These pointers are alphabetically sorted by the file names to which they point. This list of pointers starts at the beginning of sector 1 and ends with a pointer value of 0.

K.3 File Descriptor Record (FDR)

Byte #	1st Byte	2nd Byte	Byte #
0 8	File Name (10 characters padded on the right with blanks)		1 9
10	Reserved		11
12	File Status Flags	# of Records/Sector (0 for program)	13
14	# of Sectors currently allocated (not counting this FDR)		15
16	EOF Offset (bytes in last Sector)[28]	Bytes/Record	17
18	# of Records (Fixed) or # of Sectors (Variable)—bytes are in reverse order		19
20 26	Reserved		21 27
28 254	Data Chain Pointer Blocks (3 bytes/block encoding two 12-bit numbers that indicate cluster start and highest, cumulative sector offset)		29 255

There can be as many as 127 file descriptor records (FDRs) laid out as in the above table. There are no subdirectories. FDRs will start in sector 2 and continue, at least, until sector 33, unless a file allocation requires more space than is available in sectors 34 – end-of-disk, in which case the system will begin allocating space for the file in the first available sector in sectors 3 – 33. This is done "to obtain faster directory search response times"[29]. Each FDR beyond 32 files will be placed in the first available sector.

Byte 12 contains file status flags defined as follows, with bit 0 as the least significant bit:

28 A zero value for the EOF Offset indicates 256 bytes in the last sector.

29 *Software Specifications for the 99/4 Disk Peripheral (March 28, 1983)*, p. 19.

Bit #	Description
0	Program or Data file (0 = Data; 1 = Program)
1	Binary or ASCII data (0 = ASCII, DISPLAY file; 1 = Binary, INTERNAL or program file)
2	Reserved
3	PROTECT flag (0 = not protected; 1 = protected)
4–6	Reserved
7	FIXED/VARIABLE flag (0 = fixed-length records; 1 = variable-length records)

The cluster blocks listed in bytes 28 – 255 of the FDR each contain 2 12-bit (3-nybble[30]) numbers. The first points to the beginning sector of that cluster of contiguous sectors and the second is the sector offset reached by that cluster. If we label the 3 nybbles of the cluster pointer as $n_1 - n_3$ and the 3 nybbles of the cumulative sector offset as $m_1 - m_3$, with the subscripts indicating the significance of the nybble, then the 3 bytes are laid out as follows:

Byte 1: n_2n_1 Byte 2: m_1n_3 Byte 3: m_3m_2

The actual 12-bit numbers, then, are

Cluster Pointer: $n_3n_2n_1$ Sector Offset: $m_3m_2m_1$

For example, the following represents 2 blocks in the FDR for a file with 2 clusters allocated:

Actual layout in the FDR: **`4D20h 5F05h F060h`**

1st Cluster Pointer: **`04Dh`** (77_{10})[31] Record Offset: **`5F2h`** (1522_{10})

2nd Cluster Pointer: **`005h`** (5_{10}) Record Offset: **`60Fh`** (1551_{10})

The above example represents a file, the data for which occupies 1552 sectors on the disk. If we assume that no files have been deleted in this case, you should also be able to deduce that there are only 3 files on the disk because the second cluster starts in sector 5 and occupies all sectors from 5 – 33, which should tell you there are 3 FDRs before this cluster was allocated: Sector 0 (VIB), sector 1 (FDIR), sector 2 (FDR of first file), sector 3 (FDR of second file), sector 4 (FDR of third file and sector 5 (second cluster start of the third file, the first two occupying sectors 34 – 76 by inference). Furthermore, the disk contains 1600 sectors because that is the maximum and the first cluster ended in the 1600th sector of the disk (1st cluster starts in sector 77 and ends 1522 sectors later in sector 1599).[32]

30 A nybble (also nibble) is half of one byte (8 bits) and is equal to 4 bits. The editor prefers "nybble" to "nibble" because of its obvious relationship to "byte". 2 nybbles = 1 byte.

31 The subscript, 10, indicates base 10 (decimal).

32 This example is taken from one of my (Lee Stewart's) Compact Flash volumes.

Appendix L Notes on Radix-100 Notation

fbForth 2.0 floating-point math routines use radix-100 format for floating-point numbers. The term "radix" is used in mathematics to mean "number base". We will use "radix 100" to describe the base-100 or centimal number system and "radix 10" to describe the base-10 or decimal number system. Radix-100 format is the same format used by the XML and GPL routines in the TI-99/4A console. Each floating-point number is stored in 8 bytes (4 cells) with a sign bit, a 7-bit, excess-64 (64-biased) integer exponent of the radix (100) and a normalized, 7-digit (1 radix-100 digit/byte) significand for a total of 8 bytes per floating point number. The signed, radix-100 exponent can be -64 to +63. (Keep in mind that the exponent is for radix-100 notation. Those same exponents radix 10 would be -128 to +126.) The exponent is stored in the most significant byte (MSB) biased by 64, *i.e.*, 64 is added to the actual exponent prior to storing, *i.e.*, -64 to +63 is stored as 0 to 127.

The significand (significant digits of the number) must be normalized, *i.e.*, if the number being represented is not zero, the MSB of the significand must always contain the first non-zero (significant) radix-100 digit, with the radix exponent of such a value that the radix point immediately follows the first digit. This is essentially scientific notation for radix 100. Each byte contains one radix-100 digit of the number, which, of course, means that each byte can have a value from 0 to 99 (`0` to `63h`) except for the first byte of a non-zero number, which must be 1 to 99. It is easy to view a radix-100 number as a radix-10 number by representing the radix-100 digits as pairs of radix-10 digits because radix 100 is the square of radix 10. In the following list of largest and smallest possible 8-byte floating point numbers, the radix-100 representation is on the left with spaces between pairs of radix-100 digits. The radix-16 (hexadecimal) internal representation of each byte of the number is also shown:

- Largest positive floating point number [hexadecimal: `7F 63 63 63 63 63 63 63`]:

  $$99\ .\ 99\ 99\ 99\ 99\ 99\ 99 \times 100^{63} = 99.999999999999 \times 10^{126}$$
  $$= 9.9999999999999 \times 10^{127}$$

- Largest negative floating point number [hexadecimal: `80 9D 63 63 63 63 63 63`]:

  $$-99\ .\ 99\ 99\ 99\ 99\ 99\ 99 \times 100^{63} = -99.999999999999 \times 10^{126}$$
  $$= -9.9999999999999 \times 10^{127}$$

- Smallest positive floating point number [hexadecimal: `00 01 00 00 00 00 00 00`]:

  $$01\ .\ 00\ 00\ 00\ 00\ 00\ 00 \times 100^{-64} = 1.000000000000 \times 10^{-128}$$

- Smallest negative floating point number [hexadecimal: `FF FF 00 00 00 00 00 00`]:

  $$-01\ .\ 00\ 00\ 00\ 00\ 00\ 00 \times 100^{-64} = -1.000000000000 \times 10^{-128}$$

The only difference in the internal storage of positive and negative floating point numbers is that only the first word (2 bytes) of negative numbers is negated or complemented (two's complement).

A floating point zero is represented by zeroing only the first word. The remainder of the floating point number does not need to be zeroed for the number to be treated as zero for all floating point calculations.

Appendix M Bug Fixes as of fbForth 2.0:9

The following bug fixes have been made over a period of time and are in no particular time order:

- The insert-blank-line function, ***<CTRL+8>***, in the 40/80-column editor would not blank the entire new line if the cursor were not located in the first column.
- The character-copy function in the 40/80-column editor would cause **fbForth 2.0** to crash if the line-insertion and line-deletion functions were used on the last line of a block. The problem was not testing for a copy-count of 0 before copying the first character, causing the count to pass 0 before the test if the function was passed a count of 0, which it is on the last line.
- **SGN** would yield +1 for -32768 (**8000h**), the largest single-precision (16-bit) negative number possible on the TI-99/4A.
- **SSDT** was improperly setting the address of the Sprite Pattern Descriptor Table. **SSDT** is the easiest way for a user to change the Sprite Pattern Descriptor Table in graphics mode to a different location from the the default **800h**. The default, **800h**, is coincident with the text Pattern Descriptor Table. It is easy enough to change the **SSDT** in code, but it is not trivial. Besides, **SSDT** not only changes the user variable read by the constant, **SPDTAB** , but also changes VDP register #6 to the proper value and executes **DELALL** to initialize sprites.
- **SPRPUT** was setting the *x* position to 255 (rightmost position) if *y* was 0.
- **MOTION** was setting the *x* | *y* vector to -1 if the *y* | *x* vector was negative.
- If sprite automotion was not stopped in Graphics mode, blinking text appeared in Text, Text80, Bitmap and Split modes. Automotion was not stopped when changing VDP modes. For some reason, if sprite automotion is enabled and sprites are left defined, Text80, Bitmap and Split modes show blinking areas on the screen that correspond to those sprites, particularly those defined with patterns in the text PDT area.
- **BSAVE** was not explicitly saving the pointer to the last word in each of the Forth and Assembler vocabularies.
- **BSAVE** and **BLOAD** were not saving and loading, respectively, the vocabulary link fields of the Forth and Assembler vocabularies.
- **DELALL** was only marking the first 8 sprites as deleted, *i.e.*, *y* = **D0h**, when it should have been doing it for all 32! The upshot of this bug was that, as soon as sprite #7 was defined, all of the remaining sprites were suddenly defined as char 0, transparent and positioned at (0,0)!
- **CPYBLK** (loaded from FBLOCKS) was copying blocks from previous blocks files if the corresponding blocks were in block buffers. **EMPTY-BUFFERS** was added to fix it.
- **M/** was improperly setting the sign of the remainder to that of the divisor by default.